Between the Norm and the Exception

Between the Norm and the Exception

The Frankfurt School and the Rule of Law

William E. Scheuerman

The MIT Press Cambridge, Massachusetts London, England

This book was set in Baskerville by the Maple-Vail Book Manufacturing Group and printed and bound in the United States of America

Library of Congress Cataloging-in-Publication Data

Scheuerman, William.
Between the norm and the exception : the Frankfurt School and the rule of law / William E. Scheuerman.
p. cm.—(Studies in contemporary German social thought)
Includes bibliographical references and index.
ISBN 0-262-19351-5
1. Frankfurt school of sociology. 2. Welfare state. 3. Rule of law. I. Title. II. Series.
HM24.S356 1994
301′.01—dc20 94-8309
CIP

To the memory of
Amelia Lind Scheuerman

Contents

Acknowledgments

Many scholars on both sides of the Atlantic generously helped me, but three played a special role in this study. Seyla Benhabib encouraged me and provided insightful comments over the course of nearly four years. Ingeborg Maus shared her encyclopedic knowledge of twentieth-century German political thought. Judith Shklar, who passed away just as I completed the study, gave graciously of her enormous energy and tremendous knowledge of western political thought. I hope that something of her critical spirit can be detected in these pages.

I am also grateful to the Mellon Foundation, German Academic Exchange Service, and Center for European Studies at Harvard for funding. I thank *History of Political Thought, Philosophy and Social Criticism, Politics and Society,* and *Praxis International* for allowing me to borrow selectively from some articles that have previously appeared there. Finally, archivists at the SUNY Albany German Emigré Collection and the Max Horkheimer and Herbert Marcuse Archives at the Frankfurt Stadt- und universitätsbibliothek provided access to a number of important unpublished documents.

Introduction

Recovering the Rule of Law

Evidence mounts that the liberal rule of law may be destined to disintegrate under the conditions of the modern welfare state. In every advanced capitalist democracy, law takes an increasingly amorphous and indeterminate structure as vague legal standards like "in good faith" or "in the public interest," standards incompatible with classical liberal conceptions of the legal norm, proliferate. Everywhere a troublesome conflation of traditional parliamentary rule making with situation-specific administrative decrees results. The emergence of extensive state intervention in an unprecedented variety of spheres of social and economic activity has not only undermined the classical division between state and society presupposed by early liberal views of the rule of law but also broadened the scope of highly discretionary administrative and judicial decision making in many areas of state action. If a minimal demand of the ideal of the rule of law was always that government action should take a predictable form, contemporary liberal democracies probably do less well in living up to this standard than commentators suggest.

For nearly seventy-five years, this trend has been the object of a heated debate among sociologists, political scientists, and legal scholars. In *Economy and Society,* Max Weber argued that "anti-formal" tendencies in regulatory law point toward an ominous fusion of legality and premodern conceptions of morality unsuited to the dictates of a "disenchanted" moral universe and likely to undermine political freedom. At midcentury, conservative scholars like Carl Schmitt and Friedrich Hayek built on Weber's initial anxieties about so-called deformalized law to argue that the emerging democratic welfare state and the rule of law were basically inconsistent. According to Hayek, liberal democracy confronted a dramatic choice between "a road to serfdom" (whose way would allegedly be paved by the disintegration of formal law) and economic laissez-faire. A host of left-liberal and radical scholars have since offered provocative responses to their conservative peers. In *Law and Modern Society,* Roberto Unger acknowledges the accuracy of much of Weber's description of contemporary trends in legal development. But he insists that formal law's decay should be seen as an opportunity for developing an egalitarian legal alternative based on what he describes as "indwelling right." In his account, "increasing equality" conceivably "makes possible an ever more universal consensus about the immanent order of social life," which might allow us to replace "bureaucratic law or the rule of law by what in sense could be called custom."[1] More recently, Jürgen Habermas claims that Weber's original analysis of deformalized law rests on a truncated concept of rationality. Weber exaggerates the significance of the systematic and coherent structure of the legal order while obscuring the centrality of the rational argumentation that, in Habermas's view, makes up the core of a broader complex of practices and institutions essential for democratic legitimacy. Consequently, Weber overstates the dangers of deformalized law.[2]

Curiously, the pathbreaking contributions to this very much unresolved debate by a pair of long-forgotten authors have been largely ignored. This study intends to correct that fault. My aim here is to show how the political and legal analysts of the early Frankfurt school, Franz L. Neumann and Otto Kirchheimer, can help us understand the ongoing transformation of the rule of law in the capitalist mass democracies of Europe and North America. Although the world of the early Frankfurt school is in many ways distinct from our own, Neumann and Kirchheimer provide a number of crucial insights about legal development in the twentieth century that a critically minded democratic theory would do well to heed.

The mainstay of modern conceptions of the rule of law is the notion that state action must be based on cogent general rules, or what Weber called formal law: only clear general norms restrain and bind the activities of the state apparatus, provide a minimum of legal security, and counteract the dangers of a "creeping authoritarianism." If state action is to be rendered normatively legitimate, many of the giants of modern political thought argue, we need to make sure that law takes a form capable of carefully regulating bureaucrats, judges, and other state agents. Poorly constrained state action undermines political and social autonomy. Unlike those who say formal law is little but an anachronism from an archaic liberal past or a mere institutional supplement for illegitimate power inequalities, Franz Neumann and Otto Kirchheimer suggest that we need to preserve something of the classical demand for formal law even in a world profoundly unlike that which first generated such law. A genuinely democratic society requires a high degree of legal regularity and predictability to achieve autonomous and uncoerced political deliberation and action. The unavoidable expansion of the administrative apparatus and the appearance of new modes of public/private authority in our century should not lead us to underestimate the virtues of the classical liberal call for calcuable, norm-based state action. Faced with the horrors of fascist law (and the sins of one of its architects, the authoritarian Carl Schmitt), the Frankfurt-school jurists articulate an idiosyncratic but highly innovative interpretation of legal deformalization in the twentieth century that provides at least one important lesson for us: if contemporary law is undergoing a gradual deformalization, this is as much because formal law conflicts with powerful social and political interests as it is a consequence of the complexity of the welfare state. Formal law today is threatened at least partly because it contains critical elements that challenge capitalist-based social inequalities and a number of deeply undemocratic trends in contemporary political systems.

1

Who were Franz Neumann and Otto Kirchheimer? Today their names are at best faintly familiar to a North American audience. Despite a resurgence of critical legal scholarship in the United States, the jurists Neumann and Kirchheimer are little appreciated in law schools—notwithstanding the fact that the relatively sophisticated German equivalent of the American Critical Legal Studies movement takes them to be its chief intellectual predecessors. But even in Germany, an adequately systematic study of their intellectual development and contributions to a critical theory of democracy has yet to appear. Too many of their most sensitive commentators still downplay Neumann's and Kirchheimer's broader theoretical concerns.[3] I hope to help overcome that lacuna here. But before moving on to examine the details of our story, I first need to provide a quick summary of Neumann's and Kirchheimer's personal histories. Especially in the case of these authors, biography and thinking are woven inextricably together.

During the late thirties and forties, Neumann and Kirchheimer were affiliated with the neo-Marxist Institute for Social Research and maintained more or less cordial cooperation with Max Horkheimer, Theodor Adorno, Frederick Pollock, and Herbert Marcuse. They later taught in New York City and influenced a considerable number of social-science students at Columbia University and the New School for Social Research. Marcuse once wrote that Neumann "was in a rare sense a political scholar," and that "politics was a life element" for him.[4] He could just as easily have used the same words to describe Kirchheimer. Both were socialized in the heated political atmosphere of early twentieth-century Germany: Neumann was born in 1900, Kirchheimer in 1905. Following a brief bout as a soldier in World War I, Neumann, like many of his peers, chose revolution over imperialism and participated actively in the armed soldiers' and workers' uprisings that swept across central Europe in 1918 and 1919 and helped generate Germany's first experiment in republican government. In subsequent years, as a law student at Breslau, Leipzig, Rostock, and Frankfurt, he seems to have exerted a great deal of his considerable energies not only in struggling with the ideas of Karl Marx, Max Weber, Hans Kelsen, Carl Schmitt (as well as his own teacher in Frankfurt, Hugo Sinzheimer, a contributor to the Weimar Constitution and an important social democratic jurist in his own right) but also by participating in the Social Democratic Party (SPD) and in organizing left-wing student groups. Later, he recalled that his earliest experiences in the hallowed halls of the traditional German university involved organizing "students to combat anti-Semitism openly preached by university professors" at Rostock in 1918, and then at Frankfurt "the very first task with which [he] was faced was to help protect a newly appointed Socialist professor from attack—political as well as physical—by students secretly supported by a considerable number of professors."[5] The experience seems to have taken a toll on Neumann; he chose to pursue a career as a labor lawyer. German professorships in the twenties were rarely accessible to Jewish Socialists with modest social roots, and a legal career undoubtedly offered the best means of gaining a measure of personal independence. Neumann went on to open a law practice (with another important political intellectual from his generation, Ernst Fraenkel) in Berlin, teach and lecture extensively at labor union colleges like the Hochschule für Politik, work as a legal advisor for the SPD, serve as a judge in the state of Prussia (where the SPD remained politically dominant until 1932), draft a number of parliamentary laws (and even appear at the Reichstag to argue for them), all the while managing to write prolifically on legal and political issues for a stunning array of juristic and left-wing political journals.

The broad outlines of Kirchheimer's biography from this period are strikingly similar. Perhaps that was the basis for the collegial friendship that began when they met in Berlin in 1930 or so and continued until Neumann's premature death in 1954. Early on, Kirchheimer was active in socialist politics, and his intellectual interests were, like Neumann's, intensely political. As a student in the twenties, he sought out politically outspoken teachers like Carl Schmitt and Hermann Heller at Münster, Cologne, Berlin, and Bonn. In subsequent years, he also practiced law, taught at German trade union colleges and became a vocal representative of the party's left wing, while publishing widely in its journals. He and Neumann attended university seminars offered by Schmitt in Berlin during the early thirties and reportedly took part in an informal political-discussion group centered around the social democratic journal *Die Gesellschaft.* Other participants may have included Herbert Marcuse, Hannah Arendt, Paul Tillich, and Walter Benjamin.[6]

Neumann was a "rising star of reformism" in the Weimar SPD during its final years, whereas Kirchheimer looked forward to a successful legal and political career in the party's left wing. Yet all this was brought to an abrupt end when Hitler seized power in January 1933. Forced to flee Germany in 1933 (Kirchheimer for Paris, Neumann and his family for London), they soon joined the ranks of those rendered stateless by fascism. As Neumann himself would sardonically remind intimate friends in later years, he was among the first group of German citizens to have his citizenship stripped by the new regime. He did not return to Germany until August 1945, when, heavily guarded by American GIs, he arrived to commence his duties as First Chief of Research for the War Crimes Unit of the Office of Strategic Services (OSS); both Neumann and Kirchheimer spent the war and immediate postwar years at OSS figuring out how to defeat the Nazi "behemoth"—and thus the misleading accusations of both Soviet hacks and New Left sectarians in the sixties that the Frankfurt school was an instrument of the CIA and the American national security apparatus. In any event, Neumann's contributions to the Nuremberg Trial were surely of more than professional or even political significance to him; his mother, many friends, and other relatives had died in concentration camps.

The basic composition of Neumann's and Kirchheimer's intellectual production corresponds to the structure of their personal biographies. The authors' reservations about what C. Wright Mills once called "Grand Theory" and their preference for contemporaneous analyses of concrete political issues and interventions into topical political debates are more than a matter of intellectual training or proclivity. Like their lives, their intellectual work is fragmentary. One is sometimes reminded of another neo-Marxist intellectual from their generation, Antonio Gramsci, whose work similarly consists, to some extent, of a mass of disparate topical writings. Writing in an era whose basic contours were defined by the experiences of fascism, political asylum, the Holocaust, Stalinism, and the darkest days of the Cold War and McCarthyism, the Frankfurt school's resident jurists never achieve an architectonic political theory.

Systematization or orderliness is not, however, the only criterion of intellectual excellence. The distraught reflections of a crisis-ridden moment occasionally turn out to be more valuable than a stable era's self-satisfied clichés. Most of the classics of political thought emerged in the context of great political and social upheavals. We cannot build a complete political theory merely on the experience of the emergency situation, but we would do well not to ignore its lessons.

2

My central interest here lies in demonstrating the relevance of Neumann's and Kirchheimer's analysis of the transformation of the rule of law in the twentieth-century capitalist welfare state. Two auxiliary themes are developed as well.

First, an examination of the political and legal thought of Neumann and Kirchheimer suggests the necessity of revising some widely held misconceptions about the Frankfurt school and its controversial quest to develop a critical theory of contemporary democratic societies. Neumann's and Kirchheimer's political and legal theorizing points to a theoretical "missed opportunity"—an alternative and long-forgotten Frankfurt "school"—in some respects superior to both the profoundly pessimistic version of critical theory offered by Horkheimer and Adorno, and sketched out most dramatically in *The Dialectic of Enlightenment,* and to the odd brand of revolutionary theory associated most closely with Herbert Marcuse. Any attempt at an overall assessment of the early Frankfurt school's legacy must take a closer look at Neumann and Kirchheimer. It is simply not true that the early Frankfurt school was unconcerned with issues of political and legal theory.[7] To a great extent because of their real appreciation for the liberal political tradition, Neumann and Kirchheimer take significant strides toward developing a sophisticated view of contemporary democratic politics and toward breaking with many of the most troublesome aspects of traditional Marxist theory. Indeed, they break with that tradition to a far more satisfying degree than their better-known colleagues. The widespread view that Neumann and Kirchheimer were representatives of a more dogmatic and orthodox brand of Marxism than Horkheimer, Adorno, or Pollock is not only misleading but, in some ways, a reversal of the actual state of affairs.[8]

Second, an examination of Neumann and Kirchheimer is absolutely indispensable if we are successfully to take on the intimidating intellectual and political figure of Carl Schmitt, who was not only Weimar Germany's premier right-wing authoritarian political thinker but an active Nazi after 1933 and an important theoretician of many facets of fascist law. Earlier scholars' harsh assessment of Schmitt is being forgotten. Although Schmitt continued to have a significant impact on conservative legal thinking in Germany after World War II, most North American scholars in the immediate postwar era insisted on linking his shameful political choices to deeper structural flaws in his theory.[9] But forty years later, the fascist experience apparently having become little more than an obscure historical footnote for some, the editors of the radical journal *Telos* announce that the Left needs to learn from Schmitt, and those who question the prudence of borrowing from fascism's most impressive political thinker are subjected to name-calling and nasty, rambling polemics.[10] On the right, William Buckley's *National Review* tries to outdo *Telos's* "Schmitt-boosterism": Paul Gottfried insists that "Americans should take Schmitt seriously," because he correctly grasped "the self-destructive tendencies of modern democratic societies" and the need for "genuine community," and by this the author seems to mean, like Schmitt himself, that a morally and politically homogeneous community and a corresponding concept of political legitimacy should have priority over "individual liberty" and the purportedly value-free principle of formal legality. In Gottfried's view, Schmitt's attack on democracy's preoccupation "with balancing the interests and settling the grievances of contesting parties and strident minorities" was downright "prescient."[11]

A self-described "post-Marxist" responds to interpretations of Schmitt like Gottfried's by arguing that Schmitt's theory offers a basis for a genuinely pluralist political theory. For Chantal Mouffe and a growing number of postmodern writers, the liberal idea of a universal rational consensus resting on free discussion is implicitly authoritarian; because Schmitt was purportedly such an insightful critic of liberalism, radicals now should build on his friend/foe "concept of the political" as an alternative to liberalism. Mouffe seems to forget that pluralism itself always presupposes some minimal shared agreement to respect "difference." Furthermore, she is disturbingly unmoved by the fact that Schmitt's own attack on the Enlightenment and political liberalism culminated in radical nationalism, virulent racism, and a romanticization of violence. In her view, the real totalitarians are John Rawls and Jürgen Habermas, and the menace they present to "difference" everywhere can allegedly only be defeated if we join hands with the best-kept secret of twentieth-century intellectual history: meet Carl Schmitt, theorist of radical pluralist democracy.[12]

Followers of Leo Strauss also now seem eager to show that Strauss exerted a significant influence on Schmitt during the early thirties. This is a curious undertaking considering Schmitt's actions after 1933, but that does not seem to bother the Straussians too much.[13] Writers in Italy, France, and England are busily rediscovering Schmitt as well.[14] But the American Schmitt renaissance has been pioneered by two intellectually and politically mainstream writers. For the intellectual historian Joseph Bendersky, Schmitt was a traditional authoritarian, a modern-day

Hobbesian perhaps, but hardly a dedicated Nazi. Despite the fact that under the Nazis Schmitt adamantly defended German fascism as state councillor for Prussia and an influential and outspoken professor in Berlin (both until 1945), then as editor of a major legal publication *(Die Deutsche Juristenzeitung)* and a leader in the Nazi professors' guild (until 1936, when he fell into disfavor with hacks in the SS), "Schmitt's political theory was not irrational, and he never promoted irrationalism or nihilism as a political doctrine."[15] Despite Schmitt's long list of nasty anti-Semitic diatribes in the thirties, George Schwab similarly insists that Schmitt was just forced to engage in "lip service" for his Nazi bosses. Schmitt was a German Abraham Lincoln, intent on saving the Weimar Republic but appreciative of the fact that crises require illiberal and authoritarian means.[16]

The relationship between everyday political trends and intellectual discourse is always extremely complicated. Nonetheless, it is striking that Schmitt is becoming a fashionable intellectual figure in some circles precisely when an array of viciously nationalistic and even neofascist political movements are experiencing a series of political victories. Can we be so sure that the Schmitt renaissance is as harmless as it first seems? Might it not be expressive of deeper and more worrisome trends in contemporary politics?

One of the aims of this study is to offer a theoretical response to misleading interpretations of Schmitt that are rapidly gaining ground in Europe and the United States. Both Franz Neumann and Otto Kirchheimer had intimate and complicated intellectual ties to Schmitt, and a study of their thinking provides a fine vehicle for starting to develop the correspondingly multifaceted answer to Schmitt that we very much need today.[17] Both authors initially borrow from Schmitt's theory, generating, as I show in part I, profound problems for their Weimar-era attempts to develop a critical political and legal theory and a conception of what Neumann describes as the "social rule of law." Even during the most arresting stage in its evolution, in the late twenties, Schmitt's theory conflicts with a minimally defensible view of the rule of law. Only in the thirties, as we see in part II (which focuses on the more general question of the appropriate relationship between legality and legitimacy), do Neumann and Kirchheimer break with Schmitt. But even after that break, the centerpiece of their theorizing remains a subtle and easily overlooked dialogue with Schmitt. Neumann and Kirchheimer concede that there are at least some correlates to Schmitt's political and legal theory in the everyday empirical universe, but, in contrast to Schmitt, they believe that a radical political project, complemented by a critical theory of society, should undertake to rid the political and legal status quo of them. Schmitt's anti-universalistic decisionism reifies a number of troubling empirical trends by seeing them as constituting the core of political and legal experience, whereas Neumann and Kirchheimer trace such trends to irrational social and political tendencies which, in their view, can be attacked. Arguably, the most valuable facet of the liberal political legacy—the rule of law and a set of complementary institutions essential to it—is severely threatened today. Schmitt makes that crisis the starting point for an attack on liberalism and opts for a fascist alternative, whereas Neumann and Kirchheimer (more subtly than Schmitt) acknowledge the seriousness of the crisis of political liberalism but defend the unfulfilled and, in their view, implicitly subversive universalism of classical liberal political thought and champion and restate the rule of law-ideal. Partly because political-theory students had little interest in Schmitt until recently, this aspect of Neumann's and Kirchheimer's intellectual project has long gone unnoticed. Now that Schmitt has returned to haunt us, we need to recall and restate that project.

I generally treat Neumann and Kirchheimer separately. Although they shared in many ways a common intellectual agenda and worked together at the Institute for Social Research, significant differences naturally distinguish these authors. Indeed, it seems to me that these differences are helpful for illustrating how fascism and the demise of Weimar democracy constituted a pivotal "learning experience" for the first generation of Frankfurt-based critical theorists. At many junctures in the narrative that follows, I emphasize those differences. As a result, the historical and conceptual stories tend to merge. My analysis of Neumann's and Kirchheimer's break with an idiosyncratic type of Schmitt-tinged Marxism and the gradual articulation of a critical theory of mass democracy can be illustrated by means of a chronological analysis of the authors' intellectual development.

I

Carl Schmitt Meets Karl Marx

1

A Totalitarian Concept of the Political

What explains the lifelong fascination of two of our century's most provocative left-wing political theorists with the shady figure of Carl Schmitt? Why would a pair of authors intent on recovering the emancipatory implications of the modern rule of law be so obsessed with its meanest critic?

Franz Neumann and Otto Kirchheimer devote much of their impressive intellectual energies to analyzing the ongoing crisis of the rule of law. They describe the disintegration of classical formal law and its replacement by worrisome discretionary administrative decrees; they show how parliamentary institutions no longer play the role that early liberal defenders of the rule of law envisioned for them; they argue that the demise of the liberal state/society division demands a new "social rule of law," making the unfinished quest for social and economic equality its centerpiece; most originally and radically, they suggest that capitalism is ultimately incompatible with the unfinished project of the rule of law, and that as long as we refuse to challenge capitalism, the rule of law will at best be flawed and incomplete. For the mature Neumann and Kirchheimer the centrality of the dialogue with Schmitt stems from this broader project. In their eyes, not only does Schmitt's legal and political theory constitute a vicious critique of those ideals that they think critical social theory must learn to take seriously, but the very conceptual structure of Schmitt's theory unambiguously expresses key features of the present crisis of constitutionalism. Schmitt's argument for the primacy of the "the exception" vis-à-vis the "norm" parallels a number of real trends in twentieth-century legal development; his brand of political decisionism has some concrete correlates in a political universe where situation-specific emergency law plays a key role; his anti-universalist friend/foe model of politics matches too many of the bloody tribalisms so familiar to our political universe; his critique of traditional conceptions of state sovereignty corresponds to an ambiguous and worrisome demise of traditional forms of state authority; his mocking deconstruction of discursive conceptions of parliamentarism unfortunately mirrors the fact that certain traditional liberal institutions no longer provide adequate means for institutionalizing political debate and exchange. However horrible its normative structure, Schmitt's attack on the rule of law unfortunately corresponds to a variety of empirical trends suggesting that liberal constitutionalism is under attack and that we have yet to develop a suitable replacement for it.[1] A defense and reconceptualization of the constitutionalist agenda thus must aggressively challenge Schmitt, not only showing that his theory is the product of an illiberal and antidemocratic author intent on negating the West's most valuable political achievements, but also demonstrating how we can counteract empirical tendencies in contemporary law and politics embodied in his theory. We need more than a restatement of liberal political values reminding us of how Schmitt obviously stands opposed to them. We also need a critical theory showing us how we can begin to drive the specter of Carl Schmitt from the horizons of political experience.

Precisely that critical theory is what the mature Franz Neumann and Otto Kirchheimer offer us, and an interpretation and critical analysis of its strengths and weaknesses constitutes my central theme. But before we can begin to examine its main features we will have to take a closer look at an earlier moment in the relationship between Schmitt and the Frankfurt school's resident political theorists, a moment well before either Neumann or Kirchheimer had developed an adequately critical view of Schmitt or an appropriately appreciative assessment of the rule of law. While the mature Neumann and Kirchheimer distinguish clearly between the normative ills of Schmitt's decisionist theory and what it sometimes implicitly tells us about the sad state of twentieth-century politics, neither author at first succeeds in making this distinction incisively enough. During the late twenties and early thirties, both of them disastrously integrate core features of Schmitt's theory into their own normative theorizing. As we will see, both the young Kirchheimer's uncritical appropriation of Schmitt (discussed in this chapter) and Neumann's more subtle borrowing (analyzed in chapter 2) prove intellectually fatal for both writers during this period.

Were it not for the sudden revival of interest in Carl Schmitt, we probably could simply dismiss this early moment in the history of the Frankfurt school as little more than the "sin of youth" that Jürgen Habermas has recently dubbed it.[2] But contemporary attempts to "learn from Schmitt"—at times strikingly like those of the youthful Kirchheimer and Neumann—have suddenly given their early brand of "left-Schmittianism" a new significance.

Because of the centrality of Carl Schmitt's "concept of the political" both for his own theory and for Neumann's and Kirchheimer's appropriation of it, I begin with a critical exegesis of it (part I). I then offer an interpretation of Kirchheimer's Schmitt-Marx medley that focuses on its explosive fusion of a number of antimodern ideas with characteristically modernist theoretical moves (part II). I argue that the young Kirchheimer's Schmitt-inspired model of an alternative socialist legal order unfortunately points to key components of Schmitt's own vision of an explicitly fascist system of law. Whatever Schmitt's explicit political preferences during the 1920s, central elements of his theory early on anticipated some of the most onerous facets of totalitarian law (part III).

1 Carl Schmitt's Concept of the Political

In Max Weber's political and legal theory, we find a foreshadowing of the crisis of the liberal rule of law. Weber's mammoth *Economy and Society* appreciatively chronicles the emergence of a secularized system of "rational legality" made up of general legal norms like those whose advantages liberal political philosophers long emphasized, yet Weber's discussion ends with an anxiety-ridden analysis of new modes of regulatory "social law," which he thinks undermine the coherence and calculability of bourgeois formal law and could lead to its demise. Weber offers a cautious restatement and defense of both the separation of powers and the ideal of an independent judiciary, but he also nervously admits that the demands of twentieth-century politics are probably destined to generate an unprecedented accumulation of legislative power in the hands of legal experts and maybe even a bureaucratic "shell of bondage" making us "as powerless as the fellahs of ancient Egypt."[3] Prophesying a decline of parliamentary institutions that arguably has continued unabated since his death, the German liberal doubts that a central representative legislature can play the dominant role that classical defenders of the rule of law imagined for it. In clear tension to his respectful appropriation of the parliamentary tradition, Weber comes to think that modern democracies need awesome "caesaristic" leaders outfitted with a tremendous variety of powers if they are to survive.

Most significantly for our discussion, Weber suggests a view of politics only minimally tied to the Enlightenment and the rule of law generated by it. In Weber's view, the Enlightenment's political and legal theory succumbed to a faith in universalistic natural law unacceptable in a disenchanted universe like our own.[4] Although for authors in that era the generality of law was a guarantee of its expressing the common good or general will, for Weber it becomes little more than an instrument for providing minimal legal security for individuals in his view unavoidably battered about by the massive public and private bureaucracies of the modern world. For those in the Enlightenment who endorsed some version of the social contract, political legitimacy rested, at least implicitly, on a decision-making process involving autonomous, equal, and rational agents. Less hopefully, the "late liberal" Weber leaves us with a concept of politics indebted more to Nietzsche than to Rousseau or Kant: "Politics means conflict," he dramatically announces.[5] Doomed to suffer (and enjoy) the ambivalent freedoms of modernity, we are necessarily left without verifiable universal certainties about our most basic values. Only resolute "final decisions," incapable of being universally justified, now provide us with an orientation for moral and political action. Weber struggles to show that the scientific method can still help us gain clarity about the nature and implications of value choices made in the "iron cage" of modernity, and he certainly believes that science legitimately demands that we confront the possibility that a specific course of action might be inconsistent with a particular set of value preferences. But his analysis in some respects ultimately emphasizes more the limits of science than its capabilities. In Weber's view, the political arena is essentially a battlefield for representatives of competing value choices, each of whom accumulates possibilities for (state-based) coercion, which may at some point have to be used against those with alternative value preferences. Politics is a "final instance" or juncture where competing ideologies wage a battle for control over our hearts necessarily left unresolved by science's modest and incomplete attempt to conquer our minds. In part because modernity permits no universally acceptable standards for mediating between competing political alternatives, the political sphere is inevitably conflict-ridden and potentially violent. And where science grows silent, the dictates of political struggle speak ever more loudly by demanding that we commit ourselves to some set of "choices."[6]

Carl Schmitt's pivotal work of 1927, "The Concept of the Political," draws much of its underlying inspiration from key elements of Weber's view of politics.[7] But Schmitt radicalizes all the most troublesome aspects of Weber's decisionism while abandoning those features that still made Weber a true liberal.

This becomes clear at the very outset of "The Concept of the Political," where Schmitt makes a claim for the autonomy and distinctiveness of alternative forms of human activity, forming spheres that he insists are based on a unique set of criteria. Weber argues analogously that "rationalized" modern societies are characterized by the emergence of spheres of activity organized according to internal logics distinct and autonomous from those of competing "life" or "value" spheres, and, just as Schmitt does here, he focuses on the inevitability of potentially violent conflict for making sense of the dynamics of politics.[8] In his elaboration, Schmitt argues that in the aesthetic sphere we distinguish, for example, between "beautiful" and "ugly"; this distinction allegedly encapsulates what the practice of aesthetics is all about, namely the attempt to separate the beautiful from the ugly. Similarly, morality is concerned with the problem of "good" and "evil," whereas the basic dynamics of economic activity are captured by the criteria of "profitability" *(Rentabilität)* and "unprofitability." Schmitt postulates that politics should also be seen as a sphere of human activity with an underlying criterion all its own: thus his distinction between "friend" and "foe." In Schmitt's view, politics is essentially conflictual, and most fundamentally a struggle between political allies and enemies. The criterion of friend versus foe cannot be equated with or reduced to antinomies like "good versus evil" or "productive versus nonproductive." Just as those criteria describe the essential characteristics of autonomous and relatively distinct forms of activity, so too does the criterion of friend versus foe capture the essence of political activity and the basic rules of the political universe. For Schmitt, a world without friends or foes would therefore be a world without politics.[9]

Now this is not to claim that political struggles are unrelated to moral, economic, and even aesthetic conflicts. Though basically independent, the political sphere is not altogether insulated from other facets of social existence. But because politics is ultimately concerned with the question of life or death, and whether a political agent or entity survives or not, politics is, in an important sense, superior to competing value spheres. Despite the fact that politics borrows themes from other spheres of human activity it nonetheless has a logic of its own prior to theirs.[10] When morality, aesthetics, or economics appears to have become of central importance for politics, this is, in Schmitt's view, only because they have come to be governed by the criterion of friend versus foe. "The concepts of friend, foe, and struggle only gain their real significance through the fact that they relate in particular to the real possibility of killing" the other. "War is only the utmost realization of enmity" in politics.[11] The political foe is characterized precisely by the fact that he or she may at some point need to be killed and is thus an opponent or enemy in the most intense possible sense of the term. If spheres of activity that at first seem nonpolitical dominate the political sphere, this merely shows that moral, economic, or aesthetic conflicts have been subdued by the logic of friend versus foe and that such tensions have become so heated that there is a "real possibility" of killing economic, moral, or aesthetic opponents. Normally, such disagreements do not result in murdering one's opponent. But if they take an "intense" (and potentially violent "political") character, they might. Antagonistic social classes are now ready to wage war against each other on the basis of what classical liberalism once considered private concerns about the economy; religious differences suddenly take a nasty turn and different sects prepare to go to the barricades and do battle. In such moments, economic and moral conflicts transcend the value spheres from which they emerge and now concern, in Schmitt's view, the eminently political question of "existence."

The most immediate source of Schmitt's belief that the "real possibility" of violence is essential for understanding politics lies in his distaste for the moralistic "fictions and normativities" of those who aspire to create an alternative political world where violence has somehow been tamed and is no longer a common way to resolve intense political conflicts. For Schmitt, the "real possibility" of violence is a permanent and determinative feature of political existence. The quest to change this undeniable precondition of politics is either irrelevant as far as grappling with existing political contingencies is concerned or, worse, representative of a form of politics that, in its self-righteous striving to rid the world of violence, inevitably destines humanity to fight even more brutal wars. In making use of moralistic talk about ending all wars and about humanity's "universal" interest in establishing a peaceful world community, liberal universalists in Schmitt's view are forced to wage the most brutal wars of all.[12] Schmitt radicalizes Weber's decisionist theory and thus is even more dismissive of the role of "normativities" in politics than the idiosyncratic liberal Weber ever was. Despite his own insistence on the limits of universal normative truths for politics, Weber nonetheless claims that an "ethics of responsibility" follows from the very structure of the modern political sphere. Though normative certainties have been banned from modern politics, politics still implies a minimal ethics deriving, however paradoxically, from its own basically disenchanted structure. Because force is the means or tool distinct to politics, a political agent necessarily has to grapple with the problems posed by violence, in particular the fact that an agent's basic intentions inevitably manifest themselves in contradictory and unforeseen ways in a world "governed by demons" and haunted by the specter of force. Insofar as political action ultimately rests on the possibility of employing force, gaps between the actor's intentions, the actual form taken by political action, and the real-life consequences of action properly have an overriding importance for the political actor. In Weber's view, those who refuse to grapple with the implications of political violence are thus nothing but political "children"; this is why he famously demands that political agents act "with the head" and with a sense of "measure." Weber struggles to counteract the more radical and worrisome implications of the decisionist outlook. Insofar as we "choose" to act politically, we should obey the dictates of the political sphere, just as those who choose religion or science should obey their basic rules. The most important of these rules is that we consider the implications of that medium (violence) particular to politics with reflectiveness and care, just as the religious person can be expected to respect religious rituals or the scientist the general standards of the community of scholars.[13]

In contrast, Schmitt doubts that a consistently decisionist outlook leaves us any room for even a modest ethics of responsibility, and no signs of it can be detected in his concept of the political. His decisionism lacks even the barest echoes of the "old European rationalism," which still haunt Weber. As we will see, a glamorization of violence, and not simply Weber's rather worrisome acceptance of the centrality of violence for understanding politics, results. For Schmitt, the foe "is simply the Other, the Alien, and it is enough for his being that he is in a particularly intensive sense existentially something Other and Alien, so that in the case of a conflict he means the negation of one's own form of existence and therefore must be guarded from and fought off, in order to preserve one's own appropriate form *(eigene, seinsmäßige Art)* of life."[14] Mainly because Schmitt believes that the political sphere is fundamentally distinct from morality, the determination of the foe can have nothing whatsoever to do with "fictions and normativities": to see politics as being regulated by "normativities" (universal moral claims, for example) would deny its autonomy.[15] The final decision about who the foe is can be legitimated on the basis of any conceivable ground, and it suffices for Schmitt to comment that "[the foe] is simply the Other, the Alien," and that political action gains guidance from "a pure decision not based on reason and discussion and not justifying itself, that is, . . . an absolute decision created out of nothingness."[16] Having eliminated the most minimal ties between politics and morality, Schmitt reduces the core of politics to an abstract and formal "choice" capable of taking on any conceivable content; indeed, Schmitt's own widely acknowledged political opportunism is likely one consequence of this conceptual move, emerging in part from his insistence on the centrality of "intensity" for determining political action's "authenticity." Even if we can detect the prospect of this development in Weber's more moderate decisionism, only in Schmitt's theory do the dangers of a political sphere liberated from all normativities manifest themselves most unambiguously: modern politics, it seems, is doomed to the vagaries of a political existentialism whose chief aim lies in warding off "alien" forms of "life."

The basic argument of *The Crisis of Parliamentary Democracy* (1923) is little more than an empirical gloss on a more profound and nasty attack on the possibility of "government by discussion," an argument which derives from the more fundamental ideas articulated in "The Concept of the Political." Given Schmitt's view of politics, the idea of a universal moral consensus resting on a process of rational will formation has to be interpreted as just another universalistic normativity with no rightful place in the political sphere. In his view, an authentic political theory has no room for naive moralistic ideas like that of the social contract or a set of related (universalistic) conceptions about political equality, the rule of law, or any of an array of liberal political institutions. The problem with parliamentarism is not simply that it has been overwhelmed and rendered anachronistic by a set of sudden and unexpected social and political transformations, but that its preference for negotiation, compromise, and debate conflicts head-on with the decisionist core of all genuinely political experiences.[17]

Schmitt's reformulation of the concept of sovereignty, which makes up the central theme of his *Political Theology,* is similarly implied by the structure of the concept of the political. Because Schmitt believes that the political universe is unavoidably divided into alien friends and foes tortured by the ever-present threat of violence, refusing to make a decision about who those friends and foes are is equivalent to ignoring the basic laws of the political sphere. In direct contradistinction to Weber's sober call for political responsibility, Schmitt tells us straight out that it is much more important to make a decision than that it be a particularly reflective or correct one. By valorizing a "sovereign decision" above and beyond any normative principles, Schmitt thereby points to a reconceptualization of sovereignty in terms of the person "who decides on the exception."[18] The insurmountable break between morality and politics culminates in the vision of a political universe dominated by the experience of the "norm-less exception," meaning, most dramatically, a moment of crisis when the existence or life of a political entity is seriously threatened, but referring more broadly in Schmitt's view to a diverse variety of political phenomena incapable of being captured or subsumed under a set of universally applicable normativities or norm-based legal rules. Judicial action, for example, always involves an irrational indeterminate decisionist moment, and the traditional liberal view that judicial decisions are properly subordinated to general norms is profoundly misleading.[19] Analogously, no set of general constitutional norms can cover the unpredictable exigencies of the political crisis: "There exists no norm that is applicable to chaos."[20] It can never be ascertained beforehand what a political emergency (or legal chaos) requires of a particular political entity. As a result, the typically constitutionalist attempt to place legal restraints on the exercise of political authority during an emergency is not only theoretically ill-founded but potentially disastrous politically. How can constitutionalists be so sure that a political entity might not require an unprecedented centralization of authority, or an exercise of violence necessarily unforeseen by any constitutional clause or general legal norm? Because the possibility of arbitrary and unrestrained force can never be eliminated from the political universe, sovereignty must be redefined in terms of that political agent who monopolizes "the last decision," or that actor capable of taking on all the potential dangers of a political universe as unavoidably irrational and violent as our own; the guarantee of sovereignty necessarily belongs to the core of any genuine mode of politics. Insofar as existentially authentic politics is characterized precisely by its liberation from all normativities, the height of political action—sovereignty—needs to be defined in terms of the command of that moment or exception where normativities (or norm-based legalisms) are most irrelevant. But if the sovereign alone "decides whether there is an extreme emergency as well as what must be done to eliminate it," he or she must also have the power to determine when a situation of normalcy exists.[21] In this way as well, the exception is primordial vis-à-vis the norm.

Essential to sovereignty is what Schmitt describes, in "The Concept of the Political," as political "unity." Political entities are not threatened simply by external foes. Domestic or internal foes and the possibility of civil war also constitute a potential challenge to "one's own, appropriate form of life."[22] Divided political entities have no chance of surviving in an unstable political universe, and they often suffer the consequences of this failing: "That a folk no longer has the power or the will to maintain itself in the sphere of the political does not mean that politics disappears from the world. Only a weak folk disappears."[23] A far-reaching and substantial uniformity, or "homogeneity" as Schmitt often describes it, in the political sphere is a key presupposition of political strength. A mere shared commitment to any set of formal political procedures is inadequate if a political community is to rest on an unambiguous friend/foe constellation.[24] In developing this claim, Schmitt refers to Rousseau, but he strips Rousseau of any of his more defensible features. The eighteenth-century French philosopher allegedly sensed the centrality of homogeneity for authentic politics in arguing that a true democracy exists only where it presupposes a "homogeneous folk" and where there is no real basis for distinct political parties, religious differences, special interests opposed to the general will, or relatively stable majority/minority constellations.[25] In Schmitt's theory, homogeneity ultimately refers to a substantial sameness of themes or issues having a political significance. Given the tremendous diversity of potentially political issues in the contemporary world, Schmitt has to demand, ultimately, that homogeneity be extremely extensive. It is striking that he criticizes Rousseau's original formulation for still including a number of liberalistic and individualistic moments: insofar as Rousseau's reliance on the metaphor of the social contract is based on the picture of an agreement between individuals who first must enter into it, it still is predicated on some degree of political pluralism.

Because Schmitt's anti-universalism prevents him from excluding the possibility of any specific configuration of friend/foe relations, he admits that homogeneity can take many equally legitimate forms and that its manifestation depends merely on what issues have taken a truly intense and potentially explosive form at any particular juncture.[26] Not only does his hostility to normativities in the political sphere leave him helpless to criticize racism or virulent nationalism, but he generally ends up arguing that ethnic or national homogeneity is to be preferred given its manifest intensity in the contemporary world as a basis for friend/foe constellations and as a source of political unity.[27] Schmitt would like us to think that this tendency to privilege irrationalist forms of political identity is simply due to the fact that such conflicts are so common in the rather ugly terrain of contemporary politics. But this self-defense at the very least obscures his tendency to reduce the "ought" to the "is": Schmitt's belief in the basic irrelevance of universalistic normativities to politics repeatedly leads him to fuse normative and empirical claims in a confusing and irresponsible fashion. Obviously, much of real-life politics involves arbitrary and irrational racist and nationalist conflict. The real question is whether it should stay that way.

Having denied normative issues any autonomy in the political sphere, Schmitt cannot even begin to answer that question.

2 Modernist Antimodernism

If Schmitt's "Concept of the Political" undoubtedly constituted an implicit attack on the Weimar Republic and its failed aspiration to realize Germany's first constitutionalist liberal democracy, his precocious young student Otto Kirchheimer's reconstruction of Schmitt's ideas, undertaken for a set of socialist journals generally affiliated with the left wing of the SPD (with which Kirchheimer identified) during the late twenties and in the 1930 volume *Weimar—and What Then?* was explicitly so.[28] In 1927 Kirchheimer attended a seminar offered by Schmitt at the University of Bonn on "the concept of the political," and the ideas Schmitt articulated in the seminar clearly had a direct impact on the twenty-two-year-old radical. Kirchheimer combines Schmitt's concept of the political with a set of classical Marxist ideas and then outfits this theoretical fusion with a far richer empirical analysis than can be found in Schmitt's own writings from the twenties. The result is not only quintessentially left-Schmittian but appropriately explosive.

This is most clearly the case in "The Socialist and Bolshevik Theory of the State," a fiery 1928 polemic unfavorably contrasting the moderate socialism of the Second International with the (allegedly) more authentically political theory and practice of bolshevism. Originally part of a doctoral dissertation written under Schmitt, it is Kirchheimer's most explicitly Schmittian work, and, in both its rhetoric and theoretical categories, it reveals his teacher's inordinate influence. Kirchheimer dramatically announces in the essay that social democracy's basic flaw is its refusal "to decide": in its willingness to compromise with bourgeois political foes, it obfuscates the very nature of politics by closing its eyes to the fact that only a decision to act ruthlessly against the bourgeois foe guarantees socialism any future. According to the Marxist reworking of Schmitt undertaken in the essay, the friend/foe divide of our time lies between a working class forced to sell its labor power and capitalist property owners who buy it, and the great error of moderate social democracy (and the Weimar political order itself, which rests on a class compromise between liberal middle-class and reformist working-class groups) is the failure to recognize the full import of the basic enmity between the proletariat and the bourgeoisie. Repeating Schmitt's own claim that revolutionary socialism à la Sorel or Lenin constitutes a left-wing doctrine with strongly decisionistic overtones, Kirchheimer goes so far here as to praise Leninism for advocating, in contrast to reformist socialism, "a doctrine of unmitigated, all-embracing struggle," and he enthusiastically applauds the Soviet Union for pursuing a brand of politics that ruthlessly distinguishes friend from foe.[29] "Of fundamental importance for every political theory . . . is to what extent it takes account of, and admits into its texture, the principle of emergency."[30] Soviet strategists understand the centrality of the emergency and, faced with internal and external threats, are ready to act ruthlessly against their enemies without qualms about establishing a dictatorial regime as a way of undertaking the crucial task of integrating their supporters according to a set of far-reaching shared ideals. Relying on Sorel, the young Kirchheimer commends the Bolsheviks for evoking a myth glorifying the virtues of world revolution, claiming that it helps unveil and clarify the real structure of friend/foe antagonisms and aids the working classes in their struggle for liberation. Mythical thought demasks the normativistic "individualistic ethics" and "unreal, intellectually motivated class consciousness" of the Second International, showing it be to an inauthentic mode of "third-class liberal" politics, inferior to Sorel and Lenin's insistence that ethics must be subordinated to the dictates of the political struggle. Soviet mythmaking is, in any case, more effective than reformism's philistine "medley of economic development and democracy, of majority vote and humanitarianism."[31] Again echoing Schmitt, Kirchheimer tells us that Marx himself was an old-fashioned moralistic rationalist, whereas Sorel's irrationalism and Lenin's militant, myth-inspiring socialism realize the true kernel of Marx's theory, namely, the doctrine of the class struggle. Socialism should dump the Enlightenment heritage from which classical Marxism drew its normative energies; Marx's real achievement stemmed from his acknowledgment of the existential intensity of class-based friend/foe antagonisms.

Like many other fledgling democracies in the West, the indecisive Weimar Republic is a "mere shell" of the state. The state apparatus there is "something less than itself," because it continues to tolerate, and even debate with, its foes.[32] Because Weimar attempts to bring together truly antagonistic political groupings with radically distinct worldviews, Kirchheimer argues that it surrenders its political character by failing to achieve homogeneity and guaranteeing the preconditions of Schmittian-style sovereignty. This manifests itself directly in the fact that the state apparatus has been given as little real decision-making prerogative as possible, and that state authority is broken up and dispersed among an amorphous mass of distinct, decentralized administrative units (for example, social welfare agencies and new labor and welfare courts) pursuing diverse and sometimes even contrary goals. Weimar sacrifices its "will" and "substance" in favor of "formalistic" institutions: the democratic state "tends to disappear behind its own legal mechanism."[33] The emerging German welfare state and the imperatives of the politics of class compromise it depends on inevitably result in the "impossibility to find, in our age of formally democratic structures aiming at social equilibrium, a satisfactory answer to the question of who is the wielder of sovereignty, that is, who makes the actual decision in a conflict situation."[34] When state authority is spread thin among subsidiary administrative institutions aspiring to mediate and tame explosive conflicts by legal means, who can really be said to be sovereign? Where could authority be adequately centralized so as to take on the exigencies of the emergency?

In a series of articles, written on the occasion of the tenth anniversary of the Weimar Constitution on 1929 and then in the fascinating *Weimar—and What Then?*, Kirchheimer elaborates upon his Schmitt-Marx medley in order to trash the fragile republic's constitutional structure.[35] Like social democracy, the Weimar Constitution refuses to acknowledge the basic laws of friend/foe politics. Naively undertaking to combine liberal, socialist, democratic, bourgeois, and even religious viewpoints, the Weimar Constitution is "without a decision" and destined to fail in what many of Kirchheimer's contemporaries on the German Left (Franz Neumann being prominent among them, as we will see) take to be the constitutional endorsement of a transitional postcapitalist social and political order. Little more than the legal embodiment of the necessarily momentary political constellation of war-weary Germany, the constitution fails to bring together the country's diverse and antagonistic political forces according to a set of common political views and a common program for "action," and it is thus not merely formalistic but downright morally relativistic. The figure of Hans Kelsen haunts Kirchheimer's argumentation here. The neo-Kantian and moderately left-wing Kelsen had argued that modern democracy was appropriate to a relativistic worldview that could no longer rest on the acknowledgement of any set of absolute values. A belief in moral absolutes leads to political authoritarianism, Kelsen insisted, whereas a recognition of the possibility of intellectual fallibility implies the virtues of political tolerance, free speech, and political equality; anyone's view, after all, could turn out to be correct. The democratic "method" corresponds to a disenchanted, fallibilistic conception of knowledge.[36] From Schmitt's perspective, Kelsen's relativism expresses a profoundly and typically liberal antipolitical nihilism. Kirchheimer builds on his teacher's own views in arguing that the Weimar Constitution's alleged embodiment of a related constellation of ideas is a sign of its confused moral and political status. For Schmitt's young protégé, the Left would do well to stop fetishizing the constitution. Socialists should instead prepare themselves to wage a revolutionary struggle with the aim of establishing a homogeneous socialism alone capable of guaranteeing a stable and genuinely political regime.

Now it is hardly difficult to imagine why Schmitt's theory was attractive to Kirchheimer as he struggled to develop a radical critique of the Weimar Republic in the late twenties. The German republic was, in fact, besieged by a threatening constellation of right-wing and nationalist foes, and Schmitt's view that a genuine, politically authentic democracy needed to rest upon homogeneity struck his young student, unsurprisingly, as a sensible starting point for a socialist alternative. Haunted by the specter of an ambiguous and incomplete revolution and the "real possibility" of civil war, the everyday universe of Weimar politics must have seemed to confirm for Kirchheimer Schmittian insights about the primacy of the "norm-less exception." In any case, it had to appear more concrete and politically astute than the self-confident platitudes of official liberal and social democratic rhetoric. Finally, if nineteenth-century Marxism was too often dismissive of formal democracy and the so-called bourgeois rule of law and far too blind to the dangers of its own Jacobin-inspired assumptions about the virtues of a homogeneous, conflict-free postcapitalist order, Carl Schmitt's concept of the political must have seemed to offer the perfect complement to Marx's critique of capitalism for a young Marxist like Kirchheimer.[37]

Whatever the immediate roots of Kirchheimer's attraction to Schmitt's ideas, the results serve only to demonstrate the ruinous consequences of a theory that takes the ugliest facets of the political status quo as a normative starting point; the realism misleadingly attributed to Schmitt by writers like Paul Piccone and G. L. Ulmen is not necessarily an intellectual virtue when political reality at a specific historical juncture takes a particularly inhumane form.[38] Kirchheimer's Schmitt-Marx synthesis relies, in fact, on a set of implicit and unacceptable normative claims incompatible with the very presuppositions of a defensible conception of a modern political universe. If some elements of this intellectual constellation indeed do correspond to certain trends in our world, that should be taken as evidence for the unsatisfying and normatively undeveloped status of contemporary politics and by no means as a sign of the sophistication of Schmitt's theory. To a great extent because of its Schmittian features, the young Kirchheimer's fiery polemics too often amount to a mere foil for attacking a more formidable foe than either reformist socialism or liberalism—namely, the most minimal normative achievements of modernity itself.

The Schmittian quest to decouple politics from morality at first glance seems, as we have seen, to be a characteristically modernist theoretical move. Did not Weber himself persuasively argue that contemporary politics can no longer legitimate itself on the basis of substantive worldviews, such as the religious-inspired systems of natural law so crucial to the history of Western political development? Is it not, in fact, difficult to imagine how a modern, morally pluralistic community could ground itself on something like Christian natural law or classical natural right? It seems to me that Weber is right to doubt that these possibilities are acceptable to us today. But the real question is whether this situation has to leave contemporary politics in the Schmittian, normative limbo of radical decisionism, where the mere intensity of an abstract decision or choice becomes the central standard by which we can allegedly determine the correctness (or, more precisely, authenticity) of political action. Must the demise of the relatively far-reaching value homogeneity of the distant past leave us with a vague and disturbing brand of political existentialism? Are we thus forced to choose between the Scylla of substantial, premodern value homogeneity and the Charybdis of political existentialism, or might there be a more defensible alternative available to us? In subsequent chapters, we will see how the mature Otto Kirchheimer and Franz Neumann try to sketch just such an alternative in the form of a critical model of the democratic rule of law. But let me suggest that the answer provided by Schmitt and his eager leftist pupil here is a highly peculiar antimodern existentialism. However paradoxically, the Schmittian project combines *both* the ills of the Scylla of premodern value homogeneity *and* the Charybdis of a typically modernist brand of political existentialism. Indeed, Schmitt's theory is so explosive precisely because it gives an antimodern program a modernist gloss.

As we have seen, both Schmitt and the young Kirchheimer insist on the importance of homogeneity for preserving political unity and guaranteeing truly sovereign political action, and both give the concept of homogeneity extremely substantial overtones and link it to a broader anti-universalistic political existentialism.[39] For Schmitt, homogeneity can take a number of forms, but he repeatedly emphasizes the advantages of common ethnicity or nationality as a prerequisite for authentic friend/foe politics. Despite his own anti-universalistic proclivities, the young Kirchheimer does not share his teacher's interpretation of homogeneity, yet his version of it nonetheless continues with its own deeply troubling implications. Socialism à la Carl Schmitt does not refer simply to an egalitarian distribution of social and economic resources. Kirchheimer insists, in "The Socialist and Bolshevik Theory of the State," that a truly democratic and socialist society is fully integrated on the basis of a basic decision for a set of substantive common values, or an "agreement on fundamental values," and he explicitly contrasts his Schmitt-inspired vision of a socialist "value democracy" *(Wertedemokratie)* and the related idea of a homogeneous socialist people that has heroically avoided third-class, universalistic normativities to the purported moral relativism of liberal democracy and its failure to choose substantive moral values existentially. Though Kirchheimer's conception of values is admittedly far from being perfectly unambiguous, and despite the fact that the description he offers of a socialist value democracy remains in many ways undeveloped, he, like Schmitt, explicitly insists that a tacit agreement on the rules of the game as emphasized by formal democracy's defenders is inadequate. If socialist value democracy is to distinguish successfully between friends and foes, something much more substantial and far-reaching in quality is called for.[40] In any event, Kirchheimer's socialism would probably not be a particularly pluralistic or tolerant utopia. It likely implies a broadly shared common ethos and a far-reaching existentially determined consensus (emerging during what Kirchheimer dubs the "creative act" of revolution) not only about the basic structure of the decision-making process but about the outcome of policy itself and the form of much of everyday activity. The key assumption for the Marxist Kirchheimer is that values correspond to social position, hence an homogeneous social order automatically generates an high degree of cultural, moral, and political homogeneity: social homogeneity means value homogeneity. But, as an eager Schmittian, Kirchheimer also sees existentially based homogeneity as alone capable of providing the strength needed by political entities in a universe haunted by the specter of the political emergency.

Despite its modernist overtones, Schmitt's concept of the political implicitly privileges a vision of politics disturbingly reminiscent of the close-knit, small-scale, relatively homogeneous communities of the distant past, when universalistic modes of thought and praxis remained similarly undeveloped. Like Weber, Schmitt at first seems to see the secularization of the political sphere as undeniable and irreversible. Unlike Weber, the Catholic Schmitt interprets this development in terms of a dramatic regression and as evidence for the basic sinfulness and bestiality of human nature.[41] Yet Schmitt's hostility to modernity differs essentially from that of most religious authoritarians, and it is striking that he does not openly endorse a blatantly theocratic dictatorship. A real nostalgia for the relative value homogeneity of the distant past (Christian medieval Europe perhaps?) and a rebellion against the disenchanted political universe and the interrelated "fact of pluralism" can undoubtedly be detected here as well, but Schmitt's attack on modernity takes the somewhat more subtle form of a demand for substantial homogeneity.[42] The rather formalistic structure of the concept of the political—recall that intensity is the main criterion for determining the political character of a specific problem or theme—seems to liberate politics from morality, but then Schmitt and his pupil slip in a set of hidden assumptions that tend to embody all the most problematic features of the crudest conceptualizations of the relationship between politics and morality. They do this in part by underplaying the normative significance of the idea of homogeneity: Schmitt suggests that homogeneity is a political, and thus, in his theoretical system, an explicitly nonnormative, category. As a result, Schmitt's emphasis on the importance of homogeneity need not appear to contradict the argument for a radical separation of politics and morality. Nonetheless, the idea of homogeneity plays a role here strikingly like that of the substantial ethos of the underdeveloped, parochial, ethnocentric community of the distant past, when a relatively high degree of moral, cultural, and political sameness functioned to eliminate a broad variety of potentially conflict-ridden themes from the political agenda and preserve stability at the cost of eliminating real moral and political diversity, which is the source of many of the political conflicts characteristic of the modern world. Like a primitive community still primarily regulated by a set of simple indwelling customs and mores, homogeneous value democracy can allegedly do without complex institutionalized modes of political deliberation and exchange—at least the nasty Schmittian attack on discursive conceptions of liberal parliamentarism suggests as much. Homogeneity makes unity possible, but it does so at the cost of removing many identifiably political forms of action from the political sphere.[43]

Since Hegel, we know that attempts to rebel against the basic conditions of modernity necessarily culminate in terror.[44] Unsurprisingly, violence in Schmittian theory too often is envisioned as making up the very apex of politics. If intensity is the chief standard by which we are to determine how genuinely political something has become, what could possibly be more truly political than political violence? Revolution is seen by Kirchheimer as being more than the tragic, yet at times necessary, quest to right terrible wrongs. It is a creative act, an authentically existential decision (in contrast to the vacillations of compromise-based democratic politics), and he offers effusive praise for Sorel's *Reflections on Violence* and believes that revolutionary socialism is right on the mark in picturing its opponents as alien and inhumane "infidels," who will have to be ruthlessly destroyed. Kirchheimer admires Sorel and Lenin for acknowledging the necessity of a brutal last battle between socialism and capitalism and has only the most flattering of compliments for the

Soviets for crushing their foes instead of bickering or arguing with them.[45] Schmitt repeatedly praises nineteenth-century Catholic reactionaries like de Maistre and Donoso Cortés for calling for a "bloody decisive battle . . . between catholicism and atheist socialism," "a definitive dispute" capable of extinguishing the authoritarian Right's foes from the political scene.[46] In his formulation, consistent decisionism should culminate in a feverish moment when violence is unleashed against the foe and attempts to avoid the final decision amount to nothing but a normativistic antipolitical cowardice. In his introduction to the timely *Crisis of Parliamentary Democracy,* Schmitt expressly tells his German audience that a true democracy never hesitates to "eliminate" and even "exterminate" *(vernichten)* heterogeneous elements, and, to make sure his readers understand precisely what he has in mind, he mentions Turkey's driving of ethnic Greeks from its shores.[47] Again and again, he favorably contrasts the choice of a "decisive bloody battle" with liberalistic parliamentary debate, negotiation, compromise, and an Enlightenment vision of a "monstrous club," where political debate and discussion take place in every interstice of society. Even though he explicitly claims, in "The Concept of the Political," that he intends no glamorization of violence, his broader theoretical scheme inevitably transforms violence into not only a legitimate political instrument but probably a privileged one.[48] Kirchheimer is awed by Lenin's readiness to act brutally against those unwilling to accept the basic contours of a social and political order characterized by an all-encompassing Bolshevik-imposed homogeneity; Schmitt admires Aristotle's political philosophy—not because of Aristotle's vision of the political sphere as resting on relations of mutual reciprocity and debate, but because it does not hesitate to distinguish between Greek and barbarian.[49] The modern principle of the equality of all persons is allegedly a normativistic and antipolitical idea that denies the primacy of profound, existential conflicts between people, Schmitt thinks, who often *are* profoundly different and alien.

At least premodern worldviews tended to place normative restraints on political violence. Characteristically, Schmitt does not bother to tell us that his own romanticization of political violence is missing from Aristotle, for example, whom Schmitt otherwise thinks he can borrow from. As far as the problem of violence is concerned, the break between politics and traditional morality in Schmitt's theory seems real enough. Here, as on numerous other occasions, blatantly antimodern intentions are given a modernist packaging. Not only is an archaic idea of homogeneity advanced by means of a political existentialism that, somewhat paradoxically, itself seems to presuppose a radical break between morality and politics and, on some level, the dissolution of substantive premodern worldviews, but the idea of homogeneity itself is interpreted with categories borrowed from the experiences of modern nationalism and authoritarian socialism. The anti-universalistic ethnos of the distant past becomes the "nation" (or "proletariat"), now given a fittingly anti-universalistic interpretation, and, in accordance with Schmitt's insistence on the primacy of the political exception, it is pictured in a highly anti-traditional manner as unlimited, all-powerful and incapable of being restrained or shackled by constitutional or legal standards.[50] Similarly, both Schmitt and Kirchheimer acknowledge the primacy of the principle of popular sovereignty that was ushered in by the American and French Revolutions, yet their ideas about democracy have little to do with the universalistic core of modern democratic theory. Instead, they repeatedly hearken back to traditional views of democracy as an irrational and supralegal "rule of the many." If the greatness of the classical socialist political tradition derives from its aspiration to complete the unfinished and characteristically modern quest for universal autonomy, for the young Kirchheimer it becomes little more than a violent struggle for a degree of social and moral uniformity undesirable under contemporary conditions.

The mix is an alarming one, and the parallels to totalitarian thought and practice, whose synthesis of antimodern and modernist themes is strikingly similar, should be evident enough. Schmitt and the young Kirchheimer would like us to believe that the contours of political existence are by necessity determined by the normless exception—"characterized as a case of extreme peril, a danger to the existence of the state"—but this would only be unreservedly true in the political universe implied by their theory.[51] In a world overrun by political entities obsessed with recapturing mythical homogeneities and hunting down heterogeneous foes, and freed from anything resembling the universalistic normativism mocked so disdainfully by both of them, universalistic visions of a common humanity would indeed start to look like silly liberalistic myths. Political violence might conceivably become constant—and the apex of political experience.

3 The Making of Totalitarian Law

In 1933 and 1934 Carl Schmitt led a chorus of German jurists who enthusiastically endorsed the new Nazi regime.[52] Like many of his colleagues, Schmitt soon busied himself with making constructive suggestions about how the German legal order could be reorganized so as to fit the needs of the emerging homogeneous "national folk community." Predicated on what he described as the "the bankruptcy of general ideas," his legal proposals constituted a complement to the Nazis' own rabidly anti-universalistic nationalism and racism.[53] Centrally, Schmitt demanded the dissolution of the "abstractions" allegedly characteristic of modern formal law and a new system oriented toward the immediate exigencies of the "concrete situation" and the special needs of the equally particular German "folk." Vague and indiscrete legal standards (for example; "in good faith") purportedly alone could provide state officials with the flexibility denied them by "lifeless" modern law as endorsed by modern authors from Locke to Bentham. According to Schmitt, the Nazis would do well to make such legal clauses the centerpiece of their alternative to normativistic liberal law. While arguing that it should draw its inspiration from a moment in the history of medieval German common law before being influenced by formalistic Roman law and a set of "alien" (in particular, Jewish) ethnic influences, Schmitt simultaneously announced that his model constituted a theoretical advance over the anachronistic rationalism of the Enlightenment. In other words, the Nazis should be outfitted with a legal system that openly abandoned all the merits of modern formal law; it should give state authorities as much room as possible for intervening in all facets of social and personal existence in any way the "situation" (whose exigencies, of course, only the Nazis would be empowered to interpret) required. Even though the new political elite should look back to the blatant irregularities of the fourteenth-century common law of the German folk in order to construct it, fascist law was supposedly more modern than any other legal system in the world.[54]

In forthcoming chapters, we will take a closer look at what led Schmitt to embrace this position. But we can already begin to point to why Schmitt's Nazi-boosterism during the thirties was implied by the constellation of ideas from the twenties that I have tentatively, and far too incompletely, analyzed in this chapter. Well before Schmitt himself sketched out the intricate details of a totalitarian fascist legal model, Kirchheimer anticipated a vision of law with a number of disturbing similarities as early as 1928. This suggests that an identifiably totalitarian system of law is latent in the Schmittian concept of the political—or at least the young Kirchheimer's careful exegesis of the legal implications of his teacher's theory implies such an interpretation.

A conceptual configuration valorizing a normatively unregulated sovereign "decision" probably has to see the modern rule of law's self-proclaimed aspiration to regulate state action by means of cogent general norms ultimately as just another attempt to enslave politics to moralistic normativities, and hence as a hindrance to authentic political action. From this viewpoint, the idea of the separation of powers can only amount to a challenge to state unity and sovereignty; an independent judiciary probably has to be seen as a way of circumventing political decisions in the name of a dubious antipolitical belief in neutrality; the very contrast between a rule based on impartial norms and that of particular individuals must be conceived of as a quest to deny the irresistible truth that politics fundamentally concerns concrete, existential conflicts. As Schmitt explicitly notes, in "The Concept of the Political," "the sovereignty of law only means the sovereignty of those men who draw up and administer the law."[55] If the core of friend/foe politics is the experience of heated and even explosive conflict, attempts to resolve nasty political disagreements by means of peaceful legal mechanisms have to be interpreted as an inappropriate attempt to "juridify," as Kirchheimer dubs it, spheres of human activity unsuited to its logic.

The young Kirchheimer's reflections about the rule of law rigorously pursue this line of analysis. He interprets modern political liberalism's alliance with constitutionalist modes of thinking as a sign of its political ineptness and insufficiently political character. Reformist socialism repeats liberalism's errors by pursuing an overly legalistic agenda that tends to neutralize friend/foe conflicts that it would best exploit.[56] Most problematically, "The Socialist and Bolshevik Theory of the State" offers an alarmingly appreciative interpretation of Soviet law that glamorizes its arbitrary, radically discretionary, and potentially totalitarian features. In Kirchheimer's apologetic portrayal of an authoritarian socialist alternative to the normativities of modern law, the rule of law indeed is reduced to nothing more than Schmitt's "sovereignty of those men who draw up and administer law." Every feature of modern law that implies the possibility of taming or superceding an arbitrary "rule of men" in favor of a universally acceptable rule of rational law is tossed to the wayside. In subordinating the legal order to the ever-changing dictates of a political elite, law in this model is directly subjected to the particularities of the concrete dynamics of friend/foe politics and the irregular decisions of a narrowly based political elite. Embodying the logic of Schmittian decisionism, legality can no longer claim to be clearly distinct from facticity.

"The Socialist and Bolshevik Theory of the State" argues that whereas the explosion of legal instruments (in the form of new labor and social welfare courts, for example) in the West is expressive of democracy's antipolitical refusal to make a decision in favor of a set of common interests and values, Lenin admirably sought instead to restore "the image of the substantive character of law which in Europe, since the age of liberalism, has tended to disappear." Law in the Soviet Union is directly linked to the Communist party's program and is made, as Lenin notes, "an instrument for education and for imparting discipline."[57] Leninist legality mobilizes support among actual and potential friends and ruthlessly punishes its foes, and Kirchheimer approvingly describes how the Bolshevik legal system is based on ever-changing "temporary law." Cogent modern formal law is jettisoned for short-lived decrees issued by the Leninist party, and law becomes "so dependent on the government objectives at any given time that the suggestion even was made to limit the validity of the new Soviet Civil Code to only two years."[58]

But this means that legal practices long associated with a crisis situation now become normal and that the legal exception indeed becomes "more interesting than the rule. The rule proves nothing; the exception proves everything."[59] Consequently, any real distinction between law and physical coercion becomes blurred: the exigencies of the emergency could require the most violent of means, and the legal system at times needs to be subordinated as directly as possible to the logic of violence. Lenin does not mince his words: "The court is not to abolish terror . . . but it should make it understandable and should elevate it to a legal rule, as a matter of principle, clearcut, without hypocrisy and without embellishments."[60] The young Kirchheimer praises the Bolsheviks for openly admitting that law is a mere political instrument, a weapon for suppressing those who have yet to accept the imperatives of the new homogeneous socialist value community. As the party leadership's plans change (and during a crisis they are destined to alter at a rapid pace), new decrees as temporary as the previous ones will have to be issued; revealingly, any distinction between public standing law and military-style commands becomes obscured as well. Judges are denied any real independence. When written law gets in the way of the leadership's goals, it is simply tossed aside, Kirchheimer appreciatively notes, and whether or not judges act in accordance with public norms is less important than that they possess the appropriate revolutionary consciousness.[61]

It is not clear from this unfortunate essay that the twenty-three-year-old Kirchheimer appreciated the full implications of his vision of an alternative socialist legal order. Law here becomes just another form by which existing power inequalities manifest themselves, an alternative tool with which a privileged constituency (in this case, a political party falsely claiming to represent humanity's universal interests) acts coercively against its opponents. Given that any set of normative regulations will have to stand in at least some tension to factual inequalities, Kirchheimer's picture of the Soviet legal system does its best to dissolve that tension. And if political violence represents the apex of Schmittian politics, law here is fittingly reduced to little more than another means of exercising force.[62]

Although somewhat more subtle in structure, the antimodern implications of this model are equally disturbing. Kirchheimer writes that in the Soviet Union the correctness of a basic set of substantive values is "assumed to be beyond discussion," and he thinks that elections there are nothing but a "tool for the integration of the masses into the state" and therefore something altogether different from those in the heterogeneous democracies of Western Europe. Whereas the principle of majority rule in the West constitutes "rape" of political minorities because of the moral and social heterogeneity of political life there, Soviet law rightly claims to express the collective will of a truly homogeneous community.[63]

In other words, Soviet law is ultimately little more than a concretization of an underlying and preexisting consensus or, at best, an instrument for applying a far-reaching consensus to a particular problem. Like the underdeveloped communities of the distant past, the young Kirchheimer's socialism apparently does not need to rely upon complex processes of conflict-ridden lawmaking in order to come up with reasonable policies. If socialism solves all real political problems a priori because of an ill-defined commitment to "value democracy," why would legislation need to be anything more than a limited technical instrument for expressing those values? If we all were to agree about everything, why worry about the fineries of an autonomous civil society and the legal protections needed to preserve it? Carl Schmitt's totalitarian model of law explicitly appeals to the experience of premodern law; the young Otto Kirchheimer's anticipation of that idea does so at least implicitly. In spite of its characteristically modern emphasis on the fact that law is made or produced by human actors, there is more than a faint echo here of a distant moment in the history of legal development in the West. Long ago, law was not yet seen as something actively legislated but was discovered or found implicit in the "good" mores of everyday community life and then embodied in a system of common law.[64] In basing their actions on common law (which, not unlike Kirchheimer's model, was similarly highly discretionary), "wise" (and, in some legal cultures, quasi-divine) judges supposedly merely applied the community's accumulated moral wisdom. For Kirchheimer as well there is a privileged (and semidivine) group (the Bolsheviks, supposedly having special access to "the laws of historical development") best able to interpret the "good" mores of the homogeneous (socialist) value democracy. Law here is in some sense also discovered by them instead of being actively generated by means of an open and relatively freewheeling process of political exchange and legislation. As in premodern legal cultures, Lenin and his followers apparently can do without all the complexities of modern formal law or any of its complementary institutions.[65]

2

The Social Rule of Law

Whereas the young Otto Kirchheimer builds uncritically on the most troublesome facets of Carl Schmitt's political philosophy, the same cannot be said about Franz Neumann during the twenties and early thirties. This should hardly come as a surprise. If my analysis in the previous chapter is on the mark, it should be clear why a consistent left-Schmittianism is incompatible with a compromise-oriented brand of social democratic politics that acknowledges the legitimacy of basic formal democratic political procedures. Yet that is precisely the type of politics Franz Neumann, whose early contributions to critical political and legal thought have received far too little attention, represents during this period. While Neumann attended Schmitt's seminars in the early thirties and, as we will see, was probably influenced by him, his intellectual socialization and early career were more typical for the mainstream of German social democracy than Kirchheimer's. Neumann hardly idolized the authoritarian Schmitt, and his thinking was more directly shaped by social democratic intellectuals like Karl Renner, Hermann Heller, Hugo Sinzheimer, and Otto Bauer during his student years at Frankfurt and while practicing labor law and teaching at the *Hochschule für Politik* in Berlin. Neumann's relationship to Schmitt is more complicated than Kirchheimer's, and he brings together a great diversity of theoretical sources in articulating his vision of a "social rule of law" *(Sozialrechtstaat)*.[1]

These complexities are most immediately illustrated by Neumann's critique of Schmitt's "concept of the political" in the *Union Autonomy and the Constitution: The Place of Unions in the Constitutional System,* which, like many of Neumann's writings during this period, argues that the vision of the rule of law embodied in the Weimar constitutional order is no longer classically bourgeois but explicitly anticapitalist. After summarizing Schmitt's view of politics, he reaches an assessment somewhat similar to my criticism of Schmitt and Kirchheimer in chapter 1. The key problem with Schmitt's decisionism is that it makes a sovereign normless decision (and the unrestrained exercise of political power above and beyond any legal restraints) the centerpiece of politics, thus it must see all "inhibitions and controls on state power" as "unpolitical."[2] Because the rule of law's function lies precisely in undertaking the task of regulating and restraining the exercise of state authority, this means that politics and the rule of law have to be seen by Schmitt as contradictory. Schmitt's concept of the political devalues the legal medium. Neumann claims that this also means that Schmitt's view of politics is purely "dynamic" and one-sided. It underplays the significance of the "static" medium of positive law, playing off the dynamic facets of political reality (like the emergency situation) against more static features (the constitution or a particular set of legal norms). This is problematic, because it presupposes that dynamic and static features of political and social reality can be clearly separated from one another; that assumption, Neumann seems to believe, is what leads Schmitt to juxtapose a normatively unchecked exercise of power (the emergency) to the problem of norm-based law (and legal normalcy) as dramatically as he does. In order, then, to criticize this position, Neumann follows the social democratic theorist Hermann Heller in insisting that meaning-constitutive human activity shapes and structures the social world ever anew, thus social and political life is always both dynamic and static, always fusing both "the is" *(Sein)* and "the ought" *(Sollen),* facticity and normativity, and being and becoming.[3] Like Heller, Neumann worries that too much of contemporary political and legal thought artificially transforms these interlinking pairs into crude antinomies. In contrasting the dynamic and normless facets of political existence to a static legal order, Schmitt separates facets of social existence that are, in fact, inextricably intermeshed. His model thus distorts the nature of political experience and, by means of a misleading valorization of one facet of it, generates a potentially irresponsible romanticization of a "normless will"—hence Schmitt's and Kirchheimer's readiness to abandon Weimar democracy.[4]

The result for Neumann is that Schmitt obfuscates the centrality of the (norm-based) legal order for politics. Law and politics are deeply and unavoidably intermeshed, and legal normativities are by no means necessarily antipolitical. Only an alternative view that captures the inherently political character of law is true to the way social being and becoming, and static and dynamic facets of social life are intermeshed. According to Neumann, the most obvious manifestation of this interrelatedness is that the modern judiciary is active in making unequivocally political decisions, and that judicial activity increasingly has little to do with the classical model of judicial decision making offered by political philosophers like Montesquieu. Particularly in an era when law is ever more amorphous and open-ended, judges cannot simply read off legal norms without injecting their own political concerns into the process. But the intertwining of law and politics also manifests itself in more subtle ways. Despite his debts to Max Weber, Schmitt had explicitly argued, in "The Concept of the Political," that Weber's conception of politics was overly state-centered: Weber defines politics in terms of "striving to share power or striving to influence the distribution of power, either among states or among groups within a state."[5] In Schmitt's view, Weber's statist theoretical biases stemmed in part from his refusal to see that only when existentially intense friend/foe antagonisms happen to correspond to boundaries between nation-states does the nation-state remain the dominant and most intense (political) entity. If friend/foe divisions were suddenly to fall along different cleavages (for example, between religious sects or class groups), the contemporary nation-state might lose its dominant place in the political universe, and the "real possibility of killing" would then be directed against supranational foes. A new constellation of genuinely political entities would have emerged. Neumann sides with Weber against Schmitt here. He does so by posing a straightforward and even simple question: can a party to a political conflict be allowed to determine whether a specific antagonism is political, or should it be someone outside the immediate scope of a conflict who makes this determination? Neumann appreciates that it may be in the interest of a particular "friend" or "foe" to deny his or her opponent "political" stature. Claiming that a conflict is basically private can be an effective instrument for squelching a political enemy. Indeed, "isn't it perhaps the case that the state first determines which antagonism is a political antagonism?"[6] In Neumann's view, the (state-centered) constitutional order helps ascertain which issues and conflicts are political or nonpolitical and rightfully plays a dominant role in defining a particular configuration of political cleavages. The immediate example Neumann is thinking of is the Weimar Constitution, which he believes explicitly ordains a program of radical social and economic reform. Pace his conservative opponents, he wants to show that this program concerns truly political issues that demand active state attention. The Weimar Constitution predetermines the antagonisms between opponents of the Left's reform project and its defenders, and suggests the possibility of compromise with otherwise hostile political forces nonetheless willing to accept the basic principles of the constitutional order. The legal order can function, as he thinks Schmitt implicitly concedes, to relativize political conflicts. It seeks to make sure they are not allowed to become so explosive that the political order's own preconditions are questioned. Insofar as a particular constitutional system can determine which issues should remain nonpolitical (religion, for example), it can moderate and tame potential political antagonisms.

In other words, democratic legal mechanisms are an effective instrument of friend/foe politics, and substantial social change can sometimes be achieved without violence. Despite the harsh criticisms of reformist politics and the radical antilegalism of writers like Kirchheimer, it is ridiculous to see law as inherently "reactionary." "Law is in and of itself a form, an empty form," and it can serve many conceivable purposes, reactionary or radical, conservative or liberal.[7] The fact that the constitutional order relativizes political conflicts and helps defuse potentially explosive cleavages reveals how democratic law can reconcile otherwise hostile political forces. Indeed, legally mediated compromises with potential foes are occasionally both possible and beneficial, and tactical compromises can be an effective tool in the political struggle. Against Schmitt and Kirchheimer, negotiation and compromise are hardly intrinsically antipolitical. Significantly, the Weimar constitutional order rests on just such a compromise between reform-minded middle-class parties and the democratically inclined section of the working classes.

Many of the young Neumann's observations here are undoubtedly perceptive. Still, his criticisms of Schmitt remain at times surprisingly cautious and incomplete. Indeed, they reveal as much about the limitations of his own thinking during this period as the failings of Schmitt's. Though Neumann thinks he can rescue a reformist democratic-socialist political project by revalorizing peaceful democratic legal procedures, he seems unperturbed by either Schmitt's basic claim that politics concerns "struggle, and in the final instance a bloody struggle, not competition, not discussion," between friends and foes or, as we will see, the perils of a concept of social homogeneity that has a number of troublesome characteristics.[8] Neumann's concern primarily lies in rescuing democratic legal mechanisms from their extremist critics and showing that peaceful legal reforms offer a puissant political instrument to be wielded against antireform forces. But like Kirchheimer, he seems to think that certain aspects of Schmitt's authoritarian political and legal theory are consistent with socialist politics. He, too, often ignores the problem of separating Schmitt's partially valid empirical insights about contemporary politics from the more onerous normative claims with which they are intermeshed.

As I will try to show in this chapter, this failure to break more radically with Schmitt had fatal consequences for Neumann's attempt during Weimar's final years to develop a defensible critical vision of the rule of law.

1 Toward a Postbourgeois Rule of Law: Forgotten Voices of the Weimar Republic

In later years, Neumann described the idea of a social rule of law, developed in partnership with Hermann Heller as a direct response to Schmitt's and Kirchheimer's attack on the Weimar Constitution. In contrast to Schmitt and Kirchheimer, Neumann and Heller focus on demonstrating the consistency of the constitution's medley of classical liberal rights, new forms of popular democratic (plebiscitary) decision making, and socially reformist features (like its call, in article 165, for workers and capital jointly to manage the economy).[9] The Weimar Constitution is neither, as Schmitt had argued, a series of badly defined compromises that if it had made any "decision" at all it was for an explicitly bourgeois version of the rule of law, nor, à la Kirchheimer, an altogether indeterminate "decisionless" document. Rather, it embodies a coherent attempt to supplement political democracy with a substantial and even unprecedented degree of social and economic equality, which Neumann and Heller deem essential to the transitional postcapitalist order allegedly sought by the constitutional order's architects in the immediate aftermath of the revolution of 1918. On the one hand, the social rule of law derives from classical Marxism's demand to outfit so-called formal democracy with an egalitarian postcapitalist social substructure, and its main social agent is predictably identified as the industrial proletariat: "the social rule of law was thus the rationalization of labor's demand for an adequate share in the political life of the nation."[10] On the other hand, what clearly distinguishes the project from more orthodox Marxist analyses is its sophisticated view of the relationships among legal institutions, legal norms, and social and economic life. Law here is no passive plaything of an underlying "material base," determined mechanically by the dynamics of capitalist economic production and doing little more than buttressing its exploitive mechanisms; neither Neumann nor Heller hesitate in accepting the relative autonomy of law from economic and social relations. The starting point of their alternative model is the suspicion that when nonbourgeois social strata pose a real threat to capitalism, middle-class groups might abandon the most notable contributions of their own political legacy—parliamentarism, the division of powers, and a measure of legal security—for a dictatorship guaranteeing the sanctity of capitalism and right-wing economic policies. Correspondingly, Neumann and Heller examine the question of how institutions traditionally associated with the rule of law could be reconceptualized and then given a new social and political base sturdier than what its traditional (bourgeois) carrier decreasingly seemed capable or willing to provide.

With the specter of fascism taking on very real shape throughout Europe in the late twenties and the thirties, Heller and Neumann clearly have contemporary trends in mind when articulating this idea, and their own theorizing repeatedly gives expression to the immediate contingencies of the political crisis that overwhelmed Europe then.[11] Yet its contemporaneity should not lead us to miss its lasting insights. In his *Rule of Law or Dictatorship?* Heller shows that the ideal of the modern rule of law transcends its immediate social origins. A measure of legal security is essential not simply to the functioning of a capitalist market economy (as Marx and Weber had argued) but to any complex modern economy having a complicated division of labor. Every identifiably modern economy hence has an "elective affinity" with key features of the modern rule of law. Similarly, the separation of powers remains basic to the preservation of a minimum of political autonomy. Thus, signs that privileged social groups are abandoning these achievements in favor of vague promises from "neofeudal" political authoritarians are alarming indeed: if the neofeudal "irrationalists" get their way, humanity will have betrayed one of its most precious political accomplishments. The task of a socialist political and legal theory is, therefore, both to defend the rule of law against a growing number of "romantic aesthetic" critics on both the Right and the extreme Left (including, according to Heller, both Schmitt and Kirchheimer) and to figure out how best to preserve and restate it under contemporary conditions. In Heller's view, as in Neumann's, this means that the rule of law can no longer legitimately be linked to a defense of capitalism. Reducing the multifaceted rule of law to a support for bourgeois property forms and policies, as many on the political Right do, likely damns it in a world rightfully beginning to seek economic alternatives to capitalism. If the rule of law is to survive in the contemporary world and continue to guarantee a measure of political freedom, new legal institutions will have to extend it into the private economic sphere, making sure that its basic intentions are preserved in social and economic affairs as much as anywhere else. Private power can be as despotic as state power, thus the rule of law's noble struggle against despotism now needs to include an aggressive offensive against unregulated economic privilege and the ultimately unacceptable "inhumanity" of capitalism itself.[12] If social democracy fails in this undertaking, one should expect that the socially exploited will be ready to accept radical solutions. Existing democratic institutions could be jettisoned for a left-wing authoritarianism that, like its fascist counterpart, is not likely to have qualms about disbanding the rule of law.

Many of these ideas can be made out in Neumann's version of a social rule of law. Yet his model takes a somewhat richer institutional form than Heller's, and its grounding is in some important ways distinct. Not the least of reasons for this is Neumann's intellectual debt to the Austro-Marxist Karl Renner.

Already relying upon Renner in his 1923 dissertation, Neumann appears to be one of the first voices on the Weimar Left to have grasped the importance of Renner's *Institutions of Private Law and Their Social Functions,* arguably still, nearly three-quarters of a century after its publication, the most impressive attempt at a theory of law written from a traditional Marxist viewpoint.[13] What Neumann borrows most directly from Renner is the insight that "the content of every legal decree is capable of functional alteration," that its "wording can remain unchanged for centuries, while the content and social meaning of a legal institution can experience decisive transformation."[14] Like Renner, Neumann believes that a Marxist-inspired legal theory need not interpret the relationship between legal and social reality in accordance with an overly mechanistic reading of Marx's base/superstructure dialectic. There is no automatism between social and legal reality. Legal institutions do not always correspond to a particular socioeconomic context, and there are countless historical cases in which a surprising gap emerges between the two. Indeed, it should be a central concern of a neo-Marxist legal sociology to focus on this problem.[15] For Renner and Neumann, a critical theory of law seeks to understand how and why legal norms and institutions may or may not "fit" a particular configuration of socioeconomic practices, and it is concerned with explaining how some facets of the legal system come to take on operations in one set of social circumstances distinct from those they played in a previous social universe and unforeseen by their originators.

Renner's own study undertakes to illustrate this view by analyzing the central category of modern private law, namely property. According to his interpretation, the continental legal concept of property fit the conditions of an early bourgeois social and economic organization made up of relatively equal individual economic agents that has long since vanished from the historical scene. The dominant legal definition of property in Europe whereby a particular person has an absolute right to make use of a specific object once directly underpinned the rights of a small-scale producer who needed to have immediate and absolute control over a particular object (a specific tool or a plot of land) in order to engage successfully in economic activity. In a relationship of nearly perfect correspondence, early bourgeois legal views of property (as well as a set of auxiliary institutions upon which it rested) and the social world of "petty-commodity production" (Marx) constituted a harmonious whole.

The great irony of modern legal development is that capitalism has since undergone profound transformations, yet most of its complementary legal institutions remain formally unchanged. Early twentieth-century lawyers work with the same concept of property that their predecessors hundreds of years earlier did. For Renner, this disparity cannot be without significance, and he tries to show that it masks the fact that the legal institution of property no longer has very much to do with the economic functions essential to contemporary capitalist production. As a result, contemporary legal categories have a far greater ideological role in veiling illegitimate power inequalities than they did in an earlier era. Having little meaningful economic function anymore, contemporary capitalists often do little but collect stock dividends, and they very likely may never even have seen the place of production, or stepped within the doors of, their productive unit or "object," let alone engaged in some activity essential to its exploitation. The integral ties between the juridical property owner and the actual functions of property (which once involved having an essential and direct relationship to a particular object of economic activity) dissipate. All the activities performed by the classical bourgeois property owner are undertaken by very different categories of individuals (workers, managers, technicians) today, and the legally defined capitalist property owner is generally, from the perspective of the production process, the least relevant one of them all. Despite its unchanged formal structure, the legal concept of property now has little to do with its original meaning.

"The Social Significance of Basic Rights in the Weimar Constitution" is Neumann's most thoughtful attempt at defending his vision of the social rule of law by applying Renner's method. Crucial to his immediate argument there is the Weimar Constitution's article 109: "All Germans are equal before the law." Neumann argues against alternative readings of the equality clause (common, of course, to all modern democratic constitutions and, as in the Weimar Republic, hotly contested) by applying what he describes as a "sociological-historical" method explicitly inspired by Renner. In much of nineteenth-century constitutionalist thinking, Neumann insists, this clause was interpreted as merely applying to state administrative activities but not to those of parliament. It intended to say nothing about the appropriate structure of legislative norms and merely demanded that they be applied by bureaucrats and judges without bias. He notes that the social context behind this interpretation in Germany was that the bureaucracy was, until recently, heavily "feudalized" and that political forces in the legislature (increasingly sympathetic to bourgeois political and economic interests) wanted to make sure that their potential opponents in the administration accepted the supremacy of the legislature by applying its rules as mechanically as possible. The prevailing conception of the relationships among parliamentary law, the administration, and the judiciary implicitly expressed a particular constellation of social classes. Although sympathetic to this reading of the equality clause (in part because it implies giving the legislature, where working-class political groups are best represented, broad powers), Neumann is unsatisfied with it. He cites Weber's claim that the significance of it today "would be equal to zero," because every existing *Rechtsstaat* can probably already satisfy the demand to apply laws irrespective of individual persons.[16] Although recognizing that his alternative view seems reminiscent of right-wing criticisms of new nonclassical forms of social and economic legislation, Neumann nonetheless argues that the equality clause should be read as applying to legislative rule making and is an enjoinder directed at lawmakers, demanding that they act in a specific manner. Whereas right-wingers accept a (superficially) similar reading of the equality clause in order to challenge the legitimacy of new types of specific legislation addressed to the special needs of subordinate social constituencies (thus, in their view, discriminatory and illegitimate), Neumann insists that the clause should be read as a call for legislators to undertake a program that realizes "positive social and economic equality."[17] Although directed at the legislature, the equality clause provides no check on specialized forms of legislative decision making. On the contrary, it is a demand for the legislature to reconstruct social and economic life in a more radically and explicitly anticapitalist manner. Right-wing writers correctly recognize that the equality clause has to be directed to parliament if it is to have any real meaning today, but they ignore the crucial point that "every legal decree is capable of functional alteration" and that the equality clause needs to be interpreted differently than in the past. Neumann's argumentation here relies on two alternative strategies. First, it makes use of the tools of traditional constitutional exegesis. Because he thinks the Weimar Constitution embodies a left-wing vision of a social rule of law, he believes he can turn to the constitution in order to combat his political foes, and he dismisses their antireform gloss on the equality clause as being inconsistent with the constitution's aspiration to realize a political order situated, in his view, somewhere "between capitalism and socialism." This is a familiar strategy in Neumann's work during this period, and it points to the centrality for him of Renner's idea that legal reality (like the norms embodied in the Weimar Constitution) can stand in a substantial degree of tension to existing structures of social and economic inequality. Although Weimar Germany obviously remains capitalist, the constitution expresses the principles of a social rule of law aiming to transcend the social status quo. Constitutions can "be a step ahead" of existing social reality, thus the critical intellectual can rely upon traditional juristic methods in criticizing opponents.

Neumann's second argument is somewhat more interesting, in part because it is directly applicable to all modern democratic constitutional systems. Reading the equality clause as a call for legislators to avoid differentiating in favor of subordinate social groups effectively means that the social status quo is to be preserved. In Neumann's view, this interpretation of the idea of the generality of law is unfaithful to the original aim of early bourgeois conceptions of legal equality. The social substructure implicit in classical liberal political thought was that of a small-scale competitive capitalist economy consisting of relatively equal economic competitors—Neumann's corollary to Renner's vision of an early capitalism dominated by relatively equal and independent producers—in which the market offered real chances for advance to most economic actors. In that long-ago world, legal institutions and norms were meant to preserve more than a mere set of formal opportunities and rights. Classical legal freedoms represented not only formal but also "factual" liberties; the notion of equality before the law was intended to give actors a "factual chance" of taking advantage of them.[18] The transformation of small-scale classical competitive capitalism into a heavily monopolized organized capitalism, dominated by mammoth corporations with unforeseen power advantages vis-à-vis most of the population, robs classical legal institutions of the social substructure that once helped give them their original meaning. Today the free entrepreneur is replaced by cartels and syndicates of which he or she is little more than a functionary; capital and management functions tend to separate; the self-regulating "natural" market declines and state intervention becomes widespread in the economy; elimination of many economic risks for the largest economic units results.[19] In Renner's terms, the equality clause is unchanged in structure, but its social functions have necessarily been profoundly transformed.

Specifically, the idea of "equality before the law" originally presupposed not only an idea of formal legal equality but also the implicit hope that legal subjects would in fact be relatively equal in concrete social and economic terms and able to take full advantage of the potential benefits of formal equality. Conservative readings of the equality clause, as a check on legislative attempts to produce a more egalitarian distribution of resources, consequently make a mockery of the original spirit of classical liberal legal thought, turning the equality clause into a defense of precisely the opposite of what it was meant to uphold, namely, a political community in which both formal and a relative degree of factual equality supplement each other. It follows that if the equality clause is to remain faithful to its original spirit, it will have to be interpreted as providing a justification for the legislature's endeavour to reconstruct social and economic relations along radically egalitarian lines. The heir to the classical liberal conception of the rule of law becomes a left-wing vision of a "social rule of law," and the real traitors to the liberal legacy are not Neumann and his socialist comrades but those who speak in the name of liberal legal values while ignoring that our world is radically different from that envisioned by Adam Smith.[20]

Neumann undertakes to sketch out the broader institutional details of this project in a number of more technical essays. Contemporary capitalism can be transformed—by means of new forms of workplace democracy, labor courts, and joint labor/capital representation in quasi-public planning bodies—so as to recapture at least something of the social homogeneity once characteristic of its earlier competitive phase, and Neumann can endorse a set of transitional corporatist structures as part of an economic democracy conceived of as a stepping stone to a socialist economy based on self-administered economic units.[21] Pivotal here is the unusual concept of an "economic constitution," referring, for Neumann, to a set of state norms that outline the principles and organizational structure for a transitional postcapitalist economic system and aspire to preserve legal regularity and predictability. Insofar as the private sphere is a site of potential oppression and concerns genuinely political issues and concerns, and is not the site of the equal autonomous agents located by classical liberal theory there, the distinction between "public" and "private" loses any systematic justification in contemporary law. Traditional conceptions of constitutionalism no longer suffice, and the constitutionalist agenda has to be expanded into areas traditionally deemed private by liberalism. This by no means implies for Neumann that we can do without private law or an autonomous private sphere.[22] But it does mean that a traditional constitutionalist agenda risks becoming outdated if all potential despotisms, including those emerging in the capitalist "private" sphere, are to be successfully regulated. Like traditional liberal constitutions, Neumann's economic constitution demands that state intervention take a cogent and calculable form; unlike those constitutions, his model acknowledges the ongoing fusion of private and public authority in organized capitalism and the dangers of both unregulated private power and new modes of public/private power, and it seeks to subdue them by means of participatory and judicial innovations.[23]

Neumann's concern about the dangers of ill-organized and unpredictable state intervention is hardly coincidental. Indeed, his vision of a social rule of law includes a number of surprisingly contemporary features, not the least of which is his remarkable anticipation of some of the basic features of present-day radical criticisms of bureaucratic forms of state intervention.

In recent years, it has become common on the Left to accuse European social democracy of having had far too little awareness of the dangers and worrisome side effects of bureaucratically organized forms of regulation in the era of the welfare state. Although Michel Foucault has probably played the key role in inspiring this genre of criticism, even Jürgen Habermas, who surely does not represent anything like the idiosyncratic anarchism that seemed to motivate Foucault, now claims that mainstream social democracy long underestimated the extent to which inappropriate forms of bureaucratic intervention undermine political and social autonomy and at times are at best ambiguous and at worst downright counterproductive. In Habermas's view, the Left correctly remains concerned about the dangers of capitalist-based inequalities for democratic politics, but the enigma it now faces is that its traditional tool for challenging capitalist domination (bureaucratic regulation) has been robbed of the innocence it once seemed to possess. If the democratic Left is to overcome its present impasse and offer a real alternative to neoconservatism, it will have to break with an overly statist political legacy and grapple with the significance of the real dangers of bureaucratic regulation.[24]

Neumann's early model of a social rule of law suggests that this criticism, at least, needs to be qualified and that there were always subterranean strands in European socialism sensitive to many of the types of problems rightly identified by contemporary analysts of the welfare state. This probably becomes most clear in an intriguing 1925 essay, in which the young Neumann precociously acknowledges many of the limits and perils of bureaucratically organized social regulation. The piece focuses on the rather technical legal issue of compulsory state-backed labor settlements, but Neumann soon transforms it into a vehicle for addressing a number of broader concerns.

In the essay, Neumann opposes the practice of state-enforced agreements between capital and labor because he is convinced that it undermines the independence of labor unions and the working-class constituencies represented by them. Legally organized state intervention into relations between businesses and unions is absolutely necessary, because it alone can provide a degree of what Neumann calls "social freedom": far-reaching state intervention in society is imperative if broad masses of the population are to be guaranteed a minimum of social and economic independence. Simultaneously, Neumann recognizes that bureaucratic intervention poses a number of very real problems. The central state cannot try to intervene in society in every conceivable way. Only governmental regulation that is likely to be effective should be undertaken, which means here that the central state should only attempt action when it is likely to succeed in carrying it out. Because Neumann claims that strong labor unions might be able to ignore the compulsory state contracts in question, such contracts will probably prove ineffective. Furthermore, state regulation generally challenges, in an obvious way, the autonomy of those it hopes to regulate. It demands of them that they abandon specific classical private freedoms in favor of accepting new forms of state conflict resolution. Compulsory contracts, for example, undermine a labor union's right to strike, while providing it with new state-organized and state-centered means for settling conflicts between labor and capital, and it is crucial that the actors involved consider whether the forms of state control they are willing to accept are really worth the trade-offs. In the example examined here, because the right to strike is the very centerpiece of union autonomy and working-class economic action, Neumann thinks unions should be more than a bit suspicious about state-endorsed compulsory contracts.[25] Finally, there are more subtle dangers at hand as well. The proliferation of direct state regulation risks generating a "spirit of servility" *(Untertanengeist)* among social actors: they may come to count on state representatives to resolve political conflicts and thus lose an adequate sense of the significance and complexities of political struggle and the centrality of "responsible" political action.[26] This is all particularly dangerous, because, as Neumann restates on a number of occasions, "Germany is today de facto more bureaucratically dominated than ever before." But "socialism without democracy, without the participation of autonomously formed social forces . . . is not imaginable." Socialism does not seek "statization" *(Verstaatlichung)* and the negation of social autonomy, but hopes to realize social and political autonomy by means of state intervention, however paradoxical that may admittedly be, given the ambivalent structure of regulatory instruments.[27]

Neumann's analysis here points to what is arguably the central paradox of the modern interventionist state. On the one hand, extensive state intervention in social life constitutes a necessary presupposition for providing a basic degree of political and social freedom for broad masses of the population. On the other hand, the state risks intervening in facets of social life in ways sure to fail, and its interventionist activities at times threaten to engender new forms of inequality and dependence. As I read Neumann here, he provocatively suggests that the democratic Left needs what we might describe as a "self-restraining" rule of law.

Only state-organized legal regulation of social life can generate the autonomy essential to modern democratic politics, but the state must restrain itself by organizing its many, and generally absolutely necessary, activities in such a way as not to counteract the very political and social autonomy it seeks to preserve and expand. If there is any solution to the paradoxes of the modern interventionist state, it lies in part in how legal forms function to structure and organize the exercise of political power. The form of state action—for example, the legal structure of state imperatives or the legal institutions involved in particular types of regulation—is essential for preserving political and social autonomy. Poorly articulated and vague legal norms may provide administrators with too much leeway, making it easier for them to act in incalculable, irregular, and arbitrary ways.[28] Or the state may need to organize a particular type of regulatory activity in a relatively decentralized manner; otherwise, legal instruments may prove too crude for producing the desired effects. In short, developing a defensible conception of the rule of law capable of confronting the exigencies of contemporary social life means that legal and political theory has to focus on how the state's legal forms, norms, and institutions can function to protect political and social independence while recognizing the absolute necessity of extensive state action.

This insight clearly underlies Neumann's analysis of the institutional configuration of the social rule of law. He thinks that economic democracy must consist of a relatively decentralized system of diverse decision-making bodies, in part because the central state cannot directly resolve every conceivable conflict that emerges amidst the complex interstices of the modern economy. Direct state regulation of every facet of the economy would not only prove ineffective but generate a broader statization of social relations incompatible with autonomous political and social action.[29] Economic democracy should involve "self-administration," by means of new modes of worker representation and courts that offer a training ground for the working classes to enter the complexities of contemporary politics. Workers undergo a process of self-education about democratic politics only through "active participation in political, social and economic life," and labor courts offer a bridge between representative political institutions and broad segments of the population otherwise alienated from state-level politics. In educating the working classes about politics, they help make sure that they remain an independent political force.[30]

2 Authoritarian Laborism?

Despite its many absorbing features, Neumann's model of a social rule of law must ultimately be considered a failure. Although Neumann later claimed that his project "combined the heritage of civil rights, legal and political equality" with a project of social democratic reform, its commitment to civil rights turns out to be ambivalent at best.[31] It is undoubtedly true that the roots of this weakness lie in Neumann's classically Marxist assumptions, yet it is also the case that Schmitt's brand of antiliberalism shapes the contours of Neumann's left-wing hostility to the liberal-rights tradition and at times even provides him with the analytical tools for criticizing it.[32]

Schmitt had long insisted on the incompatibility of democracy and liberalism. Democracy means the "identity of the ruled and rulers" or, as noted in chapter 1, a "substantial homogeneity of the people." This identity can be constructed by many possible means and can take distinct forms, but civil liberties, legalism, parliamentarism, and the liberal belief in the sanctity of free discussion and compromise are by no means essential to it. Mass-based dictatorship could very well also realize it. Liberalism is based on a bourgeois and individualistic conception of freedom, whereas democracy is principled on the idea of equality, which is another expression for the necessity of homogeneity in a system based on the identity of ruled and rulers, or "the people and its state." Furthermore, equality must be understood in substantialist terms and cannot refer to the (antipolitical) formalistic universal equality espoused by the intellectual giants of modern political thought. The liberal conception of universal equality ignores the unavoidability of existential friend/foe antagonisms, and democratic identity is most effective when based on national or ethnic features. Democracy is also a genuinely political concept, whereas its opposite, universalistic liberalism, is antipolitical. As I outlined in the previous chapter, the peculiar antimodernism implicit in this constellation of ideas is the major source of both Schmitt's and

Kirchheimer's hostility to modern formal law, and it is implicated as well in their preference for systems of mass rule liberated from all legalistic shackles.

Given his emphasis on the centrality of the problem of political and social autonomy, it is surprising that Neumann relies explicitly on the Schmittian liberalism versus democracy dichotomy but nonetheless simply restates Schmitt's claim on a number of occasions. Like Schmitt, Neumann does so not merely to outline the tensions between a privatistic and explicitly bourgeois variant of liberalism and modern democratic politics. Liberalism in this formulation does not refer simply to bourgeois property rights but to an extensive set of classical political rights (including free speech, the right to political assembly, habeas corpus, and so on).[33] If Neumann even bothers to offer an explicit defense of this dichotomy anywhere, it remains, unfortunately, a rather simplistic one: basic rights justify individual freedom, whereas democracy aims to legitimize what he repeatedly and vaguely describes as "state coercion" *(staatlichen Zwang)*.[34] What this appears to amount to is that Neumann—again in a manner reminiscent of Schmitt, whom he continually cites in his discussion of this theme and whose peculiar categorization of political rights in the 1928 *Versfassungslehre* he directly borrows from[35]—thinks that liberal rights are essentially "prestate" and even "antistate" and are based on the idea that individual freedom is in principle unlimited in relation to the state, whereas democracy implies the legitimacy of extensive state intervention in society as a way of realizing identity between the rulers and the ruled ruled. Both Schmitt and Neumann accept an extremely privatistic interpretation of political rights, precisely so that they can then minimize the importance of basic civil liberties for contemporary mass democratic politics. Whereas Neumann's broader justification for restating the modern rule of law relies on the persuasive insight that classical legal ideals need to be reconstructed in the face of unprecedented social transformations in order to remain faithful to their original intent, he does not seem very intent on applying this maxim in his hostile criticism of so-called private, individualistic (freedom of assembly?) and antidemocratic (free speech?) rights.

Neumann is surely more uneasy about juxtaposing democracy to liberalism than Schmitt is, and at least at some junctures he seems troubled by its implications. In an essay for the SPD journal *Die Gesellschaft*, for example, he comments that "ultimately liberal ideology has performed good services for the socialist movement, and today certain liberal ideas . . . [for example, free speech] . . . still are essentially linked to socialist ideology." Minimally, liberal rights are of tactical value to the Left, and, if only for historical reasons, they cannot be "thought out of existence."[36] Yet even in this essay, he ultimately emphasizes the contradictions between liberal basic rights and democratic (and socialist) politics, and what seems to motivate him, as it did Schmitt and Kirchheimer, is the unfortunate illusion that modern mass democracy could do without institutionalized liberal political rights. Although more sensitive than Kirchheimer to the immediate political dangers that their suspension might pose for the (minority) social democrats, Neumann is, unfortunately, similarly inspired by the image of a postcapitalist socially homogeneous order in which allegedly antistatist liberal rights no longer need to perform any services for the socialist movement. Indeed, he explicitly concedes this in his revealing *Union Autonomy and the Constitution,* where all the most troubling implications of his intellectual dialogue with Carl Schmitt come to an explosive head. As long as contemporary society is missing "social homogeneity, the substrate of every true democracy," some social group or another inevitably appeals to the merely formal rights of the liberal tradition as a way of buttressing its claims against the status quo.[37] Liberal rights are an instrument of political struggle, something needed by a political minority or oppressed group in order to raise claims against its rulers, but once social homogeneity (a concept never explicitly explained here by Neumann but clearly referring to some postcapitalist condition of substantial social and economic equality) is realized, any real justification for individual rights disappears. Social homogeneity means social and political harmony, and when achieved the liberal-rights tradition would have fulfilled its worthwhile, but limited and now anachronistic, function.

The fateful consequences of this position manifest themselves unambiguously in Neumann's writings during the early thirties. Amidst the Weimar Republic's fateful last political crisis, it becomes the basis for a peculiar defense of what we can only describe as authoritarian laborism.

After abandoning political power in 1930 because of a fight over unemployment benefits, the SPD literally handed over governmental responsibility to right-wingers who had long openly sought an authoritarian solution to the Weimar Republic's long-standing political and social ills. Obsessed by the danger of worse things from the Stalinistic Communist party and the rapidly growing far Right, the SPD (for which Neumann soon served as a legal advisor) pursued its infamous course of political toleration vis-à-vis Heinrich Brüning's constitutionally dubious presidential semidictatorship. Like many others in the mainstream of German social democracy (including Hermann Heller), Neumann seems to have been convinced of the necessity of this ultimately disastrous political option. Although it would be unfair to read his *Union Autonomy and the Constitution* as an apology for Brüning, it does show why Neumann fell into the easy trap of accepting a form of quasi-authoritarianism as an answer to Weimar's ills. Carl Schmitt, unfortunately, plays more than a modest role in this tragedy.[38]

Schmitt had forecast that the time would come when social democratic thought would be forced to choose from among its distinct and allegedly incongruous liberal, democratic, and socialist elements; Neumann's *Union Autonomy and the Constitution* eerily fulfills Schmitt's forecast. The book is intended as a restatement of Neumann's doctrine of the social rule of law, but his formulation of it is striking in that it abandons any adequate concern for the civil rights that the social rule of law allegedly synthesizes with a broader left-wing reform project. Neumann begins by repeating Schmitt's views about the incongruity between liberalism and democracy, but he develops this argument by means of an interpretation of the Weimar Constitution that privileges some of its legal elements over others.[39] His argument is that those facets of the Weimar Constitution providing a constitutional base for social democratic reformism and the corporatist project espoused by Neumann are "dictatorship-proof" *(diktaturfest)*. Although the Weimar Constitution's emergency clause (article 48) allows dictatorial inroads on many basic political liberties, Neumann adamantly insists that its social-reform-oriented authors could not have intended the emergency clause as a check on the constitution's endorsement of radical social and economic change (as set out in articles 159 and 165). Whatever its status as a work in constitutional exegesis, the argument's Schmittian overtones are striking: Neumann attributes the greatest legal weight to those clauses of the constitution aspiring to realize the "positive social and economic equality" essential to a true socially homogeneous democracy. A homogeneous democracy based on substantive (economic) equality is privileged in relationship to liberalism and basic political rights, and the category of (social) equality is given more substance than (political) freedom. Perhaps most astonishingly, Neumann seems to have few qualms about the potential dangers of the new "commissarial dictatorship" and its inroads against political rights.[40] What really bothers him is that dictatorial emergency powers could be employed against the social democratic reform project and its main vehicle, the democratic labor unions. He goes so far as to apply the idea of an institutional guarantee (or the view that a constitutional document can protect and preserve the essential features of a particular institution) in order to justify the privileged status of the labor unions. In his view, the constitution outfits unions with a set of complementary rights that not only allow them to exercise all of their basic economic functions but give them more extensive political freedoms than other groups.[41]

With this move, the social rule of law's alleged attempt to fuse classical political rights with socialist reformism takes a peculiar turn indeed. Only those political forces making up part of the Left's reform coalition, it seems, are to have any meaningful political freedoms.

Of course, one could offer a more sympathetic reading of the book. Is this not the voice of someone trying to preserve some autonomy for the battered republic's only real democratic force, namely, the SPD and its union allies? Given the undeniable authoritarian proclivities of the German middle classes during the early thirties, were there any real historical alternatives to this? Might not the polarized conditions of crisis-ridden Weimar indeed have required some type of temporary executive-centered government, but a more defensible one than that which actually emerged in 1930? If so, can we not read Neumann as trying to offer an argument for a more humane alternative to the actual right-wing semidictatorships of pre-Hitler Germany?

These crucial historical questions will, unfortunately, have to remain unanswered here. More significant for our task are the theoretical sources of Neumann's problematic conception of basic political rights. Notwithstanding any historical justification which we might find for it, it sadly remains a crude conception.

Striking about Neumann's analysis is how it corresponds to the logic of the tamed version of Schmitt's concept of the political, suggested by

Neumann in *Union Autonomy and the Constitution*—a version, by the way, undoubtedly consistent with many features of classical Marxist political thinking. Rights are basically a tool of political struggle, an instrument employed by political forces against their foes, often (for Neumann) foes who dominate state institutions, hence the antistatist character of rights. In tune with the Schmittian concept of the political's valorization of political struggle and violence, they are also seen as being most essentially coercive, a weapon directed against a hostile political opponent against whom one seeks to mobilize political muscle. Predictably, they are then counterposed to a "true" homogeneous form of democracy, in which rights presumably become unnecessary. Neumann reasons that in a homogeneous (socialist) community there would no longer be any real friend/foe hostilities, thus no need for legal rights, whose main function is to serve as an instrument of political struggle. Nor would there be a need for rights to check and restrain the exercise of political authority. The state, it seems, would now be sure to act in the community's transparent collective interest. Neumann is certainly much more hesitant about making these claims than Kirchheimer is, yet it is undeniable that his view contains the dangerous suggestion that social homogeneity frees the polity of the need for serious political exchange and that socialism necessarily generates a "good" order destined to solve all major political problems. If Kirchheimer's socialism can be read as an attempt to recapture something of the homogeneity characteristic of premodern existence, Neumann's utopia is probably at best a somewhat more benign version of the same indefensible idea.

Indeed, the "autonomy" Neumann makes central to his formulation of an alternative social rule of law ultimately refers to little more than the freedom of action of a particular social agent, namely, the industrial working class. If his analysis suggests at times that autonomy (a term repeatedly used by Neumann) might mean something more, all doubts are put to rest in *Union Autonomy and the Constitution.* Despite his inflated claim to have combined liberal political rights with a broader project of radical social and economic reform, the centerpiece of the social rule of law is really "the promotion of the rise of the working class, securing liberty and property only insofar as they do not hinder the advancement of this class": the political liberty of other political agents can, as we have seen, be legitimately abandoned if it gets in the way of the working classes and an authoritarian system allegedly representative of its interests.[42] Wrapped in problematic traditional Marxist assumptions about the privileged status of the working classes and sketched out by means of categories permeated with Schmitt's brand of authoritarian decisionism, Neumann's social rule of law, unfortunately, eventually reduces the crucial idea of social and political autonomy to little more than the "ability to fight" *(Kampfbereitschaft)* of a particular social interest.

A defensible conception of the democratic rule of law clearly has to abandon the problematic idea of homogeneity found here as well. A more thorough break with Schmitt might have suggested to Neumann that political rights are not simply individualistic and that democracy amounts to more than identity, state-directed social reform, or a transitory step toward some vaguely defined socialism. The working classes do not represent humanity's universal interests; instead, democracy realizes universality in a more complicated fashion than Neumann ever manages to conceptualize. Democracy flourishes on the basis of mutually enabling common action, on a reciprocally transformative and educative process of give-and-take. It alone is fully capable of institutionalizing the unhindered debate and exchange on which effective political action is based, thereby fully rationalizing state authority. The rule of law and the institutionalization of basic political rights essential to it function to protect and buttress debate and independent political action, enabling citizens to engage in political action and exchange with the heterogeneous Other so essential to the political reflection and learning on which democracy depends.

3 Exile In England and the Specter of Carl Schmitt

Hitler took power in January 1933. His life in danger, Neumann—a prominent Berlin labor lawyer, socialist intellectual, SPD advisor, and Jew—soon fled Germany for England. Having just defended a number of prominent social democrats (including the Prussian Minister-President Otto Braun and Secretary of the Interior Carl Severing) in the courtroom against the Nazis, Franz Neumann was one of the first Germans to be stripped of his citizenship by the new dictatorship. Closely watched by Nazi spies in England, Neumann soon became active in SPD exile politics, began work on a massive study on the rule of law (under the guidance of Harold Laski at the London School of Economics), and contributed a number of essays to British and left-wing exile publications.[43]

Unsurprisingly, these essays are more radical in tone than his Weimar writings. He incisively attacks the policies of the Weimar SPD, and his comments take a refreshingly self-critical tone. The "great mistake" of the union movement "was to believe that economic democracy was possible without political democracy." Indeed, "industrial self-government itself failed." Why? "The main point is that the trade unions lost their freedom and independence. Legally, they were completely independent of the state. . . . But in fact they were . . . dependent upon the state."[44] Neumann thinks that Weimar social democracy's endeavour to realize a self-restraining mode of social and economic regulation proved disastrously unsuccessful and that the Weimar welfare state statized autonomous social relations and undermined key political groups' capacity for independent action. The democratic Left's own legal and institutional failures contributed to the rise of fascism.

Most significantly, Neumann concedes that his own vision of a social rule of law is implicated in this political catastrophe—but he concedes this for all the wrong reasons. In "The Rule of Law, the Division of Powers, and Socialism," he writes that the "destruction of all constitutional guarantees by the fascist system compels us to examine whether . . . the idea of the rule of law is compatible with Marxist-socialist ideas."[45] Neumann's answer here is "no." After trying to show that the modern rule of law, defined here primarily by its emphasis on the generality of legal norms and a clear-cut division of powers, is bourgeois, he convincingly shows how the dual emergence of mass democracy and monopoly capitalism "denatures" the liberal rule of law and transforms it into something distinct from what it was intended to be. General law is abandoned in the face of massive capitalist monopolies necessitating modes of regulation that effectively take the form of individual measures, parliamentary sovereignty is replaced by a political system dominated by the executive branch, and the judiciary usurps extensive legislative functions by exploiting the possibilities offered by vague deformalized legal norms. When a radical labor movement appears on the historical scene, "the importance of basic political freedoms decreases continuously."[46] Neumann made many similar observations in his Weimar writings, and his method is again reminiscent of Karl Renner's emphasis on the "functional transformations" undergone by legal institutions amidst far-reaching social changes, but crucial here is the fact that Neumann abandons any real interest in developing a conception of the rule of law more in tune with the requirements of mass democracy. After Weimar's demise, the very possibility of a legal order suitable to a transitional social order seems altogether naive to Neumann; the onward march of fascism necessitates a militant socialist response from the democratic Left. In fact, he directly concedes that his own project of a social rule of law failed, in part because the criticism of writers like Kirchheimer and Schmitt was correct.[47] He then repeats his characteristically left-Schmittian claims that democracy and liberalism, and thus equality and liberty, are contradictory, and although he notes that "we do not want to state that democracy has to dispense with any form of securing the freedom of its citizenry, that the idea of the rule of law has to disappear entirely . . . it will be 'superseded,' that is, at the same time obliterated and transferred to another, higher sphere,"[48] he never tells us exactly what this "supersession" should look like. Although at times uneasily looking beyond its Schmitt-influenced Marxist categories and claims, the essay nonetheless remains imprisoned in them, and Neumann probably relapses to a vision of the ties among democracy, socialism, and the rule of law in some ways more similar to Kirchheimer's than to that found in Neumann's own Weimar writings. Here, the rule of law is a bourgeois check on the socialist project and its dream of a socially homogeneous democracy. If it has any future, Neumann does not deem it important enough to discuss anymore.

With this move, the problematic Schmittian Marxism represented by Kirchheimer and Neumann comes full circle. If they are to offer a more defensible conception of the rule of law, they clearly will have to break out of that circle. Kirchheimer's investigations into the relationship between legality and legitimacy (the subject of chapter 3) as well as Neumann's theoretical contributions during the late thirties and early forties, while he was a member of the Institute for Social Research (chapters 4 and 5), show that they both came to recognize this.

II

Legality and Legitimacy

3

Parliamentary Legality or Plebiscitary Dictatorship?

For Carl Schmitt, the emergency situation constitutes nothing less than the apex of politics. It unleashes the underlying antagonisms and conflicts of the political sphere, freeing them from the antipolitical confusions that may have kept their full significance from view. If politics is ultimately about normatively irresolvable existential friend/foe conflicts, they manifest themselves most completely during a crisis.

Given that Otto Kirchheimer was one of the most fervent of Schmitt's followers, it is fitting that he quickly becomes the fiercest of Schmitt's critics: having accepted much of Schmitt's vision of politics, he must obey the laws of its polarized political universe. Kirchheimer grasps that the bourgeois parties' break with the SPD-led Müller government in 1930 constitutes a new stage in the history of the Weimar Republic, and—with the possibility of a right-wing dictatorship taking on very real proportions in Germany and Schmitt having become the most sophisticated advocate of an authoritarian alternative to liberal democracy—Kirchheimer breaks with his former teacher and abandons his Schmittian-inspired attacks on Weimar.[1] As he outlines in a set of spirited essays for the Hilferding-edited *Die Gesellschaft* during the republic's final years, the plebiscitary presidential regime promoted by Schmitt has all the makings of mass-based dictatorship. While Schmitt proceeds to batter away viciously at the republic's genuinely democratic features, Kirchheimer tries to save them—paradoxically, one of the republic's harshest critics is transformed into one of its most astute and eloquent defenders.[2]

As should be clear from part I of this study, Schmitt's writings from the early and mid twenties reveal a deep-seated hostility to classical conceptions of the rule of law. Specifically, Kirchheimer's reworking of Schmitt's thinking from this period, the central topic of chapter 1, points not only to the problematic legal consequences of his own left-Schmittianism but, if only implicitly, to many of the more immediate flaws underlying Schmitt's ideas about the rule of law during the republic's most stable period. Still, if there were any remaining doubts about Schmitt's hostility to the idea of a rule of law among his contemporaries, he soon did his utmost to put them to rest. In 1929, precisely when the republic begins to flounder, Schmitt starts to publish a series of writings on pluralism, the legislative state, and parliamentary legality, offering a somewhat revised and sociologically better informed—but also more direct and ruthless—attack both on the battered republic and on the rule of law. It is this restatement of Schmitt's views that is crucial for Kirchheimer's break with his former teacher, and our discussion will have to start there (section 1). It should demonstrate why it is simply not the case that Schmitt, as his contemporary defenders still insist, hoped to save the Weimar Republic. We can then focus on the central facets of Kirchheimer's critique of Schmitt and his attempt to develop an alternative conception of the relationship between democracy and the rule of law (sections 2 and 3). He abandons those features of Schmitt's theory that hearken back to a premodern political universe, and this allows him to acknowledge the importance of the rule of law for democratic politics. Although this is hardly what Schmitt hoped to teach him, Kirchheimer undoubtedly learned something from his former teacher, and it is a lesson we also need to take seriously: homogeneous democracy, freed from anything resembling the rule of law, is another name for dictatorship.

1 The Rule of Law under Siege

The modern rule of law includes a number of independent elements and has taken diverse concrete, historical forms. The rule of law surely plays a different role in Locke's political theory than it does in Hegel's, and American constitutionalism in many ways is clearly distinct from its continental European counterparts. Nonetheless, its centerpiece has always been the idea that governmental action must be rendered calculable and restrained: it was the exercise of arbitrary power, of despotism as they dramatically labeled it, that worried liberals as diverse as the bourgeois Locke and the rabble-rousing Paine, the aristocratic Montesquieu and the state-building Madison. In the ominous shadows of all too real experiences of political tyranny, they all came to recognize that poorly regulated and unpredictable state action made even a bare modicum of political and social autonomy impossible, and they busily set about envisioning institutional instruments with which state action could be made predictable and thus more humane. The modern rule of law has its genesis in their imaginative and historically unprecedented attempt to grapple with this task.

Locke's answer is in many ways the paradigmatic one. Arbitrary government can only be prevented if the political order is governed by "promulgated standing" laws, a separation between the legislature and executive, and an independent judiciary. In this classic statement of the rule of law, the legislature must be dominant: this guarantees a "government by law" and not, as Locke and his peers feared, one dominated by executive "decrees" or "prerogative." Governmental action must be based on clearly formulated, publicly declared rules. But, crucially, the legislature must also be restrained. It, too, can be a source of irregular inroads on individual freedom and property, and uncontrolled legislative majorities can prove as oppressive as unrestrained monarchs. Like the natural law whose purpose it is to uphold, positive legislation must therefore be general; an important part of this ideal is that it cannot take the form of vague and amorphous "extemporary dictates and undetermined resolutions." Undetermined law is similar to an irregular decree insofar as it provides excessive leeway for state representatives to act in a potentially arbitrary, nongeneral fashion.[3] Thus, the legislature is not permitted to issue situation-specific measures or decrees, meaning (for Locke) action directed against individual persons or objects. Otherwise, the "civil state" might turn out to be as unpredictable and miserable as the "state of nature" had become in its final stage, and government could be allowed to run roughshod over those freedoms whose purpose it is to protect.

The idea of the general legal norm, hence, plays a crucial role in this early liberal formulation of the rule of law, and it is arguably the pillar of the famous contrast between a "rule of men" and a "rule of law." Only if legislation does not refer explicitly to particular persons or objects but is issued in advance and meant to apply potentially to all cases and persons in the abstract, can it succeed in depersonalizing the exercise of state authority, and only then can government action be truly impartial. Political authority is regularized and tamed when general norms and not the particularistic and passion-ridden dictates of an executive or all-powerful assembly guide state action: if legislatures are permitted to undertake individual acts, nothing prevents lawmakers from pursuing oppressive acts (against a particular property owner, for example) incapable of being applied generally and thus lacking a universal justification. Indeed, insofar as general positive legislation is supposed to correspond to the similarly general imperatives of the "law of reason" (natural law), the rule of law can even be said to embody humanity's quest to model its order on the divine rationality that Locke, rather traditionally, still sees as embodied in the universe. It is what makes us most like God. The rule of law represents the hegemony of *ratio,* in contrast to mere *voluntas.* But this is all lost if state action "be varied in particular Cases . . . [and if we] . . . have one Rule for Rich and Poor, for the Favourite at Court, and the Country Man at the Plough."[4] Then humanity has succumbed to the rule of passion and, indeed, has turned away from God.

Despite their increasingly secular character, more recent versions of the rule of law have maintained this emphasis on clearly formulated general legal norms. From Montesquieu to Bentham and then Weber, the deceptively simple demand for cogent, general (or formal) law has remained a core component of the rule of law. Although God has generally disappeared from the picture, the general norm has stayed in place. It helps explain the abiding emphasis on the idea of a separation of powers—which, of course, has also taken countless forms. But central to most of them has been the notion that calculable and restrained government presupposes a division between executive and legislative power as well as an independent judiciary. Abstract and clearly formulated general norms should only be "applied" to particular cases that administrators and judges have to confront; blurring these functions might confuse the crucial distinction between impartial (or general) and particular acts and thus contribute to irregular and, therefore, potentially despotic action. As Max Weber noted, administrators and judges were ideally to be like "an automaton into which legal documents and fees are stuffed at the top in order that [they] may spill forth the verdict at the bottom along with the reasons, read mechanically from codified paragraphs."[5] Despite the slightly sarcastic tone with which Weber describes this classical idea, and although he rightly recognizes that it expresses more a noble aim than legal reality itself, he, too, thought it worth defending and saw it as constituting a basic presupposition of modern, "rational" legal authority and a minimum of legal security. Only when legal norms are coherently formulated and general can administrators and judges be expected to act so as to minimize inconsistent and arbitrary state action.

When developing his revised attack on the "legislative state" *(Gesetzgebungsstaat)* and "parliamentary legality" during Weimar's final years, Schmitt has such modern conceptions of the rule of law in mind. In his view, the liberal rule of law contradicts the concrete realities and most basic imperatives of contemporary politics. Based on a set of morally vacuous, formalistic, and antipolitical "normativistic illusions," thus probably doomed from the very outset, the modern rule of law is profoundly anachronistic. Indeed, we can—and must—do without it.[6] As I hope to demonstrate, Schmitt's exposition "trashes" the rule of law without acknowledging the legitimate worries about unharnessed and irregular state power that generated early conceptions of it in the first place. But this one-sidedness is probably preprogrammed into his analysis. Schmitt's empirical account is embedded in a broader set of theoretical views that privilege a particular conception of friend/foe politics vis-à-vis law, homogeneous democracy versus liberalism, and the (normless) political emergency in relation to legal normalcy. His empirical half-truths thus generate a set of conclusions that by no means necessarily follow from them. Although at least some of Schmitt's empirical observations are partially correct and his description of the transformation of the rule of law addresses some real problems for those of us who do not share his normative standpoint, the fact that the rule of law now functions in a manner very different than that envisioned by its classical defenders hardly constitutes an adequate defense of the authoritarian option embraced by Schmitt in the thirties.

Influenced by Kirchheimer's early sociological reconstructions of

Schmitt's own theory, Schmitt offers a right-wing variant of his young pupil's assault on the allegedly indecisive and pluralistic modern welfare state, analogously insisting that powerful social groups have effectively colonized the Weimar Republic's political apparatus and that state intervention in the economy and Germany's federal structure have helped contribute to a catastrophic situation in which the state has lost, or at least is well on its way to losing, its institutional integrity. In Schmitt's terminology, the central state gradually surrenders its monopoly on "the political."[7] Just as Kirchheimer had lambasted the republic for surrendering its sovereign character to a variety of antagonistic social forces, Schmitt now similarly argues that Weimar is no longer capable of standing above competing political and social interests and resolutely and autonomously determining the outcome of conflicts between them; institutional structures that should allow it to do so have been effectively taken over by powerful interest groups and pluralistic special interests. Although the liberal democratic welfare state is thus at best little more than an arbitrator of bad compromises among a motley group of political and social-interest blocs, Schmitt claims admiringly that Italian fascism and even Soviet bolshevism still possess a capacity for decisive, sovereign political action. There, the state apparatus allegedly still constitutes a "higher, on the basis of its own strength and authority decisive 'Third',"[8] superior to competing social and party-based political interests and capable of dominating them when necessary.

According to Schmitt, the pluralist doctrines of English writers like Harold Laski and G. D. H. Cole contain a number of revealing insights. The pluralists' endeavour to reduce the state to nothing but one among a number of competing social institutions reflects real-life developments in contemporary politics. The pluralists' dramatic talk about "the end of the state" embodies the fact that in the contemporary era the state no longer constitutes the ultimate authority in social and political affairs. But if the situation described by them is veridical—Schmitt adds—then the contemporary welfare state finds itself (in 1930) in a historical juncture approaching civil war. The demise of a coherent, unified state apparatus, exemplified most clearly by the fact that state institutions and decision making allegedly have been divvied up among profoundly antagonistic pluralistic social and political interests, means for Schmitt that normalcy has vanished and an "ethics of civil war" should guide political action. Even if the central state itself is incapable of decisive, sovereign political action, Schmitt adamantly insists, there is no escaping the logic of friend/foe politics that he describes in "The Concept of the Political." Some conflict or cleavage is bound to take a truly intense, potentially violent political form, and some interest bloc or constituency is destined to take this political cleavage to a position of dominance. From the perspective of the concrete political actor, the very real question becomes how one can best manage to grapple with the onerous implications of the disintegration of state authority. Particularly in a situation as explosive as a crisis-ridden liberal democracy, political actors need to identify their potential foes—and then work to undermine them.[9]

For Schmitt, this crisis has long-term structural roots. Classical liberalism envisioned an autonomous and self-regulating society—clearly distinct from the state and free from its influence, while able to control state action by means of a monopoly over a freewheeling and discursive sovereign parliament, whose legislative acts were to embody the "general will" and take a general legal form. Schmitt thinks that too much of liberal democratic thought in our century naively continues to presuppose this anachronistic constellation. Particularly because of the centrality of social and economic conflicts to modern politics, Schmitt argues, extensive state activity in social and economic life has proven unavoidable; only by means of far-reaching intervention can the state hope to maintain its grip on explosive class conflicts, and any return to economic laissez-faire would inevitably prove even more disastrous politically than the status quo. With the rise of the interventionist or, as Schmitt describes it, total state, the classical separation between the state and an autonomous society inevitably collapses, and liberal democratic institutions necessarily undergo a profound functional transformation. Amidst the conditions of the contemporary interventionist state, the legislature, for example, is little more than a "showplace for pluralist interests," and no one seriously believes anymore that it articulates a general will by means of unhindered debate and exchange. Parliament is controlled by antagonistic interest groups and powerful blocs representative of distinct segments of a profoundly divided polity, lacking, like the bureaucratized parties and plebiscitary elections that put legislators into power, any interest in engaging in quaint rationalistic liberal discourse with opponents. In reality, political groupings aspire merely to register their interests with state administrators and to make sure that those of their hated foes are not represented. Who today could share the old-fashioned faith in the discursive rationality of parliament or parliamentarians? Or believe that the rule of law still functions to guarantee the sanctity of a self-regulating society?[10]

Most significantly, Schmitt relies on an interpretation of the liberal legal norm that permits him to argue that it has become anachronistic in the age of interventionist politics. It is true that modern defenders of the idea that law should take a general form, like Locke and Rousseau, envisioned (though for different reasons) a political setting where there would be little need for extensive state activity in society, and their emphasis on the virtues of general law can surely be read as an attempt to limit state intervention altogether as much as to make sure that it takes a normatively acceptable form. And at first glance the insistence on law's generality indeed seems incompatible with forms of specialized legislation (directed at a specific social group, or a branch of industry) like that common today. Yet to leave the story there would be too simple. Although one of the most eloquent defenders of modern formal law, Hegel was a believer in neither bourgeois laissez-faire nor a Rousseauian "civic religion" allegedly capable of minimizing state intervention in society, and there is surely evidence that other defenders of general law did not conceive of it as an absolute prohibition on state regulation of social and economic affairs. Even Rousseau writes, "when I say that the object of law is always general, I mean that the law considers subjects as a body and actions in the abstract, never a man as an individual or a particular action. Thus the law can very well enact that there will be privileges, but it cannot confer them on anyone by name. The law can create several classes of citizens, and even designate the qualities determining who has a right to these classes, but it cannot name the specific people to be admitted to them."[11] General law can legitimately regulate specific groups of problems or individuals ("there will be privileges") as long as it does so without naming an individual person or object and simply refers to an "abstractly" defined category. Rousseau thinks that a progressive income tax directed at "subjects as a body" or en masse (for example, all those who earn more than X francs) is perfectly legitimate if it serves the general will, but he would be worried about law directed at a particular individual ("citizen A should pay X," simply by virtue of being citizen A and having, let us say, fallen into disfavor with a particular political authority).[12] In short, the concept of general law in this version of the rule of law, as in many others, amounts to the demand for *like rules for like cases*—which is distinct from an interpretation of formal law that sees it as a hindrance to legal differentiation per se. True, Rousseau exaggerates the extent to which this distinction is always so clear-cut (what happens when only citizen A earns more than X francs?), but he—like Locke, Montesquieu, Kant, Hegel, Bentham, and many others in the modern political tradition—still sees it as a minimal check on the possibility of arbitrary state action. At the very least, the demand that law take a cogent, determinate (Hegel) nonindividual form helps keep state agents from acting randomly against particular individuals.[13]

Carl Schmitt probably underplays the complexity of this issue and, like many contemporary defenders of deformalized regulatory law, concludes that the dominant liberal conception of the legal norm conflicts with the basic requirements of extensive state intervention in social and economic affairs. In Schmitt's view, a polity forced to act in innumerable spheres of social life, and which no longer simply regulates the broadest contours of societal activities but itself takes over many activities once left to the private sphere, cannot rely on an instrument as blunt as the classical general norm. More specialized, unprecedented forms of lawmaking and broad grants of legislative authority to administrative bodies are absolutely imperative after the demise of the classical state/society distinction. Such regulation rarely can be considered classically general. The fact that much of contemporary law not only is explicitly individual (directed, for example, at a particular firm or bank) but relies on what Locke described as worrisome "undetermined resolutions" ("in good faith," "in the public interest") that provide far-reaching room for potentially arbitrary administrative discretion is taken by Schmitt as evidence that the core of the liberal rule of law—the generality of the legal norm—has become obsolete, and that the idea of the separation of powers, which relied so heavily on it, no longer makes any sense. If the view of judges and administrators as passive automatons was probably highly deceptive in classical liberalism, it certainly is today, when law is destined to take an increasingly amorphous, nonformal structure. Administrators and judges no longer passively apply general rules that demand an unambiguous type of action on their behalf. In part because both legislative and administrative actors inevitably undertake discretionary action against specific individuals and particular objects, Schmitt concludes, the distinction between legislative and administrative activities necessarily is robbed of any real justification in our era.

Schmitt's view of this problem had been different just a few years before, when he had sided with Weimar conservatives hostile to nonclassical forms of state intervention. He then denounced, for example, the Left's popular call to socialize royal property, as an act of revolutionary violence, insisting that it constituted a measure directed at a particular person, which the liberal tradition (rightly, he then argued) had denied legislative authorities the power to enact. Such measures, as Locke and so many others had insisted, were contrary to parliamentary government (at least, he revealingly hinted, during the normal situation) but properly belonged to the realm of acts legitimately undertaken by the state during a profound political crisis. Governmental acts against the Prussian princes would open the door to similarly arbitrary measures against particular interests or objects—a specific newspaper, perhaps, or a vocal critic of the regime—and thereby put us on what Friedrich Hayek (who developed strikingly parallel arguments some fifteen years later) ominously describes as the "road to serfdom."[14]

Like Schmitt, Hayek makes the distinction between the individual measure and general law the centerpiece of his legal analysis. But while arguing, like Schmitt, that the welfare state and formal law are inconsistent and similarly attacking contemporary pluralistic legislatures for being colonized by powerful social and political blocs associated with the welfare state project, Hayek suggests that we can recapture nineteenth-century competitive capitalism and some type of early liberal version of the relationship between state and society and save classical general law. In *Legality and Legitimacy,* Schmitt draws very different results from a similar constellation of assumptions. Insofar as Schmitt questions Hayek's belief in the possibility of reconstructing a (romanticized) early capitalist economy, his position is in some respects the more realistic one. Given its full-scale abandonment of the minimal achievements of political liberalism, its consequences are far more heinous. Although Hayek's valorization of the distinction between the individual command and general norm culminates in the irresponsible ideology of the "free" market, it helps Schmitt embrace a far more irresponsible brand of fascism. If (1) the contemporary interventionist "total" state requires discarding general law (and, furthermore, there is no going back to an early liberal state-society constellation), and (2) there are still good normative reasons for preserving a distinction between general legislative norms and individual or particular measures or decrees (which should not be promulgated by a central legislature), as Schmitt still insists, then the modern interventionist state can only take one form—an executive-centered dictatorship. As Schmitt openly tells us, "the administrative state which manifests itself in the praxis of 'measures' "—by which he means the Weimar Republic and the emerging welfare state—"is more likely appropriate to a 'dictatorship' " than the classical parliamentary state.[15] Because popularly elected legislative bodies can only legitimately issue classical-style general norms, they are incapable of grappling with the exigencies of the modern interventionist state, to which dictatorial government is better suited. Parliamentarism and the liberal rule of law may have fit an early capitalist, relatively nonintervetionist state/society constellation, but they are irrelevant to the imperatives of contemporary politics.

Arguing for the necessity of an authoritarian answer to Weimar's crisis, Schmitt hence can seem to remain true to the classical belief in the necessity of discriminating between legitimate general and illegitimate individual legislative acts. While preparing the way for dictatorial government, he can rely on a partial appropriation of Locke and Rousseau.

Despite his attempt to delineate the political sphere from that of morality, in "The Concept of the Political," Schmitt's analysis lacks none of the pathos characteristic of early liberal defenses of the general legal norm. If the abandonment of general law represented for Locke a sinful attempt to flee from the imperatives of God's laws, Schmitt now does his best to match Locke. In his view, parliamentary government's abandonment of classical formal law taken together with the widespread view that legitimate parliamentary action need not take a classically general form means that "the way would be open to an absolutely 'neutral,' value-free, quality-less, empty formalistic-functionalistic conception of legality."[16] Without the minimal guarantee of justice provided by the classical legal norm's general structure, and without any legitimate reason for maintaining some faith in the rationality of parliamentary decision making or in the belief that its legal acts represent society's general interests, parliamentary legality is reduced to the empty and indefensible notion that a majority can, willy-nilly, determine what is legitimate. Lacking this most basic of restraints on legislative action, its every act would have to be considered acceptable, and, in Schmitt's view, the legal order is thereby denied any way of discerning friend from foe, or its real defenders from its opponents. Any majority-backed party, thus even those clearly opposed to the Weimar Constitution, could legitimately seize power and undertake any policies they deemed appropriate, however ridiculous, unjust, or tyrannical they might be. In short, either parliamentary government opts for general law and refuses to undertake modes of social legislation incompatible with it, or it has necessarily succumbed to moral "emptiness" and is destined to self-destruct. The paradoxes of parliamentary legality are thus twofold. Not only is the interventionist state essential to modern politics and (simultaneously) incompatible with parliamentary politics, but parliamentarism's unavoidable abandonment of classical liberal notions of the legal norm probably dooms it.

Schmitt relies on Weber—as noted, a paradoxical, yet nonetheless forceful defender, of much of traditional liberal legalism—in sketching the broad outlines of an alternative to liberal parliamentarism. Weber had tried to make sure that the Weimar Constitution would leave room for a powerful popular executive, outfitted with instruments allowing him to appeal above parliamentary and party institutions, both of which Weber thought most likely to be overrun by the politically stultifying process of bureaucratization. Parties and legislatures would likely fail to produce the charismatic leadership allegedly essential to modern mass democratic politics, the importance of which (in part because of his rather limited faith in the rationality of popular decision making) Weber came to emphasize with a particular vengeance during his final years.[17]

In juxtaposing plebiscitary legitimacy with parliamentary legality, Schmitt clearly has this context in mind. As we will see, his interpretation of parliamentary legality is intended as a critique of Weber. But, significantly, Schmitt radicalizes Weber's views here, as in "The Concept of the Political."[18] Whereas for Weber the idea of a mass-based charismatic leader stands uneasily alongside more traditional liberal conceptions of legality, Schmitt sheds Weber's tension-ridden constellation of its most defensible features.

Because the emergence of radically pluralistic politics and the concomitant abandonment of state "substance" in Weimar represents an emergency and perhaps even a civil war, Schmitt concludes that the Weimar president should be outfitted with unprecedented powers that permit him to issue executive measures of a far-reaching political and legal significance. Schmitt thinks not only that Hindenburg should be provided with lawmaking powers, effectively making the regime's executive decrees dominant in everyday politics and in the crucial sphere of social and economic policy making, but that he also *can legitimately overrule constitutional norms;* Schmitt thereby furnishes the Weimar executive with the power to undertake profound constitutional revisions.[19] Classical general legal norms are to make way for (normless) executive and administrative decrees, and the idea of legislative supremacy, thus one of the centerpieces of the original liberal rule of law, should be surrendered. Only such unprecedented emergency powers, Schmitt now claims, might allow Hindenburg to become the "higher" and "neutral" force, so desperately needed by substanceless Weimar Germany, capable of standing above the political system's antagonistic social and political factions and the paralyzed legislative bodies overwhelmed by them. Because the Weimar president is directly elected by the entire people, he alone truly expresses the political unity of the population, and only he embodies the constitution's original vision of a homogeneous *folk,* as opposed to the heterogeneity of the pluralist party structure, the colonized and divided parliament, and the antipolitical and outdated rule of law that helps keep it afloat. In other words, the ("political") principle of plebiscitary legitimacy, which is intimated in some sections of the Weimar Constitution, should replace ("normativistic") liberal conceptions of legality, and the legacy of the complex and multifaceted Weimar Constitution should be inherited by some form of mass-based executive-centered regime. How will this regime legitimize itself after having abandoned anachronistic conceptions of parliamentary legality and the rule of law? Schmitt tells us that charisma, or perhaps "the authoritarian residues of a predemocratic era," should do the job.[20] They alone can provide the popular support for preserving the German *folk*'s fragile political substance.

In short, homogeneity is to be recaptured, and the Weimar Republic is to be "saved"—by gutting it of any features making it recognizably republican.[21]

2 In Defense of Parliamentary Democracy

In part I of this study, I argued that the Schmittian concept of homogeneity especially was linked to many of the more problematic features of the legal theorizing of Kirchheimer and, though more distantly, Neumann. Their reception of the idea of homogeneity takes distinct forms, but for both authors the view that socialism could amount to a basically conflict-free homogeneous community proves crucial. It is this belief that ultimately leads them to underplay the significance of many liberal legal ideals.

Appropriately, it is Kirchheimer's criticism of the Schmittian idea of homogeneity that is decisive for his rethinking of the relationship between democracy and the rule of law. If one can no longer share the worrisome faith in the possibility of freeing the political sphere of real and potentially productive conflicts, classical conceptions of the rule of law necessarily take on a renewed significance. Then there is no longer any reason to assume that political institutions can automatically represent a political community's (mythical) transparent homogeneous interests, that legal institutions intent on regulating and controlling the exercise of state authority are ultimately unnecessary, or that complex forms of conflict resolution, like those provided by an independent judiciary, can be jettisoned in favor of something reminiscent of premodern common law. The traditional problem of regulating state authority again takes on significance. Indeed, given the inescapable necessity of unprecedented forms of state intervention in contemporary politics, the old-fashioned problem of legal security becomes even more pressing than it was in Locke's day, when government both needed to intervene less in social and economic affairs and lacked the unprecedented tools of mass manipulation now at its ready disposal. Recognizing this does not mean, as Morton Horwitz has recently argued in response to E. P. Thompson's description of the rule of law as an "unqualified human good," that we have necessarily succumbed to "Hobbesian pessimism" or the terrible illusions of a "conservative doctrine." There is nothing manifestly pessimistic or conservative in worrying about how state action can be effectively regulated. It is instead the belief that we can do without anything resembling the classical rule of law—so often evocative of worrisome and implicitly antimodern views of politics, as we have seen—that is arguably the truly conservative view.[22]

The homogeneity that Schmitt is intent on recapturing in his attack on pluralism is not necessarily racial or explicitly nationalistic. Kirchheimer so vigorously criticizes it in part because it arguably constitutes a reactionary mirror image of the social homogeneity that he had once seen the Soviet Union as trying to realize. Schmitt's argument here suggests a form of homogeneity guaranteed by an authoritarian state seeking to defuse real social and economic conflicts. It is inspired by a belief, common to many brands of twentieth-century right-wing authoritarianism, that the explosive class conflicts of modern capitalism can be tamed by means of a "strong" state lacking any qualms about relying on coercive political instruments in order to manufacture social and economic harmony: whereas the natural harmony of competitive capitalism was relatively spontaneous, now it is to be imposed from above by means of state coercion.[23]

Kirchheimer grasps the problematic character of this. He criticizes Schmitt by arguing that "the structure and accountability" of Schmitt's purportedly neutral executive are unspecified. Despite Schmitt's self-interpretation, the powers attributed by him to the *Reichspräsident* imply "a constitutional revolution" destructive of the republic's genuinely democratic core and likely to replace it with a "postdemocratic" brand of "caesarism."[24] It is insufficient that the Weimar president possesses a relatively popular political base in order to legitimize the overarching position Schmitt grants him: "not only legal origins, but above all the lawful exercise of power define the concept of legality," and those, like Schmitt, who ignore the significance of this nuance obscure the difference between parliamentary democracy and dictatorship.[25] A popularly elected executive can attack basic political rights and usurp the powers of competing political instances and thus undermine practices essential to a genuinely democratic regime. If political elites are given unrestrained chances to control the process of consent formation, an authoritarian regime can of course succeed in developing a popular base. Some variety of mass-based dictatorship has to be what Schmitt has in mind. He never denies the necessity of popular participation in modern politics, and he repeatedly insists on the democratic quality of his plebiscitary-based alternative to parliamentarism. But he also tells us that "the people can only say yes or no, it cannot counsel, deliberate, or discuss. It cannot govern or administer, nor can it posit norms; it can only sanction by its 'yes' the draft norms presented to it. Nor, above all, can it put a question, but only answer by 'yes' or 'no' a question put to it."[26] The idea of free consensus is a silly, liberalistic myth: consensus can be manufactured from above by means of diverse "economic, pedagogical, and psychotechnical" instruments.[27] In Kirchheimer's view, Schmitt thereby reduces democratic decision making to nothing more than "an unorganized answer which the people, characterized as a mass, gives to a question posed by an authority whose existence is assumed."[28]

Kirchheimer dryly reminds his readers that this obviously was not the intent of the Weimar Constitution when it declared its belief in the principle of popular sovereignty, during the relatively hopeful days of 1918 and 1919. It certainly assumed more than a stupid, passive, "worn-down" *folk,* whose only function would be to engage in occasional bouts of well-orchestrated ceremonial acclamation. Schmitt's analysis succumbs to the same Jacobin logic that he had described with great care in his own discussion of democratic theory, in *The Crisis of Parliamentary Democracy:* he "substitutes what the people objectively ought to think for what they do think subjectively."[29] In spite of the wide support for the so-called pluralistic parties and their representatives in federal and local institutions even during the republic's final months, and notwithstanding the fact that Hindenburg only gained an electoral majority in 1932 because the SPD unenthusiastically considered him a lesser evil vis-à-vis Hitler and the Stalinist Thälmann, Schmitt claims that these pluralistic institutions conflict with Weimar Germany's true homogeneous interests—represented, of course, by the reactionary Hindenburg, whose bourgeois and authoritarian proclivities Schmitt shares. Although the Weimar Republic is clearly losing its social base among middle-class groups, Kirchheimer argues, there is still no clear consensus in favor of an alternative dictatorship. In fact, this is in part why Schmitt and his cronies have to rely on blatantly unconstitutional methods in pursuing their agenda.[30]

Kirchheimer then undertakes a more systematic critique of the Schmittian conception of homogeneity. In his fascinating "Remarks on Carl Schmitt's 'Legality and Legitimacy'," published in one of the final issues of *Die Gesellschaft,* right before the Nazis banned it and Kirchheimer was forced to flee Germany, he identifies Schmitt's troublesome tendency to merge lines of criticism best kept distinct. Homogeneity is both an empirical and a normative category for Schmitt, tied to claims both about what true democracy should be and an empirical analysis of actually existing liberal democracies. Schmitt wants both to claim that democracy needs to be homogeneous if it is to be genuinely democratic and, perhaps most clearly in *Legality and Legitimacy,* to show that a democracy needs homogeneity if it is to function empirically and, ultimately, to survive.

The latter claim, Kirchheimer shows, is most easily disposed of. From multiethnic bilingual Belgium, to class-divided France and England, there are many cases of relatively heterogeneous democracies. Despite being torn by profound ethnic and class tensions, they still function more or less effectively. As an empirical hypothesis aiming to explain Weimar's decline, Schmitt's insistence on substantial homogeneity is a dubious one. At best it is a half-truth mirroring the instability of liberal democracy when the hegemony of bourgeois groups lacking "natural democratic behavior" is threatened by radical movements from below.[31] Restating Marx's classic analysis of the origins of Bonapartist-style dictatorship, Kirchheimer tries to show that it is not social, ethnic, or national heterogeneity per se that is destroying the Weimar Republic.[32] Although the republic's failure to guarantee a broader degree of social equality and lessen capitalist-based social antagonisms remains crucial to understanding its disintegration, Kirchheimer no longer thinks the Schmittian concept of homogeneity best describes the type of social equality necessary for assuring democratic stability. Socialism, he seems to imply, should no longer be associated with a perfect or even far-reaching social sameness, and classical socialist demands need to be made consistent with social pluralism and heterogeneity: social equality is not homogenization. Socialism cannot realize Schmittian-style homogeneity, because the "entire elimination of divergent views" and "private interest" constitutes "the elimination of the fact of individuality,"[33] and it is thus a "utopian" idea, having little relation to the imperatives of "a time of increasing social and national heterogeneity."[34]

As far as Schmitt's broader normative claim about homogeneity is concerned, it is similarly problematic. Schmitt justifies the centrality of homogeneity by seeing it as essential to producing the identity or equality between rulers and ruled that he takes to be characteristically democratic. But, as Kirchheimer notes, this distorts the basic intention of the modern democratic tradition. From Rousseau to Hans Kelsen, Kirchheimer writes, democratic theorists aspired to realize both freedom and equality, both collective autonomy and equality. Democracy was conceived of as collective self-determination, and not solely or even primarily as substantive sameness. Converting them into crude antinomies, Schmitt distorts the interrelatedness of the concepts of freedom and equality, and hence underplays the fact that the modern democratic tradition was always importantly concerned with the issue of how state action could come to correspond to "the freely formed subjective independent will" of "the people."[35] Because Schmitt falsely sees the idea of freedom as basically bourgeois, individualistic, and antipolitical (and as sharply distinct from democratic equality), he obfuscates the importance of all those institutions functioning to help make sure that democratic will formation is as uncoercive as possible. Schmitt sees basic rights as being individualistic and antipolitical, and not as institutions essential for securing an uncoerced mode of will formation.[36] Similarly, Schmitt misses the underlying intention of the principle of majority rule, arguing that it involves political "rape" in heterogeneous democracies: given heterogeneity, majority decisions manifest an alien set of values unacceptable to minorities. In Kirchheimer's view, a more sympathetic interpretation would see the idea of majority rule as having correctly presupposed the necessity of widespread political differences, but as nonetheless aspiring to achieve the greatest possible political freedom given those conditions. Relying on Kelsen to make this argument, Kirchheimer claims that when a majority determines the contours of governmental decision making and when basic rights guarantee a relatively uncoerced process of will formation and the possibility that other political interests have a chance to become majorities as well, more than half of society's autonomous wills can be said to determine state action. The principle of majority rule allows us the best practical, real-life approximation of the idea of a fully autonomous community in a conflict-ridden political world, where on many issues there is likely to be nothing approaching universal agreement.[37]

This criticism provides the basis for a more specifically constitutional one. According to Schmitt's *Legality and Legitimacy,* the Weimar Constitution itself is divided into "value-free," formalistic elements outlining the basic procedures of (liberal) parliamentary rule making, as well as a (contradictory) anticipation of some features of a value-laden, substantial, plebiscitary authoritarian alternative found in its supplementary "Basic Rights and Basic Duties of the Germans."[38] Beyond arguing, as we have seen, for the primacy of the latter features, Schmitt insists that this contradiction necessarily has immediate practical consequences. In his view, it is responsible for many of the empirical dysfunctionalities of Weimar democracy. Without risking a host of inane concrete political conflicts and crises, a constitution cannot institutionalize "material" special protective clauses (for marriage, religious freedom, or a social democratic model of "economic democracy") functioning to hinder the regulation of certain spheres of political existence while postulating a formalistic value-neutral view of parliamentary legality according to which any conceivable political grouping or viewpoint has an "equal chance" to exercise state power.[39]

Kirchheimer responds that this constitutional argument ultimately rests on Schmitt's flawed juxtaposition of freedom with equality and normativistic autonomy with political homogeneity. Specifically, it is doubtful whether a potpourri of special legal protections like those articulated in the Weimar Constitution's second section (for religious freedom or the right to set up private schools or a job) have always destabilized democracy in Weimar or anywhere else. "For heterogeneity implies the necessity of protection" like that provided by such constitutional clauses.[40] By helping to remove some problem areas from the immediate scope of a simple parliamentary majority, they sometimes "reduce the area of friction, and therefore tend to increase the functional capacity of democracy." Groups (like religious dignitaries attracted to the constitution's protection of religious freedom or union members supportive of a constitutionalized vision of economic democracy) whose privileges are thereby made relatively secure "will consequently be led into a positive relation to democracy," which otherwise might not be the case.[41]

Certainly, excessive controls on parliamentary decision making can pose serious problems for a democracy as well—as we will see, Kirchheimer himself argues that Weimar's disintegration is tied to an attack on the supremacy of parliamentary rule making, grounded in an appeal to selected legal and constitutional standards with an explicitly antimodern gloss—but Schmitt's view of this complicated issue is both one-sided and overly dramatic. After examining a diversity of examples, Kirchheimer concludes that "it must be said" that the material-legal clauses of the second part of the constitution "do not permit an unambiguous statement with regard to their effect on the functional capacity of democracy."[42]

Kirchheimer could not rest satisfied with simply having unmasked Schmitt's justification of an authoritarian plebiscitary alternative. If he was to convince his German audience of the importance of defending the battered republic, he also had to produce some positive arguments on its behalf. Otherwise, Schmitt's vicious attack on contemporary parliamentarism and the rule of law would be left unchallenged. Regardless of how dreary a portrait Kirchheimer and others succeeded in painting of Schmitt's authoritarian alternative, crisis-ridden Germany might opt for it anyhow.

Kirchheimer's post-1930 Weimar-era essays undertake this task in part by questioning Schmitt's interpretation of the classical liberal legal norm. Schmitt, he tells us, "tries with great emphasis to make generality a necessary characteristic of every parliamentary law, concluding from the erosion of this corollary of parliamentary rule that parliament must give way to the dictatorship of the administrative state."[43] There are a number of problems with this view. First, it subverts the original intention of the rule of law while claiming to remain faithful to it. An authoritarian interventionist state ruled by a mass-based executive and a set of bureaucratic cadres might prove more efficient in regulating contemporary social and economic affairs, but in Kirchheimer's assessment it is not clear that anyone (and not even the privileged strata so enthusiastically supportive of an authoritarian solution to Weimar's crisis) would be willing to accept the loss of political and social autonomy entailed by it. Furthermore, Schmitt's view fails to demonstrate adequately that the generality of legal norms must remain a necessary feature of the rule of law. If Schmitt's own argument is any real guide, this position is likely to cripple the legislature at a historical juncture where only widespread state action is capable of guaranteeing a minimum of individual autonomy and personal security, which was always the rule of law's underlying aim. In a fascinating set of publications on the legal aspects of expropriation, Kirchheimer insists that personal autonomy today presupposes extensive regulations of the private economy; freedom presupposes that individuals not be subjected to the whims of (potentially despotic) corporate power and the capitalist market. In his view, the state regulation needed to challenge these societal mechanisms may very well be incompatible with the demand for general legal norms.[44] How, for example, is a reform-minded government to regulate an individual bank or massive corporation whose functions are peculiar to it, yet which might legitimately be controlled in the public interest? Are there, then, any real alternatives to legislative action that might at times look similar to the individual measures so disliked by classical authors?[45] Finally, why should we simply assume, like Schmitt, that the legal order's universality or generality today should still be located in the (general) semantic structure of the legal norm and not in its general (that is, democratic, broadly participatory) origins? Is the generality of contemporary democratic law not necessarily different than that of early (inadequately democratic, bourgeois) liberalism?[46]

This theoretical move places a special burden on Kirchheimer. He will have to defend the mainstay of the liberal conception of the rule of law—the idea of legislative supremacy—in a more far-reaching manner than classical liberalism ever undertook. It is, after all, representative legislatures that claim to make most rules in contemporary democratic polities. If modern social and economic conditions necessitate abandoning the check on legislative decision making provided by the generality of the legal norm, which, at least according to liberal doctrine, contributed to its legitimate character, we now need to demonstrate that we can have even more faith in the rationality of parliamentary rule making than classical liberals did. Only then will we still be able to deem parliamentary rule making acceptable. Two basic—and very provocative—attempts at this can be gleaned from Kirchheimer's essays.

First, Kirchheimer seems willing to defer to at least some of Schmitt's sociological observations about contemporary parliamentarism. He accepts Schmitt's view that the modern legislature, dominated as it is by powerful, well-organized, and antagonistic bureaucratized political and social blocs, is no longer a site (if it ever was) of open, freewheeling and unrestrained debate and discourse. The idea of legislative supremacy cannot legitimize itself today on the basis of the high quality of debate that goes on within parliament's corridors.[47] Yet Schmitt's overly stylized picture of early liberal parliamentarism as a middle-class debating club, Kirchheimer insists, is irrelevant and not even very important for the defense of parliamentary supremacy now provided by most democratic theorists. Like Schmitt, many of them actually presuppose that the electoral process is increasingly plebiscitary; issues are formulated in a simple and easily accessible manner and bureaucratic parties then attempt to mobilize mass support within a highly segmented electorate.[48] Parliamentary politics is increasingly plebiscitary.

At first glance this seems paradoxical given his own anxieties about Schmitt's plebiscitarian views, but the immediate significance of this is that Kirchheimer can emphasize the similarities between parliamentary and directly democratic decision making and then suggest that Schmitt is unjustified in playing off the mass-based plebiscitary Weimar president (and forms of plebiscitary decision making easily manipulated by political elites) against rationalistic parliamentary legality: both sets of institutions are democratic, and the Weimar political order is based on a common principle simply given distinct (plebiscitary and representative) institutional manifestations by its founders: "It is a case of different organizational forms for the same legitimacy."[49] Both the system of parliamentary legality Schmitt so dislikes and that of plebiscitary legitimacy he promotes are alternative forms for the central principle and aim of democratic politics, namely, the noble ideal of collective self-determination. Kirchheimer can make this claim, as we have seen, because he questions Schmitt's endeavour to eliminate anything remotely liberal from the concept of democracy. Schmitt valorizes plebiscitary decision making, ultimately, because it is more appropriate to his antiliberal and anti-universalistic vision of democracy, and he simultaneously belittles parliamentary legality, because the latter represents for him typically bourgeois, individualistic, normativistic, antipolitical values. But if one questions Schmitt's juxtaposition of liberalism (and the normativistic ideas of freedom and the rule of law allegedly associated with it) with democracy (and substantial equality or homogeneity), none of this necessarily obtains any longer.

On the basis of a conception of political representation following, in his view, from acknowledging the centrality of freedom to democracy, Kirchheimer tries to show that parliament, despite its increasingly plebiscitary character, is actually more fully democratic than either an elected executive or any of the alternative forms of plebiscitary decision making envisioned by Schmitt. Broadly based elected institutions more accurately acknowledge the population's heterogeneity and are thus better able to make sure that all interests are represented in the decision-making process. A single executive cannot possibly stand in for all social and political interests. A system relying on a variety of larger and more diverse elected bodies (a national legislature or local and state institutions) is likely to be more effective in representing or reflecting all facets of a divided society. Similarly, Schmittian-style plebiscites, in which the people are allowed simply to say "yes" or "no" to proposals made from above, are necessarily even less representative of the polity's diverse opinions and interests; despite the undeniably plebiscitary features of modern parliamentary elections, they still provide more room for expressing a greater diversity and depth of views than Schmitt's model. This may not be much in comparison to the ambitious aspirations of classical discursive parliamentarism, but it does guarantee a degree of collective autonomy in contemporary politics that is hardly insignificant in scope: if political freedom manifests itself in the extent to which state action accords with all of the population's interests, a parliamentary system more effective at standing in for these interests is normatively superior to Schmitt's plebiscitary alternative. Even in contemporary polities, where pluralistic organized interests dominate parliamentary institutions, Kirchheimer suggests, we can still expect that a sizable number of relatively freely formed "subjective wills" succeed in having their concerns considered by the governmental apparatus.[50]

Kirchheimer's second argumentative strategy is somewhat more complex. We recall that Schmitt's juxtaposition of plebiscitary legitimacy with parliamentary legality has some similarities to Weber's call for an overarching and charismatic executive, capable of effectively challenging bureaucratized parliamentary and party institutions. As has been widely thematized in the literature on Weber, his reflections on the Weimar presidency stand in some tension to his more sober view, in *Economy and Society,* that a disenchanted "rational legal authority," in contrast to traditional and charismatic forms of legitimacy, constitutes a quintessentially modern answer to the problem of generating belief in the rightness of a particular polity: in a world liberated from premodern religion-inspired worldviews, only a belief in enacted rules and in those who are allowed to make these rules can guarantee obedience. Weber correspondingly thinks that rational legality need not take a democratic form. It can be based on "agreement or by imposition," that is, derived from democratic processes or dictated from above.[51] The dissolution of substantive morality, which is characteristic of the transition to modernity, inevitably undermines any conceivable normative basis for democratic politics. In contrast to mainstream modern political thought (which always gave the rule of law an explicitly normative grounding), Weber argues that a characteristically modern conception of legality has no real normative basis outside of its own structure. We believe in legal rules (and in those authorities who issue them) simply because they are legal. Given the disenchanted structure of our world, legality must be conceptualized in a thoroughly value-free manner, and its normative base cannot claim to rest on anything more far-reaching.[52] When Schmitt refers to the purported nihilism of parliamentary legality, it is surely intended as a jab at Weber, Kelsen, and other contemporaries whose theories have some parallels to Weber's own legal positivism.[53]

In "Legality and Legitimacy," Kirchheimer confronts this facet of Schmitt's view head-on. He explicitly borrows Weber's concept of rational legality but gives it an unabashedly democratic gloss: "the specific characteristic of a rational legal order which is no longer feudal and tradition-bound" is that it guarantees formal legal equality. This implies a subordination of administrative to legislative functions like that which parliamentary democracy has long sought to establish.[54] Kirchheimer takes this restated concept of rational legality to be the historical product of a "rationalization" of the idea of the right to resistance that culminated in the supremacy of parliamentary lawmaking.[55] In his view, the ills of Weimar democracy stem not from rational legality's (allegedly nihilistic) refusal to take on the republic's dangerous (primarily left-wing) foes, as Schmitt argues, but from the disintegration of rational legality, which Schmitt actively supports. Semi-authoritarian legal practice after 1930 relies on right-wing ideology and limited, carefully chosen sections of the Weimar Constitution in order to institutionalize a system of "supra-legality," which privileges dubious, premodern, substantive legal standards allegedly possessing "eternal validity" and "indisputable rectitude," and the guarantee of formal equality to every political group is jettisoned for blatant discrimination toward specified (primarily left-wing) political constituencies by means of such standards.[56] The democratic system of parliamentary rational legality is traded in for a nationalistic and belligerently bourgeois conception of executive-centered substantial legitimacy. Exploiting anxieties about its unstable character, the republic's true foes—led by openly antidemocratic and antireform forces entrenched in the executive branch, the judiciary, and state bureaucracy—undermine parliamentary democracy, by taking advantage of this trend so as to make themselves the real lawgivers. It is they, after all, who claim the authority to determine who falls under the rubric of the "revolutionary party" or any of a variety of similar clauses. Most ironically of all, this is all done in the name of saving the republic from its authoritarian enemies, whereas in fact it paves the way for a full-scale dictatorship.[57]

While Schmitt buttresses his own plebiscitary dictatorial model, by appealing to Weber's views about the advantages of powerful, charismatic leaders in a "heartless" bureaucratic world, Kirchheimer builds on Weber's more sober reflections about the recognizably modern qualities of rational legality. Kirchheimer sides with those features of Weber's analysis suggesting that charismatic and traditional forms of legitimacy are incompatible with the exigencies of contemporary politics, and this leads him to deem Schmitt's call for a mass-based popular leader profoundly anachronistic.[58] It is not the idea of parliamentary legality that is quaint and outdated but the quest to establish a mass-based dictatorship appealing to eternal values and a static social ideal in a dynamic and disenchanted universe. Rational legality can incorporate "the dialectic of historical development more smoothly than legitimate domination," such as that sought by the authoritarians and their allies in the bureaucratic apparatus.[59] Contra Schmitt, parliamentary democracy better suits the imperatives of modern politics than dictatorship does.

Schmitt's derogatory portrait of "the folk," for example, is predemocratic. "West European democracy only became possible through a transformation of the masses from merely passive objects of history into an active, organized force," and Schmitt wants both to ignore this accomplishment and to set Europe back centuries. His pessimistic and ahistorical conception of human nature is contradicted by the fact that "democracy changed the structural character of the masses decisively and with a speed that contradicts all theses about the unchangeability of human nature."[60] It is unlikely that the masses can be made as passive as they once were. The democratic experience has heightened their capacity for autonomous and relatively sophisticated forms of political action. Is a dramatic political "leap backward" ultimately possible? Will people be satisfied with simply answering "yes" or "no" to questions posed to them by a set of distant rulers? Opposed to the democratic tide of contemporary history and bent on undermining the dynamic process of social and economic change that is part and parcel of it, Schmitt's system of plebiscitary legitimacy suppresses dynamism in favor of an illusory static social status quo it hopes to preserve.[61] But can we be so sure that the existing state of social and economic affairs is permanent? Could a dictatorship succeed in convincing the population of the sacredness of the existing capitalist social order in a world where nothing is sacred anymore? Amidst the rapidly changing social and economic conditions of the modern world and given the politicized state of popular consciousness, a leader appealing to premodern authoritarian residues or personal charisma cannot be as easily institutionalized as Schmitt thinks. "A lost battle, an aborted economic plan, or the death of an officeholder will bring a great upheaval," and it is unlikely that charismatic or tradition-based leadership in a traditionless world can survive such crises. Many critical things should be said about existing capitalist parliamentary democracy, but the "popular safety valve of elections" guarantees that it is "the sole form of government which constitutionally makes possible the cooperation or the alternation of different groups" during a period of widespread politicization, tense class conflict, and rapid and unprecedented social transformation.[62] However inadequately, existing representative democracy responds to the imperatives of contemporary politics, and "often ignored by its enemies" is the fact that it is "a practical organizing principle for a class-divided country" whose functions a dictatorship cannot effectively fulfill.[63] Germany's semi-dictatorial regime rests on an "appeal to its indisputable rectitude," on the claim that the administrative branch has monopolized knowledge of "eternal values," but this transcendent form of legitimacy is illusory. Immanent democratic forms of parliamentary legality are more responsive to the ever-changing imperatives of political and social development and far more capable than a tiny elite could ever hope to be.[64]

3 Deformalized Law: An Introduction

Otto Kirchheimer lost his political battle with Carl Schmitt. At about the time that Schmitt chose to embrace the Nazis, the twenty-eight-year-old Kirchheimer had to pack his bags for the insecurities of political asylum abroad. True, the political defeat was by no means an intellectual one. Kirchheimer's forceful critique of Schmitt demonstrates that clearly enough. Yet few in Germany cared about that very much by 1933. Authoritarian political interests—and their allies in the intelligentsia—had made sure that the state of emergency had become very real and that normativistic debate had been robbed of its rightful place in politics.

But this does not exempt us from the necessity of critically scrutinizing Kirchheimer's own ideas. If we are to develop the positive features of Kirchheimer's thinking from this period more defensibly later on, we first have to acknowledge its limitations.

In *Economy and Society,* Max Weber argues that the rule-bindedness of the administration is a basic precondition of modern rational legal authority. In "Legality and Legitimacy," Kirchheimer agrees with this view and even relies on it to show how the (authoritarian) fusion of administrative and legislative power that emerged in Weimar's final years undermined rational legality. In Kirchheimer's view, the disintegration of the separation of powers destroys the dependence of the administration on impersonal and abstract formal parliamentary law. The "specific character of legality—the scrutiny of the administration by the application of the standard of the law" is subverted when administrative and legislative functions are badly blurred and when state action comes to be guided by ever-changing situation-specific emergency decrees.[65] For Kirchheimer, Weimar in its final years was, hence, a "government freed of the bounds of law."[66]

But how does this fit with Kirchheimer's claim in 1930 that the old-fashioned demand for general law is now anachronistic?[67] With the demise of the classical state/society divide and the emergence of organized capitalism and the welfare state, there has been, as Roberto Unger correctly notes, a "rapid expansion of the use of open-ended standards

. . . in legislation, administration, and adjudication. For example, the courts may be charged to police unconscionable contracts, to void unjust enrichment, to control economic concentration so as to maintain competitive markets, or to determine whether a government agency has acted in the public interest. Such indeterminate prescriptions have always existed in law," but they have taken on a new prominence in our era.[68] Like many others on the Left in our century, Kirchheimer convincingly suggests that we need to be suspicious of demands that law always take a general, nonindividual (semantic) form while ignoring that democratic law gains its legitimacy primarily from its general or universal participatory origins. If general law is transformed into a check on specialized social and economic regulation, as some political conservatives demand, it is indeed irrelevant in a world where the most basic measure of personal autonomy presupposes vast state activity. Still, it is striking how Kirchheimer's analysis risks underplaying, at least on some occasions, the potential perils of deformalized "materialized" regulatory law as well as the possibility that vague nonformal social regulation law, like that commonplace in the contemporary interventionist state, could make a mockery of his own insistence on the importance of the administration's subordination to law. Can this subordination amount to very much when an administrator is told simply to decide what the public interest amounts to or when a judge is asked to determine what is unconscionable about a contract? Might not the rule of law be more honestly described as a "rule of indeterminate resolutions," and does not the distinction between legal and illegal administrative action risk becoming unclear? There can be no broad agreement about what "good morals," "good faith," or "unconscionable" action means in complex, morally heterogeneous societies. Yet welfare state law makes use of these curious categories and countless others like them. Often akin to the amorphous legal standards used by the authoritarian Right (and rightly criticized by Kirchheimer) in its battle against parliamentary government in Germany during the early thirties, their language is reminiscent of a premodern antipluralistic substantive morality. In many settings, they have been interpreted by judges and administrators accordingly.[69]

Indeed, the seeds of at least some of the problems plaguing the contemporary welfare state can be detected here. Legislative bodies, undertaking necessary forms of intervention but altogether overburdened by the task of regulating a complex social world, today outfit bureaucracies with extensive and poorly defined legislative powers; judges are forced to interpret vaguely formulated blanket clauses that are incapable of any consistent interpretation; perhaps most worrisome is that well-organized and privileged corporatist and bureaucratic elites are given extensive (oftentimes poorly articulated) grants of political authority by means of quasi-political forms of decision making. Increasingly, the legislature is supreme only in legal documents and civics textbooks prescribed to high school students, while in real life it has abandoned many of its powers to relatively isolated an impervious public/private bodies. Amidst the vast bureaucratic expanses of the interventionist welfare state—where, importantly, most citizens are more likely to face the state than anywhere else—governmental action may seem increasingly irregular and even arbitrary.[70]

We need to look beyond the young Kirchheimer's underdeveloped sense of the dangers of deformalized law. Franz Neumann's theorizing during his affiliation with the Institute for Social Research, from 1936 to 1942, which is the subject of chapter 4, helps us do that.

4

The Unfinished Agenda of Rational Law

In *Natural Law and Human Dignity,* Ernst Bloch argues that one reason fascist movements in the twenties and thirties were so effective at dismantling liberal legal institutions was that they tapped into a "popular mistrust of positive law (which continually reappeared from the time of the adoption of Roman Law)." In Bloch's view, this resentment stemmed from the very real fact that in most cases "the law lets the powerful get away while it hangs the weak." The rule of law is too often a sham in a society with vast social and economic inequalities. Fancy lawyers make sure that the well-to-do criminal remains unpunished, whereas the poor lack the social and economic resources to take advantage of their formal rights. "Just like the 'anticapitalist nostalgia' " that midcentury fascism proved so adept at manipulating, a penetrating popular-based judicial skepticism became a powerful instrument in the attack on liberalism.[1] Propaganda directed against the "lifeless," "cold," and "formalistic" rule of law helped guarantee fascism a broad political base, in part because it demagogically exploited legitimate discontent with the legal system.

Similar thoughts must have run through Franz Neumann's mind while in exile in England at the London School of Economics and, after 1936, at the Institute for Social Research in New York. Must there not be something flawed about the liberal rule of law if millions were so eager to junk it?

This historical context is crucial for understanding Neumann's innovative theoretical project during the late thirties and early forties. First,

Neumann undertakes an investigation of the genesis and structure of the modern rule of law. He does this by means of a reconstruction of Max Weber's analysis of the process of legal disenchantment in his *Governance of the Rule of Law* and in a number of related publications for the *Zeitschrift für Sozialforschung* between 1937 and 1941.[2] Neumann defends the alarming thesis that the dissolution of the rule of law was always intimated in its classical formulation: even the most humane of liberal writers were ready to abandon rational law in favor of sovereignty, and the rule of law in favor of brute, unregulated state power. The source of this failing is political liberalism's traditional alliance with capitalism. If the rule of law is to be reconstructed and saved, as Neumann hopes, it now must be linked to a project of radical social and economic reconstruction. The rule of law can only be made perfect if the causes of unchecked sovereignty are eliminated; Neumann believes that the establishment of an egalitarian postcapitalist democracy could guarantee this. Only then might the admirable utopian aspirations of the classical doctrine of the rule of law finally be fulfilled.

Having suggested a positive program for an alternative rule of law, Neumann undertakes the second part of his broader project. He sets out to identify the political and social trends responsible for the rule of law's ongoing disintegration, which he thinks is most clearly, though by no means exclusively, evident in German fascism. His thesis is that powerful tendencies in contemporary politics point to the demise of anything that deserves to be described as law. Moreover, this nightmarish trend represents the practical fulfillment of Carl Schmitt's decisionistic legal and political thought. In order to defend social and economic privilege in the most direct and brutal manner conceivable, fascist theory and practice abandon the more humane facets of the contradictory legacy of classical bourgeois legal thought. Like Schmitt, German fascism opts for unharnessed sovereignty (and capitalism) over the rule of law. Significantly, Schmitt becomes Neumann's theoretical antipode, and Neumann's writings from this period aim especially at developing a critical response to "the most intelligent and reliable of all National Socialist constitutional lawyers."[3]

In this chapter, we will examine the first part of this complex project. The problem of fascist law and ideology, as well as Schmitt's role there and its broader contemporary significance, is reserved for chapter 5. In developing an analysis of legal rationalization, Neumann allies himself with Weber as well as much of classical liberalism in emphasizing that the coherence and systematization of legal norms are essential to a defensible conception of the rule of law. Legal rationality for both authors presupposes the supremacy of clearly formulated general legal norms that do "not mention particular cases or individually nominated persons, but which [are] issued in advance to apply to all cases and all persons in the abstract."[4] Whereas his colleagues Horkheimer and Adorno build on Weber to offer a traumatic and one-sided portrayal of Western rationality and development, Neumann uses Weber to determine what needs to be salvaged from classical liberalism.[5] At the same time, Neumann's reworking of the story of legal development constitutes an implicit criticism of Weber's views, and he offers a conception of the rule of law notably distinct from Weber's model of legal-rational authority. Social equality and radical democracy are made its indispensable presuppositions. Otto Kirchheimer similarly intimated, in 1932 and 1933, that Weber's views about modern law might be reconstructed in an explicitly democratic fashion, but Franz Neumann now makes this task the mainstay of his theoretical program (section 1). Having described Neumann's pioneering reconstruction of Weber and the differences between the two authors, I focus on its more problematic features (section 2). In particular, Neumann's reliance on Rousseau proves troublesome. Although in many ways impressive, Neumann's ideas still suffer from a dependence on antimodern views about politics and law: no adequate modern theory of democracy, no rule of law.

1 Reconceiving Legal Rationalization

In Max Weber's view, modern law is denied any transcendent normative base. The problem of legitimacy in the modern world is a question of legality: the structure of rational legality itself guarantees its legitimacy. Most importantly, modern law rests on a set of tightly organized and clearly formulated general legal norms, in which "every concrete legal decision . . . [is] . . . the 'application' of an abstract legal proposition to a concrete 'fact situation' " according to a formalized set of abstract legal propositions and legal logic.[6] Such a legal system can be described as rational for a number of reasons. Its systematic character presupposes the (rational) scientific activity of legal experts, who play a pivotal role in its development and cultivation. Furthermore, modern law's formal structure corresponds to the disenchanted quality of our world, and it thus suits the needs of a social order where instrumental rationality has become predominant. Exceptionally predictable and calculable, rational law facilitates the pursuit of private subjective interests and values, while acknowledging that its own structure cannot embody any universally defensible moral values. In other words, it reflects a typically modern privatization of value preferences and makes law an instrument for the pursuit of those preferences.

The process by which we have reached this juncture was arduous and complex, and—if we read Weber's *Economy and Society* carefully—in many ways, far too obscure. Weber emphasizes a number of factors in explaining the demise of legal particularisms (feudal-style privileges, for example) and the emergence of rational legality: an alliance between market-oriented (bourgeois) strata and bureaucratizing political elites and their "power needs," the universalism of Roman law and Christian natural law, and the intrinsic intellectual needs of legal experts. In any case, only in the West did these distinct ingredients get mixed in just the right way so that the recipe of legal disenchantment was successful. Things seem to have worked out differently in England given the relative tenacity of traditional legal forms there, but Weber thinks he can still show that the odd case of England—where nonformal common law remained dominant, despite the fact that modern capitalism first flourished there—does not undermine his view that capitalism and formal law need each other.[7]

This landmark cultural achievement is now under attack. Because of his conception of the relationship of science to morality, Weber never undertakes an explicitly normative defense of legal-rational authority in *Economy and Society*. But he does not hesitate to embellish his analysis with dire warnings about the possible consequences of that authority's corrosion. Weber's famous discussion of antiformal tendencies in modern law argues that growing demands for social and economic equality are likely to lead to the proliferation of open-ended, amorphous modes of relatively informal law and legal decision making, which not only undermine the legal security guaranteed by classical formal law but are based on "emotionally colored ethical postulates" inconsistent with modern law's fragile triumph over irrational and morally substantive legal forms. The welfare state and its increased reliance on vague legal terms suggests the resurrection of something disturbingly reminiscent of Islamic Kadi justice, whose ad hoc adjudication was based on a confused mix of emotional, ethical, and legal grounds. Weber thinks that judges and lawyers eagerly support these efforts because they buttress their own power needs by trusting legal experts with vast de facto legislative powers: not only does legal deformalization challenge capitalism but it threatens parliamentary supremacy as well. And if formal law is one of the greatest achievements of modernity, its disintegration potentially prepares the way for the decline of a whole set of characteristically modern institutions.[8]

Weber's position has since defined the terms of a heated debate on the pros and cons of welfare state law in the twentieth century. Right-wingers like Carl Schmitt and Friedrich Hayek latch onto Weber's anxieties and try to show that the consequences of legal deformalization are even more problematic than Weber's analysis suggested. They accept his claim that the contemporary interventionist state and classical general law are inconsistent: Schmitt opts for an authoritarian interventionist state that abandons formal law altogether, whereas Hayek wants us to dump "materialized" welfare state law in favor of a (mythical) early capitalist utopia, allegedly lacking all the problems that even Adam Smith was ready to acknowledge and thus any need for new forms of nontraditional legal regulation. Interestingly, most of the welfare state's defenders accept the logic of Weber's argument as well. Many of them see extensive social and economic reform as necessarily undermining formal law, but they are willing to accept this loss as a necessary side-effect of the social autonomy promised by the welfare state.[9]

This makes Franz Neumann's restatement of Weber's analysis of legal rationalization all the more provocative. Neumann does not belong to either of these camps. He wants both radical (and explicitly anticapitalist) social and economic reforms *and* all of the virtues of liberal general legal norms. Neumann tries to show not only that social and economic equality and classically liberal legal modes are compatible but that they need each other. Weber's view that there is always a fit between capitalism and formal law is ahistorical and misleading. The real elective affinity is between social democracy and formal law.

Like Weber, Neumann describes "the process of the divorce of positive from natural law, by which positive law became self-sufficient and autonomous."[10] He shares not only Weber's view that a complex series of concrete actors and struggles (the church and emerging nation-state, distinct religious groups, and, in particular, emerging bourgeois strata) is crucial to understanding the historical dynamics of legal rationalization, but also Weber's claim that the role of intellectuals should not be underplayed. This is why the history of legal rationalization can be effectively examined by recourse to a sociology of political ideas from Aquinas to Hegel (inspired in part by Karl Mannheim), tracing the development of the theory and practice of the modern rule of law.[11] "This process of disenchantment is no unbroken one, progressing uninterrupted through the years. Relapses are frequent; law and morals, law and natural law are often confused,"[12] but its underlying pattern and direction can nonetheless be made out by means of a synthesis of political and legal theory, the sociology of ideas, and social history.

The key conflict underlying this process is that between "force" and "law," or sovereignty and the rule of law. Law regulates and binds state power, making its exercise rule-based and potentially humane. Law is not simply a manifestation of that power but embodies a noble and unfinished attempt to make state authority tolerable. If it fails, state sovereignty (and more or less unregulated types of state action having deleterious consequences) gains the upper hand; if it succeeds, state-based power can be made normatively legitimate. When a central political apparatus emerges and is outfitted with impressive instruments of manipulation and violence, state sovereignty is potentially an "undelegated and unlimited power."[13] "Only if sovereignty exists can we speak of the state as such. . . . Only the modern state . . . conquers new markets, and produces the inner unity of administration and law; it destroys local and particular powers, squeezes out the Church from the secular sphere, holds the struggling social groups within definite boundaries."[14] Historically, none of these progressive achievements would have been possible if state action had only taken a cogent general form—in other words, if the ideal of the rule of law had always been truly supreme in political affairs. Although acknowledging the crucial role played by unharnessed state sovereignty in the emergence of the modern political and economic universe, Neumann tries to suggest how it now can be tamed. In his view, modern politics still needs state organs holding a monopoly on the instruments of coercion (and law, unlike morality, must still be backed up by the possibility of state-based force), yet he hopes that this monopoly can take a significantly more acceptable form than it has in the past, and that the state should no longer need to act in a manner incompatible with general legal norms or above and against a system of neatly codified formal law.[15] Neumann's intention here is not, à la Carl Schmitt, to romanticize the political exception or emergency and the violence that often accompanies it. On the contrary, Neumann thinks that normless decisionist power decisions can be effectively eliminated from politics, and he sees the central, and as of yet incomplete, task of both political practice and thought in the West as the abolition of such decisions. Neumann's project is to show how legal rationalization could make all those ugly facets of political existence, embodied in the very core of Schmitt's theory, unnecessary.[16] With the exception of one crucial type of political doctrine and what Neumann sees as its matching political and social program, all of modern Western thought succumbs to the flaw of allowing some spheres of political existence to be dominated by the exercise of power that is effectively unregulated by satisfactorily binding legal rules. At some point, discretionary normless commands or individual measures, which for Neumann (as for Locke, Rousseau, and many others) constitute the clearest manifestation of unchecked absolute sovereignty, are tolerated.[17] Virtually all political theories contain loopholes, permitting those in power to do pretty much as they please, and in every political theory, unrestrained sovereignty is allowed to rear its ugly head at some juncture or another. In other words, nearly all of modern political theory contains more or less blatantly decisionist elements. Schmitt's intellectual mistake is to radicalize and reify this tendency instead of recognizing its roots and trying to eliminate them. Neumann's project, in contrast, involves showing how the specter of decisionism—particularly as it manifests itself by means of normless individual power commands—can be driven from the political universe.[18]

From this perspective, the history of Western legal development is the story of the struggle to rid it of vaguely defined legal standards—like "necessity," "national security," or "public interest" and "in good faith"—facilitating potentially arbitrary, situation-specific forms of state action in some ways like those traditionally associated with the practice of raison d'état. Like Weber, Neumann emphasizes the growth of coherent and systematized legal norms and formal procedures, but unlike Weber (or Marx), Neumann is convinced that this praiseworthy trend is destined to remain incomplete within the confines of a bourgeois social and economic order: bourgeois formal law is not especially bourgeois at all. A central and identifiably Marxist feature of Neumann's study is the idea that the antinomy of law and sovereignty constitutes the very core of a bourgeois legal order. Neumann never tries to derive legal forms from the contradictory dynamics of the capitalist mode of production. His position is both more straightforward and more complicated. Indeed, only because its theoretical structure is so simple can Neumann adequately acknowledge the tremendously complex ways in which the tension between capitalism and rational law manifests itself in modernity. As we recall, Neumann follows Karl Renner in arguing that the legal superstructure need not mechanically reflect or express the imperatives of the socioeconomic substructure, and that legal institutions and social and economic reality often do fall into a state of disequilibrium. But he still thinks there is a fundamental tension between the critical, unfulfilled universalistic idea of legal equality (and the derivative view that legal norms must be clear and general) and the deep social and economic inequalities generated by capitalism. In this view, unchecked state sovereignty results from this tension: it is bourgeois society's sad attempt to overcome the gap between its implicitly egalitarian legal ideas and real social and economic inequalities by means of sacrificing the former for the latter. When the state abandons cogent general law in favor of, situation-specific action, capitalism gains the upper hand over the fragile, constantly threatened aspirations of the liberal political tradition. Because capitalism and rational law conflict, the defense of capitalist-based inequality precipitates recourse to irregular legal action.[19]

Neumann's alternative analysis of legal rationalization commences with medieval Europe. Medieval natural law is doomed, because it identifies what exists with what should be; Thomist natural law, for example, can be read ideology-critically as a theoretical codification of the feudal order. Its immanent flaw is that as soon as the pace of social development picks up in the later Middle Ages, specific institutions no longer appear divine or natural. At the same time, Christian natural law contains morally universalistic elements that transcend the immediate historical context in which they emerge. The recognition of universal equality has a "dynamic" quality tending to undermine all forms of political and social hierarchy, and Neumann approvingly cites Ernest Barker's view that "if the slave can be treated as a man in any respect, he ought to be treated as a man in all; and the admission, that he can be regarded as a man, destroys that conception of his wholly slavish and non-rational (one might say non-human) character, which was the justification of his being treated as a slave."[20] When natural law later takes a more secular form (in Hobbes, for example) and is based on a conception of human nature and not a set of preconceived transcendent norms on which political and social life should be modeled, these universalistic elements manifest themselves in the "social contract," with critical implications. Even Hobbes's authoritarian interpretation of the contract reveals its emancipatory potential: Hobbes has to concede that a legitimate political order must be grounded in a (democratic) consensus.[21]

Yet the gradual disintegration of natural law poses more immediate problems. If social and economic fluidity suggests the arbitrariness of classical natural law, it also implies that law itself is a mere artifact, lacking any transcendent or divine qualities. A characteristically modern conception of positive law begins to emerge. But this hardly constitutes an unambiguous step forward. On the one hand, it represents a crucial acknowledgement of the untenability of traditional religious worldviews, and it is fitting that theorists (like Marsilius of Padua or Nicholas of Cusa) who early on developed this idea with surprising rigor made up the most progressive political voices of the late-medieval period. On the other hand, the possibility of a purely political concept of law simultaneously arises, according to which law is robbed of any intrinsic normative value and every state act, "whether just or unjust, convenient or inconvenient," is acceptable.[22] As traditional morality declines and the structure of a replacement for it remains unclear, the makings of a radically decisionist system of law based on nothing but arbitrary prerogative begin to take shape—as absolutism and a genre of theorizing emphasizing law's "command" qualities unambiguously show. Political law is the legal complement of unrestrained sovereignty and an institutional expression of the worrisome idea that law can have no ties to morality.

The key problem for the Western political tradition becomes confronting this challenge: having abandoned natural law, the West has to find a normative replacement for it.[23] On my reading of *The Governance of the Rule of Law,* Neumann sketches at least two historical answers to the problem of legal disenchantment—what I will call here the "classical liberal" and "authoritarian legalist" paths—as well as a third possibility—a radical "social democratic" path—which he thinks has only been hinted at in political thought and practice. Later on, and as we will see in chapter 5, he acknowledges a fourth (ominous) possibility, namely, a fascist path suggested by Carl Schmitt's decisionist theory. Neumann describes (1) Locke as the theorist of the classical liberal path of eighteenth- and nineteenth-century England, (2) the intimations of an authoritarian legalism—the nineteenth-century Prussian *Rechtsstaat*—in Kant's legal philosophy, and (3) the foreshadowing of a radically egalitarian social democratic option in Rousseau, which Neumann clearly thinks that we should opt for. Each path offers a distinct answer to the dissolution of natural law; each replaces it with a more or less secularized version of the modern rule of law. In contrast to Weber, for whom rationalization, though now threatened, is essentially complete, Neumann sees the process of legal rationalization as an unfinished task. While Weber insists that modern rational law necessarily lacks a normative base, Neumann argues that the rule of law should not burn all of its bridges to the natural law tradition. Notwithstanding legal positivism's historically progressive features, its "division of the world into an is and an ought is philosophically a rather doubtful affair,"[24] thus it will be possible to attribute what Neumann describes as an ethical function to a key facet of the modern legal order.

The classical liberal path is intimated in Locke and more fully worked out by Blackstone and Dicey as well as English political practice in the eighteenth and nineteenth centuries.[25] Here natural law is eventually abandoned and replaced by the idea of parliament as absolutely sovereign and the belief that parliament can only issue general legal norms. Despite first appearances, Neumann argues, these tenets are not contradictory given the social configuration presupposed by them. Neumann sees the demand for general norms as essential to guaranteeing economic calculability in early capitalism, and he insists on an elective affinity between a liberal legal order based on them and a competitive bourgeois economy consisting of relatively small- and medium-size entrepreneurs. The early liberal state generally does "not intervene by individual measures because such an intervention would violate the principle of the equality of competitors" so sacred to early bourgeois economic ideology.[26] From this perspective, it is unsurprising that parliamentary institutions sympathetic to capitalist economic development, like those then found in Britain, limit themselves to issuing norms that undermine the absoluteness of their sovereignty. "The contradictions and ineffiencies of Dicey's" classic theoretical attempt to synthesize absolute parliamentary sovereignty with legally conceived self-limitations to legislative power "have been conclusively proved" by countless authors, but what all of Dicey's critics miss is the sociological feature of the problem at hand, which alone makes it coherent.[27]

Emphasizing this version of the rule of law's role in disguising the hegemony of privileged bourgeois strata, Neumann is quick to point out its shortcomings. Political participation is limited to a narrow group of property owners, and the general legal norm does little more than help preserve early capitalist economic calculability and conceal the concrete power claims of an emerging bourgeois economic elite. "In paying reverence to the 'law,' one can conceal the act that the 'law' is made by man," and a tiny group of rich and privileged "men" at that.[28] Neumann supports the view that this construction of the rule of law provides little legal security to the lower classes, using an innovative analysis of English common law, complementing that developed by Weber in *Economy and Society* but going beyond it in a number of ways, which demonstrates that it remained irregular and traditional precisely in those areas where its systematization might have generated real security for broad masses of the population.[29] According to this view, formal law was discarded whenever the basic imperatives of the bourgeois order were threatened or when it came to justifying colonialism. Unchecked state sovereignty surely has not vanished here. Locke's "prerogative" "in the main coincides with the sphere of competence of the federative power"—that is, with foreign policy making, and Locke's own willingness to trade in the rule of law for lawless state action on the theoretical level is all too representative of real-life English imperial practice.[30] Despite the emphasis on cogent formal law in this path, its benefits never accrued to the poor, the socially excluded, or the colonized.

Although Neumann's discussion of this developmental path focuses on debunking its ugly bourgeois underside, the structure of his critique depends on taking the classical liberal legal norm seriously. Crucially, the problem here is not the general norm per se but the failure and even impossibility of extending its advantages to all classes in a highly antagonistic social setting. Only this explains why Neumann tries to identify some redeeming qualities even in this sadly bourgeois rendition of the rule of law and why, even here, he tells us that classical law "has in the first place the function of establishing equality," albeit an equality primarily among the propertied.[31] At least as far the economically privileged are concerned, general law provides an important measure of legal security, and insofar as it matches and helps perpetuate a developing capitalist economy characterized by a relatively wide dispersion of economic resources, it preserves a measure of economic equality. Even in its most explicitly bourgeois form, general law is always more than a mere veil for power inequalities, and even here there are intimations of a historically transcendent "ethical function." When the legislator need not act according to general norms—if he "can issue individual commands, if he can arrest this or that man, if he can confiscate this or that property"[32]—the most basic measure of legal security is badly undermined.

In a second authoritarian legalist path, whose theoretical contours Neumann locates in Kant's tension-ridden political philosophy, natural law has similarly vanished, but only a dreary form of authoritarianism has replaced it. With the nineteenth-century Prussian *Rechtsstaat* in mind, Neumann describes the tragedy of the failed and defensive German middle classes, "politically in a state of subjection and . . . content with making money," who trade off the right to control parliament for the mere promise that legal security is to be guaranteed by the demise of situation-specific law.[33] Arguing against Weber and others who underplay the significance of law's genesis for determining its legitimacy, Neumann thinks this path demonstrates that the replacement of natural law with the mere demand for systematized formal law is a dreadful recipe for authoritarianism, although an authoritarianism nonetheless predictable. The lesson here is that the universalistic legacy of natural law should culminate in both the demand for "equality before the law" (and general law) as well as a mode of decision making based on universal participation. According to Neumann's peculiar (and by no means unproblematic) reading of him, Kant is seen as failing to tie his ethical theory to his legal and political philosophy adequately, and this is taken to be the crucial source of the democratic inadequacies of Kant's thought as well as exemplary of the ills of nineteenth-century Prussia. Specifically, Kant's distinction between external (legal) acts and duties and internal (moral) ones not only foreshadows the emergence of legal positivism but, in fact, represents a positivist position: the mistaken and politically troublesome quest to separate the problem of legality from that of democratic legitimacy is already found here. Kant's formalistic moral theory and the vision of the social contract resulting from it must hide implicit substantive assumptions about the sanctity of private property (in which case its alleged formalism is a fraud), or the Kantian social contract has to be interpreted in such a formal manner that it is capable of being used to justify pretty much anything. In discussing Kantian-inspired attempts to deduce a theory of punishment from his model of the social contract, Neumann tells us that all "these deductions are arbitrary, because from the principle of the social contract no concrete conclusion can be derived. . . . But just as one can prove the logical necessity of the death penalty, so to speak as a logical catharsis, so also one can prove a genuine claim on the part of the murderer to be executed."[34] Relatedly, Kantian formalism can provide no real checks on state authority; it is ultimately impotent in the face of the exercise of unrestrained sovereignty, and the innumerable compromises with the Prussian status quo implicit in Kant's own political writings provide evidence enough for this systematic flaw. The social contract has been transformed into a "transcendent idea"—an abstract and overly formalistic idea that need not result in real-life political democracy and is incapable of undermining irrational authoritarianism. "The natural law has disappeared; but with it, democracy also."[35]

Neumann's description of a third path, based on a sympathetic exegesis of Rousseau, intends to show how we might overcome the weaknesses of its historical competitors and simultaneously provide a guide for democratic socialist practice. "At the frontier of bourgeois thought," that practice's outstanding characteristic lies in anticipating an egalitarian postcapitalist order that allegedly lets us complete the liberation of the legal order from irregular, nongeneral raison d'état type of law. Here, the general legal norm takes on "an entirely ethical function." As Rousseau's theory implies, cogent general legal norms embody a democratic general will only given far-reaching social and economic equality, in which there are no "differences between rich and poor, between owners of the means of production and dependent workers, between monopolists and non-monopolists."[36] Amidst inequality, it may well be in the common good to undertake situation-specific legislative action: "If the state is confronted by a monopoly, it is pointless to regulate this monopoly by general law. In such a case the individual measure is the only appropriate expression of the sovereign power."[37] This is indeed why Weber's view that formal law complements capitalism obtains only for a particular moment in its history—and even then, as we have seen, only to a limited extent. It is also why denying popular legislatures the right to undertake individual acts under contemporary conditions (as Schmitt in the twenties and Hayek after World War II seek to do) transforms the implicit egalitarian energies of the rule of law into a check on precisely those reforms, such as the socialization of a large monopoly, that facilitate the emergence of a truly ethical system of formal law.[38] Given the non-egalitarian structure of contemporary capitalism, nongeneral law at times becomes a necessary evil, but something conscientious legislators cognizant of the virtues of the legal security provided by classical general law should struggle to avoid. In any case, only in an alternative, postcapitalist world (or so this social democratic revamping of Rousseau posits) does Rousseau's argument work. Only then does general law express a genuinely democratic general will; only then would there no longer be any need for nonclassical law (directed, for example, at a particular bank or corporation). General law could finally be universalized, its virtues accrue to everyone, and its rule made perfect. Neumann himself formulates this far more dramatically: "the sovereign power then ceases to be sovereign, it is no longer an external power confronting the subjects. It is rather society which governs and administers itself. . . . Rousseau's theory is, in fact, an interpretation of the Marxian theory of the withering away of the state; of the emergence of a society free from external rule."[39] On this path to rational legality, the state itself has finally been tamed and the epic struggle between law and sovereignty resolved. In a world of democratic republics, substantial economic equality, and a legal order limited to clearly formulated general norms, unregulated exercises of state authority become both unnecessary and impossible. The state would nominally maintain its monopoly on coercion, but why must this monopoly result in any of the unpleasant characteristics of contemporary political experience generally associated with it?

Neumann implies that only this incomplete rationalization option might fulfill the classical liberal demand that state action be bound to the dictates of the legal norm. In a fascinating discussion of the American legal realists, in *The Governance of the Rule of Law,* he concedes that Montesquieu's view of the judiciary as passively subsuming individual legal cases under general legal norms is undoubtedly exaggerated. Still, in a legal order based on cogent general law like that demanded by theorists from Locke to Bentham, discretionary decision making could be minimized. The proliferation in our century of theories valorizing the creativity of the legal decision maker in part reflects the failure to fulfill the classical demand for a legal system whose norms might provide legal experts with clear guidance and whose "real existence" they could acknowledge.[40] Again, Neumann very much has Schmitt in mind when making this claim. Whereas Schmitt had long offered a caricatured reading of liberal ideals of judicial decision making—in *Political Theology* he sarcastically noted that a "legal ideal cannot realize itself"[41]—Neumann seeks to preserve its rational core. The legal decision maker cannot be an "automaton into which legal documents and fees are stuffed at the top" so as to mechanically produce a steadfast solution.[42] Nonetheless, relatively clear general standards *can* provide meaningful direction to decision makers and guarantee an important degree of legal regularity; this, Neumann worries, is obscured by the one-sided deconstruction of liberal legal ideals like that undertaken by Schmitt. Especially given that this deconstruction contributed to Schmitt's insistence on the irrelevance of the normativistic rule of law and encouraged him to advocate an authoritarian alternative, Neumann thinks it crucial to acknowledge the liberal view's worthy features.

Like Weber, Neumann acknowledges the partially illusory quality of traditional conceptions of legal decision making, but he also believes they still contain an underlying insight essential for maintaining an adequate degree of legal security. Again like Weber, he thinks this is put at risk when vague, deformalized legal standards are permitted to play a pivotal role in the legal order. Where decision making is based on standards like "good faith, good morals, public policy, or reasonableness," it is essentially administrative: it serves "the reconciliation of colliding interests, and not the determination of conflicting rights" according to law.[43] Kirchheimer describes a similar view of legal interpretation when he writes that "the judiciary is only a concomitant to an established body of laws which it adapts to the special needs of the community. The procedural formulas which it develops provide a certain amount of predictability. The contending individuals and groups, though they never are sure which of the many possible interpretations . . . will prevail in a given case, usually could confine their actions within such limits that these could not be said to contradict openly the wording of the law."[44] But how can the legal norm provide effective control on state action when the decision maker is told simply to see whether a government agency is operating reasonably or in the public interest, or whether collective bargaining is going on in good faith? Does not the risk of problematic forms of discretionary decision making dramatically increase?[45] The traditional liberal vision of the relationship of the legal norm to the decision maker contains a critical moment repeatedly downplayed by its critics. In some contrast to Weber, Neumann focuses on the liberal ideal's democratic implications: in a parliamentary democracy, the idea of the norm-based judge or bureaucrat carries the supremacy of elected popular bodies to its logical conclusion by aspiring to minimize the discretionary activity of relatively isolated, unrepresentative legal elites. It demands that all facets of state action be coordinated, as closely as possible, according to the dictates of that facet of the decision-making apparatus that can claim to be most popular and representative. Neumann thinks contemporary authors too often forget this but genuine democrats would do well to recall it.[46]

2 Misconstruing the Generality of Modern Law

A number of problems clearly plague Neumann's ambitious neo-Marxist restatement of Weber. I will focus on what is most relevant for our broader project. Notwithstanding Neumann's claim that this third path presupposes a democratic political setting, he says remarkably little about it. Beyond praising Rousseau for seeing the social contract as "an ideal to be realized in history" and making a number of odd references to an undefined vision of a "decentralized organic democracy" (in contrast to "atomistic constructions of democracy"), we are told nothing of substance about the nature of democratic politics in his social democratic legal utopia.[47] This is hardly accidental. Here, "the individual will and general will coincide"; Rousseau's ''theory resembles that of Marx. . . . Marx has filled in Rousseau's logical structure with history," and as in Marx's overly antipolitical and antipluralistic utopia, Neumann likely believes that a particular mode of social and economic organization guarantees this coincidence without political conflict and exchange (like that essential to a genuinely democratic mode of politics) having to play much of a role.[48] Like Rousseau, Neumann conceptualizes general law as expressing a substantial general will directly extant in social and economic life. It is a legal superstructure for a set of transparent general interests allegedly realized by means of the social and economic homogeneity of the substructure. Even the more technocratic features of Marx's original political vision may resurface here: Neumann tells us that in his Rousseauian democratic socialism, society "administers itself."[49]

The criticisms of Rousseau's position are legion, and many of them can be directed against Franz Neumann as well. Only simple and underdeveloped communities conceivably manifest a general will in as direct a manner as this. Even Rousseau knew that. In a world governed by traditional worldviews and static modes of social organization, we could indeed "look into our hearts," as Rousseau hoped, and have a good chance of finding the general will and intuitively grasping what the mores of a particular small-scale community demand of us. In such a setting, our hearts would tell us pretty much the same thing. But in what respect can a legislative act—taking a classical general semantic form or otherwise—be seen as embodying a univocal common good or general will in societies necessarily characterized by a high degree of value heterogeneity and significant political antagonisms? Neumann's answer to this familiar dilemma probably must look like Rousseau's, and it likely would be forced to partake of all its familiar authoritarian implications. The outvoted would have to admit that the political majority had always been right; a religious minority defeated on a particular issue might have to concede that its opponents had always been correct; proponents of state-directed economic policy might "look into their hearts" to discover that the free-marketeers represented the very pinnacle of economic thinking.

When our hearts can no longer speak with one voice, the idea of a democratic general will must be formulated in a less concretistic manner. The concept of a democratic consensus needs to be located in the democratic political process and not in its results—in those procedures and preconditions guaranteeing an open and unrestrained process of consent formation. In complex, necessarily divisive modern political communities, the idea of consent cannot refer to an end: "the core intuition behind modern universalizability procedures is not that everybody could or would agree to the same set of principles, but that these principles have been adopted as a result of a procedure, whether of moral reasoning or public debate, that we are ready to deem 'reasonable and fair.' "[50] Burdened by a set of antimodern presuppositions, Neumann's position unfortunately remains more traditional. Because he assumes that the general will is concretely realizable in everyday social and economic existence, he inevitably underplays the complexities of democratic consent formation and misleadingly reduces democratic politics to little but a (passive) "transmission belt" by which universal social homogeneity is given a corresponding universal (or general) legal form.

Interestingly, *The Governance of the Rule of Law* opens with a refreshingly appreciative assessment of the social contract tradition in Western political thought, telling us that "even if . . . no state ever was established by contract, the category of the Social Contract might be a methodological principle necessary for the justification of the state or freedom from it." The concept of the social contract, Neumann argues tentatively in the work's opening pages, offers the starting point for a rational theory of political legitimacy, and he comments that he agrees with Carl Friedrich that "the juridical category of the contract is easily overemphasized. What is decisive is not the juridical category of the contract, but its meaning, its secular and rational justification," and the fact that it conceives of a "justification deriving from men, their wills and ends."[51]

But this insight is never fully worked out. Neumann goes on to embrace characteristically Hegelian criticisms of the formalism of the Kantian social contract, and, in the closely related "Types of Natural Law," he reduces the significance of the contract to a question of philosophical anthropology: "Every social contract reduces the will of the state to the wills of the individuals and must thus have a definite view of man's character prior to the conclusion of the social contract."[52] This move allows Neumann to criticize authoritarian writers like Schmitt, whose theories he sees as being tied to unjustifiably pessimistic views of human nature,[53] but it concurrently leads him to postulate that alternative conceptions of political legitimacy, based on competing models of the social contract, can be evaluated merely on the basis of the conceptions of human nature implied by their natural law presuppositions.

Again, Neumann's relationship to Weber is illuminating. We recall that in Weber's own gloss on the process of legal development, he had analogously argued that a perfectly formal or value-free social contract freed from any substantive natural law elements is illusory. Such a view of the social contract would have to depend on a conception of natural law consisting "entirely of general legal concepts devoid of any content."[54] Its presuppositions would have to be so abstract that they could only generate the most trivial of conclusions. Now, both Weber and Neumann raise legitimate reservations about formalistic conceptualizations of the social contract; those conceptualizations rightly remain controversial even today.[55] Still, the immediate consequences of this position for both authors nonetheless remain problematic. In the case of Weber, the critique of the social contract is partly responsible for the well-known democratic deficiencies of his theory. Convinced of the impossibility of freeing the idea of the social contract from traditional moral presuppositions, he is ultimately less interested in the contract's underlying insight—namely, the fact that it posits a mode of implicitly democratic decision making between truly free and equal persons—than that it contains substantive moral views no longer universally tenable under the conditions of a disenchanted universe. Neumann similarly (although distinctly) becomes preoccupied with the substantive moral presuppositions of the social contract tradition. Like Weber, he obscures its core intuition that political legitimacy derives from a set of procedures securing the free and equal participation of all.[56]

For both authors, this generates a rather one-sided assessment of deformalized welfare state law. Weber has nothing to say about the potential benefits of new forms of nontraditional social and economic regulation based on "undetermined" legal prescriptions. The democratic lacunae of his theory clearly lead him to neglect the significance of the fact that welfare state kinds of legal programs aspire to make sure that the political process involves authentically free and equal participants: social inequalities must be challenged if freedom and equality are to be realized and democratic decision making is to be based on a genuinely uncoerced mode of will formation. Insofar as deformalized modes of legal regulation can be shown to further this end, they are consistent with the underlying aims of the social contract and its implicit vision of a system of rational political legitimacy. Neumann tries to offer a democratic alternative to Weber and acknowledges that existing liberal democratic capitalist society lacks the features of Rousseau's theory that, in his view, alone guarantee the general legal norm's fully "ethical" character, and he openly concedes that social and economic legislation today must take nonclassical forms: "In a monopolistic economic organization the legislature is very often confronted with only one individual case or with a limited number of monopolist undertakings. The legislature often can and must use individual regulations in order to do justice to these specific circumstances."[57] Nonetheless, he argues that the generality of the legal norm in contemporary society has "besides its task of veiling power and of rendering exchange processes calculable, a decisive ethical function which is expressed in Rousseau's theory. . . . All three functions are significant and not only, as is maintained by the critics of liberalism, that of rendering economic exchange processes calculable."[58] Because full-scale social democracy might be able to reestablish the hegemony of liberal general law, the proliferation of vague, open-ended, purpose-oriented legal statutes in the twentieth century contitutes a temporary historical aberration, and there is no reason to attribute any lasting significance to it. In contrast to Weber, Neumann has no qualms about locating an "ethical" moment in the rule of law, but he identifies this normative feature with the semantic generality of the legal norm. Democratic politics is ultimately merely a presupposition, though a crucial one, allowing the general legal norm to manifest its (implicit) ethical qualities. Not altogether unlike Weber, Neumann thinks that rational legality provides its own legitimacy; the difference between the two authors is perhaps little more than that Neumann's version of rule-based Weberian rational legality aspires to be somewhat more democratic and socially critical than the original. For Neumann, the universalistic legacy of natural law is inherited primarily by the general (or universal) legal norm. The general legal norm is its favored child, whereas universalistic democratic decision-making processes are at best a distant cousin.

Having obscured the democratic energies of the social contract tradition, Neumann, like Weber, is often more concerned with demonstrating the dangers of new types of deformalized law than their potential benefits. His assessment of legal deformalization is, on occasion, as uneven as Weber's: "As for the opinion . . . that arbitration [i.e., welfare state administrative decision making and corporatist-type legal structures] is superior over rational judicial decisions, I do not share this view." General rational law is superior to equity-based considerations, "to the weighing of antagonistic interests instead of the deciding of conflicting claims" on the basis of clearly formulated general legal norms. Indeed, "the little rationality which the law still has gives a minimum of the liberal guarantees which are in the process of disappearing."[59] For Neumann, deformalized law represents a terribly frightening attack on the minimal rationality provided by the liberal legal system; as we will see, Neumann's analysis of German fascist law ultimately leads him to attribute, as Weber did earlier, nothing less than catastrophic significance to it. At the same time, Neumann's concession that general law can only be of limited significance in contemporary nonhomogeneous social settings makes his position even more peculiar than Weber's: at least Weber's old-fashioned bourgeois hostility to deformalized law corresponded to his hostility to anticapitalist (deformalized) forms of social and economic regulation. Intent on emphasizing the ethical significance of the general legal norm, yet having to concede that law today often cannot take a classical structure, Neumann's alternative analysis acquires nothing less than tragic qualities. Social and economic reforms, which are progressive insofar as they aspire to produce substantive social and economic equality, are at times doomed to take a regressive (nongeneral) legal form until social and economic homogeneity has been recaptured and there is no longer any need for nongeneral law. Democratic socialism's means are in conflict with its ends, and the precious hegemony of a perfect rule of law presupposes a period in which the rule of law in part dissipates.

Unlike Hayek and Schmitt, Neumann properly appreciates that many traditional views of formal law are not a priori inconsistent with extensive social and economic legislation—if, as we recall, such legislation carefully avoids the mention of specific individuals and merely "considers subjects en masse and actions in the abstract."[60] Not all modern defenders of general law supported laissez-faire economics or nonintervention in the private sphere. Nonetheless, even in a social world substantially more egalitarian than our own, there will still be a need for legislation directed against individual objects, and early modern political thought's traditional contrast between general and individual law undoubtedly tends to obscure this fact. How else is a democratic polity to undertake much-needed regulation of a particular branch of industry, and influential individual bank, or an important university that alone fulfills a particular set of functions? Far too conventionally, Neumann tends to see such individual acts as being inconsistent with the rule of law and as evidence for its ongoing demise. Yet does the classical distinction between individual and general legal acts always best capture the idea of arbitrary and discretionary bureaucratic action, which rightly worries Neumann? Must the noble demand for cogent formal law necessarily foreclose the possibility of highly specialized types of individual state action? In chapter 5, I will suggest how we can reformulate liberalism's insistence on the generality of the legal norm by means of a somewhat more modest emphasis on the merits of semantic clarity and cogency in regulatory law. But before I do that, it should be clear—despite Hayek's warnings about a "road to serfdom," whose way would be paved by means of nonclassical individual state acts, or Schmitt's mean manipulation of liberal defenses of the general legal norm so as to justify fascism—that many of the individual laws undertaken by elected legislatures in the era of the democratic welfare state fail to match the horrible images of state despotism conjured up by contemporary conservatives. There are countless examples of massive individual economic units actually requesting special aid from the state, or where—as in the expropriation that took place in Western Europe after World War II—extensive political debate about the pros and cons of a particular individual legal act preceded it. In such cases it becomes very difficult to see what is intrinsically unpredictable or irregular about individual law. Indeed, if there is only one major railway or an automobile manufacturer that has a special role in the economy, there may be nothing intrinsically nongeneral about legislative acts directed against it in the first place; because the legislator confronts an individual situation, an (individual) legal act that regulates it does not violate the principle of equality before the law. As noted in chapter 2, this ambiguity could already be detected in early formulations of the idea of general law. Rousseau claims that the generality of the legal norm is compatible with instituting privileges as long as it does not confer them on any individual by name, but what happens when only one conceivable person or object falls under a particular abstract category? When only citizen A earns more than X francs? Or only corporation B performs a specific set of services? Why must the principle of equality before the law then imply state inaction, as many conservatives claim? That was hardly what writers like Rousseau or Hegel had in mind when developing powerful defenses of determinate formal law.

This is clearly not to deny that deformalized welfare state law includes a number of troublesome features or that legal deformalization brings with it a set of potential perils. Whatever the other faults of his restatement of Weber, Neumann always understood that, and his ideas remain a refreshing corrective to so many self-satisfied welfare state liberal, and mainstream social democratic, defenses of nonformal law.

In chapter 5 we will turn to a more systematic examination of the dangers of deformalized law. They have probably never been revealed as unambiguously as in Nazi Germany, where such law played a pivotal role in facilitating terroristic dictatorial rule.

III

Sovereignty and Its Discontents

5

The Permanent State of Emergency

Franz Neumann's monumental study of the anatomy of German fascism, *Behemoth: The Structure and Practice of National Socialism,* has had a peculiar history. Lavishly praised by reviewers when it first appeared in 1942, it catapulted Neumann into a position of prominence in comparison with his colleagues at the Institute for Social Research. While they remained obscure figures on the intellectual scene in the United States, it helped him gain a position at prestigious Columbia University. Neumann, and not Horkheimer or Adorno, was the first of the Frankfurt émigrés to receive such an offer. Soon thereafter, the American government asked Neumann to participate in coordinating the Office of Strategic Services' crucial Research and Analysis Bureau, a division of the federal government given the task of analyzing the political situation in Nazi Germany and providing policy proposals to elected officials and military authorities. At the end of 1942, the neo-Marxist Neumann (soon followed by Kirchheimer, Herbert Marcuse, and the institute's economist, Arkadiji Gurland) headed off to Washington, D. C.: as Barry Katz has aptly described it, the Frankfurt school had gone to war. Neumann's *Behemoth* then played a central role in the Research and Analysis Bureau, where the empirical work undertaken by the German émigrés and their American coworkers at times represented little more than an attempt to elaborate on its main theses and make them palatable to government officials otherwise unfamiliar with twentieth-century radical thought, let alone known for their Hegelian-Marxist sympathies. In what is undoubtedly one of the most curious moments in the otherwise sordid history of the American Secret Service, not only was a group of exiled socialists responsible for much of the OSS' research, but a study with clear Marxist features was contributing, however indirectly, to American war policy.[1]

The appreciative American reception of *Behemoth* stands in stark contrast to that of the Frankfurt school's own "inner circle" (Max Horkheimer, Frederick Pollock, Theodor Adorno, and Leo Löwenthal). In their view, Neumann's inquiry remained imprisoned in the categories of a far too traditional mode of Marxism, perhaps not unlike that which the Institute for Social Research had stood for during most of the thirties, but which its dominant figures were becoming increasingly unsatisfied with. Whereas Neumann and Kirchheimer continued to insist on the socially antagonistic and unstable "monopoly capitalistic" character of Nazi Germany, by 1941 they had opted for an alternative "state-capitalist" explanatory model emphasizing the Nazis' success in overcoming all the tensions that had plagued earlier forms of capitalism. Dramatizing contemporary state-directed capitalism's unprecedented capacity for subduing seemingly subversive social trends and groups, Horkheimer and Adorno soon gave this shift in their thought a more dramatic philosophical form. Their *Dialectic of Enlightenment*—unappreciated when it first appeared, unlike Neumann's study, but today considered a classic, whereas Neumann's work has been forgotten—was composed in southern California during the early forties. While Neumann and his friends on the East Coast were busily trying to figure out how to take advantage of the schisms and contradictions immanent in the Nazi political economy, Horkheimer and Adorno were already well on their way to formulating the philosophical framework for the theory of the "totally integrated" or "administered" society that later made them famous. The geographical distance separating the two groups had come to correspond to real political and theoretical differences: the original Frankfurt school had ceased to exist.[2]

The dual character of this reception is illuminating. Much of *Behemoth*'s argumentation is undoubtedly traditionally Marxist, and, in many ways (and especially in the discussion of the German "totalitarian monopolistic economy," which makes up part 2 of his book), Neumann succumbs to an overly economistic interpretation of fascism's nature and dynamics: "The complete subjugation of the state by the industrial rulers could only be carried out in a political organization in which there was no control from below, which lacked autonomous mass organizations and freedom of criticism. It was one of the functions of National Socialism to suppress and eliminate political and economic liberty . . . thus forcing the whole economic activity of Germany into the network of industrial combinations run by industrial managers.[3] Put (only somewhat) more crudely, monopoly capitalism necessitated fascism. Still, it is revealing that Neumann's colleagues seem to have been altogether unappreciative of *Behemoth*'s more innovative features, in particular, its vision of Nazi Germany as a "non-state, a chaos, a situation of lawlessness," where a terrible fourth and final answer to the problem of legal disenchantment, whose basic features Neumann saw intimated in Carl Schmitt's decisionist theory, was tried out. I will argue that this blindness is hardly coincidental. The theoretical project that Neumann's colleagues began sketching, by means of a state-capitalist interpretation of fascism, lacks the tools necessary for developing a satisfying understanding of politics and law. Indeed, it is conceivable that it is precisely this second, and somewhat distinct, facet of Neumann's project that so excited the primarily radical American intellectuals who greeted his study with such enthusiasm. Having been spoon-fed on Paine, Veblen, and Dewey, they were better able to appreciate Neumann's sophisticated legal concerns and his attempt to salvage the utopian aspirations of the bourgeois political tradition. Much of Neumann's study reads like a eulogy for the unfulfilled aspirations of political liberalism. In responding to fascist attacks on the "abstract" and "lifeless" universalism of liberal political thought, he notes that "to abandon universalism because of its failures is like rejecting civil rights because they help legitimize and veil class exploitation, or democracy because it conceals boss control."[4] In his view, a radicalized version of the modern rule of law could finally allow us to complete the utopian (universalist) agenda of bourgeois political thought; that, too, is the message of *Behemoth,* and Neumann's American peers proved far more sensitive to it than the Hegelian-Marxist émigrés from Frankfurt.[5]

Although Neumann's social and economic analysis cannot be separated from his description of the Nazi legal "chaos," it is primarily *Behemoth*'s little-appreciated legal and political theory that is of interest here. In section 1, I complete the story left unfinished in chapter 4 and examine Neumann's analysis of the origins and structure of the fascist path of legal development. Because Neumann sees Schmitt as "the most intelligent and reliable of all National Socialist constitutional lawyers,"[6] the critique of Schmitt is central to his analysis of fascist law. Rarely recognized is that *Behemoth* can be read as a neo-Marxist anti-Schmitt work and, thus, as a corrective to the ongoing Schmitt renaissance. In section 2, I criticize Neumann's Marxist reconstruction of the sources of deformalized law while acknowledging its lasting insights. Deformalized law does pose real dangers, and any reconstructed model of the rule of law will have to consider how postclassical legal forms can avoid succumbing to all the horrors suggested by German fascism's (and Schmitt's) decisionist variety of nonformal law. Finally, in section 3, I focus on Neumann's relationship to the Frankfurt school's inner circle and suggest, in contrast to much of the interpretative literature, that despite its problematic features, the version of critical theory developed by him during the late thirties and early forties remains superior to theirs.

1 Capitalism instead of Law: The Nazi Experience

Long before focusing his considerable intellectual resources on the problem of fascism, Neumann had criticized nonclassical forms of law. As early as the late twenties, Neumann had insisted that the proliferation of amorphous, deformalized legal standards undermined legal security and posed a threat to the working-class movement and the struggle for democratic socialism. Vague, undetermined legal terms, like those whose dangers Locke had warned us about and long associated with poorly regulated raison d'état of state action were making their way into the sphere of legal normalcy and being exploited by the most privileged social interests. True, Neumann did concede that such standards posed more of a threat in an authoritarian setting than in a democratic one: "At least in democracy there is the formal possibility of structuring governmental decrees in a social manner. That also succeeds [for example, in the Weimar Republic] to some extent".[7] But even in a democracy, their dangers remained real enough. A democratic socialist legal alternative, thus, should aspire to eliminate them, thereby making formal law hegemonic and completing the process of legal rationalization.

In developing this position, Neumann, as we have seen, gives Weber's views on legal development a radical gloss. In a similar vein, his alternative interpretation of the proliferation of nonformal law and of the blurring of the distinction between law and administrative decree in the twentieth-century is intended as a response to Weber. We recall that Weber saw legal deformalization's main source as political and social democratization, and his anxieties about welfare state types of materialized law conveniently corresponded to his suspicious view of the popular-based reform movements that Weber took to be its political base. The new social law is incompatible with the rationality of a capitalist market economy, formal legality, and modern bureaucracy, just as the demand for it stems from an essentially antimodernist attack on such institutions. Welfare state law comes "from below" and shares all the irrationality of allegedly emotion-based popular political action, which Weber so loved to dwell on in his polemics against the Left. Of course, this view poses problems for the left-wing Neumann, particularly given that he considers many of Weber's anxieties about deformalized law sound. In contrast to Weber, he argues for an elective affinity between materialized law and organized, or monopoly, capitalism. Put most simply, "legal standards of conduct [blanket clauses] serve the monopolist. . . . Not only is rational law unnecessary for him it is often a fetter upon the full development of his productive forces. . . . [R]ational law, after all, serves also to protect the weak".[8] During his affiliation with the Institute for Social Research, Neumann repeatedly focuses on the advantages of deformalized legal modes for the privileged and powerful: where the rules of the game are unclear and inchoate it is generally the biggest kids on the block who will take advantage of them, and in the sphere of social and economic law (where deformalized legal norms first emerge and eventually gain preeminence) that means that the core, or monopoly, sector of the economy is best positioned to exploit the flexibility touted by the defenders of "soft" postclassical regulation. Consequently, subordinate social strata are better off sticking to classical modes of formal law.

This alternative interpretation allows Neumann to turn the tables on Weber. Irrational legal trends come "from above" and "not below." The most secure core sector of the capitalist economy, not popular groups demanding radical social and political reforms like those deplored by

Weber, are the real beneficiaries of nonclassical law. They, not the working classes, represent the main obstacle to the unfinished process of legal rationalization. Democratic socialism, not Weber's authoritarian brand of liberalism, alone can complete that project.

Two observations lead Neumann to support this subversive reworking of Weber. First, he thinks he can locate deformalized law's sources in an economic transition ignored by Weber. Weber is right to argue that capitalism and formal law require one another, but he misses that this is only true for the *competitive capitalist* juncture in economic development.[9] When the economy becomes dominated by massive monopolies posing highly particular problems and, thus, needing to be regulated by means of legal acts that are effectively individual, liberal general law tends to disintegrate. Formal law's social base vanishes. Contemporary capitalism depends on more or less irregular administrative commands, not the liberal rule of law. This is also why Neumann harshly criticizes Ernst Fraenkel's *Dual State,* which anticipates many features of Neumann's own study but insists on the dualistic face of Nazi law: arbitrary situation-specific measures facilitating the power claims of the Nazi elite function alongside significant elements of the norm-based rule of law in the sphere of civil law. Similarly concerned with demonstrating the organic links between Schmitt's theory and Nazi legal experience, Fraenkel concedes that the emergency-centered "prerogative state" (like that anticipated by Schmitt's political thought) is supreme in relation to the "norm-based state" (the rule of law); his work describes in great detail how the dictates of the Nazi political elite at times lead arbitrary administrative commands to oust general law even in those spheres where general law tends to be dominant. But like Weber, Fraenkel believes that capitalism presupposes a high degree of legal regularity and, hence, some features of the liberal rule of law. Insofar as German fascism remains capitalist, Fraenkel concludes, it preserves certain minimal characteristics of modern legal rational authority that can be identified in the sphere of private law. In contrast, Neumann traces the disintegration of rational law to the socioeconomic sphere itself. Consequently, Neumann must embrace a more radical and disturbing picture of the Nazi legal order than his friend and colleague. From Neumann's perspective, Fraenkel remains the prisoner of an anachronistic Weberian view of the relationship between capitalism and formal law that obscures the full significance of the transition from competitive to organized capitalism. Furthermore, Fraenkel's study—based on research from the mid thirties—allegedly misses the radicalization of the disintegration of the rule of law during the regime's mature period and final years.[10]

Second, Neumann relies on one of Weber's own observations about the decline of liberal parliamentarism in order to criticize Weber's insistence on the democratic, anticapitalist significance of nonformal modes of interventionist state regulation: "Weber pointed out that sabotage of the power of parliament begins once such a body ceases to be just a 'social club.' When deputies are elected from a progressive mass party and threaten to transform the legislature into an agency for profound social changes, anti-parliamentary trends invariably arise in one form or another".[11] In Neumann's view, Marx's classic analysis of French Bonapartism can be applied to twentieth-century politics and used as a starting point for a critique of deformalized law. Nonclassical law becomes widespread precisely when mass-based working-class political parties make their way into parliament; parliament's effective abandonment of legislative power to subordinate decision making institutions (the administration, courts, various corporatist set-ups), which nonclassical blanket clauses outfitting administrators and judges with extensive discretionary powers facilitate, should be interpreted as a manifestation of the tendency to disempower potentially radicalized parliamentary bodies in an era of mass-based class politics. Indiscriminate legal standards emerge, because parliamentary supremacy (and classical modes of formal law supportive of it) now poses a threat to hegemonic social interests. According to this view, although right to identify regulatory law's immediate roots in the democratization process, Weber obscures its intrinsically antidemocratic nature.

Neumann's retelling of the story of contemporary deformalized regulatory law provides the backdrop for *Behemoth* and his endeavour there to bring together an analysis of the Nazi German political economy, emphasizing its monopoly capitalist character, and a vivid illustration of all the dangers of nonformal law. Because Neumann locates the main hindrance to the unfinished project of rational law in contemporary capitalism's economic substructure and its resultant social antagonisms, he thinks these somewhat distinct problems are two sides of the same coin; the fact that fascist Germany is both aggressively (monopoly) capitalist and ruthlessly substantializes law simply reinforces his suspicions about the capitalist functions of nonformal law. Not only does the new German legal order make materialized modes of law absolutely supreme, but Germany's brand of highly monopolized organized capitalism takes a profoundly contradictory and explosive form: "the antagonisms of capitalism are operating in Germany on a higher and, therefore, a more dangerous level, even if these antagonisms are covered up by a bureaucratic apparatus and by the ideology of the" folk community.[12] The most vicious renaissance of particularisms in law corresponds to a social and economic order in which a set of narrow (particular) interests altogether dominates social and political affairs. Contra Weber's expectations, the specter of refeudalized law shows its ugly face most insolently in an advanced capitalist setting and neither in a democratic welfare state situated somewhere between capitalism and socialism nor in full-fledged democratic socialism. Unharnessed sovereignty (as facilitated by formal law's demise) runs amok where the motor of capitalist exploitation is least restrained.

German capitalism sheds those features of political liberalism that had always provided some minimal restraint on the inequalities generated by it. The formalistic rule of law should not be seen as merely providing a front for substantive inequalities: "Equality before the law is merely formal or negative . . . but it does contain a minimum guarantee of freedom and must not be discarded. Both functions of the generality of law, calculability of the economic system and guarantee of a minimum of freedom and equality, are equally important; not the first alone, as the theories of the totalitarian state [and crude Marxist analyses] maintain".[13] By demanding that power be allowed to express itself only in accordance with a set of general norms, even under contemporary conditions, the rule of law provides real checks on capitalism's injustices. Social inequalities can be mediated by the rule of law's normative restraints, thereby deflecting their dangers to some extent. Even in a socially antagonistic setting, the rule of law is always more than mere ideology. Though by no means consisting merely of privileged economic elites or driven exclusively by economic motives, the Nazi power elite (in the NSDAP, monopoly capital, upper civil service, and army) is most fundamentally a counterrevolutionary coalition directed against the democratic achievements of the German working classes; imperialist expansion and the transformation of much of Europe into one horribly exploitive capitalist sweat shop is the glue that ultimately holds its distinct and potentially antagonistic components together. Because the rule of law is incompatible with exploitation and plunder on such a scale, Neumann posits, the Nazis have to abandon it.

Furthermore, German fascism realizes core components of Carl Schmitt's legal and political thinking, because Schmitt's theory gives expression to some of the most worrisome tendencies toward nonrational modes of law identifiable in contemporary society.[14] Deeply rooted social trends underlie the reemergence of particularistic law and a legal order where the imperatives of the (normless) exception or concrete situation become its centerpiece. While Schmitt's decisionist theory gives these empirical processes an abstract theoretical form and reifies them, by suggesting that they make up the very essence of authentic political experience, Neumann thinks we can counteract their sources and thereby avoid all of their horrible consequences. If Schmitt's theory seems more realistic than "lifeless" universalistic liberalism, in Neumann's view this simply suggests that political and social reality should be transformed in a radically democratic and anticapitalist manner. Legal decisionism must be robbed of its social base so that the universalism of the modern rule of law project can flourish.

Much of *Behemoth* is devoted to an analysis of the particularistic structure of Nazi law, its elective affinity with the underlying structural dynamics of the Nazi political economy, and its compatibility with much of Schmitt's theory. Just as Schmitt long suggested that an authentically political community would have to dump universalistic normativities, essential to Nazi law is that it junks even the remnants of the universalism of the Western political tradition.[15] Despite their similarly authoritarian and bourgeois character, even legalist development paths (like the Prussian *Rechtsstaat*) remained loyal to the classical ideal of the generality of the legal norm. In Neumann's view, traditional authoritarian regimes were still able to provide a minimum of legal security. The totalitarian Nazi behemoth—a "non-state, a chaos, a rule of lawlessness and anarchy," like that described by Hobbes, three hundred years earlier, in his analysis of the English Civil War[16]—fails even on this score. It fails largely by giving vague legal standards and oddly moralistic blanket clauses an unprecedented significance: "Having formerly been stepchildren of law, they now become its darlings."[17] Pursuing one possible implication of arguments emphasizing liberal law's allegedly indeterminate core, Schmitt and others make a virtue of necessity and begin to restructure German law so that it *does* take a profoundly indeterminate, amorphous—and unpredictable, arbitrary—form. Whereas Neumann identifies the great unfinished task of the process of legal rationalization with the quest to rid law of vague terms that provide a legal front for the exercise of badly managed state power, Nazi law represents an unparalleled attempt to subordinate the entire legal order to such standards and thus represents a historical regression of unheard of proportions. And while Schmitt had insisted on the primordiality of the exception and the exigencies of the emergency situation, Nazi law transforms this idea into a practical political program: Germany now finds itself in a permanent state of emergency. Essential to this development is not only the increased role given many preexisting blanket legal clauses but the fact that the regime supplements them with new naturalistic and racist ones—"the racial feelings of the people," "the folk community," the "life interests of the folk."[18] Even more so than in the case of those blanket clauses taken over from Weimar, the amorphousness of such standards helps guarantee unprecedented leeway for manipulation: what can "the racial feelings of the people" amount to except what a group of administrators take them to be at any given moment? Today the term justifies persecuting Jews and Communists; tomorrow, mildly critical Bavarian Catholics. Neumann repeatedly emphasizes the role of ambiguous and premodern legal standards in allowing Nazi law to take what he had earlier described, in *The Governance of the Rule of Law,* as a purely political form: "whether unjust or just, convenient or inconvenient" every decision of the power elite is to be considered legitimate.[19] Given that "in present-day society there can be no unanimity on whether a given action" corresponds to indiscriminate concepts like racial feelings, such clauses provide an appropriate legal basis for a system in which every one of the elite's concrete decisions is to be deemed lawful.[20]

Neumann persuasively shows how Nazi legal ideologues effectively concede all this. Institutionalist modes of legal thought flourish, according to which legal decision making should correspond to the situational exigencies of particular spheres of social existence (for example, the family, workplace). From the perspective of the proponents of this school, liberal general law is necessarily static and lifeless,[21] always having misleadingly denied the necessity of flexible modes of decision making complementing "concrete orders" or particularistic communities, which, in their view, cannot be effectively regulated by modes of judicial and administrative action borrowed from liberalism. Abstract universal norms fail to capture the exigencies of concrete life; it is due time that legal thinking recognize this fact. Specifically, judges should ignore written law when it conflicts with national socialist ideology, and the judiciary should be reorganized so that it is not independent of directly political instances. Judicial decisions should be overruled by the party or police if they deem them unsuitable to the imperatives of the broader "folk community." Indeed, the German folk community itself has concrete needs qualitatively distinct from those of alien nations; the presuppositions of universalistic international law are thereby rendered obsolete as well.[22] Neumann shows how the exponents of such ideas become incoherent as soon as they try to explain precisely how situation-specific law can provide any real standards for legal decision making. By itself, the concrete situation tells us very little, and institutionalist or concrete-order legal thinking merely functions to assure that the system's "decisionist elements are preserved and enormously strengthened."[23] In relinquishing universalistic normativities, Nazi law can provide no rational standards for determining the legitimacy of a particular course of action.

The death of rational law is simultaneously accompanied by the demise of the institution that helped make it possible. A profoundly confused set of conflicting and overlapping power blocs without a central coercive authority, Nazi Germany lacks even a state apparatus in any defensible modern sense of the term. If it is a minimal precondition of a characteristically modern political universe that it possess some central instance where conflicts can be resolved in a binding manner (and backed up by the possibility of force), the monstrous four-headed Nazi behemoth surely lacks such an institution:

In an absolute monarchy, in a constitutional system, and in a democracy, the compromises between various groups claim and have universal validity. If it is necessary for the state to coordinate and integrate hundreds and thousands of individual and group conflicts, the process must be accomplished in a universally binding manner, that is, through abstract rational law or at least through a rationally operating bureaucracy. Under National Socialism, however, the whole of society is organized in four solid, centralized groups (the party, upper civil service, army, and monopoly capital), each operating under the leadership principle, each with a legislative, administrative and judicial power of its own. Neither universal law nor a rationally operating bureaucracy is necessary for integration. . . . There is no need for a state standing above all groups; the state may even be a hindrance to the compromises and to domination over the ruled classes.[24]

Each of the behemoth's four power blocs speaks a distinct, particularistic legal language, makes different demands on the population, and stands in a tension-ridden relationship to its competitors, and each has an impressive set of coercive instruments at hand. "Each group is sovereign and authoritarian; each is equipped with legislative, administrative, and judicial power of its own."[25] With the emergence of a set of distinct sovereign power blocs, however, the death of traditional state sovereignty must follow.[26]

Given Neumann's statement, at the outset of *The Governance of the Rule of Law*—"both sovereignty and the rule of law are constitutive elements of the modern state," but that "both . . . are irreconcilable with each other, for highest might and highest right cannot be at one and the same time realized in a common sphere. So far as the sovereignty of the state extends there is no place for the rule of law"—his emphasis on the purported absence of sovereignty in Nazi Germany at first seems odd.[27] Is not sovereignty expressive, in Neumann's view, of the nonrationalized face of power and domination in modern politics and a consequence of the liberal political tradition's sad tendency, as he argued in *The Governance of the Rule of Law,* to abandon its more utopian aspirations for a defense of capitalism and the inequalities generated by it? Why then emphasize the irrelevance of sovereignty for understanding fascism?

Again, Neumann's dialogue with Schmitt is essential for understanding the complexities of his position here. In *The Governance of the Rule of Law,* it turned out that both "highest might" and "highest right" could be synthesized—if we finally chose to pursue a social democratic path to rational law capable of making modern formal law fully hegemonic. Sovereignty and law, or power and freedom, had always been irreconcilable in the modern state, but this allegedly could be changed if social and political democratization allowed parliamentary democracy to free itself from emergency legal regulations and other modes of irrational, normless law. Incompletely rationalized alternative versions of the rule of law had always contained some more or less Schmittian moment. Each had left some room for normatively unrestrained state action, and the specter of Schmitt's definition of sovereignty as "he who decides on the exception" haunted them all. Schmittian-style sovereignty is really what disturbs Neumann, and it is Schmitt's radicalization of the idea of an unrestrained sovereign *voluntas* (acting beyond the normative restraints of *ratio*) that he takes to be the real threat to the rule of law and whose vestiges he wants to drive from the political universe. Radical social democracy allegedly guarantees the hegemony of coherent general legal norms, Neumann seems to believe, as well as the absolute supremacy of that institution (a popularly elected parliament) that the rule of law's classical defenders had always seen as essential to it. Amidst social homogeneity, a popularly based legislature purportedly resolves all potential conflicts in a universally acceptable manner and thus secures the elusive supremacy of rational parliamentary legality.

Neumann never doubts that the functioning of the rule of law presupposes a central, coherently organized institution with the capacity for resolving conflicts authoritatively and potentially coercively. Insofar as the idea of sovereignty has traditionally been associated with some version of this vision, Neumann on one level merely intends to defend a conventional view of the state, like that offered by Weber, against Schmitt's radically decisionist concept of sovereignty. According to Neumann, such an apparatus is a necessary but insufficient precondition for overcoming the possibility of lynch justice or civil war and for a further rationalization of political power. The possibility of violence can never be altogether eliminated from the political sphere. Yet centralizing and then subjecting coercive instruments to relatively calculable state norms is necessary if force is to be tamed; at least Hobbes and other theorists who justified the modern state as it began to emerge were right about that.[28] Indeed, Nazi Germany is interpreted as providing a vivid example of all the dangers of the pre-Hobbesian framework. Coercive authority there is distributed among a confused medley of competing sites of power, each intent on maintaining its "turf" against the others and each outfitted with particular instruments of coercion that can be unleashed against potential foes. More akin to a system of gang rule, in which each "gang" (the NSDAP, army, upper civil service, monopoly capital) constitutes an independent sovereign, than any characteristically modern system of state domination, Nazism's distinct power interests only get along with each other as long as there is enough "booty" (that is, the produce of German imperialism) to go around. Loose and uneasy compromises, not a shared commitment to rational law, keep them united. In place of the rational, universalistic facets of state authority found, although inadequately, elsewhere, "nothing remains but profits, power, prestige, and above all, fear" as a cement between Nazism's power blocs. "Devoid of any common loyalty, and concerned solely with the preservation of their interests, the ruling groups will break apart as soon as the miracle-producing Leader meets a worthy opponent."[29] Under an altered set of political circumstances, the deceptively monolithic face of the fascist power elite could easily dissipate, and the system's drive to make the state of emergency a permanent affair manifest itself even more horribly.[30]

As in Schmitt's conception of sovereignty, the exercise of power in fascism is freed of any rational or normatively universalistic features whatsoever. Hence, it breaks decisively with even the most unsatisfying modern conceptions of state sovereignty, all of which envision at least some intermeshing between *ratio* (rational law) and *voluntas* (will). The radical decisionist system of unharnessed power found in Germany is "not based on reason and discussion and not justifying itself" but simply on pure power decisions "created out of nothingness" and unjustified by any universal normative standards.[31] While Schmitt originally hoped this view of sovereignty as whoever decides on the exception would buttress the political executive in its struggles against parliament, Neumann effectively counters by suggesting that the implications of Schmitt's view are much more far-reaching: Schmittian-type sovereignty does not merely undermine democratic conceptions of parliamentary supremacy but helps facilitate the disintegration of the most minimal, defensible features of the modern state apparatus. In insisting on the normless character of sovereignty, it denies even the political executive any real possibility for challenging the power claims of competing power blocs by means of universally binding claims; in making the experience of the political emergency its core, it cannot ground any lasting system of political hierarchies. Any interest or power bloc that proves factually capable of exercising power in a particular situation has to be considered sovereign, according to Schmitt's definition. But the executive is by no means the sole institution in contemporary society outfitted with impressive de facto coercive instruments. Capitalists can close down factories and throw thousands out of work, the military often gains a relative degree of autonomy in relation to other societal institutions, and political parties can quickly organize and mobilize mass shows of public support and private militias. The valorization of the normatively unregulated concrete situation effectively means that concrete de facto power inequalities are given free reign and that *voluntas* can be fully freed from *ratio.*

Neumann's argument for a fit between Schmitt's theory and Nazi political reality leads him to develop a provocative critique of Harold Laski's pluralist socialism. Schmitt's ideas suggest the most horrible consequences of surrendering the Western political tradition's fragile and incomplete universalistic features, but for Neumann worrisome analogous trends can be detected even in purportedly progressive writers like Laski. However admirable his aspirations, Laski's critique of sovereignty threatens to accelerate parallel trends toward a refeudalized political and social universe.

Laski criticized monistic conceptions of state sovereignty, which, in his view, (1) normatively implied attributing a moral preeminence to the state, like that once possessed by the Church and that thus downplayed the complications of moral experience and the unavoidability of conflicts between political and moral obligations, and (2) increasingly had little to do with the factual realities of an ever more complex social world. The state had "become a kind of modern Baal to which the citizen must bow a heedless knee" and incompatible with the spirit of liberal political values. Only a radical break with the ("grim Hegelian") myth of an all-powerful, undivided, morally supreme sovereign could ground a participatory decentralized alternative better able to realize the ideal of self-government and more in tune with the needs of a universe in which political and social decision making is necessarily ever more localized.[32] Though having altogether different intentions, Schmitt had accepted some features of Laski's empirical analysis when arguing that the contemporary welfare state had fallen victim to a pluralism, like that in fact sought by Laski, in which political decision making was increasingly fragmented and state sovereignty seemed to have vanished. As we recall, Schmitt thought the welfare state lacked a decisive center capable of acting effectively against political foes. Powerful social and economic constituencies had colonized the state apparatus, making it impossible for the state to engage in authentically political forms of action. Against Laski, Schmitt concluded that only a (sovereign) dictatorial alternative, relying on overtly authoritarian means, could reestablish the state's political character and free it from the suffocating grip of interest-based corporatist politics.

In a fascinating discussion, at the outset of *Behemoth,* of the demise of the Weimar Republic, Neumann initially seems to acknowledge the legitimacy of at least some of Schmitt's anxieties. Weimar indeed granted extensive public authority to a series of decentralized institutions (labor courts, new forms of workplace democracy, and so on); in Neumann's view, Weimar, very much in correspondence with English pluralist doctrine, mistakenly tried to transform the state into little more than one among a number of competing and roughly equal institutions. Neumann is little concerned with developing a systematic normative critique of Laski's views; he thinks he can demonstrate their failings by describing pluralism's disastrous real-life empirical consequences.[33] "Once the state is reduced to just another social agency and deprived of its supreme coercive power, only a compact among the dominant independent social bodies within the community will be able to offer concrete satisfaction to the common interests".[34] In a deeply antagonistic society, such a compact is likely to prove fragile. Consequently, Laski's pluralism threatens to exacerbate the fragmentation of traditional instruments of self-rule, such as a central parliament, and contribute to political paralysis, in part because it presupposes a degree of social harmony unrealizable under contemporary capitalism. In Germany, the state bureaucracy filled the ensuing decision making vacuum, as witnessed by the unprecedented significance taken on by emergency decrees and the executive branch. The decline of the central legislature and the increasingly decentralized character of political authority there, both of which were endorsed by pluralist theory, played into the hands of a bureaucratic elite best suited to exercise de facto power on a day-to-day basis. In spite of its praiseworthy democratic and anticapitalist aims, Laski's pluralism is implicated in the emergence of something far worse than a system of democratic parliament-centered authority. In underplaying the advantages of central state institutions and classical modes of formal law for facilitating the resolution of political conflicts in a universally binding manner, it leaves us unarmed against the specter of a political world overrun by mean, irrational particularisms.

Neumann distinguishes his reading of Laski from Schmitt's by pointing to a number of factors suggesting that even a parliamentary system as class-divided as Weimar Germany did not have to succumb to authoritarianism. Although this is illustrative of worrisome general trends, there were more than enough elements specific to German political development and Weimar itself that played a crucial role in its demise, and, problematic as they undoubtedly were, pluralist tendencies alone did not do the job. Various untried reforms might have succeeded even in Weimar in guaranteeing the "fuller utilization of the potentialities inherent in Germany's industrial system," which Neumann sees as essential to maintaining a system of parliamentary legality during a crisis like that which destroyed democratic systems throughout Europe in the thirties.[35] Most fundamentally, even though Nazi Germany embodies many of Schmitt's own ideas about sovereignty in its institutional core, it is even more overrun by all the dangers Schmitt had claimed his brand of authoritarianism could challenge. Neumann's portrait of German fascism as a chaotic behemoth aims to demonstrate that even the worst-functioning parliamentary democracy is less ravaged than fascism by all the most dreadful side-effects of corporatist interest-based politics, and a central and rarely appreciated thesis of his study is that Schmittian-style decisionist sovereignty is likely to exacerbate the dangers Schmitt claims it can solve. In fascist Germany, state institutions, allegedly securing general aims in the economic sphere, are in reality dominated by privileged elites pursuing a narrow set of private interests. Economic decision making is far more egotistical and irrational than it was even in the battered Weimar Republic. Notwithstanding Nazi ideology, Hitler is not really a decisive and all-powerful leader.[36] Even those decisions in which he seems to have a significant say sometimes constitute little more than uneasy compromises between the social order's competing sovereigns, each of which is more worried about protecting its particular turf and narrow set of interests. The fascist state is colonized by particularistic interests to a greater extent than was ever the case under parliamentary democracy. Neumann thinks that even the regime's ideologues have to acknowledge this: "we have . . . shown that Nazi constitutional theory, especially that of Carl Schmitt . . . denounced the Weimar Republic for its pluralism and praised Nazism for its unity. Now, even Nazi constitutional lawyers occasionally express grave doubts" about fascism's capacity for overcoming pluralism. " 'The German people,' says one, 'has fought long and hard for its full unity. Shall the field of the constitution of the courts be now dominated by—I venture to say—vertical pluralism?' The author refers to the extensive departmentalization of the judiciary, . . . the coexistence of many jurisdictions and court systems, phenomena that express the same shapelessness of Nazi constitutional life."[37]

Formalistic parliamentarism proves, even under the worst circumstances, better adapted to the demands of contemporary organized interest-based politics than Schmitt's brand of authoritarianism.

2 The Ills of Deformalized Law

Neumann's analysis of a fourth fascist legal path helps us identify the immediate sources of the author's interest not simply in reconstructing the rule of law, but in developing an alternative model of it that aspires to reestablish the privileged position of formal law. With Carl Schmitt preaching the virtues of the "death of general ideas" to enthusiastic audiences of young fascist legal scholars and eagerly telling them that nonformal substantialized Nazi law represented a theoretical and practical advance insofar as it alone took a systematically situation-specific form, Neumann takes it upon himself to defend a central feature of the legacy of classical liberal legalism more aggressively than most liberals themselves bothered to do. While Neumann had been suspicious of deformalized law well before the Nazi rise to power, the experience of German fascism soon transformed him into one of its fiercest intellectual opponents.

Can Neumann's Marxist-Weberian interpretation of legal deformalization justify his intense hostility to it? Just as Weber influenced generations of conservative critics of welfare state law, so, too, has Neumann shaped the contours of much of the left-wing hostility to it, especially in central Europe; the question thus has immediate significance.[38] Certainly, the basic argument remains a dramatic one. Regressive (from the standpoint of a line of modern thinkers extending from Locke to Bentham) modes of materialized law are based in (reactionary) organized capitalism. Capitalism in its most developed form radically contradicts all of the liberal tradition's most defensible features, and those strata intent on advancing an unabashedly antisocialist political and economic agenda try to dump the rule of law. Though most developed in fascism, such trends are found in all interventionist capitalist polities. Finally, since Carl Schmitt's decisionism makes the inadequacies of universalistic liberal legal ideals its very centerpiece, and because the trend toward substantialized postformal law can be traced to contemporary capitalism, Schmitt can be demasked as a bourgeois ideologue. His is a quintessentially bourgeois theory. In Neumann's own words, the "legal theory and legal practice of bourgeois society are, as Carl Schmitt put it, *Situationsjurisprudenz*"—in other words, increasingly in organized capitalism "law is a mere technique for the conquest and maintenance of power."[39]

Alas, the argument is too crude in this form. Rather than repeat criticisms raised elsewhere against traditional Marxist legal theorizing like that engaged in by Neumann here, we can see this merely by focusing on the immanent weaknesses of Neumann's own exposition.[40] Most clearly, his interpretation of fascism is overly economistic. Neumann can emphasize the economic functions of radically deformalized law in organized capitalism because he makes the unacceptable assumption that the Nazi power elite, if only "in the last instance," primarily seeks to preserve monopoly capitalist domination. But this position contains a number of serious empirical weaknesses.[41] Furthermore, it is striking that Neumann's analysis obscures one of the sources of the renaissance of democratic politics in postfascist capitalist societies after 1945. Not only did the postwar welfare state prove essential to guaranteeing democratic political forms a popular base, but it relied extensively on precisely those forms of law that Neumann, like Weber, so vehemently criticizes. Deformalized law and far-reaching discretionary administrative and judicial action have flourished to an unprecedented extent in organized capitalist liberal democracies. In the United States, administrative bodies are given the power to regulate trade so as to undermine "unfair or deceptive practices," the workplace in order to "assure . . . healthy working conditions," the environment according to "standards consistent with national environmental goals," and energy production so that rates are not "unduly discriminatory," and many authors have powerfully argued that such vague standards have given administrators and judges heightened opportunities for acting in relatively irregular, situation-specific ways.[42] It is undoubtedly true, as Neumann would have predicted, that many of these regulations involve capitalist economic monopolies; by the same token, what sphere of contemporary capitalist social existence does not at least to some extent? Yet it would be misleading to see deformalized welfare state law as fundamentally constituting a legal superstructure for the hegemonic position of monopoly capital. At the very least, we would then have to ask why so many subordinate social groups long supported governmental programs made possible by it, or why mammoth corporations have been so resistant to some forms of welfare state law.

The phenomenon of legal deformalization is more ambivalent than Neumann ever concedes during the thirties or forties. Like Weber, he correctly recognizes that substantialized law takes on prominence when subordinate social strata gain a real say in parliamentary affairs and the modern interventionist welfare state starts to emerge, but his obsession with its economic functions leads him to skirt a number of difficult questions. How, for example, would it be possible for the interventionist state to organize its activities in distinct and complicated spheres of social and economic life without recourse to broad, open-ended and potentially discretionary purpose, or result-oriented, law? The multiform structure and complex dynamics of social spheres now regulated by the welfare state is the apparent source of many deformalized legal clauses, and the common view that "it is unrealistic to suppose that unambiguous legislative standards . . . can be achieved when the government plays a large role in human affairs" needs to be countered in a more convincing way than by offering a vague picture of a homogeneous socialist alternative.[43]

At the conclusion of chapter 4, I criticized Neumann's problematic reliance on a distinction between general and individual law and argued that because he obscures the *participatory* generality of democratic law's origins (and obscures the democratic implications of the modern social contract), he locates modern law's universalistic normative features primarily in the legal norm's semantic generality. This conveniently corresponds to the underlying anti-Schmittian thrust of his entire theoretical project: insofar as Schmitt interprets the arbitrary individual measure as nonuniversalistic, authentically political, and thus as the appropriate centerpiece for fascist law, Neumann thinks he can counter Schmitt's decisionism by trying to salvage liberal general law. Schmitt's valorization of the (normless, particular) exception can be attacked by means of a defense of the (general) legal norm.[44] But Neumann thereby underplays the fact that even an individual law partakes of modern political thought's universalistic elements when it is founded on a relatively broad-based process of democratic will formation or when it broadens the openness and noncoerciveness of democratic politics. The legacy of universalistic natural law is more multifaceted than Neumann grasps. Despite what he too often suggests, the abandonment of law's semantic generality is thus not evidence per se of the disintegration of its rational character. Admittedly, this point is of limited significance as far as Neumann's own analysis of Nazism is concerned, since fascist law obviously did not rest on even the most minimal general democratic base. Still, it is important to recall if we are to determine the wider implications of Neumann's model of legal rationalization.

At the same time, Neumann is rightfully terrified by Schmitt's alternative vision of an arbitrary and purely situational mode of law. Schmitt's theory certainly does illustrate how legal deformalization could culminate in a brutally decisionist system in which state action no longer is bound or regulated effectively by a set of determinate legal norms. Rather than carelessly concluding, from the criticism of Neumann's position I just sketched, that we can dismiss his old-fashioned concern with the structure of the legal norm—as far too many authors intent on defending the welfare state in our century have—let me try to suggest how Neumann's defense of liberal general law can be given a more modest but more defensible gloss.

Inspired by the justified anxieties of many modern political thinkers about vague, indeterminate, nonformal law, Neumann can be read as developing an argument for what I described in chapter 2 as self-restraining law. Locke warns us of the dangers of undetermined resolutions in the legal order; Hegel discusses the need for determinate generality in contrast to the "monstrous confusion" of traditional law; Bentham mocks the "Egyptian hieroglyphics" that make up the core of much of the legal order. In a similar spirit, Neumann believes that excessively ambiguous legal standards are unlikely to provide sufficient guidance to state actors. Highly discretionary—and potentially arbitrary—forms of state action may result. When excessively vague, law constitutes little more than a blank check, which bureaucrats and judges are left to fill in; judges and administrators may end up regulating *like cases in unlike ways.* One way of regulating state authority effectively is by means of the legal norm. Law is the language of state power, and if its use of this language is confused or unclear, its authority is likely to be exercised by subordinate state and quasi-public bodies (administrators, judges, corporatist units at times dominated by privileged and well-organized private interests) in a correspondingly inchoate fashion. The German legal scholar Jürgen Seifert has recently summarized this view by noting that legal norms only fulfill a "reasonable function when the scope of interventionary authority is clearly identifiable for the citizen and the preconditions, according to which an act of intervention can occur, are so fixed that they can be verified by a court."[45] In a similar vein, John Rawls writes that the meaning of law must be clearly defined, because if "statutes are not clear in what they enjoin and forbid, the citizen does not know how he [or she] is to behave."[46]

If government bureaucracies are permitted to act inconsistently, the judiciary is left to make sense of blanket clauses that can be interpreted to mean pretty much anything, and private groups are outfitted with broad and ill-defined grants of state authority, then new forms of poorly harnessed power are bound to emerge. The possibility of autonomous social and political action most certainly will be undermined. True, even the most precise legal terminology is open to alternative interpretations. A critical democratic theory will have to offer an analysis of the rationality of judicial interpretation and decision making.[47] Nor, obviously, does precision in law guarantee that the substance of the legal norm will be just. Still, this should not lead us to throw the baby out with the bathwater, as happens when we ignore the potential significance of the qualitative leap into legal indeterminacy that deformalized legal standards might make possible. Even if we need to criticize the economism and manifest democratic deficiencies of Neumann's Marxism here, he is probably right to suggest that increased discretionary state action, like that facilitated by deformalized law, poses difficult questions for democratic politics.

Democracy needs more than cogent, determinate law. By the same token, it is hard to conceive of a political order with energetic publics, vigorous debate, and a responsive set of institutions when poorly regulated state and new forms of public/private authority are allowed to run amok in society. Ineffectively constrained state bodies threaten to drain the wellsprings of political and social autonomy. Coherence in law provides one way of carefully channeling their activities. Democratic politics requires an adequate degree of legal calculability and predictability if decision making is to be genuinely broad-based and noncoercive; cogency in law may help us assure that calculability. Democracy also demands that citizens have a right to be able to find out what rules regulate their activity; clarity helps attribute to law the *public* character so often emphasized by traditional defenders of formal law. Admittedly, it has generally been authors on the political Right (like Hayek) who have pointed to the dangers of materialized law—precisely because they hope to undermine the welfare state, whose unprecedented forms of interventionary activity such law seems to facilitate. Meanwhile, many progressives rush to defend deformalized law—in order to fight off vicious right-wing attacks on the welfare state. But perhaps it is time that those intent on developing a humane alternative to both laissez-faire capitalism and the disappointing welfare state status quo recognize the limitations of this divide. At a juncture where disgust with the welfare state administrative apparatus and its exceedingly discretionary, and at times disabling and disciplinary, regulatory activities has become omnipresent, Neumann's idiosyncratic left-wing defense of formal law may take on fresh significance.

Although it would be manifestly outrageous to associate terroristic fascist law with contemporary deformalized welfare state law, many recent analysts of it have pointed to perils like those that worry Neumann.

In the sixties, Grant McConnell described how the decline of formal law in the twentieth-century United States facilitates the colonization of regulatory bodies by organized private interests, and he demonstrated that the result too often has been "arbitrary and discriminatory action" in the name of an ill-defined public interest.[48] Clearly formulated legal norms help make sure that the biggest players on the field have to play according to the same rules as everyone else and at least keep the weaker players from being altogether subjected to their whims. More recently, Theodore Lowi shows how ambiguity in regulatory law not only results in parceling out poorly regulated public power to the best-organized and most privileged social groups but paralyzes democratic policy making. Empty legislative statutes fail to advance a coherent set of goals and fail to aid those whom they claim to. Despite American liberals' characteristic dislike for rigid modes of formal law, progressive public policy needs more, not less, legalism.[49] Ingeborg Maus demonstrates how deformalized law in contemporary Germany engenders discretionary action favoring the most powerful social and economic interests. According to her account, blanket clauses in environmental law tend to provide a means by which large corporations can thwart demands for ecologically sensitive action. Polluters prefer vague deformalized law to clear legal directives, because it allows them to get away with behavior more in tune with capitalist economic rationality than with ecological sensibility.[50] While conventionally arguing that formal law is too inflexible for effectively regulating something as complex as environmental protection, Alfred Marcus can be read as suggesting that Maus's view applies to the United States as well. Marcus documents how the semantically coherent elements of American environmental regulation have been systematically abandoned over the past twenty years in favor of standards and situation-specific law when they conflict with industry's demand for so-called economic realism. Big corporations rebel against law demanding clear changes in corporate behavior and prefer a case-by-case approach, allowing them to get away with more than tight, codified legal rules permit.[51]

Although fascist law has little to do with the concrete realities of contemporary forms of state intervention, it remains a powerful reminder of all their potential dangers, particularly given the fact that our societies are also characterized by a confused overlapping of private and public authorities and deeply anti-egalitarian political and social structural trends. Even though Neumann gives it an overly economistic interpretation, Schmitt's theory illustrates all the threats posed by the demise of classical formal law and the proliferation of flexible, deformalized, situation-specific law. Like Neumann, we would not go altogether wrong in seeing Schmitt as a theoretical antipode—precisely because the theorist of the exception, like the exception itself, does prove revealing, and because we, unlike Schmitt, want to keep the state of emergency from becoming an everyday affair.

Indeed, artificial contrasts between a rights-based interpretation of the rule of law and a view of it emphasizing the importance of clear rules, like that advanced by Ronald Dworkin, can be criticized from this viewpoint.[52] Political rights (for example, free speech and habeas corpus) are necessarily institutionalized, interpreted, and fought over by real-life state bodies and agents, and the problem of how to make sure that the regulation and interpretation of basic rights remains normatively acceptable was long inextricably tied to the question of the structure of the legal norm. Constitutionalist thinkers long accepted possibilities for regulating free expression (even if that just meant setting up minimal and rather liberal basic rules for registering demonstrations or publishing a newspaper), for example, but it was simultaneously established that such "interference with the rights reserved to the individual is not permitted on the basis of individual but only on the basis of general laws."[53] In other words, the demand for formal law was one way to challenge illegitimate and arbitrary inroads on basic rights, and formal law was seen as a powerful instrument for protecting political rights. A constitution can declare an abstract and universal right to free speech, yet if state bodies are permitted to regulate that right by means of deformalized legal norms generating highly discretionary action, it risks becoming little more than a privilege granted to whatever group state actors happen to favor at a particular moment. Easy contrasts between the rule of law's traditional concern with the structure of the legal norm and its attendant commitment to basic political rights obfuscate this interrelationship, whereas Neumann's old-fashioned defense of formal law reminds us of it.

Unlike Neumann, we cannot assume that the demise of general law necessarily paves the way for the death of the rule of law. Because democracy is not the main bequest of the modern political tradition's universalistic features in Neumann's view, he underplays the potential (democratic) benefits of some deformalized modes of state regulation. Either we preserve general law—or we get the horrors of Carl Schmitt and fascist legal decisionism. Yet precisely because existing modes of deformalized law often have extremely ambivalent consequences for democratic politics, we need to take Neumann's worries seriously. Democracy is that political form based on the free and equal participation of all, where the views and interests of everyone must be considered equally in the formulation of policy, and which aspires to guarantee political autonomy for everyone. Some version of this basic idea, and not that of the generality of the legal norm per se, certainly has to be considered the main successor to universalistic natural law and the social contract tradition. Insofar as materialized law can be shown to pose problems for the democratic process—by creating unnecessary dependencies on state administrators, or by exacerbating inequalities rather than destroying them—democrats have a responsibility to strive to realize superior legal modes.

The modern rule of law was an anticipatory utopia from the very beginning. By demanding that rational law and not individuals rule, it pointed toward the possibility of replacing all forms of unjustifiable coercion with a system of norm-based rule that, due to its reasonableness and generality, would no longer be experienced as domination as such. The rule of law was to be anonymous and nonpersonal, not because the dynamics of an oppressive and distant state bureaucratic apparatus had become impermeable, but because political oppression had been eliminated from the universe. If democracy is to realize genuinely free and equal participation, it cannot tolerate inequalities that squelch the expression of some voices while privileging others. A reconstructed model of the rule of law will have to take this task more seriously than postwar welfare state law, with its oftentimes highly ambivalent substantialized legal modes, has. The central problem with capitalism is not (as Neumann emphasizes) that monopolies destroy the generality of the legal norm by forcing law to take an individual form, but that it contradicts the generality of the democratic process and, hence, the demand that all potential voices have an equal chance of being expressed and taken seriously in the process of policy formation. As long as capitalism—or deformalized legal standards that exacerbate capitalist injustices—continues to buttress inequalities and undermine the openness of the democratic process, it conflicts with the liberal tradition's most important gift to us, namely, the (incomplete) project of a democratic rule of law.

Like much else in *Behemoth,* Neumann's understanding of the relationship between capitalism and legal development was too mechanistic. Yet he was undoubtedly right in making it central to his attempt to defend the rule of law.

3 Neumann and the Frankfurt School: A Second Look

Were not Neumann's critics among The Institute for Social Research's inner circle right then? Are not his theoretical contributions, as Martin Jay has noted, expressive of "a more orthodox" Marxism than their own?[54] Some of my criticisms of *Behemoth* seem to support this reading.

But let us take a closer look at the theoretical alternative that Horkheimer and Pollock began to work out at about the same time as Neumann put the finishing touches on *Behemoth.* A central reason why Neumann is fixed on demonstrating the contradictory and economically unstable monopoly capitalist character of Nazi Germany is that he sees Horkheimer's and Pollock's alternative state-capitalist model not simply as intellectually misleading, but as a recipe for political paralysis. In his view, it irresponsibly exaggerates Nazi Germany's integrative capacities, wrongly suggests that state-managed capitalism could "become the millennium," and can only engender "utter hopelessness." It thereby points the way to the demise of a genuinely critical theory.[55]

Despite my own reservations about central features of Neumann's theorizing during this period, it seems to me that there are good reasons for taking these criticisms seriously.

According to Horkheimer and Pollock, a series of novel shifts in contemporary capitalism proved that "the primacy of politics over economics, so much disputed under democracy, is clearly established" in a number of settings, among them fascist Germany (the main object of their analysis), as well as both the post–New Deal United States and the Soviet Union.[56] "[A]ll basic concepts and institutions of capitalism have changed their function; interference of the state with the structure of the old economic order has by its sheer totality and intensity 'turned quantity into quality' "[57] and has thereby engendered a new form of capitalism in which control over the state apparatus becomes the real source of social power. Classical Marxism's insistence on the predominant role of the economic substructure as well as a corresponding theory of power highlighting the centrality of class-based antagonisms becomes anachronistic. Central planning replaces traditional market mechanisms; market-based prices are increasingly determined by state decrees; with the decline of private property as an independent source of social privilege, the profit motive declines as well, and a more amorphous drive for influence over the state bureaucratic apparatus replaces it. Given the state machinery's preeminent position, one's position in the social structure is now determined primarily by one's place in the "political set-up and only in a secondary way upon the extent of one's property".[58] Pollock repeatedly insists that the new order need not be threatened by all the more infamous types of economic crises plaguing traditional capitalist economies. Although acknowledging that the system's underlying social antagonisms might manifest themselves by means of irrationalities in the planning process, both Pollock and Horkheimer seem confident that this will probably not happen and that state capitalism can overcome all potential immanent threats to its basic workings. Pollock writes that in the case of Nazi Germany "I am unable to discover such inherent economic forces as would prevent the functioning of the new order. . . . Economic problems in the old sense no longer exist when the coordination of all economic activities is effected consciously instead of by 'natural laws' of the market."[59] Fascist state-directed capitalism is liberated from all the more worrisome economic consequences of the classical capitalist market economy and represents a "learning process," demonstrating to elite groups everywhere that capitalism can be successfully managed through extensive state intervention.

Horkheimer's more speculative essays from this period (1940–41) suggest the importance of these political-economic reflections for the subsequent history of Frankfurt-based critical theory. In the transitional "End of Reason" the institute's director offers an apocalyptic overview of the history of modern thought describing how reason "ultimately destroyed itself."[60] Horkheimer's new appreciation for the integrative capacities of state-directed capitalism is tied to a profoundly pessimistic cultural analysis in which fascism is seen as both the key experience of Western modernity and a logical consequence of deep trends in it. Capitalist society in its most developed statist (and authoritarian) form remains profoundly irrational, yet there are no significant social groups pointing to the possibility of its demise. As a result, the activity of critical theorists increasingly takes on hopeless, or at least melancholic, overtones. They are reduced to little more than chronicling the ongoing disintegration of "the fundamental concepts of civilization" without being able to point to any real alternative. Offering an even more dramatic critique of Western rationality, *Dialectic of Enlightenment* radicalizes the story of the "End of Reason" and, in the process, develops the philosophical fundaments for Horkheimer's and Adorno's well-known postwar theory of "total integration" (or, in the elder Marcuse's rendition of it, "the one-dimensional society"), according to which all major institutions of the capitalist welfare state are overrun by an all-pervasive, irresistible logic of domination. At least implicitly, the experience of total fascist state-capitalist integration is given general significance: for postwar critical theory, the specter of fascist one-dimensionality continues to haunt liberal democracy. Critical theory increasingly exhausts itself in a backward-looking defense, as Horkheimer and Adorno revealingly describe it in their preface to *The Dialectic of Enlightenment,* of "the residues of freedom . . . even if these seem powerless in regard to the main course of history."[61]

In retrospect, Neumann's anxious warnings to his colleagues about the implications of the state-capitalist model take on a prophetic character. Inevitably, they suggest a set of speculative questions. Were other more satisfying analytical routes available to the first generation of critical theory? Might they have been intimated in some features of its work, which a "pearl diver" (Arendt) might fruitfully recover? Did critical theory have to culminate in the dreary and much criticized theory of total integration, or one-dimensionality?

From this perspective, Neumann's critique of the state-capitalist model takes on fresh significance. In part 2 of *Behemoth,* he offers a fiery response to his colleagues' views. He tells them that "the very term 'state capitalism' is a *contradictio in adiecto*".[62] If the state is the de facto owner of the means of production (and this *is* what the state-capitalist model implies), it no longer makes any sense to call the system capitalist. Thoroughgoing state control of the economy on this scale is inconsistent with any defensible conception of capitalism's basic dynamics. More ambitiously, Neumann undertakes the tiresome chore of demonstrating that all the bureaucratic institutions important to Nazi economic coordination are, in reality, often dominated by a relatively conventional capitalist elite. The "primacy of politics" that Pollock and Horkheimer identify by pointing to the omnipresence of the state administrative apparatus remains more fiction than reality. Political groups do play a crucial role in the power structure but not to the exaggerated extent claimed by Pollock and Horkheimer. Most disturbingly, their basically unsubstantiated speculations about the integrated quality of German fascism reproduce the Nazis' own misleading propaganda about the system's stability and potential longevity. Not only is the chaotic behemoth not as perfectly integrated as they argue, but it is even more tension-ridden and potentially explosive than capitalist liberal democracy.

The basic conceptual problem may look like the following. Despite its break with a Marxist view of the primacy of production, the state-capitalist thesis in fact reproduces some of the worst features of classical Marxism. Traditional Marxism saw the political sphere as being subordinated to the functional imperatives of the economic substructure; politics constitutes a mere superstructure dominated by the capitalist "base." Horkheimer and Pollock transform this constellation by making the state—which, in their analysis, seems to refer to little more than a central bureaucratic authority—its focal point, but the underlying functionalist logic characteristic of too much Marxist thinking about politics and law remains unquestioned in this model. It is now the state that, willy-nilly, dominates social and economic affairs, and it is now outfitted with all the social-structural omnipotence Marx tended to attribute to the capitalist substructure. Indeed, all of the model's most basic categories are concepts taken from Marxist political economy, which the authors just invert or turn upside down: the "plan" supposedly replaces the "market"; the "dictate" takes over the function of "prices"; the "profit motive" is jettisoned for a "power motive"; "buyers and sellers" are replaced by "commanders and commanded." Yet even more so than in the case of Marx, this leads not only to a one-sided empirical analysis of the sources of power and social privilege but to a truncated conception of politics:

politics here amounts to little but the (pretty much automatic) process by which the administrative apparatus assures that its basic imperatives have been satisfactorily fulfilled; all the facets of social existence potentially conflicting with this functionalist logic lack the conceptual autonomy appropriate to them here, just as an earlier economistic Marxism denied any real conceptual independence to questions of culture, psychology, politics, or law. The political sphere—where competing social visions are fought over and contested and the very definition of functionalistic social mechanisms (and the possibilities for regulating or altering them) is a matter of dispute—is of little interest to Pollock and Horkheimer, given their underlying faith in the integrative capacities of the state bureaucratic "base." Nineteenth-century Marxism's original weaknesses are actually exacerbated because the social sphere constituting the base (the state) is additionally outfitted with all the positive properties that traditional socialist thought naively attributed to administrative planning and bureaucratic modes of organization. Very much in that tradition, Horkheimer and Pollock picture the planning process as having impressive capacities for overcoming all conceivable problems it might be forced to confront; there is probably even less reason here than in classical Marxism for developing any real appreciation for the significance and relatively autonomous dynamics of political culture, political institutions, or law. How else are we to explain why the authors group Franklin Roosevelt's United States, Hitler's Germany, and Stalin's Russia into one social type? This only makes sense if they assume that the obvious differences in political and legal institutions and culture separating these examples are, "if only in the last instance," irrelevant. Just as the "totally integrated society" allegedly has no real place for genuine political conflict or exchange, so, too, must a theory obsessed with encapsulating the experience of total integration obscure the meaning of these phenomena as well.

From this angle, Neumann's relationship to the Frankfurt school's inner circle begins to look more complex than is suggested by most of the secondary literature. Without doubt, his views are far too orthodox at times. Yet the eclectic character of much of Neumann's thinking—probably best demonstrated by his real appreciation for Max Weber and Enlightenment thinkers like Montesquieu, Locke, and Rousseau—nonetheless puts him in a far better position to grapple with political and legal questions than his colleagues are. The German philosopher Axel Honneth may be going too far in seeing the makings of Habermas's theory of communicative action in Neumann's and Kirchheimer's work, but Honneth is certainly correct to suggest that we need to develop a renewed appreciation for both authors if we are to reach a more adequate understanding of the Frankfurt school's failings and missed chances.[63] Put somewhat more polemically: an acknowledgement of the crucial role played by the state bureaucracy in contemporary society does not a political theory make. However inadequately, all of those questions that Horkheimer, Pollock, and Adorno deem unimportant to social thought are precisely those taken on by Neumann and Kirchheimer.[64] Neumann was rightly unconvinced that even the Nazi German political and social system was totally integrated.[65] He rightly considered the attempt to put New Deal reforms in the same category as Nazi and Stalinist state interventionism as careless and misleading.[66] Although his interpretation of the demise of liberal democracy in Europe during the thirties parallels much of the Institute for Social Research inner circle's interpretation from the same period, he supplements it with a rich discussion of the political and historical idiosyncracies of Germany that anticipates much of the postwar debate about German exceptionialism, as well as a fascinating attempt to describe the problems posed by organized corporatist-style pluralist politics.[67] Horkheimer explicitly criticizes Neumann for emphasizing the relatively autonomous political dynamics of this development. In a letter to Neumann, he accuses him of underplaying "our [the inner circle's] conviction that fascism is the result of basic social trends" and not, as he thinks Neumann unduly exaggerates, a set of historically specific political failures that might have been avoided.[68] Yet the demise of classical competitive capitalism clearly did not necessitate an epoch of either fascist or postfascist total integration, and Neumann's richer understanding of the autonomous workings of politics and law placed him in a better position to understand why. Though Neumann might have assented to the inner circle's Hegelian-Marxist view that liberal democracy needs to be "superseded" *(aufgehoben)* by a future socialist alternative, he clearly had little patience with the political and legal vagaries of his colleagues' version of this idea. It is difficult to imagine Neumann, so intent on defending the rule of law and trying to show how it might be preserved, arguing that "with the advent of justice" in socialism "law disappears,"[69] or believing even for a moment that council communism offered any real political option for modernity.

In *The Governance of the Rule of Law,* Neumann appreciatively describes Rousseau as an author who "stands at the frontier of bourgeois thought" and is still caught up in some of its key assumptions, while uneasily looking beyond them.[70] It seems to me that the same needs to be said about Neumann's relationship to classical Marxism—and, as far as developing a defensible theory of law and politics is concerned, certainly far more so than for most of his colleagues at the Institute for Social Research.

6

Beyond State Sovereignty

In 1940 Max Horkheimer seems to have asked his colleagues at the Institute for Social Research for feedback on an article on state capitalism that he was busily writing, and Otto Kirchheimer soon obliged him with a brief but arresting essay on what was soon to become Horkheimer's "The Authoritarian State." In subsequent years, Kirchheimer would raise a number of criticisms of the state-capitalism paradigm both in the *Zeitschrift für Sozialforschung* and in more traditional academic journals, but most of them did not extend much beyond Franz Neumann's core objection to the Horkheimer-Pollock line of argumentation: the state-capitalist model exaggerates the integrative capacities of new modes of political regulation emerging in capitalist countries as a consequence of the economic crisis of the thirties. Like Neumann, Kirchheimer acknowledges that the state bureaucracy now plays a central role in coordinating the capitalist economy, but he similarly refuses to concede that the Nazis had established a nightmarish, "perfectly administered" political and social order. Although the balance of power between organized private groups and political institutions "is definitely shifting in favor of government," as he notes in "Changes in the Structure of Political Compromise,"[1] and despite the fact that there are therefore legitimate reasons for labeling the evolving configuration of state-society relations "state capitalism,"[2] neither the Nazis nor the far more benevolent administrators of the democratic welfare state had eliminated capitalist-based social strife; that, at least, the Nazis would not succeed in exterminating. Characterized by a tendency to fuse private and public power, the emerging order remains socially antagonistic. In Kirchheimer's view it is chiefly the new form taken by social conflict that is unprecedented. Struggles between massive interest blocs, merging private power and public organization in a fashion unfamiliar to competitive capitalism, replace the manifestly economy-centered class struggles of the early liberal past. In fascist Germany, quasi-public power groupings (monopolists, for example, whose privileged position is given government sanction) belong among the main social and political actors. Horkheimer and Pollock are right to focus on the active role of the state in monopoly capitalism but wrong to argue that the political superstructure takes on characteristics like those attributed by Marx to the capitalist economic base. The overall picture is more complicated. Although the social order remains capitalist, base and superstructure are welded together in a complex and at times bewildering manner.[3]

Kirchheimer's fascinating 1940 memo on Horkheimer's essay takes a pivotal step further in developing a critique of the Institute inner circle's state-capitalist paradigm.[4] In demasking a series of hidden neo-Leninist presuppositions, Kirchheimer identifies a set of theoretical weaknesses distinct from, but as worrisome as, the hopelessness Neumann perceptively saw as following from the state-capitalist model.

In "The Authoritarian State," Horkheimer tries to argue not only that the state bureaucracy is contemporary capitalism's dominant institutional focus but that long-term bureaucratizing trends in capitalist development ultimately crippled oppositional social movements and precipitated fascism's rise to power. Despite its essayistic and even impressionistic form, the article powerfully describes the sources of the Left's alleged enslavement to "the spirit of administration." Horkheimer offers a disturbing chronicle of how independent and spontaneous anticapitalist movements, forced to adjust to the logic of an ever more bureaucratic and state-organized social universe, were eventually replaced by undemocratic unions and top-heavy bureaucratic parties with little capacity for mass mobilization. Just as state bureaucratic mechanisms supplanted classical capitalism's independent entrepreneur and its self-driven "natural" market mechanisms, so, too, was the working-class movement robbed of any real autonomy.

At the same time, Horkheimer suggests that bureaucratizing tendencies themselves undermine the ruling elite (whether capitalist or "integral etatist" Soviet-type state socialist), whose privileges they had thus far buttressed. More and more the bureaucratization of the economy makes its management routine and simple. "Average technical skills" easily acquired by everyone, Horkheimer speculates, could soon undermine the last remaining rationale for political domination. With the possibility of a radical democratization of administrative tasks finally taking on real proportions, the vision of a planned socialist economy staffed by a legion of popular technician-workers leaves the sphere of bad utopianism and enters the realm of the politically feasible.[5]

Given the organized Left's subservience to bureaucratic ideology and practice, Horkheimer believes it is unlikely to pull this off. A paradoxical dialectic is at work: the bureaucratization (and routinization) of economic activities both prepares the preconditions for human liberation and denies social groups the capacity for achieving it. Bureaucratization should set us free, but instead it enslaves us. The general thrust of Horkheimer's analysis remains deeply pessimistic. If there is still a way beyond this paradox, he argues, it could only come from (unnamed) "isolated" *(vereinzelte)* individuals who have miraculously managed to escape the dark shadows of the spirit of administration. Only their unpolluted will for freedom, Horkheimer apocalyptically concludes, might still help free humanity from the repressive telos of bourgeois world history. But union bosses and staid social democratic apparatchiks surely cannot.[6]

From the perspective of postwar critical theory, "The Authoritarian State" is an eye-opener. Not only does it document Horkheimer's growing political pessimism and anticipate the postwar theory of the perfectly administered society, but it also points the way to the idiosyncratic brand of revolutionary politics most clearly represented in the history of the Frankfurt school by Herbert Marcuse's theory of one-dimensional society. It is hard to miss the similarities between Marcuse's picture of a one-dimensional world, capable of being challenged solely by the "great refusal" of isolated constituencies that for one reason or another are immune to its oppressive and all-encompassing logic, and Horkheimer's appeal to the isolated individual and what's left of a battered will for freedom, alone able to halt the regressive tide of bourgeois development.[7] Horkheimer's essay suggests two conceivable political answers to the diagnosis of total integration, and the postwar theorizing of the first generation of Frankfurt-based critical theory can be interpreted as the endeavour to develop one or the other of these options. Either, as in the case of Horkheimer or Adorno, the theory of total administration culminates in a melancholic and backward-looking attempt to save the final "residues of freedom" (as described in chapter 5, and as Neumann presciently warned his colleagues about), or, as with Marcuse, it generates a brand of fiery radicalism that can be satisfied with nothing less than overthrowing "the whole" *(das Ganze)* and ultimately incapable of finding any real redeeming qualities in any of the institutions of contemporary society or in any of its major players: Horkheimer's own half-truths about the failings of the Second International resonate in Marcuse's later (and hardly altogether unjustified) disgust with the conservative working-class hard hats who took such relish in pummeling longhaired peace activists during the late sixties. Most problematically, the idea of a totally integrated social order implies a neo-Leninist political project of educational dictatorship like that which can be detected even more clearly in Marcuse's later writings than in Horkheimer's "The Authoritarian State." How else are we to break out of the suffocating one-dimensionality than by relying on isolated groups (college students? ghetto rebels?) supposedly free from its influence? If our universe is truly one-dimensional, is not some avant-garde of outsiders going to have to force the rest of us to be free? In a 1964 letter to Kirchheimer, Marcuse concedes that "as to your comments [about *One Dimensional Man*]: indeed, the political consequences would point to an *Erziehungsdiktatur* [educational dictatorship], although not really *'auf technokratischer Grundlage'* [on a technocratic basis]. The point I wanted to make is that there is no such thing as pure (or almost pure) technological rationality—the latter is always also (and internally) political rationality. But then all the old arguments against an *Erziehungsdiktatur* since Plato are still valid. . . . Result: the pessimism expressed in the last pages."[8] Is there a more cogent summary of the political paradoxes of the theory of total integration? Either an educational dictatorship—or a paralyzing pessimism?

These are all familiar criticisms of Marcuse.[9] Less appreciated is that there were alternative voices in the first generation of Frankfurt-based critical theorists who perceptively recognized some of these problems and tried, however incompletely, to sketch out another course.

Kirchheimer's "Memo on State Capitalism" shows that, alongside Neumann, he has to be counted as one such dissident voice. Kirchheimer raises two central criticisms of Horkheimer's argument. First, he concedes that mass-based political parties have proven ineffective in undertaking the much-needed revolutionary transformation to democratic socialism. With fascism well on its way to becoming Europe's dominant political force, Kirchheimer, like Horkheimer (and Walter Benjamin as well, to whom Horkheimer dedicates his essay), has few qualms about laying a great deal of the blame for this catastrophe on the failures of mass-based left-wing organizations.[10] Yet Kirchheimer is somewhat skeptical of Horkheimer's vague reference to a "will to freedom." Given that Horkheimer's appeal to the isolated lacks any more definite political contours (who is meant here? under what conditions will this "will to freedom" be exercised?) does it not probably rely on some further assumption—in Kirchheimer's view, a faith in human nature? Considering Horkheimer's own gloomy portrayal of contemporary social and political trends and his suspicions about conventional mass-based politics, what else but such an assumption would allow him to preserve even the most minimal hope in a will to freedom? In response, Kirchheimer worries that if contemporary history suggests anything, it is that human nature has become deeply depraved. For that matter, it is not clear that Horkheimer's optimism about human nature can perform the function expected of it. If we are to make absolutely sure that the transition to democratic socialism does not take on terroristic features, more than the will to freedom of the lonely and unintegrated is called for. In order for revolutionary change to take a genuinely democratic form, Kirchheimer insists, it most certainly will have to rely on mass-based bureaucratic organizations. The real lesson of the Left's collapse in the face of fascism is not that a revolutionary project of social transformation can do without mass-based democratic parties, but that the Left will have to figure out how to keep such parties from succumbing to paralyzing bureaucratizing tendencies, which Kirchheimer sees Horkheimer as describing more or less accurately.

Secondly, Horkheimer's crucial "argument, that the victorious revolution can transform economic-political problems into purely technical ones," was advanced in a similar form by Lenin, in *State and Revolution*, and Horkheimer's analysis risks committing errors similar to those that made Lenin's original views so problematic.[11] Like Lenin, Horkheimer fails to acknowledge adequately that even a planned socialist economy cannot eliminate all questions of "value." Economic priorities will have to be set, some regions and industries developed instead of others, and such questions remain (pace Lenin and Horkheimer) intensely political. Lenin's obsession in *State and Revolution* with the example of a state-run postal service obscures this. In the post office, clear goals can be presupposed and the question of "which path is right and which path is wrong" in their pursuit often "is a technical problem."[12] But the same cannot be said for the economy as a whole. Again, like Lenin's own simplistic vision of a primitive democracy managed by technician-workers, Kirchheimer seems to suggest, Horkheimer's claim here does not give us enough reason for believing that his postcapitalist utopia could avoid the dangers of administrative dictatorship. In the earlier, closely related "Marxism, Dictatorship, and the Organization of the Proletariat" (1933), Kirchheimer had written that "the primitivity of Lenin's image of democracy, all too restricted as it was by the ideas of the Paris Commune, hardly takes into account the technical complexity of the governmental apparatus of the twentieth century," and he clearly has this criticism in mind when discussing Horkheimer's own failure to acknowledge the necessity of both complex forms of bureaucratic decision making and distinct (superordinate) democratic political institutions.[13] Conceivably, a model along the lines suggested by Horkheimer gives us reason for believing that economic power in socialism would no longer need to be buttressed by control over the state apparatus. Hypothetically, democratic socialism makes possible peaceful political transitions to an extent that capitalist liberal democracies often fail to achieve. In Kirchheimer's view, socialism means, in part, that key economic decision makers (in a planning agency, for example) could simply be "outvoted" and replaced without their economic status being threatened—in contrast to the situation in capitalism, where economic actors defeated in the competitive struggle or challenged by new subordinate social groups sometimes opt to disrupt the peaceful course of democratic politics rather than surrender their hegemonic power position.[14] Nonetheless, if the crudity of Lenin's ideas helped generate an authoritarian "oligarchical bureaucracy," by failing to recognize the unavoidability of complex bureaucratic institutions and the virtues of genuinely democratic representative institutions, as Kirchheimer had noted in his earlier criticism of Leninism, Horkheimer's view risks making the same mistake.

Here, as at many junctures, Kirchheimer—like Neumann—points to the outlines of a theoretical and practical "third way," beyond both Horkheimer's and Adorno's apocalyptic defeatism and Marcuse's odd brand of elitist revolutionary politics. Alongside Neumann, it is Kirchheimer who represents a real alternative to the mainstream of early critical theory, and it may be their legacy, not that of their better-known colleagues, that constitutes a starting point for a rejuvenated critical theory of politics.

In this chapter, I will try to buttress this thesis by focusing on the critique and deconstruction of Carl Schmitt's theory developed by Kirchheimer. Although Kirchheimer's writings here range over a tremendous variety of themes (from criminal law to fascism to the question of decree powers and sovereignty), he is intent on doing battle with Carl Schmitt's decisionism by means of a "critical political sociology of the exception," which, as I will show, suggests an interpretation of twentieth-century legal development similar to that which I have tried to defend in previous chapters: we can no longer demand (with early modern political theory) that law always take a (semantically) general form, yet we need to confront the possibility of deformalized law's leaving us with a frightening system of decisionist law like that advocated by Carl Schmitt. While recognizing the necessity of forms of legal regulation unforeseen by classical authors, we need to insist that any contemporary legal alternative integrate all the merits of cogent formal law. In Hegelian terms, we cannot merely negate traditional modes of parliamentary general law but have to preserve its core aspiration (section 1).

In preceding chapters, we broached the difficult theoretical question of state sovereignty. Kirchheimer's considerations on this theme can help us tackle some of the enigmas that are still unsolved. I described Neumann's critique of Schmitt's decisionist view of sovereignty (in terms of "he who decides on the exception") as well as his attempted resolution of the riddle of state sovereignty and law (and *voluntas* and *ratio,* or state power and right) by means of a neo-Marxist reworking of Weber's conception of legal rationalization. These two tasks turned out to be closely interrelated for Neumann. Insofar as situation-specific materialized law, like that enthusiastically endorsed by Schmitt, potentially fails to bind or regulate state agencies effectively, the corrosion of modern formal law was seen as generating a renaissance of poorly regulated modes of state action akin to those traditionally associated with unharnessed sovereignty or even "reason of state." Formal law had long been a crucial instrument for taming the state's monopoly on violence and making it normatively legitimate. Neumann shows that its apparent disintegration poses real problems for those intent on defending the constitutionalist agenda. Like Neumann, Kirchheimer now intends to take on Schmitt's fascistic conception of sovereignty by defending a democratic alternative to it. By closely examining Kirchheimer's views, we can better see the limits of both his and Neumann's own conceptualization of sovereignty. Despite the undeniable superiority of their views in relation to Schmitt's, Kirchheimer and Neumann still end up trying to restore a vision of state sovereignty poorly adapted to modern democratic politics. Nonetheless, ongoing attempts to develop a defensible modern reconceptualization of democratic political legitimacy can still learn a great deal from the early Frankfurt school's analysis of sovereignty (section 2).

1 A Critical Political Sociology of the Exception

Franz Neumann long tried to show that the contemporary legal order had taken on features disturbingly reminiscent of Schmittian decisionism and that Schmitt's theory and political program could be debunked by proving that its central features matched worrisome developmental trends in the capitalist political economy. One of Kirchheimer's main achievements during the thirties and early forties was to buttress Neumann's insistence on the links between bourgeois society, Carl Schmitt, and decisionist ideology and law. Like Neumann, Kirchheimer thinks the history of the capitalist political economy and decisionist modes of law are interconnected, and his writings can be interpreted as identifying and describing three distinct stages in the relationship between the two. An impressive set of studies on the history of criminal law describes a system of dual justice in which modern forms of formal law exist side by side with discretionary legal gaps primarily employed against the socially underprivileged (subsection A). This dualism characterizes bourgeois law until anticapitalist antisystemic movements appear on the historical scene in the early twentieth century, helping to radicalize its decisionist elements and giving the state of emergency a place in the everyday workings of the liberal legal order unlike anything desired by classical liberal constitutionalism. The flourishing of temporary emergency governments in European parliamentary politics during the twenties and thirties offers the clearest manifestation of this trend (subsection B). Finally, fascist regimes toss aside the final remnants of the emancipatory potentialities of political liberalism in order to rescue a particularly exploitive brand of capitalism: the exception becomes the norm, and the state of emergency becomes normalcy. Bourgeois society surrenders its most important legal achievements and regresses to the raison d'état ideologies and practices that accompanied its ascent. The Janus-faced modern state, in which one face speaks the language of reason and law and the other that of unrestrained sovereignty and force, becomes a violent beast (subsection C).

(A) Coauthored with the legal sociologist George Rusche, *Punishment and Social Structure* (as well as a number of related articles in French and American journals) advances two main theses.[15] First, and probably most convincingly, Kirchheimer and Rusche deflate the widespread view that the severity of punishment influences the crime rate. No empirical evidence adequately shows that harsh punishment deters crime.[16] The crime rate is conditioned most fundamentally by the structure of capitalist-based inequality: the poor and desperate are driven to commit crimes even when threatened by highly repressive modes of punishment. Furthermore, as long as liberal reformers continue to presuppose that subordinate social constituencies making up the great bulk of criminals should "fear a further decline in their mode of existence" if they break the law, criminal law reform is likely to remain extremely modest.[17] If punishment has to be more unattractive than the social and economic conditions of the least well off members of society, even a reformed system of punishment will remain highly unpleasant given capitalist-based inequalities. Second, the evolution of criminal law's disciplinary instruments can be explained by recourse to a history of the capitalist labor market. The cyclical "laws of motion" of the capitalist economy are recapitulated in a series of parallel cycles, identified by the authors, in the history of punishment. Where labor shortages exist, for example, the harshness of punishment tends to be somewhat reduced because of the advantages (from the standpoint of the propertied) of avoiding a needless waste of labor power. Conversely, punishment tends to be brutal under market conditions unfavorable to the working classes. Contra liberal common sense, the history of criminal punishment is hardly characterized by linear progress. Like the booms and busts of the capitalist economy, it continually succumbs to terrifying relapses.

From our perspective, the study is significant for a number of reasons. The authors share Neumann's esteem for the classical liberal vision of a closed system of neatly formulated and fixed legal rules, and they similarly refuse to see early demands for rationalizing law and legal procedure purely as a consequence of the functional requirements of capitalism. Unlike Neumann, Kirchheimer and Rusche focus on the problem of criminal law—in which cogent formal law is even more important than those areas of the law Neumann was most concerned with: in criminal law, the state confronts society's most unpopular constituencies, and one minimal test of the rule of law's claim to equal protection before the law certainly is the extent to which the structure of legal regulation helps preserve basic protections for the political community's most disliked elements. For many classical liberals, as for Kirchheimer and Rusche, formal law always had an important role to play in maintaining the rights of the accused. In a key chapter focusing on the Enlightenment and its contributions to criminal law, Kirchheimer and Rusche argue not only that the emergence of modern rational law was ultimately "to benefit all classes alike" but that pre-Enlightenment absolutist forms of law were more appropriate to the exigencies of a complete "capitalist rationalization of criminal law."[18] Arbitrary and irregular discretionary law, not the relatively radical views of criminal law developed by writers like Beccaria, better suits bourgeois society's interest in disciplining subordinate social groups according to the imperatives of the capitalist labor market. Simultaneously, the authors acknowledge the incomplete character of the Enlightenment and, like Neumann, see its limitations as stemming from unwarranted concessions to capitalism. In particular "the formal and rational system [of law] . . . had little to do with the actual administration of criminal justice" either in legal practice during or after the Enlightenment or in the minds of all Enlightenment authors, and substantial loopholes and harsh punishment outlived the reform period. In spite of Enlightenment-era reforms, "death or transportation was the rule for most offenses."[19] Even during the golden age of revolutionary liberalism, the tendency to abandon formal law in favor of protecting a socially unjust mode of property against vagrants, petty thieves, and other mostly small-time criminals remained all too evident, and criminals continued to suffer unnecessarily, due to political liberalism's unfortunate alliance with capitalist private property. The tragic implications of this alliance became even more apparent in the nineteenth century, as increasingly powerful and conservative bourgeois strata lost faith in so-called bourgeois formal law precisely because of its potential advantages to "all classes alike." The immediate aftermath of the Paris Commune, when bourgeois groups in France showed few reservations about establishing a repressive system of special courts and martial law, already anticipated the middle classes' impending betrayal of rational law.

Walter Benjamin, who was likely working on his "Theses on the Philosophy of History" at about the same time Kirchheimer and Rusche's study appeared in the United States, was not altogether off the mark when claiming that "the tradition of the oppressed teaches us that the 'state of emergency,' " like that which had by then become "normal" in fascist-dominated Europe, "is the rule."[20] Benjamin's theoretical intentions were certainly more ambitious than Kirchheimer's and Rusche's, but the former's sensitivity to how a crude political faith in progress could help prepare the way for political cataclysms is hardly alien to Kirchheimer and Rusche. This is made most clear in the final pages of *Punishment and Social Structure,* where they warn us about reformist proposals in modern criminal law that fail to acknowledge the necessity of far-reaching social and economic change: "The crime rate can really be influenced only if society is in a position to offer its members a certain measure of security and to guarantee a reasonable standard of living."[21] Unless linked to a broader agenda for radical social change, reform projects can only experience short-lived and probably limited successes. The disappointment likely to follow from their failure, as the authors think the advent of fascist criminal law suggests, inevitably prepares the way for a resurgence of brutal authoritarian views about criminal punishment. In fascism, "fixed criminal law" is abandoned, in part because "calculable norms of criminal law could provide the political opposition with a point of departure."[22] Kirchheimer here likely has an eye on Carl Schmitt, who was peddling an extremely pessimistic conception of human nature in order to ground his dreary portrayal of a political universe overwhelmed by unavoidably explosive friend/foe conflicts: the failures of a superficial reformism play into the hands of those arguing "for the inherent wickedness of human nature" and engender "a return to the pessimistic doctrine that [humanity's] evil nature can be tamed only by depressing the prison standard below the lowest free class. The futility of severe punishment and cruel treatment may be proven a thousand times, but so long as society is unable to solve its social problems, repression, the easy way out, will always be accepted."[23]

Not only is vicious punishment destined to remain part and parcel of the liberal legal order until capitalist-based social inequalities are attacked head-on, but liberalism may very well contribute to its own demise unless it undertakes that attack.

(B) During and after World War I, Kirchheimer wrote, "the use of extraordinary powers by the executive for legislative purposes became so widespread in Europe that constitutional theorists began to find it convenient to give up the doctrine of legislative supremacy."[24] Parliamentary enabling acts outfitted the executive branch with wide-ranging legislative powers. Parliaments were reduced in France, Germany, Belgium, and many other settings to doing little more than passively registering a long list of executive decrees. Modes of formal law declined, while situation-specific executive measures (directed at individual objects) as well as vague laws (like that passed in France, in 1939, allowing the executive to take all "measures imposed by the exigencies of national defense") proliferated.[25] As we have seen, Schmitt had been among the most enthusiastic proponents of the trend toward executive-based discretionary rule during Weimar's final days, whereas Kirchheimer had been one of its most articulate critics. It is fitting that Kirchheimer's considerations on this problem pick up where he left off there.

As in the early thirties, Kirchheimer again seems to suggest that the generality of law should be located primarily in the (universal) democratic structure of decision making that generates it, not in the generality of its semantic form.[26] A criticism of executive decision making thus cannot be based on what Kirchheimer, in some contrast to Neumann, sees as a somewhat outmoded conception of the legal norm. The real problem with vague parliamentary delegations of legislative power and executive-based discretionary decision making lies not in its nongeneral semantic structure but in its tendency to undermine the participatory base and representativeness of the decision making process. When a parliamentary majority outfits the executive with far-reaching legislative authority, the function of parliamentary minorities is undermined. A narrowly based group of cabinet members, chosen by the parliamentary majority coalition and unrepresentative of the minority, becomes the de facto legislator, and minority groups are denied any real say in the policy-making practice. While parliament-centered lawmaking at least gives political minorities the chance to have their views aired and exert some influence on the actions of the majority while laws are being formulated and passed, this opportunity is impaired in an executive-based system that puts lawmaking powers directly into the hands of a small clique. In short, the assumed generality of democratic law is badly corroded.[27]

Executive-centered rule accelerates the decline of parliamentary democracy and constitutes "an intermediate station on the road to complete authoritarianism." Barred from governmental authority, political minorities have neither reason to respect parliamentary mechanisms nor an immediate political interest in their defense. What real justification can be provided for parliamentary bodies in such a system? If they really play such a minimal role, why not dump them for an openly authoritarian regime, particularly given the much-touted "efficiency" of executive action? Completing the essay just as Nazi armies were overrunning France, Kirchheimer writes, in a footnote, that the French debacle proves beyond a shadow of a doubt that a democracy "with a dubious popular or parliamentary basis" is unlikely to prove, militarily or otherwise, capable of defending itself when decree-based government emerges and contributes to the disintegration of state policy's popular legitimacy. "The degradation of parliament to a mechanism recording votes of confidence and authorizing enabling bills only hastens the disintegration process of parliamentary government as such."[28] Like its cousin on the other side of the Rhine, the French political elite grasped this all too late.

Kirchheimer situates this institutional argument in a broader socioeconomic framework. The imperialism of the normless emergency in contemporary politics corresponds to a real crisis in the history of bourgeois society: with the emergence of radical anticapitalist political groupings in the early twentieth century, parliamentary bodies are increasingly paralyzed. Deeply divided, they cannot act effectively. Enabling acts are one answer to this crisis. More commonly, executive decision makers simply usurp legislative powers, as in Germany in the twenties, in order to deal with pressing demands that an ineffective parliament leaves unsatisfied. In Weimar Germany, for example, the executive branch was forced far too often to grapple with issues and undertake activities that parliamentary institutions, dominated by hostile class-based parties, failed to resolve. In Kirchheimer's view, this was the main source of the dominant role played by the state bureaucracy (the judiciary, national administration, and federal president) in German politics as early as 1923, when the social democrat Ebert was forced to rely on constitutional emergency powers to push through a set of social and economic measures. We recall that Schmitt himself had argued that parliamentary institutions were increasingly rendered ineffective by a set of explosive political cleavages. But in Kirchheimer's view, as in Neumann's, Schmitt's description of the polarizing consequences of "pluralism," "according to which it was the destiny of democratic government to be split up into a number of independent social powers struggling one against another, until finally all those anti-governmental and quasi-governmental forces would be crushed by dictatorship and by the erection of a totalitarianian state," is too indiscriminate.[29] For example, Schmitt's interpretation underplays a crucial factor in the emergence of quasi-authoritarian executive-centered government: middle-class political groupings in mid-century Europe show a disturbing proclivity to surrender their former liberal and democratic political aspirations in favor of preserving the social and economic status quo against demands from below. With working-class reformist parties gaining a voice in elected institutions, bourgeois groups, often possessing an impressive array of allies in the executive branch, too often enthusiastically embrace decree rule.

Decree rule itself sets into motion a relatively autonomous political dynamic destined to destroy parliamentary government. But if the responsibility for initially putting executive-centered regimes in power can be attributed to any particular social group in contemporary European politics, it would have to lie with the bourgeoisie.

(C) Like Neumann, Kirchheimer thinks that German fascism represents the culmination of trends that long pointed to the possibility of a legal and political order dominated by the exigencies of the emergency situation, and he similarly describes Schmitt as being "the theorist of the Nazi Constitution just as Hugo Preuss was the theorist of the Weimar Constitution."[30] Fascism's version of the "shift from the general law of earlier capitalism to the administrative command of monopoly capitalism"[31] and the interrelated "disappearance of a unified system of law" in favor of "innumerable steadily increasing special competences"[32] shatter liberalism's fragile quest to delineate legality from morality and thereby destroys its basic achievements.[33] Whereas liberal law guaranteed a degree of rationality by securing legal regularity and predictability for individuals and social groups, the rationality of Nazi law takes a different form. Echoing a theme central to the theorizing of his institute colleagues, Kirchheimer writes,

> [R]ationality here means only that the whole apparatus of law and law-enforcing is made exclusively serviceable to those who rule. Since no general notions prevail which could be referred to by the ruling and the ruled alike and which thus might restrict the arbitrariness of the administrative practice, the rules are being used to serve the specific purposes of those ruling. . . . This, then, is a strictly Technical Rationality which has as its main and uppermost concern the question: How can a given command be executed so as to have the maximum effect in the shortest possible time?[34]

Fascist law embodies the logic of a means-ends technical rationality distinct from more emancipatory forms of rationality intimated in the legal practices and theories of traditional liberal law.

The sources of this transformation lie in National Socialism's accelerated destruction of the social and economic correlates of the modern rule of law. Kirchheimer presupposes Karl Renner's view that the fundaments of the liberal rule of law once matched the everyday realities of an early bourgeois economy consisting of roughly equal small-scale economic competitors. The idea of the abstract legal person fit the fact that the proprietor of early capitalism was relatively independent of his or her peers; notions of the free contract suited a social situation in which agreements between similarly situated economic agents could claim to be based on a relatively high degree of autonomy and reciprocity; the principle of equality before the law had its social correlate in the actual equality existing between independent property owners. But the development of monopoly capitalism and an ensuing process in which social and economic life becomes ever more organized (as labor unions and new types of state intervention undertake to confront the problems posed by a monopoly economy) undermine these social and economic presuppositions. As a result, "it was easy for the Nazis to make fun of this conception" and its abstractness and formalism and to jettison it for a crude community-centered, racist "folk community" *(Volksgemeinschaft)*. Under contemporary conditions, liberal legal categories "usually did not offer a profitable tool for the adjustment of differences which frequently represented claims of social groups and not mere individuals."[35] Liberty of contract, for example, was early on transformed into an ideology whose main function lay in defending the privileged position of mammoth capitalist interests; in any case, it decreasingly corresponded to the realities of quasi-governmental agreements like those common in an ever more bureaucratized and corporatist mode of capitalism. In a world of social and economic giants and deep inequalities, the central place attributed to the abstract person and formal equality in liberal legal thought seemed to have lost any relation to social and economic reality.

Renner had hoped that supplementary legal institutions (for example, labor law and new modes of social welfare regulation), beginning to emerge in capitalist societies and increasingly important for contemporary law, would be able to rob what he described as the "main freedom" *(Hauptfreiheit)* of capitalist private property of its dominant place in the liberal legal order. Kirchheimer's analysis here intends to show that in fascism the main freedom of capitalist private property ominously turns *against* supplementary institutions and freedoms essential to capitalism's development but having protective elements transcending their economic functions. The idea of the legal person is never merely a mask for the capitalist property owner; formal equality is always more than a front for social inequality. The most direct confirmation of this is that even the existing "legal heaven does not consist exclusively of group claims and counterclaims." There is still need for legal protection for the individual in organized capitalism, and there are still "parallel relations among individuals and between the individual and the state" that a defensible modern conception of the rule of law hoping to preserve and broaden political and social autonomy should readily acknowledge.[36] Instead of trying to preserve these features by reconceptualizing them to suit contemporary conditions, fascist critics cheaply latch on to the discontinuities between the liberal legal utopia and capitalist social reality in order to jettison the former and radicalize all the worst features of the latter. Fascism itself belligerently defends capitalist monopolies at the cost of destroying liberal legal institutions that now pose a potential threat to it. As a result, "the increasing factual subservience to the command of the monopoly-dominated group has now become a legalized subservience."[37]

Neumann's view that rational law is dispensed with in fascism because it also "serves to protect the weak" increasingly applies to the core components of the liberal legal system as a whole.[38]

Many criticisms undoubtedly could be leveled against Kirchheimer's (reconstructed) narrative here, especially given its tendency, as in Neumann's similar theoretical reflections from this period, to rely unquestioningly on a number of traditional Marxist theoretical assumptions. At the same time, there is a good reason for claiming that an investigation of the place of the legal exception in modern politics could do worse than by linking the exception to an analysis of inequality, or by postulating that formal law at times is undermined by the irrationalities of power. Although in need of being restated, Kirchheimer's contribution remains noteworthy.[39]

Another issue is of greater immediate significance for our undertaking. With the potential dangers of deformalized law becoming all too clear in fascism, Kirchheimer now acknowledges that the disintegration of modern formal law could prepare the way for a terrible mode of decisionist law and normatively unregulated state sovereignty; this was missing from some of his Weimar-era writings. While acknowledging the virtues of formal law in binding state and public/private authorities effectively and providing an appreciable degree of legal regularity, Kirchheimer refuses to link this insight to a problematic emphasis on the semantic generality of the legal norm. He insightfully grasps that what is more crucial than law's semantic generality is the extent to which legal regulation—general or otherwise—helps coordinate and standardize state activity. In an essay published in 1934 while at the Institute for Social Research's Paris branch ("Remarques sur la théorie de la souveraineté nationale en Allemagne et en France"), Kirchheimer formulates the basic question at hand in a manner as relevant today as it was over fifty years ago. With an eye toward Nazi Germany and the makings of a legal order based on pure power decisions favoring the most privileged social and economic interests, and with Schmitt's theory in mind, Kirchheimer insists that democracies need to find a satisfying solution to the following problems: can nongeneral modes of situation-specific law, like those increasingly found everywhere in the twentieth-century legal universe, be made compatible with democratic politics? Must it, as substantialized fascist law suggests, inevitably produce a worrisome merger of executive and legislative authority?[40] And would not a similar fusion bode ill for democracy?[41]

We might add a further question as well. Despite its undeniable achievements, does the contemporary welfare state and its reliance on discretionary law give us reason enough for dismissing these anxieties? Kirchheimer plainly sees that it would be deeply misleading to assimilate the legal irregularities of the welfare state to the system of terror instituted by the Nazis. But after undertaking an exhaustive analysis of the New Deal and the emerging apparatus of the American welfare state, in "In Quest of Sovereignty," he notes that many of the new welfare state institutions, with their bewildering fusion not only of legislative and executive powers but of public and private authority, have "successfully resisted all attempts at legal formalization, regardless of whether such attempts have been made by" legislators or courts. "The antitrust policy of the United State government, for example, is comparable to an occasional wanderer in the forest, who might cut down cobwebs which a spider was careless enough to build across the path. But the spider waits patiently until the wanderer disappears and hurries to spin another web to catch up with the rest of his gang."[42] Unsurprisingly given the basic structure of his argument, he suggests that there is no satisfying resolution to this problem realizable within the confines of the bourgeois social and economic status quo. But might the incestuous ties between decisionist law and capitalist inequality be cut if an alternative social order based on "a free association for the common use of productive forces," like that vaguely alluded to by Kirchheimer, were realized?[43]

2 The Crisis of State Sovereignty

Neumann and Kirchheimer are only two among a diverse group of twentieth-century political thinkers who have done battle with some version or another of the theory and practice of sovereignty. Jacques Maritain argued long ago that "the two concepts of Absolutism and Sovereignty have been forged together on the same anvil."[44] Maritain convincingly shows that the underlying assumption of most modern views of sovereignty that there is some final, undivided, and potentially absolute power in the political community betrays its roots in the sorry politics of early modern Europe, whose omnipotent monarchs have vanished from the historical scene but whose theoretical relics (and their practical consequences) continue to haunt us.[45] For Hannah Arendt, sovereignty invokes an "ideal of uncompromising self-sufficiency," thus denying the plurality essential to politics.[46] Political action rests on mutuality and reciprocity. The absolute independence implicit in classical formulations of the concept of sovereignty, whether it be conceived of in reference to a particular nation-state or to an institution within a specific political community, is diametrically opposed to this. Decentralized and mutually enabling forms of common action, not a monistic "point" in the state apparatus where coercive instruments are centralized, ultimately generate political power.

If Neumann and Kirchheimer belong to a broader intellectual tradition, it is in far too incomplete a manner. For both authors, a critique of Schmittian decisionism is complemented by a defense of a concept of state sovereignty having a number of indefensible traditional features. We recall Neumann's view that Nazism's brutality stemmed in part from its polycratic structure, as well as *Behemoth*'s provocative description of the demise of an institutional center having a monopoly on the exercise of coercion as representative of a cataclysmic "death of state sovereignty." Neumann thought he could see a hint of this development even in Laski's left-wing pluralist political theory, and he was sure that its basic structure corresponded to Schmitt's expressly irrationalist emergency-centered view of sovereignty. Yet whatever the virtues of his surprising reading of Laski, and however justified his anxieties about "state-less" fascism, we still need to ask whether Neumann's own reliance on the problematic discourse of state sovereignty and its traditional association with some potentially absolute, all-powerful, and undivided "point" in the political community is best suited to his broader analytical aims; Neumann's own illustration of how the ideas of "might" and "right" (or state sovereignty and law) had conflicted throughout the course of Western political development should probably make us skeptical about his own project of salvaging a reconstructed, left-wing version of state sovereignty.[47] Even if the rule of law presupposes an institutional configuration guaranteeing that law is binding and potentially coercive, must we take recourse to the theoretical paraphernalia of state sovereignty? To some conception of a potentially all-powerful and undivided body or final instance in society? On the contrary, does not democratic politics aspire to subject such "points" in the political community (be it the state as a whole or a specific state institution) to a more abstract network of public debate and exchange in which public opinion is allowed to formulate and define itself? Neumann writes that he agrees with Austin's view of sovereignty as referring to a supreme power apart and truly independent of society.[48] Yet if it is precisely the aim of democratic politics that society be made fully autonomous, does not this definition probably foreclose the very possibility of a suitable view of democracy?

Governance of the Rule of Law shows clearly why Neumann continues to insist on the virtues of state sovereignty throughout his intellectual career. Although focusing on decisionist tendencies in the history of legal development, he argues that a democratic and socially critical view of the rule of law cannot do without its own conception of state sovereignty and that such an alternative needs to avoid the errors of both "the normless will of Schmitt" and "the will-less norm of Kelsen."[49]

Neumann's criticisms of Schmitt's view of sovereignty should be clear by now, but his reservations about Kelsen's neo-Kantian "pure theory of law" are less so. Kelsen thought that legal analysis had long been subordinated to crude moral theories and problematic modes of social analysis so as to have transformed it into little more than a cheap weapon for political ideologues. If the autonomy of law were to be appropriately theorized and its study to be given a firm scientific base, legal theory would have to undertake a radical break with sociology on the one hand and ethics and politics on the other. Although nineteenth-century legal positivism had undertaken a similar project, Kelsen argued that it had done so only incompletely, in part because it had not yet fully grasped the nonuniversalizability of all moral and political values, which Kelsen, like Weber, saw as essential to the modern predicament. If legal theory were to be given a more solid basis, the break with natural law needed to be more thoroughgoing. On the basis of this separation, Kelsen concluded that it only made sense to speak of sovereignty as a quality or feature of the legal order itself but not in reference to a concrete political institution allegedly standing beyond or outside the legal system; such views of state sovereignty were too personalistic and contained potentially authoritarian implications. State and law had to be seen as identical. The state was to be conceived of in terms of a hierarchy of norms stemming from a "basic norm"—defined in *The Pure Theory of Law* as "nothing more than the basic rule, according to which the norms of the legal order are produced."[50] Every state could be interpreted as a "state based on law" *(Rechtsstaat)*. Sovereignty was an attribute of the legal order, since it was "underived" *(nicht-weiter-ableitbar)*, as Kelsen noted, from any competing, higher order of norms.[51]

Though appreciative of a number of facets of Kelsen's legal positivism, Neumann thinks Kelsen depends on a methodological sleight of hand to resolve what continues to be a very real problem, namely, that state sovereignty and the rule of law often do conflict. Despite Kelsen's attempt to define the problem out of existence, it empirically remains the case that state actors and agencies act in opposition to constitutional and legal norms. Kelsen's division between legal science on the one side and ethics and sociology on the other obscures this problem. Although legal positivism's "rigid distinction between the is and [the] ought is a highly progressive principle" given the plethora of crude fusions of law and morality characteristic of twentieth-century law, Neumann, invoking Hegel, thinks it is still "philosophically a rather doubtful affair."[52] Specifically, we need to be able to distinguish between normatively defensible conceptions of the rule of law and their authoritarian rivals. An analysis of this problem must be at the core of any defensible legal theory. Our choice in favor of democracy and the rule of law over fascist decisionist law involves more than a set of nonuniversal private values.

In part because Kelsen denies the possibility of making this distinction as part of a pure theory of law, he underplays the significance of conflicts between law and sovereignty. If every legal order is a *Rechtsstaat,* the idea of such a conflict becomes nonsensical. For Neumann, understanding the contours of just this constellation is essential for comprehending the peculiarities of twentieth-century legal development—*and* the horrors of fascism.

Kelsen's hierarchy of norms is supreme, or sovereign, only because it is ultimately enforceable by means of the state's monopoly of coercive instruments: "by its coercive character law can be distinguished from custom and morality."[53] Kelsen's basic norm obtains because a particular set of political institutions makes sure that it does. Hence, the removal of an empirical analysis of state-based power from legal theory amounts to denying legal science the possibility of an adequate conceptualization of precisely that enigma that is most essential to the object at hand. Schmitt's concept of sovereignty sought to free *voluntas* from *ratio;* Kelsen inverts this view and seeks to drive an empirical account of the problem of *voluntas* (and concrete power relations) from the field of legal science altogether. Oddly mirroring Schmitt's formulation of the problem, Kelsen's definition of sovereignty must prove unsatisfying as well. In *Behemoth,* Neumann gives this criticism its nastiest form: despite Kelsen's worthy political aims, "by throwing out of account all relative problems of political and social power" his theory "paves the way for decisionism, for the acceptance of political decisions no matter what their content, so long as sufficient power stands behind them"; "the pure science of law has done as much as decisionism to undermine any universally acceptable value-system."[54]

For Neumann, sovereignty concerns both right and might, law and power, and *voluntas* and *ratio.* A defensible concept of state sovereignty cannot close its eyes to the fact that the rule of law is always predicated on the empirical possibility of (state-based) force, or, as Max Weber described it, "the chance of physical or psychic coercion resulting from the actions of a specialized staff of men who are directing their actions toward forcing the obedience or punishing the violation of such an order."[55] Against Schmitt, Neumann thinks we need to harness *voluntas* and figure out how one side of this dualism (state power) can, however paradoxically, be fully regulated by means of that institution (rational law) that it alone makes possible. Legal forms, like deformalized legal standards, providing excessive opportunities for unchecked exercises of state power, hence have to be eliminated from the legal order. Against Kelsen, Neumann argues that we need to take the significance for law of (sociologically ascertainable) state-based power seriously and cannot pretend that it constitutes a mere metajuridical problem. True, the resultant quest to tame "might" with "right" (or state power with rational law) may look like the infamous problem of trying to "square the circle," but in Neumann's view an honest acknowledgement of the depth of the paradox at hand is superior to either Schmitt's romanticization of unregulated sovereignty or Kelsen's seeming refusal to acknowledge the significance of the paradox at all. "The inter-relationships of legal and social phenomena cannot be contested."[56] Despite legitimate reasons for distinguishing among ethics, legal sociology, and the methods used by lawyers and judges to make sense of a particular legal norm or a set of legal documents, the division here can never be as clear-cut as Kelsen thinks: "A legal order for its own sake is unthinkable"; law is most basically "but one aspect of the order of human lives."[57] Because Kelsen's theory tears the study of law out of the broader social context from which it gains its meaning, it distorts what law is most fundamentally about. The "purity" of Kelsen's theory ends up impairing legal analysis more than aiding it.

In contrast to Schmitt's normless will and Kelsen's will-less norm, Neumann offers "normed will": he locates sovereignty in a social democratized, Rousseauian general will acting according to cogent general norms and thus, or so Neumann claims, in a normatively legitimate manner. This normed will is situated in "the totality of those . . . who exercise the highest legal power"—in the state and, most importantly, in a central legislature whose general norms effectively define the contours of judicial and administrative action.[58] For Neumann, a popularly elected legislature governed by the principle of rational legality and backed up by a coherently organized bureaucratic apparatus, like that described by Max Weber, should serve as the main site of the sovereign general will.[59] Hermann Heller outlined a similar project in his fascinating and now long forgotten *Sovereignty*. It is clear from *The Governance of the Rule of Law* both that Neumann's views about state sovereignty are shaped by Heller's and that he agrees with Heller's revealing description of elected representative institutions as constituting an institutional set-up "through which the people as a unity rules over the people as a diversity." Political rights and the principle of majority rule allow the people's general will to emerge autonomously, but for Neumann representative institutions (especially parliament) serve as a center where the unity of the democratic general will expresses itself most directly.[60]

If this view of sovereignty breaks with many of the more worrisome facets of absolutist theories, such as those of Bodin or Hobbes, it nonetheless succumbs to the classical error of describing, as in Rousseau's theory, a sovereign "body" having a number of troublesome premodern features. In Rousseau's original formulation, the popular sovereign looks too much like the royal sovereign that it is meant to replace: the "person" of the monarch is replaced by the (equally monistic) "body" of the people, which, like the monarch, is "single and unique, and cannot be divided without being destroyed."[61] Despite the fact that he or she has allegedly been beheaded, the absolute monarch has probably survived, as best evidenced by the demand (for Neumann, as for Rousseau) that legitimate government presupposes far-reaching homogeneity. After all, only if the people are made truly and perfectly "one" in a variety of ways, can they (or, more appropriately, it) look like the single body of the monarch the popular sovereign is supposed to replace. But the fact that a democratic sovereign consists of a collection of distinct persons (not a concrete person or body) is obscured by Neumann, as it was by Rousseau and so many others, and the logic of this argumentation leads Neumann (like those others),[62] to pursue the enigmatic project of trying to situate the (allegedly) monistic singular "people" (and its general will) in a set of core institutions—most importantly, in parliament.

Unfortunately, this distorts the novelty of democratic legitimacy. A modern and desubstantialized alternative will have to take the distinctiveness of the popular sovereign far more seriously than Neumann or Rousseau do.[63] Royalists like Filmer were undoubtedly on the mark in the seventeenth-century when they accused early proponents of popular government of underplaying the fact that "the people, to speak truly and properly, is a thing or body in continuall alteration and change, it never continues one minute the same, being composed of a multitude of parts, whereof divers continually decay and perish, and others renew and succeed in their places," but they were altogether wrong in thinking this to be to democracy's demerit.[64] On the contrary, democracy's chief virtue, as well as the key to understanding the nature of an identifiably democratic concept of political legitimacy, lies precisely in that its sovereign is only singular in a more abstract sense. In contrast to either seventeenth-century monarchies or twentieth-century dictatorships, the popular sovereign consists of a diversity of interacting subjects engaged in self-educative processes of political exchange and action, whose collective decisions are potentially superior to those of any single concrete (monarchical or dictatorial) sovereign and his or her clique of courtiers. In potentially mobilizing all conceivable talents and insights, democracy provides the preconditions for a genuinely rational exercise of power. Although lacking the immediate presence or substance found in the sovereignty of a monarchy or a modern dictatorship, it has something much more valuable: widespread and unrestricted popular debate and interchange, in which all voices can be heard and taken into consideration and in which the exercise of power might come to rest on a set of reasonable, broadly shared grounds and thus lose its coercive character. Any defensible conception of the unity of democracy must be formulated with these properties in mind. Its "oneness" can only refer to a shared commitment to the basic rules and procedures—central among which are those long associated with the ideal of the modern rule of law—that help the people make full use of their unique characteristics: first and foremost, their multivocality. Any attempt to give this unity a more far-reaching interpretation is likely to contradict the plurality of "the people" and thereby intimidate or silence this or that part of it, undermining exactly what makes democracy normatively superior to any competing political form. Democracy alone aspires for decisions based on universal and unfettered exchange, and although that obviously provides no guarantee that a particular law will be most appropriate to some problem at hand, democratic laws are more likely to "make sense" than those of any competing political form.[65]

Parliamentary mechanisms certainly make up an important instrument for facilitating political reflection and debate. If a system of democratic political legitimacy is to be primarily located in the broad and abstract process of popular discourse, a central parliament certainly has a key role to play in its exercise. Yet a central legislature (or even a somewhat broader set of state institutions) cannot constitute a single instance, or "point," that a (mythical) monistic people occupies or steps into in the same manner that a monarch steps into a palace or ballroom. Parliament can only be one of a number of tools of democratic politics, precisely because a sovereign as diverse and many-sided as the people engages in a far more decentralized and diffuse mode of political deliberation and action. Anything less misconstrues its nature and impairs the exercise of its capacities.

In a set of essays written between 1934 to 1944, Kirchheimer persuasively shows that a traditional and inadequately desubstantialized image of popular sovereignty, such as that posited by Neumann, has little to do with the everyday workings of contemporary politics. In some contrast to the justification of parliamentarism developed in opposition to Schmitt (discussed in chapter 3), he now focuses on the real failures of contemporary parliaments. With parliamentarism being swept away by fascism, a cautious defense no longer suffices.

Kirchheimer claims that "the emergence of solid economic blocs broke the political power of parliament as a unified and unifying institution."[66] In "Changes in the Structure of Political Compromise," he illustrates this claim by describing the unprecedented challenge posed by the financial community to parliaments in liberal democratic regimes in the twenties and thirties. In countries like France, virtual dual sovereignty emerged, as big banks outfitted with far-reaching power over the workings of the capitalist economy came to rival parliament. Although noting that government everywhere seemed by the late thirties to be getting the upper hand in relation to the financial system, Kirchheimer doubts whether recent institutional changes in the relationship between the two amount to much more than a shift in the form of the conflict. Even after the United States government began extensively regulating the banking community, "for the realities of political power, their evaluation and appreciation, we had to turn to the financial page" of the newspapers.[67] Feuds between elected legislatures and bankers are one of the more obvious manifestations of the conflict between capitalism and parliamentary democracy, and there is little reason to assume that any of the new regulatory institutions have eased this conflict satisfactorily or will succeed in guaranteeing elected bodies the supremacy in society that they claim to have. "In Quest of Sovereignty" focuses on a related set of threats to elected legislatures engendered by corporatist trends in the capitalist political economy. Concluding that increasingly the legislature's "usefulness is restricted to that of a meeting ground where diverse social groups find convenient gratuitous facilities for propaganda activities" but that it no longer has the dominant position attributed to it by constitutional doctrine, Kirchheimer analyzes the broader political implications of the emerging configuration of state-society relations, in which vaguely regulated, nonparliamentary interest- or group-centered decision making tends to take on greater political importance than what goes on in parliament itself.[68] Fascism radicalizes the tendencies plaguing contemporary liberal democracy, frontally attacking institutions like parliament, which, although still providing some indispensable opportunities for preserving a minimum of political freedom, have everywhere recklessly been allowed to decay. Political institutions in liberal democracies tend to be overrun, albeit less severely than in fascism, by an array of privileged and antagonistic blocs of organized private power as well, and a corporatist-style dispersion of political authority among decentralized interest group dominated regulatory agencies confuses political responsibility and subordinates it to organized private power and new blocs of fused private-public power. Perhaps most dramatically, other institutions have failed to fill the vacuum left by the central legislature's decline. With their "aura of disinterestedness," the courts seemed the best possible candidate for this vacancy, but the imperatives of judicial decision making make them poorly suited to it. The judiciary "would have had to exercise constant vigilance and quickly render orders sufficiently generalized to cover comprehensive areas of dispute, instead of narrowly constructed specific rules," like those necessarily emerging in the judicial process.[69] The case-oriented structure of judicial decision making makes the courtroom a poor source of consistent and predictable (generalized) standards like those provided by parliament in an earlier and simpler era. Thus, "is there no supreme body which may take the place of parliaments . . . as the final authority of last resort? Has no procedure developed to alleviate and control the constant pressure and counterpressures exercised by the different organizations, public and private alike, to anticipate the repercussions of each individual action and thus to balance them?"[70]

Kirchheimer interprets Schmitt's decisionist conception of sovereignty as both embodying crucial features of this crisis and offering an irresponsible response to it. *Political Theology* implicitly recognized that the "permanent subject" of a democratic, parliament-centered conception of sovereignty was disintegrating. With the demise of democratic regimes throughout Europe fresh in mind, Kirchheimer argues that both the electorate and elected representative bodies increasingly consist of an assortment of profoundly antagonistic social groups incapable of finding a shared basis for common action. In striking correspondence to this state of affairs, Schmitt's theory gave "up the hope of finding a permanent subject of sovereignty that would be intent on, and capable of, balancing the interests and volitions of different groups and factions." Of course, the disintegration of democracy's social base (or permanent subject) in itself constitutes no reason for abandoning the democratic project. A true democrat should conceive how social antagonisms are to be lessened so that a stable, norm-guided political entity could reemerge and a workable form of parliamentary democracy could be recaptured. Although correctly identifying a crisis of the permanent subject of democratic politics, Schmitt chose to attribute "sovereignty to those persons or groups that would prove able to exercise political domination under extraordinary circumstances." Where social and political life is genuinely unstable, the command of "extraordinary circumstances" (the political crisis or emergency) truly becomes all-important. During such a moment, the most powerful social and political interests may be "compelled to resort to building a machine of violence that would enable them to suppress 'undesirable' groups" if they are to maintain their hegemonic status.[71]

Schmitt responded to the disintegration of democracy's social base and the concomitant decline of institutions essential to it (such as parliament) by transforming the emergency into the centerpiece of political theory. Only a dictatorial regime making the emergency omnipresent could guarantee the elimination of "undesirable groups," like left-wing parties and labor unions, that had come to pose a real threat to the status of hegemonic social and political groups. A theoretical accompaniment to authoritarian practice, Schmitt's seemingly abstract definition of sovereignty is counterrevolutionary right to its core. Because it matched the political needs of privileged strata, for whom "*norm*-al" parliamentary politics no longer provided a secure enough guarantee for their privileged status, it was able to become a centerpiece of fascist thinking.

Despite Kirchheimer's persuasive diagnosis of a "crisis of sovereignty," his cure—unlike Schmitt's, which he rightly attacks—is tentative and undeveloped. He apparently hopes to reestablish what he repeatedly, yet vaguely, describes as a "final authority of last resort," or some "supreme body," but in any case some stable democratic institution capable of "*norm*-alizing" politics in an (exceptional) crisis-ridden era.[72] Like Neumann, Kirchheimer thinks capitalist-based social antagonisms offer the main hindrance to this project and notes that the "permanent coordination" that a sovereign should be able to accomplish presupposes a "compatibility of diverse group claims" unlike that found in contemporary capitalism. In other words: no democratic socialism, no state sovereignty.[73]

But Kirchheimer does not give us much more to go on. What is this sovereign "final authority" or "supreme body" supposed to look like? Is not his interest in recapturing some supreme institutional instance reminiscent of Neumann's problematic attempt to reestablish a (concretistically conceived) general will and a single site for it in a central parliament or at least in some set of central state institutions? As I suggested above, that is an inappropriate image for a system of democratic legitimacy. Democracy consists of interacting subjects and has a "permanent subject" in only a very limited and formal sense. Or are we to interpret Kirchheimer's hesitancy to point to an alternative concept of sovereignty as evidence of his relative theoretical and political sophistication and as a sign that he, unlike Neumann, realizes that traditional conceptions of state sovereignty can have little to do with the imperatives of modern democratic politics? He certainly seems to lack Neumann's theoretical self-assuredness. Does that suggest that Kirchheimer wants to avoid Neumann's mistakes?[74]

It seems to me that Kirchheimer provides us with no satisfying answer to these queries. Yet he may have something else to tell us. If only indirectly, his analysis shows that the demise of traditional state sovereignty not only provides potential opportunities for broadening the democratic project—we may finally be free from the deadening "body" of the absolute monarch that continues to haunt discussions of "sovereignty"—but points to a number of real dangers as well. The institutional core of many conventional views of state sovereignty—centrally, parliament—could disintegrate, but so would democracy.

"In Quest of Sovereignty" 's most disquieting thesis is that in a political and social world subjugated to bewildering blocs of ineffectively regulated, organized private interests and corporatist-style bargaining units, and where the party system tends to model itself on the consumer marketplace, "the people" can only govern itself rather ineffectively. Ours is by no means the perfectly administered or monolithically one-dimensional universe described so ominously by Kirchheimer's Frankfurt colleagues. But it does look disturbingly similar to the apologetic models of democracy developed by authors like Schumpeter, who fashion democratic politics on the purported consumer sovereignty of the capitalist market: just as consumer choice supposedly helps assure the supremacy of the consumer in economic affairs, the fact that voters have some choice among competing elites guarantees an adequate degree of popular sovereignty.[75] Kirchheimer appreciates both the economistic assumptions and the apparent empirical accuracy of this view, but he does so only in order to highlight the sad state of contemporary democracy. Consumer sovereignty is more fiction than fact in an economy in which consumer behavior is largely preprogrammed by corporate giants and massive advertising firms; by the same token, the political activity of the electorate today is profoundly undermined by "the great estates" of corporatist-style politics and its mammoth fusions of public/private power.[76] A few years earlier, he noted that "free elections not only require an absence of physical constraint and liberty to cast one's ballot as one pleases, but also the absence of those pressures, which, while not preventing the voter from casting his ballot, yet prey on his mind so vigorously and unremittingly that he finds himself totally unable to form anything like an opinion on the issues at stake. The history of the struggle for complete freedom of election is, properly speaking, the history of the progress and the failures of democracy itself."[77] "In Quest of Sovereignty" claims that the contemporary welfare state fails to live up to these aspirations. Relegated to the shadows of organized capitalism's "great estates," voters' "utterances lack the elements of precision, understanding, and resolution which alone would enable them to become volitional determinants" in the political system.[78] Complex and decentered modes of policy making replace the concrete, substantial state-centered sovereign described in much of modern political thought, but this facilitates a refeudalization of political decision making and a trivialization of political discourse rather than an expansion of possibilities for political freedom. By no means have the death of state sovereignty and the decline of elected central legislatures ushered in the stateless utopia pictured by critics of sovereignty, such as Harold Laski.

The empirical validity of this picture cannot be adequately evaluated here. But if accurate, it would suggest that organized capitalism's "great estates"—massive corporations whose functions are in fact public, bargaining set-ups in which the state-society distinction has clearly lost any significance, the poorly regulated bureaucracies directing some aspect of social existence—threaten an even more suitable and desubstantialized conceptualization of democratic politics than either Neumann or Kirchheimer ever succeed in articulating. In such a setting, the "sovereignty" of abstract, nonlocalizable processes of political exchange and action would inevitably be hemmed in, constrained, and constantly on the defensive. Contra Kirchheimer, the problem with neofeudal "great estates" would not be their incompatibility with the institutionalization of some final or supreme, state institution but their more insidious threat to a less concretistic version of democracy. Unfortunate enough to be excluded from the worlds of private privilege or bureaucratic power, many voices would be silenced. Others might succeed in shouting their views through the chinks of an increasingly impermeable political wall, but by the time they made their way to the other side, they would sound like faint whispers.

The absolutist sovereign would have been eliminated from the political universe, but his opponent, the revolutionary people, would have been killed off as well. The democratic revolution would have devoured its children.

IV

Toward the Democratic Rule of Law

7

A Democratic Concept of the Political

Franz Neumann's final writings constitute an impressive attempt at overcoming the democratic-theoretical deficits of the early Frankfurt school. During the thirties and forties, Neumann and Kirchheimer surely went further than their colleagues at the Institute for Social Research toward formulating a defensible vision of democracy, but even their ideas about democratic politics during this period were hardly flawless. Indeed, the limits of their democratic theory too often contributed to the inadequacies of otherwise creative contributions to an alternative view of the rule of law. In previous chapters, I have suggested how we might begin to compensate for those deficits. Here we need to examine how the elder Neumann himself ambitiously tackles the issue of democratic politics during the late forties and early fifties. Chapter 8 focuses on Otto Kirchheimer's complementary analysis of the legal institutions of the postwar democratic welfare state.

Neumann's "concept of political freedom"—the centerpiece of his postwar theorizing and the central theme of this chapter—is explicitly intended as a democratic antidote to Carl Schmitt's "concept of the political." Our inquiry thus comes full circle. We began with a discussion of the influence of Schmitt's fascistic concept of the political on the early Frankfurt school. We can conclude with a critical analysis of the school's most sophisticated attempt at developing a democratic alternative to Schmitt, as well as its implications for the unfinished project of reconstructing the rule of law.

1 The Concept of Political Freedom

Before his premature death in 1954, Neumann had begun work on what he hoped would be a comprehensive study of the problem of political dictatorship. Two portions of it, published posthumously in *The Democratic and Authoritarian State* as "Anxiety and Politics" and "Notes on The Theory of Dictatorship," reveal something else as well: even at this late juncture, Neumann remains intent on developing a critique of the political and legal theory of Carl Schmitt. Long unappreciated is that Neumann's more ambitious theoretical essays from the early fifties constitute an "anti-Schmitt" of sorts. Conceivably, his unfinished work on dictatorship was meant to serve as a final intellectual blow against modern dictatorship's most sophisticated theoretician.[1]

Or so those surviving remnants of the text suggest. Inspired by Montesquieu's famous typology of regime, Neumann argues in the final pages of "Notes on Dictatorship" that dictatorship has a "spirit" or "energetic principle" all its own, namely that of fear or anxiety. Irrational fear "appears in all caesaristic and totalitarian movements" and is actively exploited by those who hold power there and essential to their success in guaranteeing the obedience of those over whom they rule.[2] "Anxiety and Politics," where Montesquieu's view is buttressed by means of Freudian social psychology, gives this claim a sturdier basis in contemporary social science. Neumann accepts the dramatic thesis of *Civilization and Its Discontents* that anxiety is an inevitable consequence of the process of social and cultural development, but he insists that Freud ignores the crucial political problem at stake: the degree to which anxiety varies according to the dictates of the broader political and social setting.[3] The argument of *Civilization and Its Discontents* is too clumsy, and Neumann thinks we need to distinguish clearly between anxiety's potentially beneficial forms (that warn us of real dangers and help protect us from them) and its destructive, neurotic, and persecutory variants; the latter is what Montesquieu had in mind when describing the dependence of political despotism on fear.[4] Although warning us that we need to avoid an implicitly antidemocratic interpretation of mass politics that exaggerates its nonrational components, Neumann accepts Freud's view that much of popular politics can be explained in terms of libidinal energy. Like Freud, he argues that aim-inhibited libidinal energy offers a cement that facilitates uncritical and potentially catastrophic psychological identifications of political groups with their leaders. Unlike Freud, Neumann complements his modest psychological considerations with a number of careful historical observations. First, on the basis of a survey of mass-based movements extending from sixteenth-century radical Protestantism to the Ku Klux Klan, he concludes that even the most irrational and aggressive forms of persecutory anxiety possess some minimal basis in everyday political and social experience. Psychological and political crises are interrelated. At the basis of even the most vicious manifestation of irrational fear, one can identify a concrete reason (for example, war, poverty, or the fact that a dominant social class suddenly loses its hegemonic status) why it suddenly overwhelms particular social groups. Second, Neumann describes how popular authoritarianism relies on conspiracy theories and the vision of a "devilish" and allegedly almighty "enemy": "Just as the masses hope for their deliverance from distress through absolute oneness with a person, so they ascribe their distress to certain persons, who have brought this distress into the world through a conspiracy."[5] Indeed, "wherever affective (i.e., Caesaristic) leader-identifications occur in politics, masses and leaders have this view of history: that the distress which has befallen the masses has been brought about exclusively by a conspiracy of certain persons or groups against the people."[6] Affective Caesarism personalizes complex historical and social processes. Mechanisms of psychological identification turn out to be matched by an equally striking ego differentiation in relation to a movement's (alleged) opponents. The latter is as crucial to mass politics as the former. How else are otherwise diverse, conflict-ridden movements to be integrated "despite all cleavages of class, party, religion"? According to Neumann, often this is only possible "through hatred of an enemy."[7]

From our perspective, the significant facet of this all is tucked away in a seemingly obscure footnote: Neumann tells us that Carl Schmitt's *Concept of the Political* "made a general theory" out of the troubling psychological processes that he has tried to describe "instead of limiting it to regressive mass movements."[8] Schmitt's existential friend/foe conceptualization of politics, his emphasis on the criteria of hostility and its intensity, as well as his description of how the foe is pictured in terms of an inhumane and fiendish Other who must be extirpated, is an accurate recapitulation of how anxiety is mobilized and regenerated by mass-based authoritarianism, but it is hardly the universally applicable model of politics that Schmitt claims. The fact that Schmittian theory seems so realistic to some probably expresses the sorry status of our anxiety-ridden epoch and the fact that it is "susceptible to the growth of regressive mass movements."[9] Even "with the end of the second World War anxiety has not disappeared from the world. On the contrary, it has become even greater and more frightful."[10]

"If the concept 'enemy' and 'fear' do constitute the 'energetic principles' of politics, a democratic political system is impossible."[11] Democracy has no future if Schmitt's concept of the political has the universal quality he attributes to it. Irrational anxiety paralyzes the political actor, making him or her incapable of acting with any political efficacy. Democracy is doomed if the masses are seized by unjustified persecutory fear. It is thus incumbent on us not only that we debunk Schmitt's theory, as Neumann thinks that his writings have helped do, but that we develop a positive and proudly democratic antidote to it: the left-wing anti-Schmittian "political sociology of the exception" offered by Kirchheimer and Neumann has to be sustained by a complementary normative theory of democracy. Neumann therefore counters Schmitt's concept of the political with his own concept of political freedom. Just as "fear of an enemy" is the "energetic principle" of fascist authoritarianism, the author notes in the pivotal "Concept of Political Freedom," so does democracy have its own "integrating element" in the principle of political freedom.[12] In Neumann's view, the experience of freedom remains the best insurance against anxiety. Democracy is the only political form that makes autonomy its telos, and it "is not simply a political system like any other; its essence consists in the execution of large-scale social changes maximizing the freedom of man."[13] Only democracy holds out the promise of personal and collective "self-reliance," and only it can hope to succeed in undermining the irrational fear that Schmitt implicitly makes the centerpiece of his deceptively abstract view of politics and which his fascist allies managed to manipulate with such disastrous consequences in our century. If in the postwar era fear "has begun to paralyze nations and to make men incapable of free decisions," a broadening of the democratic project alone can help us counteract this worrisome trend.[14] Only then can we completely rob Schmitt's theory of any empirical correlates it still possesses in the everyday political universe.

Because Neumann is implicitly self-critical of many of the least defensible facets of his own previous theorizing, "the concept of political freedom" makes up the theoretical core of his postwar intellectual project, and even where not directly thematized it is nonetheless presupposed or at least hinted at. Its three-tiered, Hegelian structure, in which each separate moment ("juridical," "cognitive," and "volitional") is thought indispensable yet ultimately inadequate for what follows it, is likely more than coincidental. At times strikingly reminiscent of the mature Hegel, Neumann self-consciously undertakes to develop an identifiably modern conception of politics and, in the process, distances himself, like the elder Hegel, from modern authors whose break with the ancients remains incomplete. Most significantly, Neumann's reading of Rousseau becomes both more subtle and more appropriately critical: although remaining an inspiration to democratic theory, Rousseau relies on an antipluralistic and authoritarian idea of the full "identity of ruled and rulers" and "complete social and moral homogeneity." Like the political theorists of classical antiquity, he misses the virtues of the modern differentiation between "man" and "citizen," religion and politics, state and society, morality and legality, all of which can be minimally interpreted as taking "into account the fact that the conditions under which such (perfect moral or social) identification can be achieved have never been realized in history." Moreover, the impossibility of perfect homogeneity should not be seen as a tragic loss but as a belated acknowledgement of the romanticized and ideological picture of the Greek polis that continues to haunt us: "every society is charged with antagonisms. Even the most democratic system needs safeguards against the abuse of power."[15]

In striking contrast to Schmitt's concept of the political, Neumann's democratic response begins with an appreciative analysis of juridical freedom—in other words, the rule of law. Juridical freedom (basic rights, an independent judiciary, general law) makes governmental action predictable and helps provide a measure of legal security. The freedom embodied in the liberal formula of "individual versus the state" is not to be interpreted as antipolitical in the manner of Schmitt but as an inestimably valuable presupposition of a genuinely autonomous process of democratic will formation. Yet it is also more. Neumann repeats his thesis that the central dilemma of modern political thought is best described in terms of the dichotomy of sovereignty and law: the modern state makes “right” (rational law) possible but paradoxically relies on “might” (the state’s disciplinary apparatus) to do so.[16] The state apparatus alone can provide the presuppositions of political and social autonomy, yet its historically unparalleled accumulation of coercive instruments represents a constant threat to freedom. A defensible answer to this paradox for Neumann involves subduing might (state power) with right (a system of democratic legality). Because “the two aspects may harmonize in some historical situations . . . for some groups in society and not for others,” a critical theory of society seeks to determine what conditions prevent this harmony from being realized.[17] As we recall, Neumann’s own solution to the riddle relied on a number of enigmatic ideas unsuited to a desubstantialized modern conception of democratic politics; nonetheless, his argument here may not presuppose the more troublesome facets of the vision of state sovereignty that I criticized in chapter 6. Even if we rightly find Neumann’s own image of state sovereignty unsatisfying, it still would be mistaken to pretend that the basic paradox of the modern political situation—namely, the fact that normatively legitimate law always presupposes the possibility of state-based coercion—can ever be fully transcended, or to obscure the significance of either side of the paradox, as Neumann suggested that both Schmitt and Kelsen, though in different ways, had. Just as decisionism demonstrates the disastrousness of eliminating normative concerns about political legitimacy (or “right”) from politics, in the same vein it would be fatal to ignore the difficulties posed by the modern state and its monopoly on coercion. Some version of an identifiably modern state apparatus controlling the exercise of coercion remains a civilizational achievement worth defending; that, at least, was the basic and highly provocative argument of *Behemoth*.[18]

Because of the protections it provides against the perils of state authority, juridical freedom makes up the most direct institutional embodiment of the modern political predicament. As a result, “it is *the* element of the concept of freedom that we can never give up.”[19] If political alienation poses a threat to democracy by preparing the way for demagogues talented at exploiting political cynicism, it is equally the case that possibilities for individuals to distance or alienate themselves from a particular political community and its state apparatus also have real advantages in an epoch in which not only is "the fact of pluralism" so obvious but the state is outfitted with far-reaching manipulative instruments. There is nothing intrinsically conservative about accepting the value of basic legal and constitutional constraints on state authority. For Neumann, the truly conservative view is the opposing one. In pretending that we can do without minimal legal protections, either we implicitly ignore those features of the basic problematic of modern politics posed by the necessity of state-based coercion, or we forget that perfect political homogeneity cannot be realized today. Particularly given widespread heterogeneity, legal protections for political minorities remain a presupposition of every genuinely liberal polity.

Much of this basic argument should be familiar by now. More innovative is Neumann's sudden stress in his postwar writings on the limits and potential illusions of legalistic modes of thought and practice.

Neumann now underscores the idea that democratic politics is always more than legalism and that political freedom cannot be secured by legal security (or basic legal protections) alone. Juridical freedom is inadequate. Although it is part of the quest to realize a democratic society, it remains a mere presupposition of it and manifestly needs to be "superseded" by other features of the concept of political freedom. Insofar as defensive variants of liberalism too often succumb to an uncritical faith in constitutionalism and the rule of law, they reduce the concept of political freedom to its most limited component; although in a very different way than Schmitt suggested, such variants may turn out to be "unpolitical" ideologies. In "Economics and Politics in the Twentieth Century," Neumann rather surprisingly concedes that democracy's authoritarian critics at times rightly point to the limits of "negative" legal security and juristic freedom; but they, like Schmitt, then irresponsibly jettison it for alternatives that abandon the modern project of universalizing political freedom. A convincing, critical democratic alternative pursues a different path. It seeks to avoid the errors of a crude legalism, such as that so effectively mocked and exploited by fascism and bolshevism. There is more to politics than law, and democratic politics hardly exhausts itself in the principle of the rule of law.[20] Specifically, even in a democracy there are good reasons for accepting some version of a right to political disobedience. Democracy's claim to having made such a right anachronistic—through its institutionalization of peaceful mechanisms that guarantee freedom for political minorities and possibilities for them to become majorities—often reflects more a normative aspiration than empirical reality: "Whether or not a democracy really protects minority views is open to judgment. Different views may be held in regard to each and every one of the various types of democracy."[21] Even nominally democratic laws sometimes need to be disobeyed, and illegal action can be normatively legitimate. One reason for this is that the political sphere inevitably forces us to confront new and unparalleled challenges and thus requires action by political agents willing to take on these tasks in correspondingly unparalleled and unorthodox ways. Yet the legal order, too, often drags behind new demands placed on political actors. A naive faith in the legal status quo—Neumann has the legal demise of democracies in mid-century Europe in mind—can prove catastrophic, can even "endanger democracy itself."[22] "Naturally conservative," every legal order obviously embodies the political achievements of past struggles and previous generations. Even though a democratic system best minimizes the consequences of this natural conservatism, we can never be sure they have been altogether vanquished, and every genuinely democratic view of politics would do well to recognize this. Despite the legal order's obstinate character, "no system, even the most conservative one (in the literal meaning of the term) can merely persevere; even to persevere it must change."[23]

Carl Schmitt would probably have argued that this simply demonstrates the limitations of universalistic legal normativities. For obvious reasons, Neumann is intent on showing that this is not what he has in mind. An appreciation of the limits of the rule of law does not doom us to the irrationalism of political existentialism. On the contrary, the limitations of liberal legalism purportedly should lead to an acknowledgment of the superiority of an extremely rationalistic, cognitive element in the concept of political freedom. If the political sphere can never be rendered as calculable or predictable as legalists suggest, and if it always demands of political actors that they act in new and unexpected ways, then the questions "what do we want to use this freedom for?" and "what is supposed to be the substance of our freedom?" suddenly take on special significance. Even more fundamentally, "how can man determine himself, how can he unfold his possibilities, when he does not know himself?"[24] Only a self-reflective subject can hope to be adept at risk taking in a complicated political universe. On the level of macropolitics, democracy similarly has a central goal "taking account of the increase of knowledge, and rationally changing society to keep up with knowledge."[25] The Socratic quest for self-knowledge (more precisely, knowledge of human nature, external nature, and social and historical development) is fundamental to the project of political freedom. Freudian social psychology, which offers a way "of understanding human action in order to enable man to act freely," is an example of the first form of this self-knowledge; knowledge of external nature demystifies its workings and helps allow us to live fearlessly in the natural world; finally, an "understanding of the historical progress" (or "insight into historical necessity," in the more blatantly Hegelian terminology Neumann sometimes employs) should sensitize us to the concrete possibilities for expanding freedom in a particular political situation.[26] Freedom may mean one thing in one epoch and something else in another, and there are objective restraints at every stage of social development on the possibilities for realizing autonomy. An efficacious citizen must grapple with the practical problems posed by the fact, as Marx knew, that individuals "make their history but not under the conditions which they choose." In Neumann's view, this need not imply, as it did in traditional Marxism, a call to subordinate political action to a deterministic and fatalistic philosophy of history.

Sometimes Neumann gives the idea of cognitive freedom a limited gloss and seems intent merely on postulating that scientific freedom and probably an adequate level of formal education are essential to self-reflexive political praxis.[27] But in at least one text—a fascinating December 1952 lecture, delivered for a Berlin radio station as part of a lecture series that included contributions from Theodor Adorno, Hannah Arendt, Paul Tillich, and Ernst Fraenkel—he probably goes beyond this by explicitly allying himself with a set of thinkers (including Jefferson and Mill) for whom democracy is seen as best able to realize a mode of practical deliberative "truth seeking" and to guarantee a reasonable exercise of state authority: democracy's superiority stems from the fact that it best institutionalizes the idea that "truth emerges only through the competition of opinions, and thus that a minority position not only must be tolerated but that the minority position belongs constitutively to the concept of right political action" (insofar as it may prove to be a more accurate or correct view than the majority opinion). Democracy, like no competing political form, makes the ideal of rational discussion its core.[28] Interestingly, Neumann argues that Weber's view of science needs to be reconstructed with this in mind. Weber was absolutely right to insist that the scientific process must be clearly delineated from the everyday political and ideological tug-of-war and from a conception of the university that reduces it to a center for political education or agit-prop, but he was wrong to ground this view in a problematic value skepticism and not to see that it is tied to the fact that democracy itself rests in a belief in unhindered rational discourse and the supremacy of convictions deriving from reasonable debate. The scientific process needs to be as open as possible, in part because such a view of science corresponds to democracy's interest in truth seeking.[29] Just as "the truth of political theory is political freedom," so, too, does political freedom rely on the capacity for an effective use of practical rationality (or truth seeking).[30] Democracy is to be defined as that political form alone capable of making the exercise of state-based "might" rational, thereby making it "right" or legitimate.

Characteristically, Neumann is less interested in sketching out the philosophical complexities of this idea than in examining its immediate political implications. What most concerns him is the fact that "rational discussion presupposes the existence of an informed public opinion," which is unlikely to emerge today given the complexity and impermeability of governmental activity, the increased scope of public and private bureaucratic decision making, massive concentrations of capitalist economic power, the stupefying character of everyday workplace activity, as well as an evident "hardening of parties into machines which . . . tend to exclude newcomers from the political market."[31] Part of a much broader and alarming "crisis in political freedom," contemporary democracy's cognitive moment is threatened daily by a frightening array of trends, and Neumann supplements his typically Marxist concern about the tensions between capitalism and democracy with a set of Weberian observations about the problems posed for the democratic process by complex bureaucratic organizations.[32] In his view, a critical democratic theory has the task of scrutinizing impediments to deliberative democratic will formation and determining whether they can be undermined or eliminated. By this it hopes to show how democracy can realize its normative superiority and realize truly reasonable and universally justifiable policies.

Neumann then fleshes out some of the details of this ambitious agenda in "Approaches to the Study of Political Power," where he postulates a conception of political power, akin to that rightly criticized by Hannah Arendt, defining it as "the control of other men for the purpose of influencing the behavior of the state."[33] Yet unlike Arendt, who persuasively argues that too much of modern political theory thereby reduces power to coercion and excludes a priori the possibility of alternative forms of reciprocal and mutually enabling political action, he does not criticize the definition itself but merely comments that politics is more than power, that political action involves more than "an indifferent repetition of the endless struggle of 'in groups' versus 'out groups,' " and that the ordinary person is rightly repelled by such views of politics and correctly demands that we differentiate democratic politics "from the sale of soap."[34] Specifically, "politics is certainly the conflict between power groups. . . . But one group may, in its struggle for power, represent more than a particular interest; it may represent the idea of freedom, the idea crucial to political theory. . . . [It] transcends its particular interests and advocates (in Hegelian terms) universal interests."[35] But even that is still too simplistic, because "who can say today, and how do we know, what progress and regression" is or which groups represent particular or general interests?[36] Neumann goes on to identify a deeper problem: in a democracy, every competing interest must claim to represent general or universal interests, and politics in the democratic era thus becomes more propagandistic and "ideological than in any previous period in history."[37] Yet there are counteracting tendencies as well. Although "Marxists usually overlook" this, insofar as each political constituency today claims a universal character, political decision making tends in fact to become more general or democratic in its results. Despite the flourishing of propaganda, "the very need to appeal to social groups larger than the immediate interest group compels adjustment of various interests."[38] Whether or not a particular political group or agenda is progressive can only be empirically proven today.[39] The democratic process provides a peaceful mechanism whereby competing power groups, at least hypothetically, are given a chance to try out their ideas empirically. In an epoch when no single group can claim to represent universal interests, democracy gives us the best opportunity for determining which policies actually extend freedom.

"[L]aw limits political power; knowledge shows us the way to freedom; but man can actually attain freedom only through his own efforts. Neither God nor history grants freedom to him."[40] The concept of political freedom includes a final "volitional" element based on juristic and cognitive freedom yet superceding them. Legalism is "naturally conservative," and constitutionalism provides no guarantee that individuals will enlarge the sphere of political and social autonomy. However valuable, knowledge and political competence do not themselves generate freedom. A particular situation "may present magnificent opportunities for freedom, but they may be missed if one does not act or fails to act adequately."[41] Even though authoritarian regimes have been known to take relatively predictable constitutional forms and sometimes even provide a surprising amount of room for scientific and intellectual autonomy, they cannot institutionalize "active participation"—defined by Neumann here, following Aristotle, as the possession of an equal share in the "deliberative and judicial functions" of rule.[42] Only democracy realizes all facets of political freedom by making "active participation" truly extensive. Just as volitional freedom represents the height of the concept of freedom, so, too, does the only political form capable of fully realizing volitional freedom constitute humanity's greatest, and thus far incompletely realized, political achievement.

Neumann's definition of volitional freedom is extremely revealing: it suggests that he senses that his sharp delineation between cognitive and volitional freedom is of limited value, which explains Neumann's otherwise peculiar comment at the outset of "The Concept of Political Freedom" that its three distinct moments should be reintegrated in the future, now that he has artificially "dissected" them.[43] If deliberation belongs to the core of action, what is the fundamental difference between cognitive and volitional freedom? Why privilege the latter, as Neumann's insistence on the supremacy of volitional freedom (or active participation) implies here? Most "activist" facets of politics cannot be neatly distinguished from their cognitive features. Giving a speech at a demonstration, conversing with those who look on, and writing a letter to the editor of a political journal are clearly as much cognitive as volitional activities.

The ambiguity in Neumann's argument has two probable sources. As already noted, at times he gives the idea of cognitive freedom a rather narrow significance—as referring to little more than the activities of intellectual experts and scientists. In spite of his struggle to break with a view of it that belittles the rational truth seeking that goes on in practical, everyday political activities and deliberation in favor of the organized cognitive pursuits of scientists and experts, something of the more narrow view surely haunts "The Concept of Political Freedom." Consequently, it makes sense that its limits be emphasized: as Neumann perceives, there clearly is more to democratic active participation than expert discourse. Like Aristotle, Neumann rightly appreciates that the core of a defensible vision of political action has to include some conception of political deliberation. Nonetheless, his continuing fascination with the image of an undivided, sovereign "final instance" or "point," like that described and criticized in chapter 6, at the same time reinforces the unfortunate tendency to separate cognitive and volitional moments, by encouraging him to stress, as he does in a number of postwar essays, the importance for politics of the (oftentimes violent, nondeliberative) "struggle for the control of the coercive organizations, for police, justice, army, bureaucracy, and foreign policy" and thus the supremacy of a volitional "politics of the will," in contrast to cognitive, deliberative political activities.[44] Of course, the fact that much of the empirical reality of contemporary politics better suits this image than one making deliberation or rational discourse its core only refurbishes this problematic move.

Like Schmitt's existentialist concept of the political, Neumann's antidote places the problem of the political "will" in the foreground. Yet it would be a mistake to ignore the profound differences separating Schmitt's monological, unfettered fascist will, acting according to "a pure decision not based on reason and discussion and not justifying itself" from Neumann's alternative democratic will.[45] Neumann protests against Schmitt's view that a normatively unregulated decision always precedes a norm, and he tells us that in a democracy the "decision emerges through discussion."[46] His democratic will finds itself among others of equal stature. He reminds us that one reason why it, unlike Schmitt's, needs to be restrained by the rule of law is that juridical freedom incorporates a recognition of the pluralistic structure of modern politics. The democratic will is dialogical:[47]

> To stress merely the volitional aspect of freedom creates as dangerous a situation as does exclusive concentration on the juristic or cognitive aspect. To define political freedom simply as individual will implies the negation of the obligations which we have toward our fellow man: one cannot assert one's will at the expense of another, nor attain one's own perfection by destroying another's. The protection of minorities and of dissenting opinions is ruled out if the activist element alone is deemed the equivalent of freedom. The juristic element, therefore cannot be dispensed with.[48]

In a similar fashion, freedom's cognitive element helps protect us from the temptations of a political adventurism, represented most clearly by the anti-intellectual putschism romanticized by fascism. Nonreflective, normless action is pseudofreedom, generating political disasters and self-destruction.[49] The realization of freedom—in a world consisting of a plurality of individuals as well as a broader set of objective natural and historical restraints on freedom that need to be freshly ascertained at every moment when political creativity is called for—is not at the disposal of any particular individual will, let alone an unthinking one. This is also why political activity unmediated by cognitive freedom is not an end in itself. Direct forms of decision making may or may not be appropriate instruments for expanding political autonomy and making political authority rational: the "instrumentalities of direct democracy, like initiative, referendum, plebiscite, and recall, may or may not serve as correctives to representative government."[50]

A genuinely democratic community obviously relies on choices or decisions, but in contrast to Schmitt's existentialist normless will, the ideal democratic will is reflective and self-restraining. Democracy aspires to establish a community where collective decision making is based on reflective, self-restraining action—not because it has some hidden bias for philosophical rationalism or the mores of the bourgeois "discussing classes," but because it acknowledges that only a political will of this type can make the fullest use of its capacities and resources. Self-restraint is not the same thing as weakness; discursiveness is not equivalent to indecisiveness. The "boundlessness" of dictatorial politics is false and deceptive; in reality, it is less authoritative than the voluntary restrictions and self-binding, responsible power of democracy—notwithstanding Carl Schmitt's views to the contrary.[51]

2 Neumann's Unfinished Critical Theory

Neumann never had a chance to complete his anti-Schmittian democratic concept of the political. A fatal auto accident outside Geneva in 1954 put an end to his plans to pursue a reconstructed democratic theory synthesizing political liberalism's critical elements (and authors like Mill and Jefferson) with the subtle neo-Marxism of the Frankfurt school. Indeed, his "concept of political freedom" is far too incomplete. Neumann innovatively argues that a democratic vision of politics must grapple with the interrelationships among practical truth seeking, rationality, and the democratic process. But his model of a deliberative democracy remains institutionally unfinished and its normative grounding too simple. Provocatively, his analysis repeatedly insists on the need to distinguish between self-binding (or self-regulating) political power and limited (anti-interventionist) government, between the need for a self-restraining activist and interventionist state and an archaic constitutionalism obsessed with fencing in political power but oblivious to all the real advantages of state action in a world overwhelmed by capitalist-based inequalities. Yet the implications of this insight are never fully sketched out. In invoking thinkers like Jefferson and Mill, Neumann points the way to a vision of politics less obsessed with the problem of state sovereignty and more in tune with the dictates of modern pluralism. Unfortunately, he never fully abandons his problematic belief in the image of a sovereign final "point," or "instance."

This is not to say that we should join the chorus of commentators (including Martin Jay and H. Stuart Hughes) who see Neumann's postwar writings as evidence of a tendency to abandon a genuinely critical theoretical agenda.[52] The elder Neumann does stand, as Hughes perceptively notes, "between Marxism and Liberalism" at this juncture, but he does so much more innovatively than Hughes and others claim. This may not be the "labor metaphysics" of nineteenth-century Marxism (C. W. Mills), but neither is it a conventional mode of political liberalism. Neumann rightly becomes skeptical of Marxist views about the primacy of the economic base for social analysis (going so far as to refer to "the Procrustean bed of Marxian theory"), but he simultaneously insists on the dangers of the "fashionable" tendency "to reject Marxism root and branch" and deny oneself "a clear understanding of the relationship between economic power and political power."[53] Although interested in a wide range of phenomena whose meaning was necessarily obscured by classical Marxism (such as the problems posed by bureaucratic complexity for democracy), he continues to make the tension between political democracy and capitalism a centerpiece of his analysis. The real difference is that Neumann now sees more clearly than ever before that a Marxist-inspired critique of capitalism cannot provide us with a suitable political vision. However incompletely, the elder Neumann points the way to a new and still very much undeveloped critical theory of democracy. Notwithstanding Jay's description of the elder Neumann as an uneasy liberal or Rainer Erd's emphasis on the "resignative" moments in Neumann's thinking, there is little on the programmatic level here that is inherently defensive about his democratic concept of the political.[54] In fact, Neumann explicitly criticizes a rich tradition of "uneasy liberal" constitutionalism, inspired by Montesquieu, which he sees as having abandoned the project of subduing state-based "might" with "right" in favor of simply thwarting the meanest possible consequences of the modern leviathan, and again and again he unfavorably contrasts such ideas to his own outspoken and aggressive attempts at "squaring the circle" of state power and freedom.[55] Could not contemporary democratic theorizing do worse than develop at least some of Neumann's insights more completely? Do we not need to develop a richer conception of self-binding or self-regulating state authority? Might we not build on Neumann's link between cognitive and volitional freedom? And in contrast to the genuinely defensive views that continue to dominate democratic theory, might we not begin to develop an alternative model, appreciative of the significance of political deliberation?

One flaw in Neumann's thesis is of outstanding significance for the purposes of our study. In my exegesis above, I glossed over the more worrisome features of the author's revised interpretation of the rule of law. It is so important to our broader project that it is best to deal with it separately.

Neumann's demonstration of the limited quality of juridical freedom seems, at a first glance, unobtrusive enough. Surely, democratic politics needs legal restraints but it does not exhaust itself in constitutionalism. Autonomous political action presupposes the rule of law, yet it also requires risk taking and imaginative political action that challenges the boundaries of codified law. Neumann's argument includes a second and more worrisome facet as well. Here, as previously, his model of the rule of law is rather traditional. The generality of the legal norm—that it is "a rule which does not mention particular cases or individual persons but which is issued in advance to apply to all cases and all persons in the abstract; and . . . as specific as possible in its general formulation" (hence conflicting with open-ended legal clauses that have proliferated in recent years)—makes up its core.[56] But like many postwar defenders of the welfare state, Neumann concedes that this model can have only limited applicability in a setting necessitating extensive governmental action, and that cogent formal law today is necessarily replaced by vague legal standards and various forms of equity law and bargaining seemingly essential to the contemporary welfare state and its reliance on unprecedented forms of state intervention. Complex state activity today requires equally complex (nonformal) modes of law. And although "socialization resolves many problems," it cannot allow us to recapture some type of near-perfect social homogeneity like that which Neumann once imagined capable of providing the social substructure of a revitalized system of formal law; abandoning his belief in the possibility of a gapless social democratic rule of law, Neumann surrenders many of his reservations about the disappearance of formal law as well.[57] According to his revised position, deformalized law is here to stay, and contemporary politics needs indeterminate legal standards, which neither Locke nor Hegel would have deemed capable of regulating state action effectively. The internal rationality of law (that is, its semantic generality and resultant regularity) can never be complete: "The general law may, in its very formulation, contain an escape clause permitting purely discretionary decisions which are not the product of the subsumption of a concrete case under an abstract rule; or [during a crisis] . . . the general law may be suspended altogether."[58] The rule of law can never be rendered perfect, and legal gaps, exceptions, and irregularities are unavoidable side-effects of a social setting having particularistic power concentrations necessarily regulated by "clandestine individual measures" and administrative commands.[59] But we can still hope that because of its general origins, irregular law can be exercised, as Neumann thinks he has proven in "The Concept of Political Freedom," in a relatively rational fashion in a democracy. He now senses the truncated quality of the conception of rationality—whereby technical or purposive rationality is given a predominant position—that he takes from Weber and that has long encouraged him, as it did Weber, to emphasize the advantages of a coherent and codified system of legal norms at the cost of underplaying the rationality derived from universal political exchange. At least this is implied by his claim that rational democratic political authority no longer excludes irregular ("irrational") law.

This revised view is not without its paradoxes. While telling us emphatically that the rule of law "is *the* element in the concept of freedom that we can never give up," Neumann concedes that we inevitably have to sacrifice it each and every day.[60] If the gist of the rule of law remains the general legal norm, most contemporary law—with its reliance on vague legal standards and broad, poorly regulated grants of power—is outright sacrilege against this most sacred of political ideals. The rule of law is essential to democracy, but the author thinks that precisely those activities that help make democracy relatively humane today (social policy dependent on materialized legal forms, for example) are incompatible with it. The rule of law allegedly best protects us from the horrors of dictatorship—yet now it purportedly can have only a limited role in contemporary politics.

Neumann thinks his democratic antidote to Schmitt shows how democracy can tame state-based "might" by means of "right." Can he pull this off? Whatever its advantages over Schmitt's "concept of the political," given Neumann's own puissant insights about the fusion of situation-specific administrative decrees and formal parliamentary law in our epoch, there are some reasons for skepticism. If raison d'état forms of law ineffective at binding or restraining state actors (if only in the form of equity-style legal bargaining widespread in organized capitalism) are now an unavoidable feature of everyday legal affairs, can democracy hope to succeed in rationalizing state power adequately? Deformalized democratic law poses none of the dangers of its distant totalitarian cousin, and maybe it is true that the "dream of the liberal period . . . from the end of the 18th century to the first half of the 19th" of a legal system having a uniformly clear and codified form was a utopia that does not work, as Neumann now resolutely announces.[61] Yet does this give us sufficient reason for belittling the more disturbingly deleterious consequences of some modes of discretionary law that flourish in our epoch? How can we be so sure, as so many of the more self-satisfied defenders of welfare state law have been, that we are not simply giving up one of the more admirable demands of the liberal political tradition in favor of a concrete, albeit rather ambiguous, configuration of social power? That normativity is not once again being surrendered for brute facticity? The interventionist democratic state probably cannot do without some legal irregularities. But how much legal insecurity is consistent with a genuinely autonomous mode of democratic will formation? Surely, there is more to the rule of law than formal law. Yet can the rule of law do without formal law altogether?

Neumann never provides an adequate response to any of these questions. Intent on justifying the emerging apparatus of the postwar democratic welfare state and concerned (in the context of McCarthyism and the specter of postwar European neofascism) about the possibility of an authoritarian resurgence, he now thinks it best to place such doubts on the intellectual back burner and acknowledge, like many of his peers on the reformist Left, the apparent unavoidability of ambiguous, deformalized legal forms. These failings are then exacerbated by his refusal to consider the advantages of a number of proposed legal reforms. He begins by repeating familiar reservations about delegating legislative authority to decentralized decision-making bodies and argues that corporatist set-ups tend to become fronts for nontransparent, badly regulated public/private privilege. Legal irregularity cannot be compensated for by introducing new participatory modes of interest-centered legal decision making, and if "a nation has decided that a social activity needs governmental regulation, full responsibility should rest upon the government (the executive branch) as the decision-making body, and responsibility should not be shifted to interest groups by incorporating them into the administrative machinery."[62] But in view of the massive array of social and economic activities needing to be regulated today, is this classical view defensible anymore? Neumann is right to see that political decentralization in itself is no guarantee of greater political autonomy, as Kirchheimer similarly noted in "In Quest of Sovereignty." Decentralization can play into the hands of privileged local groups and buttress particularistic local tyrannies. Yet if a central state bureaucracy by itself is to regulate the unparalleled variety of tasks undertaken by the welfare state, the central legislature will be unable to watch over it carefully, and citizens may be transformed into increasingly passive objects of administrative control. Might not the consequences of such a model look like the infamous "Oriental-Egyptian" "shell of bondage" that results, according to Weber, if "a technically superior administration were to be the ultimate and sole value in the ordering of . . . affairs, and that means: a rational bureaucratic administration with the corresponding welfare benefits"?[63] As for recent proposals envisioning constitutionally endorsed social rights (to an income, job, health), as a way of updating the rule of law in a social and economic universe very different than that in which it first emerged, Neumann is now similarly skeptical: "It is extremely doubtful whether it is wise to designate as civil rights positive demands upon the state—whether for social security, trade union recognition, or even planning. These and similar demands upon the state have their legitimation in their social utility, which must be concretely demonstrated," whereas classical liberal rights, "in contrast, constitute the very essence of a democratic political system and need no demonstration as to their social usefulness."[64] Because Neumann himself seems to admit in the same passage that even the basic right of free expression can only be preserved today by positive governmental action—every democratic polity has been forced to concede that free speech, for example, can only be preserved if "economic imbalances" are checked[65]—his criticism rings hollow. There is rarely a clear-cut distinction now between rights demanding that government "leave us alone" and ones necessitating far-reaching state activity so as to demonstrate their value or utility. Because an ever-decreasing number of traditional liberal rights are "self-executing," liberal and social rights are no longer principally distinct and now refer at most to different points on a gradual scale.[66] If this is the case, there is no reason to assume that a standard that proclaims a right to social security, or any of a broad array of similar ideals associated with the welfare state, should necessarily be denied constitutional status. Nor does the otherwise reasonable claim that we still need to distinguish between democracy's procedural core and its social presuppositions provide a sufficient basis for criticizing conceptions of social rights. Just as we recognize that classical civil rights (to a fair trail, habeas corpus, and so on) are valuable in themselves and a necessary precondition for a genuinely autonomous and democratic mode of decision making, so, too, can we appreciate the advantages of social rights without obscuring this distinction.[67]

If we are to succeed in reconstructing the rule of law, we will need more institutional imagination than Neumann himself musters in his final years. The legitimacy of democratic law depends on how uncoerced and open the decision-making progress, but we can only hope to begin realizing this generality if we can devise adequate ways of regulating state (and public/private) authority. Franz Neumann's otherwise thought-provoking "concept of political freedom" never accomplished that task. Perhaps I can now suggest how we can begin to take it on.

3 Recapturing Formal Law?

Contemporary legal scholarship has of late energetically focused on the ills of contemporary welfare state law,[68] much of which has been the object of a brutal intellectual assault during the past fifteen years. The present study can only make a modest contribution to this debate. Nonetheless, I suggest that formal law has a greater role to play in a restructured system of contemporary legal regulation than most authors in the twentieth century have been willing to acknowledge. Neumann's and Kirchheimer's idiosyncratic critical analysis of legal deformalization may still contain a few lessons for those concerned with institutionalizing a welfare state that takes classical liberal legal values seriously. With the discretionary apparatus of the contemporary administrative state an object of popular derision, perhaps it is time to reconsider whether the welfare state's unfinished project of broadening social equality and political participation is necessarily incompatible with the old-fashioned liberal demand for predictable, cogent formal law.

Undoubtedly, there is much to be said for the common view that "it is unrealistic to suppose that unambiguous legislative standards" can be formulated when "government plays a large role in human affairs."[69] By the same token, it is too easy to shout "social complexity" every time another vague, deformalized standard makes its way into the legal system.

In his classical account of the American regulatory state, Theodore Lowi argues powerfully that highly complicated and relatively successful New Deal reforms often took a rather traditional legal form, whereas many of their politically far more precarious predecessors (such as the reforms of the Kennedy and Johnson era) broke far more dramatically with classical conceptions of law. Forms of regulation that take a traditional legal structure put the state's impressive powers to work achieving a relatively clear set of goals, whereas semantically ambiguous standards hand over poorly defined grants of legislative authority to antagonistic, organized interests. Unsurprisingly, many of the New Deal reforms proved more salient than those that followed. Lowi thinks the empirical evidence also suggests that the relative transparency of classical legal forms improves state actors' opportunities for identifying the consequences of a particular act of social regulation. In contrast, murky modes of law make it especially difficult for legislators and administrators to determine what may or may not be working. Notwithstanding the common view that deformalized law is demanded by social complexity, policy that takes a traditional legal form often better contributes to complex policy-related learning processes.[70] There is no self-evident reason why a system of insurance for the elderly, like that introduced by the Old Age Insurance (OAI) facets of the United States Social Security Act, is inherently less complex than regulation aiding poor children, such as Aid to Dependent Children (AID). Nonetheless, OAI takes a relatively traditional legal form, and its eligibility test refers to clear-cut criteria, such as the number of years you have worked and whether you have reached age sixty-five. ADC is far more discretionary: "eligibility and benefits ultimately rely on a subjective determination of resources, need, and other criteria by an individual caseworker or administrator." Its troublesome "suitable homes" standard, for example, increases "the administrative burden on caseworkers, making arbitrary shorthand judgements about the suitability of the home, as well as outright discrimination, considerably more likely."[71]

It was the libertarian Right that first proposed that some facets of the welfare state be reformed so that its legal structure could be rendered more transparent and less reliant on bureaucratic discretion. With these concerns in mind, Milton Friedman formulated the idea of a guaranteed minimum income. Of course, from the viewpoint developed here, the central problem with right-wing versions of a guaranteed income should be obvious enough. Capitalist-based inequalities contradict the most basic source of democratic law's legitimacy—the openness and generality of the process that generates it—and versions of a guaranteed income amounting to nothing more than a bribe to rapidly growing ghetto populations are, thus, not only bad social policy but bad democratic law as well. A reconstituted democratic rule of law seeks *both* legal security *and* social equality, extensive, potentially liberating state policy *without* poorly regulated bureaucratic discretion. Its defenders refuse to accept the Right's claim that legal security necessitates an openly bourgeois, noninterventionist state; the mainstream Left's (matching) view that social and economic progress requires increased legal irregularity; or a so-called radical view more obsessed with trashing the rule of law than anything else. Recent contributions suggest that this last alternative might amount to more than another dose of bad utopianism. A number of authors argue convincingly for an alternative welfare state based on a set of universalistic social programs (in particular, those relying on instruments like a guaranteed minimum income) able to undermine bureaucratic discretion while broadening the participatory generality on which democratic legality depends. Andre Gorz argues that a guaranteed basic income would not require an intrusive and complicated bureaucratic apparatus.[72] Liberals like Ralf Dahrendorf and a variety of European Greens offer distinct versions of the same idea.[73] Of course, the particularities of the various proposals are diverse and complex enough, and I cannot hope to do credit to them here. But they are significant, from our perspective, for one simple reason: each of them implies that some types of welfare state programs could be based on significantly more transparent, calculable legal forms than those we have today, that the obvious fact of social complexity and the need for complex bureaucratic and market mechanisms in contemporary society do not mean we have to rest satisfied with the rather sad status quo of welfare state law, and that a particular configuration of social and political inequalities has as much to do with the problematic structure of contemporary law than anything else. There is no a priori reason why state intervention must be legally inchoate. It is not social complexity but a particular configuration of power and privilege that often prevents environmental regulation from taking a classical form ("all corporations should cease production of PCB by year 1997") or legislatures from institutionalizing a generous guaranteed minimal income having a great deal more legal integrity than most parliamentary acts can claim nowadays. A law demanding "that all citizens be given X dollars each month" possesses greater legal coherence than, for example, the following extreme, but by no means uncharacteristic law, passed by Congress in 1970, stating, "The President is authorized to issue such orders and regulations as he deems appropriate to stabilize prices, rents, wages, and salaries. . . . The President may delegate the performance of any function under this Title to such officers, departments and agencies of the United States as he may deem appropriate."[74]

Are we to argue that the exigencies of social complexity necessitate the latter law over the former? That the latter is somehow necessarily more modern than the former? Cannot this question ultimately be answered only by political imagination and old-fashioned experimentation?

What is striking about many of the blanket clauses that worry theorists like Neumann is that they tend to appear in the most conflict-ridden spheres of social and economic life.[75] This should suggest the possibility that the source of contemporary law's deformalized structure lies in part in the unnecessary and vicious social antagonisms that continue to characterize our political universe. Because of the tremendously antagonistic nature of social relations in spheres such as the capitalist workplace, there can be no clear agreement about how to regulate conflicts emerging there; neither clear-cut formal parliamentary rules nor precise legal procedures can be arrived at that regulate labor-capital relations. The parallel implied by Neumann between everyday deformalized legal standards and terms like "prerogative" or "national security" may reveal its full significance here. Just as emergency laws remain essential to an antagonistic and insufficiently rationalized international political setting, so, too, do blanket clauses appear to mirror (fortunately more blandly) the irrational, conflict-ridden facets of contemporary social existence. Just as martial law or national security in the world of state politics too often becomes a front for badly regulated exercises of power by the most privileged state-level actors (a well-armed nation state or, in the case of a domestic crisis, the police or military), so, too, have blanket clauses in social regulation too often worked to serve the interests of hegemonic social interests. Might not a more egalitarian social order be able to do without some of the more disturbing features of contemporary welfare state law? Could an alterative social world result in political compromises more acceptable to the groups concerned, and might not those agreements take a legal structure less like imprecise norms, such as "national security," that pave the way for the most horrible forms of state action?

A second and more ambitious set of proposals openly acknowledges the necessity of delegating extensive legislative authority to subordinate decision-making bodies but suggests that in contrast to present practice this could be used as a way of undermining legal irregularity. Both a more broadly based and a semantically more cogent set of legal norms could be generated if legislative authority were placed in the hands of those most sensitive to the complexities and consequences of a particular object of state action. The central legislature already delegates extensive authority to decentralized decision makers, and the real task lies in organizing this delegation so as to make it most compatible with the basic principles of a democratic conception of the rule of law. Proposals demanding that a parliamentary center regain the all-encompassing place it once possessed too often amount to a negative utopia. A central legislature restrained by the condition that its activities only take a general form would sometimes be denied adequate opportunities for undermining inequalities of private power that constitute as much a threat to the democratic rule of law as badly regulated state authority. Yet the status quo is unsatisfying as well. An overburdened central parliament, overwhelmed by the complexity of tasks at hand, hands over its legislative authority, by means of open-ended legal standards, to poorly regulated and relatively unrepresentative bureaucrats and corporatist bargainers, whose actions in many cases corrode the very preconditions of autonomous political and social action on which democracy depends. Inevitably, the purported generality of legislative decision making and the extent to which it represents a true plurality of autonomously formulated views and interests are badly undermined.

In this vein, Ingeborg Maus provocatively argues that we need to supplement the central legislature with new, decentralized legislative bodies and introduce a division of labor between the two types of institutions,

> "according to the degree of the generality of the applicability of a mode of legal regulation. Legal norms directed at only a very limited number of addressees or which only have regional consequences could be conferred about and determined in legislative arrangements in which the parties to the conflict directly confront each other and are equipped with symmetrical negotiation-positions so as to compensate legally for the asymmetries of social power. . . . All this presupposes that the parliamentary center stays responsible for the most general function: the determination of procedural norms, according to which the contents of law emerge in decentralized legislative processes.[76]

Democratic law can be given a broader (general) basis by expanding opportunities for taking part in the legislative process. Maus believes, furthermore, that law could become far more cogent form than it is under contemporary conditions, when the parliamentary center is forced to hand over a set of regulatory problems to an administrative agency by simply proclaiming that it should be resolved "in the public interest" or "in good faith." In environmental law, for example, "what's missing presently are (not necessarily centrally determined, but) general decisions, like the simple prohibition of harmful materials," which could give the judiciary and bureaucracy clear guidance.[77] But the realization of such legal forms demands that we consider radical new ways of organizing the legislative process.

Decentralization is not an end in itself but one possible means for transforming the welfare state's "administrees" into active citizens. If "no taxation without representation" presented an appropriate democratic rallying cry in an era of parliament-centered politics far simpler than our own, perhaps it needs to be supplemented in the age of the interventionist state with something like "no regulation without representation." In accordance with the idea that the legitimacy of democratic law rests both on its semantic clarity and, more fundamentally, on the reasonableness of the process that generates it, we might restructure delegated legislative activities so that those regulated by the administrative apparatus are finally given a real opportunity for determining the formulation of administrative rules and norms, particularly given the overarching significance state activity takes on in so many lives. Instead of continuing to deny the obvious fact that parliament cannot be the all-powerful institution that it was in a far less complex era, the legislature might now openly delegate extensive authority to various subordinate bodies—while, perhaps, demanding that decentralized bodies both take a more adequately representative form and articulate more coherent rules (rules better able to guide judges and bureaucrats effectively) than overworked parliamentarians are capable of. This would acknowledge that the generality of law today can no longer be derived solely from traditional legislative politics. And it anticipates what self-binding democratic institutions should look like: a genuinely effective legislature self-consciously limits itself to determining the broadest contours and priorities of governmental policy while leaving many of the details of legal regulation to subordinate representative bodies.

Franz Neumann would have reminded us, rightly, of the countless potential complications and dangers posed by calls for decentralizing legislative authority today. But perhaps we need to recall his own words that "no system, even the most conservative one . . . can merely persevere; even to persevere it must change." That, I assume, applies to the ideal of the democratic rule of law as well.

8

Between the Norm and the Exception

In 1965 an outraged Herbert Marcuse reported that "the whole post-fascist period is one of clear and present danger. . . . I maintain that our society is in such an emergency situation, and that it has become the normal state of affairs."[1] Marcuse's controversial "Repressive Tolerance," where he makes this statement, can be interpreted as an unsuccessful attempt to avoid accepting the most worrisome consequences of this position. Marcuse's better democratic instincts tell him that any attack on basic political rights would simply make "totalitarian democracy" even more totalitarian than it allegedly is today. Nevertheless, the logic of his basic diagnosis leads him to abandon his healthier intuitions and conclude that "the exercise of civil rights by those who don't have them presupposes the withdrawal of civil rights from those who prevent their exercise."[2] If the postfascist era finds itself in a permanent state of emergency, how can we criticize oppressed groups that reach for political weapons appropriate to its logic? Of course, such argumentation is hardly unfamiliar to our story. Recall the similar claim that Walter Benjamin made in 1940: "the tradition of the oppressed teaches us that the 'state of emergency' in which we live is not the exception but the rule."[3] Or consider, more centrally, Carl Schmitt's counterrevolutionary version of this diagnosis from the late twenties and early thirties, when he argued that the disintegration of the liberal rule of law not only revealed its fundamentally antipolitical character but, more immediately, proved that the interventionist welfare state sought by his left-wing foes had driven modern polities into an emergency stage.

Unlike Marcuse's or Benjamin's, Schmitt's assessment became a self-fulfilling prophecy. Insofar as it helped justify his embrace of a Nazi alternative that truly did embody the logic of the political emergency, Schmitt's view helped make sure that the state of emergency became a very real state of affairs for most of the globe in the thirties and forties.

In this study, I have tried to show how Franz Neumann and Otto Kirchheimer develop a more subtle and defensible view of the role of the exception in contemporary politics. The details of the story shift over time, and significant differences often separate our two authors. Yet both Neumann and Kirchheimer focus on how poorly regulated state action undermines the rule of law and contradicts its utopian spirit. And at least after their break with Schmitt during the thirties, they consider how we might reconceptualize liberalism's dream of regulating state authority by rational law and thereby rejuvenate the constitutionalist agenda. In their complex alternative view, irrational raison d'état action indeed has made significant inroads on the sphere of political normalcy, even in the more humane quarters of twentieth-century politics. It may be that "the historian of the twentieth century will be less impressed by diverse propagandistic claims of various regimes as to the reign of law under their dominion than with the close cohabitation between wide stretches of certainty for mass man's daily living conditions with unheard-of areas of oppression, lawlessness, and rewards for maximum aggressiveness."[4] Nonetheless, the rule of law does provide real protection to at least a few inhabitants of our divided and bloody world at least some of the time. If we were to try to describe this configuration pictorially, we would have to rely on fewer blacks and whites—and a greater number of grays—than either Schmitt or Marcuse would have us think. "Each society has such islands where the rule of law is at best uncertain, conjectural, and often nonexistent. . . . The decisive difference, in separating a normal from a criminal state, involves the degree to which such islands are kept under control and whether they are encroaching on wider and wider fields of social activities."[5] While successfully demonstrating that capitalist liberal democracies are by no means monolithically criminal, the Frankfurt school political theorists rightly remind us that worrisome forms of exceptional, decisionistic law still haunt us.[6]

This is in part why Kirchheimer can offer a refreshingly balanced portrayal of the version of the rule of law that emerged in the aftermath of the political cataclysms of the thirties and forties. Kirchheimer's final writings, which make up the theme of this chapter, chronicle that brief moment in contemporary history when aggressive capitalist economic growth and a real decline in political tensions (or "the end of ideology," as it was prematurely labeled) seemed well on their way to solidifying the foundations of the institutional configuration described so bleakly by Marcuse in *One-Dimensional Man* and then attacked and stripped down by neoconservative political movements later on. But in the fifties and early sixties, it at least seemed possible that welfare state capitalism was destined to provide limitless consumer goods for pretty much everyone, and old social and ideological divisions certainly did look increasingly irrelevant in a world where the "Keynesian class compromise" (and the Cold War) had worked to narrow the political universe of the "overdeveloped" West. Like Marcuse, Kirchheimer avoids much of the self-congratulatory spirit of this period. Unlike his former colleague, however, he refuses to accept either a picture of the warfare/welfare state as lacking any immanent disruptive tendencies or the claim that it finds itself in a permanent state of emergency. Kirchheimer's writings between 1945 and 1965 see the legal institutions of the postwar welfare state both as an undeniable achievement and as flawed, unsatisfactory, and contradictory—in short, as situated uneasily between the norm and the exception.[7]

Of course, the political universe Kirchheimer described no longer looks very much like our own. In retrospect, the assumption of limitless capitalist growth seems naive; all the negative technological and ecological side-effects of the postwar political economy are exploding in the face of its children; old-fashioned capitalist social inequality has made an impressive comeback; political ideology is very much alive in an era when neofascism is Europe's fastest-growing political movement. But in showing us what was always wrong about the mainstream Left's modes postwar attempt to construct a postbourgeois model of the rule of law, Kirchheimer can help us develop an emancipatory version of it able to take on all its old and new opponents.

It was a lifelong concern of Neumann and Kirchheimer that the contemporary *Rechtsstaat* take an adequately democratic and socially egalitarian structure. Kirchheimer's final writings offer a further gloss on this theme. In a political universe in which the possibilities for meaningful participation remain minimal at best and the liberal "rule of (parliamentary) law" is being systematically replaced by an emerging "rule of administrative decree," Kirchheimer stubbornly insists that the agenda of the democratic rule of law should not exhaust itself in the multiplication of legal claims and a set of experts ready to enforce them; not simply more tribunality but truly "general" (broadly based, participatory) and relatively cogent law-based state action is needed today, and the contemporary welfare state would do well to give that explicitly democratic facet of the constitutionalist ideal greater significance than it has thus far. Indeed, until new institutions are devised, many welfare state legal institutions remain at best incomplete and at worst ambivalent (section 1). In Kirchheimer's view, democratic regimes in the immediate postwar era never successfully tackled the task of giving welfare state law a sufficiently participatory base. If the rule of law is to be revitalized, we will have to do better (sections 2 and 3).

1 The Ambivalent Structure of the Postwar Legal Order

It is probably no accident that Kirchheimer's vision of the postwar legal order takes its most systematic form in a contribution completed right before his death in 1965 for a *Festschrift* for Marcuse. At first glance, "The Rechtsstaat as Magic Wall" seems to cover familiar ground. Describing the fundaments of relatively democratic (Anglo-American) and authoritarian (nineteenth-century continental European) variants of the rule of law, Kirchheimer tells us that "their common denominator lies in the simple thought that the security of the individual is better served when specific claims can be addressed to institutions counting rules and permanency among their stock-in-trade than by reliance on transitory personal relations and situations."[8] But however straightforward its underlying insight, the rule of law-ideal obviously remains complicated. What exactly is a legal rule or norm, and how is it to be contrasted to modes of law that allow too many possibilities for personal arbitrariness? How much room for administrative and judicial discretion is compatible with the rule of law? Kirchheimer doubts that a perfectly clear distinction between norm-based and discretionary action is always possible in the era of the interventionist state,[9] yet he still hopes that we can counteract discretionary trends more effectively than has been accomplished so far. Admitting that there has been a fusion between authorities making general rules and those applying them, he concedes that some of the more common anxieties about welfare state law remain legitimate. In contradistinction to many who focus on such trends, however, this does not lead him to embrace an anti-interventionist, openly bourgeois alternative. Accusing belligerent "free market" critics of welfare state law, such as Hayek, of an irresponsible romanticism, Kirchheimer insists that such authors ignore the old lesson that without extensive and far-reaching modes of social regulation, everyday existence itself would not be bearable for much of humanity. In his view, there is no going back to the early capitalist market utopia stylized by the welfare state's conservative critics, and by necessity "the *Rechtsstaat* is transformed into the *Sozialrechtsstaat*" (social rule of law).[10] If realized, the conservative program of feebled legislatures and active common-law judges, allegedly able to act spontaneously and noncoercively, would produce very real social and economic misery and flagrantly violate the rule of law's most basic aspiration to provide a minimum of personal freedom.[11]

At the same time, Kirchheimer is unconvinced that the welfare state project necessarily involves leaving wide areas of social and economic existence poorly regulated: "it is not intelligible why social security rules cannot be as carefully framed and the community burdens as well calculated, as rules concerning damage claims deriving from negligence actions."[12] The welfare state itself can be organized in a manner more in tune with at least the spirit of modern formal law: "If social services may be produced for the purposes of mass consumption, the accompanying procedures guaranteeing these rights must be producible too."[13] Even if some conservative critics may be partially right in identifying a worrisome increase in legal irregularity, this should serve as a spur to reform it by developing new types of rules and procedures counteracting that trend, and not as dubious evidence for the view that legal security for the few inevitably necessitates poverty for the majority.

But the real novelty of "Rechtsstaat as Magic Wall" lies elsewhere. In a set of earlier essays, Kirchheimer described the emergency of "a universe of legally enforceable or at least legally arguable claims."[14] What he meant by this was that citizens in the emerging postwar welfare state increasingly were given opportunities for taking their individual legal claims (for social security, housing, pensions, worker's compensation, even a job) to a judge or administrator, and he argued that this tendency was both the most striking and most ambiguous facet of postwar legal development. The tremendous popularity of the move to realize T. H. Marshall's program of expanding social rights was perfectly understandable in a historical juncture where millions had just experienced the political horrors of the thirties and forties. Kirchheimer did not hesitate to describe the welfare state's chivalrous "juridification" as a "late and endangered stage of civilization" worth defending.[15] The proliferation of legal remedies for individual claims provided a real measure of security and autonomy to segments of the population long denied them. At least from the perspective of those who enjoyed its fruits for the first time, it most certainly was not the despotic "road to serfdom" described by free-market critics. Kirchheimer also described how in some settings it had helped contribute a crucial dose of political continuity essential for the difficult transition from fascism to liberal democracy in the immediate postwar years. In West Germany (the immediate object of most of these inquiries), the welfare state universe of legal claims permitted potentially divisive and explosive social and economic issues to be taken off the parliamentary agenda (thereby stabilizing parliamentary institutions) and, in good old-fashioned central European fashion, charged their management to a coterie of bureaucratic and legal experts.[16]

Still, Kirchheimer remained anxious. Although acknowledging the virtues of the emerging "universe of legal claims," he seems to have sensed that it rested on a particular set of economic presuppositions, which, as he suggested on at least one occasion, might prove short-lived.[17] Fueled by an unprecedented bout of capitalist economic growth, "the modern welfare state can now provide solutions to problems of many social groups without in the process worsening the situation of competing social groups. This weakens the old clashes of immediate interests and converts them into mere conflicts of priority in the time sequence satisfactions."[18] As the economic pie grew, the proliferating universe of legal claims could be satisfied, but the danger was that if the pie suddenly shrank, the interrelated system of welfare state claims might prove vulnerable. More fundamentally, he worried that this rendition of the rule of law complemented the flourishing civic privatism and the trivialization of political affairs that many other social critics were describing with great verve during the fifties and early sixties. If there was little doubt that the postwar world should be relieved at the obvious cooling off of domestic political tempers and a real decline in class tensions, it was still worrisome that "polls, which show only the sketchiest knowledge of legislative and administrative processes . . . indicate a higher degree of familiarity and satisfaction with the working of the courts," a trend, in Kirchheimer's view, rooted in the welfare state's unprecedented reliance on a system of legalistic individual claims.[19] But was the judiciary now of greatest immediate interest mainly because it least demanded of postwar citizens that they move beyond the role of passive clients and their typically private concerns (for a more spacious apartment, for example, or a better pension)? Did not this trend pose problems for a system based on the principle of the supremacy of elected popular institutions? Kirchheimer eagerly supported new ombudsmen-type mechanisms as a way of outfitting citizens with a greater set of legal remedies against the burgeoning welfare state bureaucratic apparatus, but he wondered if they might just help "the small fry," "who gets nowhere with his somewhat complicated and forlorn social security claims," without necessarily counteracting deeper trends toward an apolitical, privatized world of lonely consumers.[20] And sometimes the whole process clearly got out of hand, subordinating social spheres to legalistic and judicial criteria inappropriate to them: in Germany, "witness the increasing number of unlucky candidates in university exams or parents whose children flunk in lower schools and who hale professor or teacher—mostly without much success—into administrative court."[21]

"Rechtsstaat as Magic Wall" offers the most thorough interpretation of these anxieties. In order to unravel their meaning, Kirchheimer focuses on the dramatic example of postwar Germany's failure to prosecute Nazi war criminals satisfactorally. Kirchheimer certainly does not think the problems of welfare state law and the prosecution of Nazis (or, for that matter, the broader issue of political justice that occupies much of his attention during the fifties) are identical. As he knows, obscuring the crucial distinctions between them would be extremely problematic, and any analysis of welfare state law that reduces it to just another form of political repression both distorts the complexity of the historical story at hand and underplays the welfare state's real advances.[22] Nonetheless,

Kirchheimer does think he can refer to the case of Germany's failure to prosecute Nazi war criminals to make some rather general and abstract claims about the relationship between legality and democracy. The gist of the sad story retold by him is that despite a universe of juridical and bureaucratic remedies available for prosecuting Nazis, little legal action was undertaken against them, and when administrators and judges finally did bother to press charges against a small number of war criminals, the acquittal rates were nearly four times higher than in all other legal proceedings. Kirchheimer thinks it would be too simplistic to focus on the individual errors of particular persons or institutions in order to explain this set of events completely. He convincingly shows how a highly complicated and intermeshing configuration of forces came together to generate it. Although the Bundestag admirably refused to submit to right-wing demands for extensive amnesties, like many elected legislatures in other contemporary democracies it never succeeded in making sure that administrators and judges were actually upholding the law. As for the bureaucrats and legal experts, they probably took a conscientious look at most of the individual cases that reached them but never bothered to make any fuss about the system's overall failure to investigate Nazi thugs in a suitably rigorous way.[23] Despite the idiosyncracies of the German example, Kirchheimer thinks it is of more than local significance: it proves nothing less than how facile the widespread attempt to reduce the rule of law to a "universe of legal claims" is. According to him, this view of the rule of law was precisely that of the Germans, who seem to have believed that this necessary yet insufficient "*part* of what we have recognized as the traditional armor of the rule of law" (my emphasis) constituted it very core.[24] But "a rule of law, resting only on the theoretical availability of legal remedies, somehow resembles a modern house whose glass wall, the major attraction for all visitors, already stands, but whose wooden utility walls no one has so far bothered to build."[25] The possibility of "a day in court" (or, for that matter, the right to visit the caseworker or file a complaint with his or her supervisor) is a precious accomplishment and certainly not itself responsible for the ills of postwar democracy in Germany or elsewhere, but in Kirchheimer's view it is far from being enough. The rule of law has to involve more than a potpourri of possibilities for legal redress or even a mass of judges and administrators who are supposed to look after them. Where the political community, as in postwar Germany, is more concerned with distributing the good of economic growth than with developing a broader set of democratic "utility walls," the "magic" of the rule of law's "magic wall" will turn out to be a cheap circus trick—pretty to look at and even enjoy, but nothing to get very excited about. "Formal remedies" and the "substantive goals of a social order" can rarely be neatly separated. Democracy's major merit lies in its "close and constant interweaving" between legality and "its basis of legitimacy," and a political order's failure to help establish this interweaving can prove catastrophic.[26] The German Federal Republic offers plenty of legality (that is, chances for legal redress), but it conveniently obscures the full significance of the fact—Kirchheimer, crucially, clearly thinks this argument applies to the postwar welfare state as well—that the virtues of legality fully flourish only amidst a broader constellation of democratic practices and mores.

In "Private Man and Society," Kirchheimer asks what democratic consensus really amounts to in the advanced societies of Western Europe and North America. He provides the dramatic answer that even the modest conceptualization of consensus offered by most democratic theorists today remains a mirage in the world of everyday empirical politics. Consensus obviously does not take the far-reaching form envisioned by authors like Schmitt; "Private Man and Society" seems to accept that this is just as well. But even a more defensible formal conception of democratic consensus, allowing us "to haggle endlessly over substance but keep the system going via sacrosanct ways of procedure" has little to do with the self-understanding of those to whom normative theorists (at times far too unreflectively) attribute it.[27] Synthesizing the results of a variety of alarming empirical studies on the political views of working- and lower-middle-class groups, Kirchheimer argues that they suggest that most residents of wealthy, developed countries see "liberty" chiefly as a chance for "foraging around within the confines of the system for a rewarding job combination opening up maximum access to consumer goods. These men's universal liberty is, then, the liberty of the consumer's market."[28] So-called realist conceptualizations of democracy delight in this privatism and the interrelated manifestations of political apathy and tortuously try to make a virtue out of it, but Kirchheimer thinks we should take it as a warning about the depth of political alienation in contemporary society. In his analysis, it has concrete institutional roots in a "missing link between high-level decision and individual fate":[29] "while the technical and, though to a somewhat smaller degree, the social forms of human existence in the West have undergone immense changes in the last half-century, our political arsenal has been refurbished mainly with new dimensions and techniques of domination and manipulation rather than with—what is admittedly more difficult—new means of participation. . . . Political innovations that could remedy this imbalance have been rare everywhere."[30] The lesson Kirchheimer draws from this observation is not that the rule of law should be dissolved into the demand for a vaguely conceived system of mass-based popular rule (as has been common on the Left since Marx's romanticized portrayal of the Paris Commune), but that the intermeshing of legality and democratic legitimacy so essential to the "magical" advantages of the rule of law itself requires a more activist and educative system of popular exchange and decision making than that common in the postwar West. "If the hapless citizen of some Eastern lands is integrated to too great an extent into an often unwanted social fabric, the citizen of the West may miss political education and significant participation altogether," and the very ends of legality are likely to be distorted when this education and participation fail to be forthcoming.[31] The welfare state universe of claims nobly intends to free the poor and the working classes from unnecessary tutelage, yet it might become little more than a complement to the lifestyle of the "private man" of consumer capitalism unless adequately supplemented by a set of self-educative participatory institutions.

Democracy needs legality, but legality also needs democracy. Like a complicated mathematical equation we continue to struggle with but still have not solved to our satisfaction, an error on one side of it means that the other will suffer from miscalculations as well. As early as 1930, Kirchheimer had argued that a truly democratic version of the rule of law needed to locate the generality or universality of law primarily in its (democratic participatory) base or origins, and, as he is well aware, more defensible modern conceptions of the rule of law always at least hinted at this idea as well. Anglo-American views of the rule of law, for example, traditionally linked the demand for popular political participation (and the democratic genesis of law) to a privileging of broad-based parliamentary rules in contrast to executive decrees or measures. Kirchheimer's concern here, in part, is simply that the welfare state gives up too much of this multifaceted original agenda.

Recently, Claude Lefort has written:

> "Isn't the welfare state like Janus?" someone will ask. "Doesn't it have a hidden face: that of the police state?" This is a legitimate question. There is good reason to suspect not only that the repression directed against strata eroded by the economic crisis may increase, but that it is in the very nature of the welfare state to "neutralize the expression of social conflict." But let us not forget that it does have two faces . . . nor should we forget to look at the obstacles which block the expansion of the coercive state; I refer to the democratic apparatus, which prevents the agencies of power, law, and knowledge from fusing into a single leading organ. If we fail to remember that . . . if we concentrate our attention upon the increasing prerogatives of public authorities, we will no longer be able to discern the specific nature of a power whose exercise always depends upon competition between parties—with all that competition implies—and upon debate which is sustained by public liberties and which preserves them.[32]

Very much in his spirit, Otto Kirchheimer could easily have made this statement. Yet he probably would have insisted on qualifying its more affirmative features. In Kirchheimer's analysis, existing forms of political participation (or Lefort's "democratic apparatus") do not function quite as well as Lefort's comment might suggest.

2 The Politics of Friend and Foe: A Sociological Reinterpretation

In "The Waning of Opposition in Parliamentary Regimes," Kirchheimer recalls Mill's view that political "competition must be a competition of ideas as well as of interests, because without a competition of ideas and the duty to listen to them the victory of the momentarily more powerful group would always be a foregone conclusion."[33] Social privilege is no guarantee of political rationality. Political competition presupposes a battle between genuinely distinct viewpoints and not simply bargaining between established social interests. Kirchheimer argues that for late eighteenth- and nineteenth-century liberal constitutionalism, political opposition was conceptualized in terms of a "ceaseless critic," making up the core of a set of institutions and practices for augmenting a decision-making process in which a relatively open and reasonable "public opinion" could materialize.[34] In the spirit of this project, liberalism tended to demote judicial practices resulting in the suppression of discordant views. Courts became relatively tolerant toward radical critics.[35] Parliament was never quite the eloquent "debating club" idealized by its defenders (and reviled by its critics), yet in much of Europe it did become a focal point for criticism of royal, and then executive, authority.[36]

Kirchheimer's provocative thesis here is that contemporary mass democracy surrenders too many of the emancipatory features of this constitutionalist agenda. In his view, contemporary democracy generally does not institutionalize "ceaseless criticism" at all effectively, and the tolerance nineteenth-century courts showed even the most radical critics has been undermined not only by totalitarianism, as many liberals have argued, but by modern democracy's own failure to develop new modes of participation capable of supplementing traditional institutions ill suited to the demands of a universe more complicated than that of Guizot or Mill. Objective social trends and conscious efforts join together to replace the "limited public opinion" of middle-class constitutionalism with the socially broader, yet less alert and astute, "directed mass opinion" of contemporary democracy. Politics in the postwar world is of interest to few and is incidental to the liberty of the consumer marketplace. Shaped by means of a capitalist press that replaces the party press of a previous era and tends to trivialize politics, contemporary public opinion shows evidence of conformism and ethnocentrism.[37]

In my reading of Kirchheimer's typically far-flung writings from this period, it makes sense to focus on two central issues. I will first discuss the problem of political justice (subsection A) before moving on to his gloss on the crisis of parliamentarism (subsection B). Again, the ghost of Carl Schmitt necessarily haunts our narrative. In a second 1957 essay, Kirchheimer writes that Schmitt's "exclusive orientation to his eternal enemy, the *Rechtsstaat,* makes for the same grandiose one-sidedness and remoteness from reality which would pervade his eternal counterpart, a purely individualistically conceived legal order."[38] In responding to many of Schmitt's views, Kirchheimer clearly hopes to avoid a similar one-sidedness and remoteness from reality. As so often in the past, he concedes that at least some facets of Schmitt's theory have empirical correlates in a political universe showing a number of worrisome and, as far as the normative aspirations (and, to some extent, empirical reality) of eighteenth- and nineteenth-century liberal constitutionalism is concerned, regressive tendencies.[39] But he also thinks we should avoid seeing these trends as providing us with the whole story, let alone as a legitimate starting point for developing a defensible normative theory. Even if contemporary law sometimes "obliterates the distinction between normalcy and emergency," many facets of the postwar political universe still represent a precious achievement.[40] The capitalist welfare state is neither a one-sided story of legal decay nor a perfectly progressive and unambiguous step forward. In it, "the relationship of the individual to the organs of the state and interest groups is ambiguous. Services and protection, pressure and oppression, blur easily and almost unnoticeably."[41] In any event, a critical theory of society aspires to eliminate the most worrisome manifestations of normatively unregulated state action (or the normless exception) from the political universe. And if the *Rechtsstaat* is Schmitt's "eternal foe," Kirchheimer thinks that it should remain our eternal "friend."

(A) In the twenties and thirties, Carl Schmitt eagerly debunked liberal attempts to separate law and politics, and political from judicial practices.[42] Although itself expressive of an antipolitical refusal to acknowledge the supremacy of existential friend/foe conflicts, Schmitt argued, the liberal differentiation between law and politics revealed something else as well. Universalistic liberal ideals, such as judicial neutrality, were among liberalism's most insidious weapons against its foes. Who could outdo an opponent who waged battle in the name of humanity's "general interests" or who murdered only in order "to end all wars" or guarantee "universal peace"? At times, Schmitt matched the crudest of orthodox Marxist critics in seeing the rule of law as a mere instrument of political coercion. Behind it always stood a particular power group, such as the bourgeois "talking classes," who had discovered that it suited a concrete, situation-specific set of political purposes. For Schmitt, justice was always fundamentally political, and at its very core a form of friend/foe politics. Whatever the other differences between his theory in the twenties and that in the thirties, his subsequent contributions to Nazi law, which helped transform the courtroom into an administrative accessory of the racist folk community, were fundamentally consistent with this early view.

Kirchheimer's *Political Justice* analyzes those features of twentieth-century juridical experience corresponding, to a greater or lesser extent, to Schmitt's crudely instrumentalist reading of the legal system. Describing how legal instruments are employed in our era so as to transform political critics who seem to question the "particularly intensive" interests of the community into hated, alien foes—the *hostis generis humani*—Kirchheimer relies on his former teacher's language in order to debunk his views.[43] In contrast to Schmitt, he sticks to a more traditional liberal conception of the relationship between politics and law—"political action is directed towards changing or confining power relations; the apparatus of justice serves to resolve limited conflicts between individuals and the community . . . according to preordained rules"—and, on the basis of this conventional distinction, he criticizes the proliferation of forms of legal action (for example, political trials and discriminatory ad hoc legislation directed against political minorities) that make a mockery of it and too often resemble Schmitt's friend/foe model of legality.[44] Kirchheimer does concede, at the work's outset, that "every political regime has its foes or in due time creates them," and at a first glance he might be interpreted as accepting his former teacher's view that the political universe can never be freed from explosive and potentially violent friend/foe antagonisms.[45] But he clearly has something different in mind. *Political Justice* can be read as suggesting that in a world victimized by dictatorship and social inequality and where democratic legitimacy and legality rarely connect up, let alone properly interweave, some forms of political justice remain unavoidable. The very difficult practical question then becomes how such exceptions to constitutionalism are to be made compatible with democracy's broader normative underpinnings: most prominently, the Nuremberg Trials present an example of how the democratic project paradoxically can be served by legal means that, if made permanent, would clearly be inimical to it. From the perspective of liberal constitutionalist thinking, the war-crimes trials were undoubtedly problematic. Yet in helping to demonstrate the horrors of fascism and its attack on the minimal presuppositions of the "human condition, the survival of mankind in both its universality and diversity," they were justified.[46]

Kirchheimer still believes that Schmitt's reduction of law to a mode of friend/foe politics, despite its empirical base in many areas of twentieth-century juridical experience, tends to reify the most miserable features of an alterable political universe. Sustained in part by amorphous legal categories (an inflationary concept of treason, for example) giving state agencies plenty of room to obscure any meaningful distinction between real threats to the integrity of democracy and legitimate political criticism, political justice allows poorly regulated exercises of state sovereignty to make inroads on the sphere of rational law throughout the postwar West. Kirchheimer readily admits that totalitarianism—which, not incidentally, realizes the most brutal forms of political justice—poses a real threat to democracy, but he thinks it both normatively troublesome and politically problematic that purportedly democratic regimes have too often carelessly traded off core elements of the rule of law, by embracing forms of discrimination and open respression against political critics. Harsh action may be necessary against violent, authoritarian political groups, but in the spirit of classical constitutionalism, Kirchheimer thinks repression is best limited "to the repulsion of tangible and concrete threats against the public order, rather than striving towards ideological conformity." Ideally, violent extremists should only be dragged into court when they engage in a battery of specifically defined and immediately threatening acts, and if, as in the "halcyon" days of nineteenth-century constitutionalism, democratic societies once again gave legal concepts like "treason" the most liberal conceivable interpretation.[47] The immediate problem with broader and blatantly ad hoc forms of discrimination is that they generate a variety of side-effects fatal to the "ceaseless criticism" whose virtues authors like Mill rightly appreciated. Too often little more than a modern-day form of raison d'état, political justice intimidates actual and potential critics, thereby promoting a "waning of opposition" that undermines the openness and flexibility of political debate on which democracy depends.[48] The growing significance of such practices in our epoch suggests that we may be abandoning constitutionalism's justified hesitancy about silencing dissenters and regressing to a preliberal era when political elites were allowed to prosecute critics willy-nilly.[49]

Like most of Kirchheimer's final writings, *Political Justice* lacks the radicalism and theoretical precision of his earlier and more self-confidently

Marxist writings. As in the case of the elder Franz Neumann, "no Marxian utopian about things to come" probably guides him any longer.[50] But, again as in Neumann's case, a faint utopian wind still blows here: Kirchheimer comments that political justice may be nothing more than a "delusion" of "an antagonistically organized society," and when explaining why some northern European countries have relatively few authoritarian critics and still treat them so liberally, he reports that "British and Scandinavian workers don't need Communists to tell them how to establish public ownership in industry and transportation, control private investment, . . . satisfy consumer needs through nonprivate outlets (coops), . . . build an all-embracing social security system, or 'socialize medicine.' "[51] In responding to those ready to apologize for McCarthyite political justice and the social and political status quo in the United States, he sarcastically reminds them that "it is hard to see how, for example, complete or partial legal suppression of the American Communist Party would provide a quicker rate of urban renewal, eliminate racketeering, raise the intellectual and educational level of political officeholders, abolish political illiteracy all around, eradicate corruption in public life, obliterate all traces of traditional violence in labor disputes, and banish racism."[52] Even after having abandoned any easy faith in a Marxist utopia, Kirchheimer hopes that radical social democracy might undermine some of the immediate roots of political justice. However eclectic the underlying theoretical paradigm of his postwar work becomes—indeed, his portrayal of the welfare state at times seems more like the bureaucratic and privatistic bourgeois "democratic despotism" described by Tocqueville, at the conclusion of *Democracy in America,* than many of the defenses (or criticisms) of it provided by Marxist-oriented social democrats in the fifties—Kirchheimer still believes that "farreaching change within the framework of democratic institutions" might point the way beyond the sins of legal modes that represent an abandonment of the liberal political tradition's truly critical elements.[53]

This theoretical eclecticism is a healthy one in Kirchheimer's case, manifestly heightening his sympathy for the virtues and complexities of the rule of law and the basic workings of democratic political institutions, as well as his own awareness of the significance of a host of issues whose full meaning was missed by classical Marxism. Like Neumann, Kirchheimer points the way to a rejuvenated critical theory of politics appreciative of both the continuing merits of Marx's hostility to capitalism and its undeniable normative and political deficits. He also now stands somewhere between "Marxism and Liberalism." Just as this aspect of Neumann's late writings is less indicative of a "resignative" abandonment of a critical theoretical and political agenda than of an ambitious and incomplete struggle to develop an alternative critical theory suited to the exigencies of a social world distinct from that which generated classical Marxism, so too does Kirchheimer's postwar rendition of Frankfurt-based critical theory include a number of innovative features. Perhaps this is best demonstrated by his growing sensitivity to the problems posed for the rule of law by the irrationalities of the international state system, a theme whose complexities society-centered Marxism long underplayed and which even Neumann effectively ignored, despite his lifelong fascination with the renaissance of raison d'état state action and legal forms in the twentieth century. "Rechtsstaat as Magic Wall" reminds us that the rule of law in the international sphere still obtains only at the sufferance of the great powers, and it reminds us how this state of affairs inevitably results in a dangerous spillover, which undermines the rule of law in the domestic sphere as well: *Political Justice* argues that the ongoing crisis of constitutionalism stems in part from a closely related crisis of the modern nation-state.[54] Only in the twentieth century do political movements break out of the nation-state boundaries that once separated relatively isolated and provincial populations and conveniently corresponded to political elites' aspirations to act in the international setting by means of effectively unregulated practices long associated with the idea of raison d'état. Yet as national borders lose the significance they once had, Kirchheimer suggests, the separation between raison d'état and rational law begins to dissipate. As domestic political activity becomes ever more directly integrated into an irrational and divided international setting, modes of (raison d'état) law, which liberalism never succeeded in eliminating there, can make an impressive comeback in the domestic setting as well. Totalitarian movements ignoring national borders are the most obvious manifestation of an increasingly internationalized political world and the most direct incentive for introducing new forms of repressive law, but they are only the tip of the iceberg. National borders are crossed by an increasing number of citizens for a variety of reasons, and "the new universe of communications allows worldwide interest groups and political movements to escape the impact of national law."[55]

Kirchheimer suggests that this process can help us explain why, as in the McCarthyite witch hunts of the fifties, many of the most vicious attacks on the rule of law now too often garner uncritical popular support. Unsurprisingly given democracy's failure to develop new instruments for guaranteeing the rationality of the decision making process, the reaction to the "disorderliness" of a world (and, concretely, to the terrible international totalitarian movements spawned by it) increasingly both complex and intimate has been defensive and even jingoistic. Precisely as the nation-state goes into crisis, archaic nationalistic identities flourish among those groups that have the least opportunities for shaping the contours of the new order. This provincialism is strengthened by the fact that the expanding legalistic universe of claims with which the modern welfare state's clients most closely identify is still guaranteed by the bureaucratic apparatus of the nation-state, despite the globalization of so many other features of political and economic existence. In short, Schmittian friend/foe politics, in which legitimate political criticism is perceived as identity threatening and existential, is one possible consequence of the ongoing disintegration of the modern nation-state. This comes out most clearly in the political trial, which revealingly gives "the masses a more intimate sense of participation in the world of politics than present-day parliamentary performances will allow."[56] There, as the political community turns to watch a legal spectacle translating its most irrational anxieties into the easily accessible form of an entertaining (show) trial, pseudoparticipatory friend/foe politics unabashedly drives (normal) parliamentary concerns from the political stage, revealing in a sudden blast how distant and irrelevant parliamentary institutions have become to so many in the age of "directed public opinion." Deprived of suitable instruments of self-government and political self-education, the masses are ready to be whipped into a frenzy that can be directed against a fabricated, allegedly inhumane foe.

(B) Kirchheimer's writings between 1945 and 1965 conclude his lifelong exploration of the crisis of parliamentarism. As we recall, "Changes in the Structure of Political Compromise" and "In Quest of Sovereignty" asked uneasily whether the emerging capitalist administrative state was compatible with classical liberal conceptions of parliamentary government. Kirchheimer now thinks the experience of the postwar West can be interpreted as confirming many of his earlier anxieties.

The attempt to satisfy a universe of legal claims couples with the need for extensive regulatory activities to generate a massive administrative apparatus that takes over many of the activities once more directly managed by elected legislators. In contrast to de jure statements of legislative supremacy, the de facto case in many political systems in the advanced West is that "a cabinet is responsible for the political business conducted by a bureaucracy over which it has an uncertain control to a parliament which lacks any means outside the trappings of constitutional authority for enforcing such control."[57] Kirchheimer goes so far as to tell us that we now live in an administrative state: "in a somewhat grotesque sense, Engels' and Lenin's utopian prediction of the administration of things instead of the domination of men has found a certain degree of confirmation in the realities of Western industrial society," where the bureaucratic universe of claims becomes a mainstay of political and social existence.[58] Although the welfare state admirably succeeds in removing potentially explosive political and social conflicts from the parliamentary scene and helps guarantee political stability, this comes at the cost of placing much real decision making power in the hands of administrators, over whom elected political bodies have only minimal and unsatisfying controls. The fundamental problem is

> what does parliamentary control of the administration mean in an age where a medium-sized state of 45 to 50 million . . . employs from a million to a million and a half civil servants and state employees? How can the parliament, twice removed from the actual scene, exercise meaningful control? The cabinet minister and his personal staff, if they do not shun the trouble, the waste of energies, and the enmities in the administrative ranks, may call for files, summon the professional administrative echelons and . . . transfer or discipline recalcitrant personnel. The members of parliament may make a critical speech, discuss departmental problems on the days set aside for the discussion of the budget, . . . he may elicit specific information during the questioning hour. . . . But the member of parliament always remains an outsider to the precincts which he may want to police. Even if he should be an unusually intelligent man with good technical and bureaucratic background, where will he find the information to exercise his office as supreme controller?[59]

This is not to say that parliamentarism has outlived all of its useful functions. As in the past, Kirchheimer rightly insists that the overall picture is more complex than crude critics of parliamentarism (like Schmitt) would like us to think.[60] He qualifies his harsh assessment of contemporary legislatures by reminding us that some legislatures (the United States Congress, for example) have been more successful than others in counteracting these trends. Modest reforms, like the introduction of extensive American-style parliamentary investigation, underdeveloped in much of Western Europe, surely undermine the most problematic features of the administrative state.[61] Even poorly functioning legislatures give political minorities a chance to influence the legislative process, providing individual parliamentarians with a public forum for expressing dissenting views and contributing to greater democracy within the apparatus of the political party, which, like the administrative apparatus, plays an increasingly central role in contemporary politics.[62] And, of course, when election results are inconclusive, parliamentary negotiations still have a key place in establishing workable coalitions.[63]

Still, "would an emergency show that industrial mass society and its equivalent—the administrative state—assigns a secondary place to all parliamentary assemblies by sheer necessity?"[64] Might a serious and unexpected crisis prove that parliaments have become little but a hollow formality? Kirchheimer thinks the sudden death of the parliament-centered French Fourth Republic and its replacement by de Gaulle's openly plebiscitary executive-based regime in 1958 gives us reason enough for worrying that this might be the case. In Kirchheimer's view, the Fifth Republic's outfitting of the executive branch with far-reaching powers completes the logic of a process, namely, the transformation of parliamentary government into the executive-centered administrative state, apparent everywhere in the industrial welfare states of the advanced West.[65] The reason this transition proved so climactic in France was that the old-fashioned brand of liberal parliamentarism practiced by the Fourth Republic made fewer concessions to the realities of postwar politics than other Western systems. Because the incongruity between liberal constitutional norms and the administration's de facto exercise of power was so great in France, it proved most directly explosive there. But the specter of de Gaulle haunts us all. In contrast to those who welcome the devolution of parliamentary democracy into a plebiscitary executive-centered regime, Kirchheimer is anxious. Is not a regime dominated by a set of bureaucratic cadres likely to prove less flexible and dynamic than one with a broader base? Parliament is declining everywhere, but it sometimes does manage to serve as a minimal "conduit between the administration and the political process."[66] Can France do without even this, as de Gaulle's supporters seem to believe?

Although Kirchheimer is silent about how to counter trends toward the administrative state, the reader is reminded of his tentative comment from "In Quest of Sovereignty" that "new devices and institutions"[67]—as he suggests in a 1961 essay, possibly some form of worker self-determination and a cautious loan from "the Pandora's box of the referendum"—can help take on some of the job the nineteenth-century liberal parliaments tackled better than their modern-day successors.[68] Otherwise, or so Kirchheimer's angst-ridden analysis concludes, parliamentarism may well be on its way to becoming a quaint but lifeless relic of a long-lost political universe.[69]

Nor have political parties, which seem to have taken over many of the main functions of parliament, succeeded in checking trends that jar with nineteenth-century constitutionalism's vision of political opposition as a "ceaseless critic." In this sphere as well, the capitalist administrative state proves to be an ambiguous creature. On the one hand, its obvious material achievements significantly lessen social tensions. On the other hand, this success itself engenders far more homogeneous party systems than their predecessors. In Kirchheimer's analysis, Willy Brandt was describing more than the idiosyncracies of postwar Germany when he commented, in 1961, that "in a sound and developing democracy it is the norm rather than the exception that the parties put forward similar, even identical demands in a number of fields. The question of priorities, of the rank order of tasks to be solved, and of methods and accents thus becomes ever so much more the content of opinion formation."[70] Kirchheimer recognizes that the demise of the militant politics of an earlier era is not something to be deprecated cheaply. He clearly thinks that the relatively humane welfare state of postwar capitalism has much to be said on its behalf. At the same time, as the administrative state expands, political parties take on the characteristics of mere "business agents," which, like the judges and bureaucrats busily processing individual claims, are more concerned with "adjudicating" between interests than offering fresh ideas: the logic of juridification can pollute party life, keeping parties from making sure that there is a competition of ideas as well as interests.[71] For that matter, the distinction between the administrative apparatus and the political party tends to become blurred as parties rush to occupy some portion of the all-important bonanza of the bureaucratic apparatus, posing obvious problems for an institution whose basic function it is to criticize state policy. The state and political opposition sometimes fuse together, and parties risk becoming too blunt an instrument for articulating popular demands effectively.[72] Even though trends toward greater political and social homogeneity remain real, the postwar capitalist welfare state is neither the harmonious middle-class society described by its apologists nor the totally administered one criticized by left-wing critics.[73] Kirchheimer reminds us that even during times of boom significant social strata—"older people whose income has not kept up with inflation, small peasant holders, small artisans and retailers without the capital to modernize their shops, and white collar elements outflanked by many groups of manual workers"—are left out of the welfare state's universe of organized interests, and, in contrast to Adorno and Marcuse, he continues to insist that the mass culture consumed by the working classes remains in some ways contradictory and far from perfectly one-dimensional.[74] The immediate significance of this is that as political parties become mere business agents for various organized interest groups, they risk ignoring those constituencies outside the universe of organized interests most directly integrated into the welfare state. But even if parties do avoid that mistake, Kirchheimer thinks they are clearly committing a serious one in closing their eyes to "the more important problems of our time (threat of universal atomic destruction, disproportion between the living standards and the expectations of advanced and former colonial countries, impact of technological change . . .)," none of which have a home in a setting predicated on aggressive capitalist economic growth and private consumption, and whose key actor is the passive and privatistic client of the administrative state universe of claims.[75]

3 The Contemporary Relevance of Kirchheimer's Critique of the Postwar Welfare State

Nearly thirty years after Kirchheimer's death, the welfare state rule of law lies in ruins. A defense of a moderate version of the social rule of law, such as Kirchheimer describes, belonged to the political mainstream of the immediate postwar era, when politicians and lawyers from virtually all parties rushed to embody some form of it in new constitutions for France, Germany, Italy, and elsewhere. Today, talk of "freedom from want," like Franklin Roosevelt's in his famous four-freedoms speech, sounds downright incendiary, and the idea of constitutionalized social rights is something only a handful of legal and political thinkers still defend.[76] In 1966 Kirchheimer could refer to free-market attacks on welfare state law as "a rearguard skirmish."[77] In the neoconservative era, Hayek is seen as a prophet, and T. H. Marshall a forgotten nobody. Today Kirchheimer's critique seems to be the rearguard skirmish.

Kirchheimer's writings between 1945 and 1965 remarkably anticipate many of those processes that precipitated the decline of the welfare state. When economic growth sputtered, the welfare state universe of claims came under a massive attack from privileged groups always skeptical of it and now allied with constituencies long locked out of a core of organized interests on which it rested. Potential oppositional groups and parties, which for too long had uncritically accepted the logic of limitless private consumption and bureaucratic passivity, proved unable to break out of old ways of thinking and come up with imaginative responses, and the decline of political opposition indeed proved to have long-term, unexpected costs. Issues ignored by the Keynesian political universe (unrestrained technological development, the possibility of atomic war, the gender contradictions of a way life predicated on "the supremacy of one's private existence within the bosom of the nuclear family") suddenly burst on the political scene, as their poisonous consequences became increasingly unacceptable to some political constituencies.[78] As evidence by continuing declines in participation in parties and parliamentary elections throughout the West, democratic "catch-all" parties may indeed have become too blunt to express popular energies effectively. And as neofascist movements reenter parliaments, talk of a crisis of parliamentarism begins to sound far less fantastic than it did just a few years ago.

Is not Kirchheimer's critique of the welfare state politically anachronistic in such an age? Insofar as it exaggerates how much the welfare state, even in Western Europe, ever was able to realize the ambitious legalistic universe of claims that reformers like Marshall (or even Franklin Roosevelt) sought, it is surely overstated. We also might recall how the fascist Schmitt often relied on excessively idealized portrayals of early liberalism precisely in order to debunk the somewhat less glamorous reality of everyday democratic politics in the twentieth century. Does not Kirchheimer himself probably rely on his old teacher's ploy in negatively comparing contemporary "directed public opinion" with an idealized picture of nineteenth-century constitutionalist regimes?[79] (Where was this constitutionalist utopia? In the slave states of the American South, or at the American frontier, where Native Americans were brutally hunted down like buffalo? In Dickens's England?)

It still seems to me that Kirchheimer's postwar writings can help serve as a much-needed corrective to a trend increasingly widespread among liberal and left-wing intellectuals today. Unsurprisingly given the one-sidedness and viciousness of the right-wing attack on the welfare state, there are signs that it is becoming fashionable to romanticize the American New Deal and postwar European welfare state in an equally one-sided manner. Like many such authors, Kirchheimer appreciates all the real achievements of the welfare state and its new legal institutions. He, too, recognizes that the "Age of Hayek" is destined to be an "Age of Misery," incompatible with the aspirations of the unfinished democratic project and the rule of law. But in contrast to such voices, his analysis can help us explain why so many came to see "the rule of bureaucrats and legal experts," which too often makes up the real core of our rule of law today, as unsatisfying and intrusive. Kirchheimer resists a reduction of the multidimensional rule of law into a one-dimensional defense of judicial and administrative decision making, and he rightly senses that a genuinely democratic version of the rule of law requires developing new instruments of self-government. The ideals of parliamentarism and the rule of law were always intricately intermeshed. Any attempt at a new conceptualization of the rule of law necessitates reconsidering how parliamentarism can be conceived and institutionalized anew in epoch when existing legislative bodies are manifestly overwhelmed.

Kirchheimer's account should remind contemporary defenders of legally based social rights of their potential limits. Even if we dismiss other reservations that have been directed (by Franz Neumann, among others) against such proposals,[80] Kirchheimer's observation that a "universe of legally enforceable claims" threatens to generate highly ambivalent relations of dependency between an empowered administrative elite and a set of privatistic clients needs to be taken seriously. What new institutions might counteract the increased de facto authority of bureaucrats and judges that might follow from the further institutionalization of social rights? How could constitutionally based social rights be kept from becoming a basis for what Kirchheimer once described as a system of suprapositive supralegality—that is, a set of amorphous legal standards that judges and bureaucrats rely on to challenge decisions by relatively broad-based, elected representative bodies?[81]

In contradistinction to many contemporary writers, Kirchheimer can help us explain why the welfare state's failure to challenge more radically the logic of the bourgeois private consumer made it easy pickings for crude bourgeois ideologies that simply took such thinking to its logical conclusion. He would better understand those among the poor and working classes who too often experienced the administrative state as an "immense and tutelary power," like that described so brilliantly by Tocqueville, in which "the will of man is not shattered, but softened, bent, and guided; men are seldom forced by it to act, but they are constantly restrained from acting. Such a power does not destroy, but it prevents existence; it does not tyrannize, but it compresses, enervates, extinguishes, and stupefies a people, till each nation is reduced to nothing better than a flock of timid and industrious animals, of which government is the shepherd."[82]

In offering an alternative to neoconservatism, should we not take this perspective into consideration as well? Or will middle-class intellectuals once again choose to ignore it and rush off, as so often in the history of social policy making, to set up disciplinary institutions that can make us clients but not autonomous citizens?

Conclusion

The Presence of the Past

From the perspective of much of contemporary radical legal scholarship in North America, the story that I have recounted here undoubtedly seems curious. Franz Neumann and Otto Kirchheimer argued that the rule of law—as well as a set of complementary institutions—is severely threatened by a series of unprecedented political and social transformations. According to the Frankfurt school jurists, the possibility of the rule of law's demise poses profound dangers for democratic politics. It is difficult to conceive how we might realize a political order with active and critical publics, freewheeling debate, and a responsive set of political institutions when the state apparatus and new forms of corporatist public/private authority are poorly regulated. If unchecked, the decay of the rule of law threatens to leave us at the mercy of a highly discretionary—and potentially arbitrary—situation-specific mode of law akin to the "rule of the exception" suggested by Carl Schmitt's authoritarian political theory in the twenties and thirties. According to Neumann and Kirchheimer, democracy very much needs the rule of law. The real problem is how it can be freed from problematic premodern and bourgeois presuppositions and restated and institutionalized in a political and social setting distinct from that which originally produced it.

Many representatives of the Critical Legal Studies movement (CLS) are likely to dismiss the early Frankfurt school's interest in preserving the basic achievements of the modern rule of law as deriving from a set of liberalistic intellectual illusions. For them, formal law is symptomatic of a broader problem and hardly (as I have tried to suggest) an unfulfilled demand that critical social theory still needs to take seriously. Mark Kelman argues that formal law is inextricably tied to a "stereotypical masculinity"; in any event, "it is impossible to imagine any central or local legal institutions advocating a coherent, noncontradictory body of rules. *All* rules will contain within them deeply embedded, structural premises that clearly enable decision makers to resolve particular controversies in opposite ways. . . . [A]ll law seems simultaneously either to demand or at least allow internally contradictory steps."[1] An unavoidable, radical indeterminacy constitutes the very core of all legal experience. Despite the fact that Rousseau and Hegel belong among the rule of law's most persuasive defenders, Duncan Kennedy thinks formal law is fundamentally privatistic and individualistic and exemplifies one aspect of a divided and deeply contradictory liberal legal consciousness (whose other side is made up by an ill-defined altruism, which Kennedy finds somewhat more appealing) that we probably would be better off jettisoning for an unnamed alternative.[2] Roberto Unger, who gives CLS's hostility to traditional liberal law its most speculative gloss, is less hesitant about suggesting the outlines of such an alternative. Because "the experience that supports the rule of law is one of antagonism among private wills," he believes he can contrast liberal law unfavorably to (ill-defined) notions of solidarity and community and, by implication, the possibility of a system of indwelling communal values, in his view anticipated by the proliferation of oddly moralistic standards in contemporary law, which would replace the rule of law. Like the tight-knit traditional communities of the premodern world, where shared mores and not abstract law governed everyday existence, Unger proposes a modern-day counterpart, where everyday mores (an "indwelling pattern of right")—but mores always open to criticism and revision—could make the rule of law obsolete.[3] If formal law rests on illegitimate forms of patriarchal, privatistic social antagonisms, what use could a communal, egalitarian utopia possible have for it? Why not just discard it?

This is not the place to undertake the careful analysis of the Critical Legal Studies movement that its provocative contributions to contemporary legal discourse clearly deserve.[4] Yet my exegesis of Neumann and Kirchheimer does generate a number of questions CLS authors need to confront. Although much about the contemporary political universe is new and unprecedented, many facets of it remain reminiscent of those experiences that first led political and legal authors to formulate the ideal of a rule of law hundreds of years ago—and led Neumann to Kirchheimer to insist on its virtues only a few decades ago. Why should we simply assume, as many in CLS do, that an emphasis on law's (allegedly) indeterminate core *necessarily* suggests a "progressive," left-wing brand of politics? As I recounted earlier in this study, right-wing authoritarians in midcentury Germany eagerly attacked traditional conceptions of norm-based legal decision making, in order to valorize the creative activity of an administrative apparatus hostile to democratic forces. Have CLS authors done enough to distinguish their deconstruction of liberal law from that of authoritarians like Carl Schmitt? For that matter, how could we make sure that administrative and new public/private authorities would be effectively constrained and regulated after we did away with "formalistic" liberal legal rules, as many in CLS seem to believe possible? If the rule of law is to be abandoned, what could keep such authorities from acting in an arbitrary and potentially oppressive manner? What new institutions could perform the admirable functions that the rule of law, however inadequately, has performed in liberal capitalist societies? This study has focused on the early Frankfurt school's dialogue with right-wing critics of the liberal rule of law, such as Schmitt. Yet implicitly, Neumann and Kirchheimer also intended to respond to a series of orthodox Marxist theorists, who repeatedly underplayed the achievements of the liberal rule of law. As Neumann and Kirchheimer recognized early on, this failing had disastrous consequences for left-wing political practice in our century. Despite the obvious differences between Critical Legal Studies and traditional Marxism, can we be so sure that the romantic impulses of the original Marxist critique of the "bourgeois" rule of law have been adequately eliminated from contemporary CLS discourse? A "total" critique of liberal legal values, as Unger described his project in *Knowledge and Politics,* may seem emancipatory in the context of a political culture in which the Establishment has generally prescribed to legalistic values. But how critical is it in a setting where there is evidence galore that privileged elites are little concerned with respecting the rule of law as soon as it conflicts with entrenched power interests?

In an age characterized by a rapid expansion of poorly regulated executive authority, a fusion of traditional liberal law with bureaucratic decrees, a demagogic attack on the rights of the criminally accused, and a permanent state of emergency in many inner cities, Neumann's and Kirchheimer's modest contributions to critical political and legal scholarship may help provide a much-needed corrective to one-sided, purely destructive attacks on the rule of law, which today, as in the twenties and thirties, are flourishing. For a pair of authors whose times were "circumscribed by the names Stalin, Hitler, and McCarthy," as Kirchheimer commented in 1964, that certainly is not the meanest intellectual accomplishment.[5]

Notes

Introduction

1. Roberto Unger, *Law in Modern Society* (New York: The Free Press, 1976), 221–22, 238–42.

2. Jürgen Habermas, "The Tanner Lectures," in *The Tanner Lectures on Human Values,* vol. 8 (1988), ed. S. McMurrin (Salt Lake City: University of Utah Press, 1988). Habermas's recent contributions to legal scholarship should make the object of this study all the more interesting. Many of Habermas's concerns were anticipated by Franz Neumann and Otto Kirchheimer, his predecessors at the Institute for Social Research.

3. For the best account in German: Alfons Söllner, *Geschichte und Herrschaft* (Frankfurt: Suhrkamp, 1979).

4. Herbert Marcuse, preface to *The Democratic and Authoritarian State,* by Franz Neumann (New York: The Free Press, 1957), vii. See also Marcuse's obituary for Kirchheimer in the *American Political Science Review,* vol. 60, no. 2 (June 1966), 486. There are numerous helpful biographical accounts from which I have borrowed. The reader should consult the bibliography for them.

5. Franz Neumann, "The Intelligentsia in Exile," in *Critical Sociology,* ed. Paul Connerton (New York: Penguin, 1976), 433.

6. Ernst Fraenkel, *Zur Soziologie der Klassenjustiz und Aufsätze zur Verfassungskrise 1931–32* (Darmstadt, Ger.: Wissenschaftliche Buchgesellschaft, 1968), viii–ix.

7. This common view was recently repeated by the German philosopher Ludwig Siep in "Mit Radikalen vernünftig reden?" *Der Spiegel,* no. 43 (1992), 292.

8. For one influential statement of this view, see Martin Jay, *The Dialectical Imagination: A History of the Frankfurt School* (Boston: Little, Brown, 1973), 165–66.

9. For an excellent discussion of Schmitt's influence in postwar Germany, see Ingeborg

Maus, *Bürgerliche Rechtstheorie und Faschismus: Zur sozialen Funktion und aktuellen Wirkung der Theorie Carl Schmitts* (Munich: Wilhelm Fink, 1976).

10. For a sampling, see G. L. Ulmen, "Review of Bendersky," *Telos* 59 (spring 1984); and most of the articles in the *Telos* special issue on Carl Schmitt, 72 (summer 1987), but especially Paul Piccone and G. L. Ulmen, "Introduction to Carl Schmitt." See also G. L. Ulmen, "The Sociology of the State: Carl Schmitt and Max Weber," *State, Culture, and Society,* vol. 1, no. 2 (1985).

11. Paul Gottfried, "Legality, Legitimacy, and Carl Schmitt," *National Review* (August 28, 1987), 52–53.

12. Chantal Mouffe, "Radical Democracy or Liberal Democracy?" *Socialist Review,* vol. 90, no. 2 (April–June 1990).

13. Susan Shell, "Meier on Strauss and Schmitt," *Review of Politics,* vol. 53, no. 1 (winter 1991).

14. See *Telos,* no. 72 (summer 1987).

15. Joseph Bendersky, *Carl Schmitt: Theorist for the Reich* (Princeton: Princeton University Press, 1983), 59.

16. George Schwab, *The Challenge of the Exception: An Introduction to the Ideas of Carl Schmitt* (New York: Greenwood, 1989), 101. See also Schwab, "Schmitt Scholarship," *Canadian Journal of Political and Social Theory,* vol. 4, no. 2 (spring–summer 1980).

17. In the case of Kirchheimer, the relationship was at times personally intimate as well: he seems to have been one of Schmitt's favorite students during the twenties, and he visited Schmitt even after World War II at least once.

Chapter 1

1. In order to avoid potential misunderstandings, let me make it clear right away that this is not to suggest that Schmitt's empirical political and legal analyses (in contrast to his moral intentions) are defensible or especially sophisticated or that we can read his empirical analyses without an eye to his fascist political and moral goals. As we will see, Neumann's and Kirchheimer's claim is both more modest and more subtle: some facets of a crisis of liberalism in our century are expressed or mirrored within certain aspects of Schmitt's theory.

2. Cited in Ellen Kennedy, "Carl Schmitt and the Frankfurt School: A Rejoinder," *Telos,* no. 73 (fall 1987), 102. My discussion here is intended as a contribution to the ongoing debate about the relationship between Schmitt and the Frankfurt school, which Kennedy has played an important role in initiating. See also her article and criticisms by Martin Jay, Ulrich Preuß, and Alfons Söllner in "Special Section on Carl Schmitt and the Frankfurt School," *Telos,* no. 71 (spring 1987). I have also benefited from Volker Neumann, "Verfassungstheorien politischer Antipoden: Otto Kirchheimer und Carl Schmitt," *Kritische Justiz,* vol. 14 (1981).

3. Max Weber, *Economy and Society,* ed. and trans. by G. Roth and C. Wittich, (Berkeley: University of California Press, 1978), 1402.

4. Weber, *Economy and Society,* esp. 865–71.

5. Weber, *Economy and Society,* 1399.

6. Weber, "Politics as a Vocation" and "Science as a Vocation," in *From Max Weber: Essays in Sociology,* ed. and trans. by C. Wright Mills and H. H. Gerth (New York: Oxford University Press, 1946).

7. All quotes here come from the original 1927 version of the essay; Kirchheimer could only have been familiar with this version when the texts discussed here (published between 1928 and 1930) were written. Carl Schmitt, "Der Begriff des Politischen," *Archiv für Sozialwissenschaft,* vol. 58, no. 1 (1927). All translations from German texts are my own. I have consulted an extensive secondary literature on Schmitt's concept of the political. The reader should consult the bibliography for the full list. The connection between Weber and Schmitt (as between Schmitt and Kirchheimer) is in some ways a direct one. Schmitt attended Weber's lectures in Munich during 1918 and 1919 on "Science as a Vocation" and "Politics as a Vocation," as well as a *Dozentenseminar* Weber offered for colleagues. Parts of *Political Theology* first appeared in a *Festschrift* for Weber prepared by his students. See G. L. Ulmen, "The Sociology of the State," 3–6.

8. On the centrality of violence for Weber, see Hannah Arendt, *On Violence* (New York: Harcourt, Brace and Jovanovich, 1970). Arendt criticizes what she takes to be a characteristically modern tendency to reduce the category of power to coercion. As we will see, Schmitt and the young Kirchheimer are particularly adamant proponents of this view, and all of its weaknesses arguably become clear in their theories.

9. Schmitt, "Der Begriff des Politischen," 3–5, 7.

10. The 1927 version is somewhat ambiguous on this problem: politics there seems to be autonomous and distinct in exactly the same manner that other spheres of activity are: "Das politische steht nämlich selbständig als eigenes Gebiet neben anderen . . ." (p. 3). By 1932 this has been changed to, "Jedenfalls ist sie selbständig, nicht im Sinne eines neuen Sachgebiets, sondern in der Weise, daß sie weder auf einem jener anderen Gegensaetze . . . zurückgeführt werden kann" (p. 27). Carl Schmitt, *Der Begriff des Politischen* (Berlin: Duncker und Humblot, 1932). This version has been ably translated by George Schwab as *The Concept of the Political* (New Brunswick, N.J.: Rutgers University Press, 1976). There was also a 1933 version with more aggressively fascist and openly anti-Semitic tones. On the differences between the texts, see Herbert Marcuse, "Review of Schmitt," *Zeitschrift für Sozialforschung,* vol. 3, no. 1 (1934), 102–3; Karl Löwith (alias Hugo Fiala), "Politischer Dezionismus," *Revue Internationale de la Theorie du Droit,* vol. 9 (1935).

11. Schmitt, "Der Begriff des Politischen," 6.

12. Schmitt, "Der Begriff des Politischen," 19–21.

13. "Whoever wants to engage in politics at all, and especially in politics as a vocation, has to realize these ethical paradoxes. He must know that he is responsible for what may become of himself under the impact of these paradoxes. I repeat, he lets himself in for the diabolic forces lurking in all violence." Weber, "Politics as a Vocation," 125–26.

14. Schmitt, "Der Begriff des Politischen," 4.

15. As we will see, Schmitt uses the term "normativity" in a number of different senses.

Sometimes it refers to moral claims allegedly irrelevant to the existential dynamics of friend/foe politics; at other junctures, it refers to classical general legal norms such as those often seen as the mainstay of the rule of law by political thinkers like Locke and Montesquieu and by modern legal positivism. In my reading of Schmitt, central to his attack on normativities is a critique of universalistic ideals of human equality. His hostility toward general law (or legal normativities) probably follows from his more fundamental suspicion about modern conceptions of human equality.

16. Carl Schmitt, *Political Theology* (1934), trans. George Schwab (Cambridge: MIT Press, 1988), 66. On the structure of Schmitt's decisionism, see Christian Graf von Krockow, *Die Entscheidung . Eine Untersuchung über Ernst Jünger, Carl Schmitt, Martin Heidegger* (Stuttgart: Ferdinand Enke, 1965), 54–67.

17. Carl Schmitt, *The Crisis of Parliamentary Democracy,* trans. Ellen Kennedy (Cambridge: MIT Press, 1985). Much of Schmitt's critique of discursive conceptions of legitimacy was suggested in his (1919) *Political Romanticism,* trans. Guy Oakes (Cambridge: MIT Press, 1986).

18. Schmitt, *Political Theology,* 5.

19. Schmitt, *Political Theology,* 30. See also Carl Schmitt, *Gesetz und Urteil. Eine Untersuchung zum Problem der Rechtspraxis* (Munich: C. H. Beck, 1968).

20. Schmitt, *Political Theology,* 13. See also Schmitt's impressive study of the idea of dictatorship in legal and political thought in his *Die Diktatur* (Munich: Duncker und Humblot, 1928).

21. Schmitt, *Political Theology,* 7.

22. This becomes even more clear in the 1932 version of the text. Schmitt, *The Concept of the Political* (1932), esp. 32.

23. Schmitt, "Der Begriff des Politischen," 18–19.

24. The concepts of unity and homogeneity are explicitly linked on a number of occasions. In "Staatsethik und pluralistischer Staat" (1930), Schmitt writes that unity from below takes the form of a substantial homogeneity of a people, whereas from above it is guaranteed by means of command and power. Carl Schmitt, *Positionen und Begriffe im Kampf mit Weimar-Genf-Versailles* (Hamburg: Hanseatische Verlagsanstalt, 1940), 139.

25. Schmitt, *The Crisis of Parliamentary Democracy,* 13–14; Schmitt, *Legalität und Legitimität* (Munich: Duncker und Humblot, 1932), 43–44. Authors who, like Ernst Fraenkel, emphasize the parallels between Rousseau and Schmitt tend to downplay Schmitt's criticisms of Rousseau. See Ernst Fraenkel, *Deutschland und die westlichen Demokratien* (Frankfurt: Suhrkamp, 1991).

26. In particular, see Carl Schmitt, *Die Verfassungslehre* (Munich: Duncker und Humblot, 1928), 226–42.

27. Schmitt, *The Crisis of Parliamentary Democracy,* 74–75. The view common among many of Schmitt's contemporary disciples that his racist and anti-Semitic polemics from the thirties are "extraneous" to his thinking is, at best, somewhat misleading. See Paul Piccone and G. L. Ulmen, "Introduction to Carl Schmitt," *Telos,* no. 72 (summer 1987), 11.

28. On Kirchheimer within the context of debates in German social democracy, see Wolfgang Luthardt, *Sozialdemokratische Verfassungstheorie in der Weimarer Republik* (Opladen, Ger.: Westdeutscher, 1986); Joachim Blau, *Sozialdemokratische Staatslehre in der Weimarer Republik* (Marburg, Ger.: Verlag der Arbeiterbewegung, 1980); Richard Saage, ed., *Solidargemeinschaft und Klassenkampf,* (Frankfurt: Suhrkamp, 1986).

29. Otto Kirchheimer, "The Socialist and Bolshevik Theory of the State" (1928), in Otto Kirchheimer, *Politics, Law and Social Change* (henceforth *PLSC*) (New York: Columbia University Press, 1969), 11. This essay is all that remains of Kirchheimer's doctoral dissertation. Its spirit is in some ways strikingly reminiscent of Walter Benjamin's "Critique of Violence," *Reflections* (New York: Harcourt Brace Jovanovich, 1978.

30. Kirchheimer, "The Socialist and Bolshevik Theory of the State," 14.

31. Kirchheimer, "The Socialist and Bolshevik Theory of the State," 12–14.

32. Kirchheimer, "The Socialist and Bolshevik Theory of the State," 21.

33. Kirchheimer, "The Socialist and Bolshevik Theory of the State," 17.

34. Kirchheimer, "The Socialist and Bolshevik Theory of the State," 20.

35. Kirchheimer's 1930 book *Weimar—and What Then?* has been reprinted in *PLSC.* "Das Problem der Verfassung" (1929), "Verfassungswirklichkeit und politische Zukunft der Arbeiterklasse" (1929), "Artikel 48 und die Wandlungen des Verfassungssystems: Auch ein Beitrag zum Verfassungsstag" (1930) are reprinted in Otto Kirchheimer, *Von der Weimarer Republik zum Faschismus: Die Auflösung der demokratischen Rechtsordnung,* ed. Wolfgang Luthardt (henceforth *WR*) (Frankfurt: Suhrkamp, 1976). Significantly, in his own 1928 study on constitutionalism, Schmitt argues that the Weimar Constitution includes many "compromises and ambiguities which do not contain a decision." But he is (in 1928) in some ways less ruthless in pursuing this critique than Kirchheimer. Despite its ambiguities, the constitution nonetheless made a "fundamental decision" in favor of the "bourgeois rule of law" *(bürgerliche Rechtsstaat)* and against social democratic interpretations of it, like those to be discussed in chapter 2. Schmitt, *Die Verfassungslehre,* 28–36, esp. 30.

36. Although Kelsen underplays the implicit normative character of the democratic process and, like Weber, thinks that the disenchantment process has to leave us with a political sphere from which morality has altogether disappeared, Kirchheimer's own alternative remains deeply inadequate. Hans Kelsen, *Sozialismus und Staat* (Leipzig: C. L. Hirschfeld, 1923); *Vom Wesen und Wert der Demokratie* (Tübingen, Ger.: J. B. Mohr, 1929). For that matter, the views of the Weimar Constitution's authors are more complicated than the young Kirchheimer suggests, and they were by no means uniformly relativistic; see Heinrich Potthoff, "Das Weimarer Verfassungswerk und die deutsche Linke," *Archiv für Sozialgeschichte,* vol. 12 (1972); Ulrich Kluge, *Die deutsche Revolution, 1918–19,* (Frankfurt: Suhrkamp, 1985), 159–80; Hugo Preuß, *Staat, Recht, und Freiheit* (Tübingen, Ger.: J. B. Mohr, 1926).

37. Kirchheimer was only one of a number of left-wing social democrats in the twenties who thought that aspects of Schmitt's political theory could be made compatible with Marxism. See also Max Adler, *Die Staatsauffassung des Marxismus* (1922) (Darmstadt, Ger.: Wissenschaftliche Buchgesellschaft, 1964); Adler, *Politische oder Soziale Demokratie* (Berlin: Laubsche, 1926). For an excellent discussion of this dialogue, see Ilse Staff, "Zur Rezeption der Ideen der Französischen Revolution von 1789 in der deutschen Staatslehre des

20. Jahrhunderts," in *Die Ideen von 1789,* ed. Forum für Philosophie (Frankfurt: Suhrkamp, 1989).

38. Paul Piccone and G. L. Ulmen, "Introduction to Carl Schmitt," 11–12. See also Joseph Bendersky, *Carl Schmitt: Theorist for the Reich,* 92.

39. Significantly, this is what separates Kirchheimer's use of the concept of homogeneity from that of some of his left-wing contemporaries. The social democrat Hermann Heller also demands social homogeneity, but his version of this idea is not only far more pluralistic than Schmitt's or Kirchheimer's but is not grounded in an anti-universalistic decisionism like that found here. The difference is not just that Kirchheimer is a left-wing socialist and Heller a more moderate social democrat. Kirchheimer makes the normless exception the centerpiece of his theory, whereas Heller rightly recognizes the dangers of doing such. See Hermann Heller, "Politische Demokratie und soziale Homogenität," *Gesammelte Schriften,* vol. 2 (Leiden: A. W. Sijthoff, 1971).

40. Kirchheimer, "The Socialist and Bolshevik Theory of the State," 4–7, 17–18; *Weimar—and What Then?,* 40.

41. Schmitt, "Der Begriff des Politischen," 21–27.

42. For a fine discussion of Schmitt's political theology, see Ilse Staff, "Zum Begriff der Politischen Theologie bei Carl Schmitt," in *Christentum und modernes Recht,* ed. Gerhard Dilcher and Ilse Staff (Frankfurt: Suhrkamp, 1984).

43. It is worrisome that contemporary postmodern anti-universalists who build on Schmitt have downplayed the significance of homogeneity for Schmitt. This is particularly true of Mouffe. It is unclear to me how Mouffe, having accepted Schmitt's attack on universalistic normativities, can avoid succumbing to all of its well-known negative features, such as Schmitt's own inability to counter the "concrete" anti-universalistic claims to power of racists and radical nationalists. See Chantal Mouffe, "Radical Democracy or Liberal Democracy?" In contrast, Marcel Gauchet takes the problematic notion of homogeneity for totalitarian politics seriously. See his "Die totalitäre Erfahrung und das Denken des Politischen," in *Autonome Gesellschaft und libertäre Demokratie,* ed. Ulrich Rödel (Frankfurt: Suhrkamp, 1990).

44. I am thinking specifically of Hegel's criticism of the French Revolution and his arguments to the effect that it failed (for example) to acknowledge the need for a characteristically modern differentiation among the state, civil society, and a sphere of intimacy.

45. Kirchheimer, *Weimar—and What Then?,* 44; "The Socialist and Bolshevik Theory of the State," 10–14.

46. Schmitt, *Political Theology,* 59, 63.

47. Schmitt, *The Crisis of Parliamentary Democracy,* 9–10. Describing Schmitt as a theorist of compromise and discussion, as one prominent German Supreme Court justice does, seems to me to be unfounded; see E. W. Böckenförde, *Recht, Staat, Freiheit: Studien zur Rechtsphilosophie, Staatstheorie und Verfassungsgeschichte* (Frankfurt: Suhrkamp, 1991), 344–65.

48. Schmitt, "Der Begriff des Politischen," 6–7.

49. Schmitt, *Die Verfassungslehre,* 228–29. But even in the political thought of classical antiquity there are of course signs of a more universalistic worldview. Even in Aristotle's discussion of the status of women and slaves in *The Politics,* he seems to struggle, for example, with the more problematic implications of his views on equality.

50. In his *Verfassungslehre,* Schmitt seems to build on Sieyes's picture of a potentially all-powerful, legally unrestrained "nation." On this theme, see Stefan Breuer, "Nationalstaat und pouvoir constituant bei Sieyes und Carl Schmitt," *Archiv für Rechts- und Sozialphilosophie,* vol. 70 (1984).

51. Schmitt, *Political Theology,* 6.

52. Carl Schmitt, "Der Führer schützt das Recht" (1934), reprinted in *Positionen und Begriffe im Kampf mit Weimar-Genf-Versailles.*

53. Carl Schmitt, "Nationalsozialistisches Rechtsdenken," *Deutsches Recht,* vol. 4, no. 10 (May 25, 1934), 225.

54. Carl Schmitt, "Nationalsozialistisches Rechtsdenken," esp. 226; *Staat, Bewegung, und Volk: Die Dreigliederung der politischen Einheit* (Hamburg: Hanseatische Verlagsantalt, 1933), esp. 44–45; *Über die drei Arten des rechtswissenschaftlichen Denkens* (Hamburg: Hanseatische Verlagsanstalt, 1934), esp. 10, 58–59.

55. Schmitt, *The Concept of the Political* (1932), 62. Schmitt's ideas about the rule of law are rather complex during the twenties and early thirties; they will be examined in depth in chapter 3. For now we note that even then he argues for a radical tension between (an anti-universalist, homogeneous) democracy and the (normativistic, liberal) rule of law. The central thesis of the 1928 *Verfassungslehre* is that constitutional democracy tries to synthesize the "political" idea of democracy with the "bourgeois individualist" rule of law. The former must have primacy for Schmitt.

56. Kirchheimer, "The Socialist and Bolshevik Theory of the State," 3–8; *Weimar—and What Then?,* 65–67; the 1928 "Bedeutungswandel des Parlamentarismus," which rehashes some features of Schmitt's critique of parliamentarism, in *WR,* 59.

57. Kirchheimer, "The Socialist and Bolshevik Theory of the State," 17.

58. Kirchheimer, "The Socialist and Bolshevik Theory of the State," 18.

59. Schmitt, *Political Theology,* 15.

60. Cited in Otto Kirchheimer, *Political Justice: The Use of Legal Procedures for Political Ends* (henceforth *PJ*) (Princeton: Princeton University Press, 1961), 287, where he develops a critique of state socialist law (and an implicit self-critique of his early writings) similar to that offered here.

61. Kirchheimer, "The Socialist and Bolshevik Theory of the State," 17.

62. For a helpful analytical discussion of the relationships among law, power, and violence, see Alexander Passerin d'Entrèves, *The Notion of the State* (Oxford: Oxford University Press, 1967).

63. Kirchheimer, "The Socialist and Bolshevik Theory of the State," 14–17; *Weimar—and*

What Then?, 40–43. This view of the principle of majority rule is also Schmitt's, and he repeats it on countless occasions. Compare Schmitt's analogous reflections in *Die Verfassungslehre,* 238–51.

64. Fritz Kern, *Kingship and Law in the Middle Ages* (Oxford: Basil Blackwell, 1948), 151.

65. On premodern legal culture, see Stanley Diamond, "The Rule of Law vs. the Rule of Custom," in *The Rule of Law,* ed. Robert Paul Wolff (New York: Simon and Schuster, 1971), who similarly romanticizes underdeveloped communitarian forms of legal regulation.

Chapter 2

1. A fine discussion of the young Neumann's relationship to Schmitt is provided by Volker Neumann, "Kompromiss oder Entscheidung? Zur Rezeption der Theorie Carl Schmitts in den Weimarer Arbeiten Franz L. Neumanns," in *Recht, Demokratie, und Kapitalismus: Aktualität und Probleme der Theorie Franz L. Neumanns,* ed. Joachim Perels (Baden-Baden: Nomos, 1984). My differences with this interpretation should become clear here and in the following chapters: the author exaggerates the similarities between Schmitt's analysis of the demise of state unity and Neumann's criticism of pluralist trends in contemporary politics. Neumann never accepts Schmitt's view of sovereignty. His is a more traditional view, closer to Weber's (and inspired directly by Hermann Heller). For a good overview especially of Neumann's Weimar contributions, see Wolfgang Luthardt, "Kontinuität und Wandel in der Theorie Franz L. Neumanns," *Internationale Wissenschaftliche Korrespondenz zur Geschichte der deutschen Arbeiterbewegung,* vol. 19 (1983).

2. Franz Neumann, *Koalitionsfreiheit und Reichsverfassung. Die Stellung der Gewerkschaften im Verfassungssystem* (Berlin: Carl Heymanns Verlag, 1932). The discussion of the concept of the political takes place on pp. 123–29; the quote is from p. 125.

3. Hermann Heller, "Staat" (1931), in *Handwörterbuch der Soziologie* (Stuttgart: Ferdinand Enke Verlag, 1955). See also Heller, *Die Souveranität* (1927), reprinted in Hermann Heller, *Gesammelte Schriften,* Bd. II (Leiden: A. W. Sijthoff, 1971). Here and in many other texts, Heller tries to show that despite their seeming antagonisms, the theories of Kelsen and Schmitt actually complement each other from a broader perspective. In separating legal theory radically from a sociology of power, Kelsen allegedly leaves us with a formalistic "nomocratic" theory as one-sided as Schmitt's irrationalism, which makes the (normatively unrestrained) exercise of brute power its core. Schmitt's realism is a direct antipode to Kelsen's worrisome refusal to integrate an empirical analysis of politics into his theory, and each theory implicitly reproduces the failures of the other. As we will see, Neumann later develops a version of this thesis and similarly seeks an alternative to both Kelsen's positivism and Schmitt's valorization of brute power.

4. Neumann, *Koalitionsfreiheit und Reichsverfassung,* 125–26. For Neumann's criticism of Kirchheimer, see, for example, his "Social Significance of Basic Rights in the Weimar Constitution" (1930), in *Social Democracy and the Rule of Law,* edited by Keith Tribe. Translated by Keith Tribe and Leena Tanner. (London: Allen & Unwin, 1987), especially pp. 27–28, 42–43. I have altered the title given in the translation that appears in *Social Democracy and the Rule of Law* because it appears potentially misleading to me. On occasion, I have made other *minor* changes in the translations that appear in *Social Democracy and the Rule of Law.*

5. Schmitt, "Der Begriff des Politischen," 2; Weber, Politics as a Vocation", 78.

6. Neumann, *Koalitionsfreiheit und Reichsverfassung,* 127.

7. Neumann, "Der Kampf um den Zwangstariff," *Die Arbeit,* vol. 2, no. 11 (November 1925), 696.

8. Neumann, *Koalitionsfreiheit und Reichsverfassung,* 124.

9. The Weimar Constitution included articles making extensive socialization possible (article 156), and it demanded that employees and employers jointly manage the economy (article 165). Neumann directly criticizes the constitutional interpretation of Schmitt and Kirchheimer on a number of occasions, as does Heller. See Neumann's "Social Significance of Basic Rights in the Weimar Constitution" and his "Fünf Jahre Arbeitsgerichtbarkeit," *Soziale Praxis,* vol 41, no. 35 (September 1932), where he attacks the claim that Weimar is merely a formal democracy. Neumann thinks that its founders also wanted the republic to realize an egalitarian social "substance." See also Hermann Heller, "Freiheit und Form in der Verfassung," *Gesammelte Werke,* vol. 2. Neumann's underlying view of the Weimar Constitution as ordaining a social rule of law is repeated in all of his major texts from 1930 until 1933, but he provides a particularly cogent statement of it in "Reichsverfassung und Wohlfahrtsstaat," *Das Freie Wort,* vol. 4, no. 26 (1932).

10. Franz Neumann, *Behemoth: The Structure and Practice of National Socialism* (New York: Oxford University Press, 1944), 46.

11. This comes out most clearly in Heller's analysis of Italian fascism. Hermann Heller, *Europa und der Fascismus* (Berlin: Walter de Gruyter, 1929). Heller is probably the most significant social democratic political theorist from the Weimar era, and his work has rightfully garnered attention in recent years among younger German scholars attracted by a healthy eclecticism that combines an explicitly anticapitalist standpoint with a far richer analysis of legal and political institutions than that typically found in the Marxist tradition. See Wolfgang Schluchter, *Entscheidung für den sozialen Rechtsstaat. Hermann Heller und die staatstheoretische Diskussion in der Weimarer Republik* (Baden-Baden: Nomos, 1983); Christoph Müller Ilse Staff, eds., *Staatslehre in der Weimarer Republik. Hermann Heller zu Ehren* (Frankfurt: Suhrkamp, 1985). Like many in his generation, Heller did not survive fascism. He died in 1933 (at the age of 42, and probably because of health complications from fleeing Germany) in republican Spain. Neumann's intellectual relationship to Heller is an exceedingly complicated one. Although his model of a social rule of law parallels Heller's ideas, Neumann became increasingly critical of some elements of Heller's rather complicated social philosophy. For a sample of this criticism, see Franz Neumann, "On the Marxist Theory of the State" (1935), in *Social Democracy and the Rule of Law.* A crucial section of *Union Autonomy and the Constitution* was originally a paper Neumann gave at a seminar of Heller's in Berlin. Other parts of it were presented at a seminar directed by Carl Schmitt.

12. Hermann Heller, "Rechtsstaat oder Diktatur?" (1930), in *Der bürgerliche Rechtsstaat,* ed. Mehdi Tohidipur, vol. 1 (Frankfurt: Suhrkamp, 1978). In postwar Germany, Heller is generally credited with the idea of a social rule of law, which was robbed of its more radical features when given constitutional status in article 20 of the Bonn Basic Law of 1949. But Neumann begins using the term at the same time (1930).

13. Karl Renner, *The Institutions of Private Law and Their Social Functions* (1929) (London: Routledge and Kegan Paul, 1949).

14. Neumann, "The Social Significance of Basic Rights in the Weimar Constitution," 33. He repeats this phrase on many occasions.

15. On the base/superstructure problem, see Franz Neumann, *Rechtsphilosophische Einleitung zu einer Abhandlung über das Verhältnis von Staat und Strafe,* unpublished doctoral thesis Faculty of Law, University of Frankfurt, 1923 (available at the Stadt- und Universitätsbibliothek, Frankfurt), 19–26. For references to Renner, see Franz Neumann, "Richterliches Ermessen und Methodenstreit im Arbeitsrecht", *Arbeitsrecht,* vol. 16, no. 6 (June 1929), 329–32; Neumann, "Der Entwurf eines Monopol- und Kartellgesetzes," *Die Arbeit,* vol. 7, no. 12 (December 1930), 774–75. Neumann applies Renner's method directly in a number of technical legal texts: "Betriebsgeheimnisschutz," *Arbeitsrecht-Praxis,* vol. 5, no. 5 (May 1932), and "Gewerkschaften und Wirtschaftsverfassung," *Marxistische Tribüne,* vol. 1, no. 2 (November 1931). The question, of course, is whether this reading of Marx is convincing. Can a Marxist legal theory adequately grapple with the problem of the autonomy (in all of its significance) of the legal and political order? Renner seems to assume this more than he demonstrates it. His study, as he himself admits, leaves unanswered the question of the extent to which the legal and political order actively defines the contours of social and economic life and is not a passive superstructure. More significantly, his legal positivism leads him to ignore important questions about the underlying normative structure and significance of the legal order and, thus, about the relationship of legality to legitimacy. Neumann's analysis here suffers from the same problems. He assumes the flexibility of Marxist theory for developing an adequate analysis of law more than he manages to defend it. One important difference between Renner and Neumann is that the latter refers to the Austro-Marxist Otto Bauer's view (based on Marx's analysis of French Bonapartism) that the relative balance of class forces in central Europe after 1918 is responsible for a "relative autonomy" of political and legal institutions. Though certainly an interesting sociological thesis, it still does not allow us to focus adequately on the normative problem of the relationship between legality and democratic legitimacy. For both Renner and Neumann, the problem of legitimacy is simply not a central one, and the recourse to Bauer does not provide any solution to this basic weakness. This is, of course, a characteristic problem of classical Marxist theorizing about politics. Why worry about the problem of legitimacy when the industrial proletariat is destined to establish a "good" order? For Bauer's views, see his "Das Gleichgewicht der Klassenkräfte," in *Austromarxismus,* ed. H. J. Sandkühler and Rafael de la Vega (Frankfurt: EVA, 1970).

16. Neumann, "The Social Significance of Basic Rights in the Weimar Constitution," 34–35.

17. Neumann, "The Social Significance of Basic Rights in the Weimar Constitution," 32. Significantly, Schmitt was among the most prominent writers on the German right who argued during the twenties that the generality of law should also apply to the legislature. Schmitt, *Die Verfassungslehre,* 138–57. But we will have to wait before evaluating Habermas's recent charge that Schmitt influenced left-wing German political and legal thought "indirectly by means of Franz Neumann." Jürgen Habermas, *Faktizität und Geltung: Beiträge zur Diskurstheorie des Rechts und des demokratischen Rechtsstaats* (Frankfurt: Suhrkamp, 1992), 521.

18. Neumann, "On the Preconditions and the Legal Concept of an Economic Constitution," in *Social Democracy and the Rule of Law,* 46–48.

19. Neumann, "On the Preconditions and the Legal Concept of an Economic Constitution," 44–49.

20. Is this view convincing? Even if this picture of early capitalism is more myth than reality, one could argue that at least the ideal of a relatively egalitarian market economy (consisting, generally, of relatively equal and independent producers) played a crucial role in the emergence of liberal democratic political thought; perhaps this is most clear in the writings of Rousseau, Jefferson, and Tocqueville, but one can detect it elsewhere as well. Insofar as those ideas have been institutionalized in liberal constitutions and political bodies, the relationship between myth and ideology on the one side and social and political reality on the other side becomes more complicated than it first might seem. The myth of an egalitarian economy continues to structure our very real political and legal institutions, hence it is always more than mere ideology.

21. Neumann describes this project in many texts: "Gesellschaftliche und staatliche Verwaltung der monopolistischen Unternehmungen," *Die Arbeit,* vol. 5, no. 7 (1928); "Der Salzburger Juristentag," *Die Arbeit,* vol. 5, no. 10 (October 1928); "Gegen ein Gesetz zur Nachprüfung der Verfassungsmäßigkeit von Reichsgesetzen," *Die Gesellschaft,* vol. 6, no. 6 (June 1929); *Die politische und soziale Bedeutung des arbeitsgerichtlichen Rechtspechung* (Berlin: E. Laubsche, 1929); "Der Entwurf eines Monopol- und Kartellgesetzes"; "Kartell- und Monopolkontrolle," *Gewerkschafts-Zeitung,* vol. 41, no. 6 (February 1931); "Gewerkschaften und Wirtschaftsverfassung"; "Fünf Jahre Arbeitsgerichtbarkeit."

22. On public/private law, see Franz Neumann, "Zur öffentlichen-rechtlichen Natur des Tarifvertrags," *Arbeitsrecht,* vol. 13, no. 1 (January 1926); also "Salzburger Juristentag."

23. Neumann, "On the Preconditions and Legal Concept of an Economic Constitution"; "Gewerkschaften und Wirtschaftsverfassung."

24. Jürgen Habermas, "The New Obscurity: The Crisis of the Welfare State and the Exhaustion of Utopian Energies" in his *The New Conservatism: Cultural Criticism and the Historians' Debate* (Cambridge: MIT Press, 1989). Also: Claus Offe, *Contradictions of the Welfare State* (Cambridge: MIT Press, 1984), 239–51.

25. Neumann, "Der Kampf um den Zwangstariff," 698–701.

26. Neumann, "Der Kampf um den Zwangstariff," 699–700.

27. Neumann, "Der Kampf um den Zwangstariff," 698–99. On the importance of "autonomy," see *Die politische und soziale Bedeutung der arbeitsgerictlichen Rechtsprechung,* 36–40; "Gewerkschaften und Wirtschaftsverfassung."

28. Neumann, "Betriebsrisiko," *Arbeitsrecht-Praxis,* vol. I, no. 10 (October 1928); "Lohnzahlungen bei Betriebsstockungen," *Juristische Wochenschrift,* vol. 57, no. 46 (November 17, 1928); and in many other texts. Compare Ernst Fraenkel's similar anxieties about the consequences of legal deformalization for the working classes in his *Zur Soziologie der Klassenjustiz* (1927), reprinted in *Zur Soziologie der Klassenjustiz und Aufsätze zur Verfassungskrise 1931–32.* Neumann and Fraenkel practiced law together in Berlin during the republic's final years and both were active in the SPD.

29. Neumann, *Die politische und soziale Bedeutung der arbeitsgerichtlichen Rechtsprechung;* "Gewerkschaften und Wirtschaftsverfassung"; "Fünf Jahre Arbeitsgerichtbarkeit." Neumann's model of an autonomous and relatively nonstatist socialism comes in part from his Frankfurt law teacher, Hugo Sinzheimer, an author of the Weimar Constitution as well as the chief architect of modern German labor law, who originally developed many of the ideas sketched out by Neumann during the twenties. Like Heller, Sinzheimer died in exile (in

Holland); he also has recently been rediscovered by critical younger scholars in Germany. See Hugo Sinzheimer, *Arbeitsrecht und Rechtssoziologie* (Frankfurt: EVA, 1976).

30. Neumann, *Die politische und soziale Bedeutung der arbeitsgerichtlichen Rechtsprechung,* 38; "Der Entwurf eines Kartell- und Monopolgesetzes," 786.

31. Neumann, *Behemoth,* 46.

32. For an enlightening discussion of traditional Marxism's problems with conceptualizing basic rights, see Claude Lefort, *The Political Forms of Modern Society* (Cambridge: MIT Press, 1986), 239–72.

33. Schmitt, *Die Verfassungslehre,* 157–82. Neumann, *Koalitionsfreiheit und Reichsverfassung,* 9–19; "Gegen ein Gesetz zur Nachprüfung der Verfassungsmässigkeit von Reichsgesetzen," 522–24; "The Social Significance of Basic Rights in the Weimar Constitution," where he even refers to "the extraordinarily stimulating theory of Carl Schmitt," 28–30; *Die politische und soziale Bedeutung der arbeitsgerichtlichen Rechtsprechung,* 7–8. The constitutional backdrop in Weimar, as in the United States at the time, was dominated by a conservative interpretation of political rights as instruments for defending traditional capitalism, which correspondingly sought to transform the court system into a check on legislative social reform. Although the Weimar Constitution provided no legal basis for institutionalizing an American-style constitutional court with the power to overrule parliamentary legislation, right-wing political forces dominant in the legal system hoped to cripple parliament (where the Left long remained relatively well represented) in part by referring to select constitutional rights in order to challenge the constitutionality of parliamentary laws. Unsurprisingly, this development worried Neumann and many others—including Otto Kirchheimer—on the Weimar Left; Kirchheimer's astute critique of the judiciary's transformation of the Weimar Constitution's relatively progressive expropriation clause (article 153) into a defense of private property belongs in this genre (see the essays on expropriation collected in *Social Democracy and the Rule of Law*). In any event, this trend certainly helps explain Neumann's hostility to purely liberal (and allegedly undemocratic) conceptions of basic rights and the division of powers. Still, it offers no apology for the broader analytical conclusions that he draws from it. One could argue that Neumann accepts the conservative view that rights are individualistic and bourgeois but draws different political conclusions from it.

34. Neumann, "Gegen ein Gesetz zur Nachprüfung der Verfassungsmäßigkeit von Reichsgesetzen," 522; *Koalitionsfreiheit und Reichsverfassung,* 11.

35. Compare the diagram on p. 170 of the *Verfassungslehre* with Neumann's categorization on pp. 15–16 of *Koalitionsfreiheit und Reichsverfassung.*

36. Neumann, "Gegen ein Gesetz zur Nachprüfung der Verfassungsmäßigkeit von Gesetzen," 523.

37. Neumann, *Koalitionsfreiheit und Reichsverfassung,* 10–11. Neumann, "Gegen ein Gesetz zur Nachprüfung der Verfassungsmäßigkeit von Reichsgesetzen," 523–24. For an example of his use of the term "social homogeneity," see "Das geschichtliche Verhältnis von Staat und Koalitionen," *Gewerkschafts-Archiv,* vol. 9, no. 17 (December 1932), 248. Neumann's category of homogeneity lacks the explicitly anti-universalistic and existentialist elements basic to Schmitt's formulation of it. At the same time, the way it is linked to the idea of a fundamental contradiction between political liberalism and democracy (and a hostile assessment of basic political rights) probably reveals something of the imprint

of Carl Schmitt. It is striking that Hermann Heller, who articulates an influential competing argument for "social homogeneity" from a social democratic viewpoint during the same period, does not succumb to the illusion that a postcapitalist homogeneous democracy could do without basic rights. Here again, Neumann's traditional Marxist position is probably mediated by categories shaped or even borrowed from Schmitt. Compare Heller, "Grundrechte und Grundpflichten" (1924), in *Gesammelte Werke,* vol. 2.

38. From the vast historical literature, I have found the following studies most helpful: Gotthard Jasper, *Die gescheiterte Zähmung. Wege zur Machtergreifung Hitlers 1930–34* (Frankfurt: Suhrkamp, 1986); Hans Mommsen, "Die Sozialdemokratie in der Defensive: Der Immobilimus der SPD und der Aufstieg des Nationalsozialismus," in *Sozialdemokratie zwischen Klassenbewegung und Volkspartei,* ed. Hans Mommsen (Frankfurt: Athenäum, 1974) (on the SPD and its problems); Wolfgang Luthardt, *Sozialdemokratische Verfassungstheorie in der Weimarer Republik* (on the different reactions to the crisis among SPD political theorists).

39. In a revealing letter to Schmitt from September 7, 1932 (that is, six weeks after the Prussian *Staatsstreich,* in which Schmitt played a pivotal role), Neumann warmly praises the latter's (1932) *Legalität und Legitimität.* Neumann comments that he "agrees completely" with the "critical parts of the book." Neumann accepts Schmitt's claim that the principle of parliamentary legality can no longer "function" effectively in the Germany of the thirties: "if one accepts the standpoint that the fundamental political antagonism in Germany is the economic antithesis, that the decisive friend/foe constellation in Germany is that between labor and property, then it makes sense to claim that . . . rule can no longer be parliamentary." Moreover, Neumann shares Schmitt's view (as expressed in *Legalität und Legitimität*) that the "substantive" elements of the Weimar Constitution should be given priority over many of its traditional liberal democratic "formalisms". In Neumann's case, that means that some of the explicitly social democratic clauses of the constitution's second section, "Basic Rights and Duties," make up the substance of the Weimar constitutional order and should be given priority. As we will see in chapter 3, Schmitt's *Legality and Legitimacy* similarly argues for the primacy of select components of the constitution's "Basic Rights and Duties"—but *not* its social democratic elements. The letter is reprinted in *Reform und Resignation. Gespräche über Franz L. Neumann,* ed. Rainer Erd (Frankfurt: Suhrkamp, 1985), 79–80.

40. It is really only with the emergence of the Papen regime, in June 1932, that Neumann seems to recognize the dangers of the semidictatorship that had emerged in Germany. See Franz Neumann, "Recht ohne Grundlage," *Vorwärts* (morning edition), September 7, 1932; "Rechtswirksamkeit der Notverordnungen, Kampffreiheit oder Friedenspflicht," *Arbeitsrecht-Praxis,* vol. 5, no. 10 (October 1932); *Das gesamte Pressenotrecht vom. 4 Februar 1933* (Berlin: Dietz, 1933).

41. Neumann, *Koalitionsfreiheit und Reichsverfassung,* esp. 122–39. Compare Schmitt's own use of "institutional guarantees" (and Neumann's role in its formulation) in "Freiheitsrechte und Institutionelle Garantien der Reichsverfassung," in *Verfassungrechtliche Aufsätze aus den Jahren 1924–54* (Berlin: Duncker und Humblot, 1973).

42. Neumann, "The Social Significance of Basic Rights in the Weimar Constitution," 33.

43. For the biographical details, see Peter Intelmann "Zur Biographie von Franz L. Neumann," *1999: Zeitschrift für Sozialgeschichte des 20. und 21. Jahrhunderts,* vol. 5, no. 1 (January 1990).

44. Franz Neumann, "The Decay of German Democracy," *The Political Quarterly,* vol. 4, no. 1 (October–December 1933), 536, 538. Luthardt's "Kontinuität und Wandel in der Theorie Franz L. Neumanns" offers a helpful discussion of this theme.

45. Neumann, "The Rule of Law, the Division of Powers and Socialism," in *Social Democracy and the Rule of Law,* 66.

46. Neumann, "The Rule of Law, the Division of Powers and Socialism," 72.

47. Neumann, "The Rule of Law, the Division of Powers and Socialism," 68.

48. Neumann, "The Rule of Law, the Division of Powers and Socialism," 74.

Chapter 3

1. In particular, see Otto Kirchheimer, "Artikel 48 und die Wandlungen des Verfassungssystems: Auch ein Beitrag zum Verfassungstag" (1930), in *WR.* On the role of emergency legislation in Weimar Germany, see Hans Boldt, "Article 48 of the Weimar Constitution: Its Historical and Political Implications," in *German Democracy and the Triumph of Hitler,* ed. A. Nichols and E. Matthias (London: Allen and Unwin, 1971).

2. See Ellen Kennedy, "Carl Schmitt and the Frankfurt School." Eager to toss diverse left-wing critics of contemporary politics into a pot with fascists like Schmitt, she obscures many of the important differences between the two, and she ultimately must downplay Kirchheimer's break with Schmitt. Volker Neumann's "Verfassungstheorien politischer Antipoden" is superior.

3. John Locke, *Two Treatises on Government,* ed. Peter Laslett (Cambridge: Cambridge University Press, 1967), esp. chap. 11, para. 137. For a discussion providing helpful background about the immediate historical and intellectual context for this conception, see M. J. C. Vile, *Constitutionalism and the Separation of Powers* (Oxford: Clarendon Press, 1967), esp. 53–75.

4. Locke, *The Second Treatise on Government,* chap. 11, para. 142.

5. Weber, *Economy and Society,* 979.

6. Schmitt develops the ideas discussed here in numerous texts from this period, but its central features are worked out in "Wesen und Werden des Faschistischen Staates" (1929), "Staatsethik und pluralistischer Staat" (1930), "Die Wendung zum totalen Staat" (1930), and "Weiterentwicklung des totalen Staats in Deutschland" (1933), all reprinted in Carl Schmitt, *Positionen und Begriffe im Kampf mit Weimar-Genf-Versailles; Der Hüter der Verfassung* (Tübingen, Ger.: J. C. B. Mohr, 1931); and *Legalität und Legitimität.* For a helpful overview of some of Schmitt's ideas from this period, but one that does not cover their transformation during the early thirties adequately, see Rune Slagstad, "Liberal Constitutionalism and Its Critics: Carl Schmitt and Max Weber," in *Constitutionalism and Democracy,* ed. J. Elster and R. Slagstad (Cambridge: Cambridge University Press, 1988). For a more general discussion, see Richard Wolin, "Carl Schmitt, Political Existentialism, and the Total State," *Theory and Society,* vol. 19, no. 4 (1990); Wolin, "Carl Schmitt. The Conservative Revolutionary: Habitus and the Aesethetics of Horror," *Political Theory,* vol. 20, no. 3 (1992); Ingeborg Maus, *Bürgerliche Rechtstheorie und Faschismus,* as well as her essays in *Rechtstheorie und politische Theorie im Industriekapitalismus;* Volker Neumann, *Der Staat im Bürgerkrieg. Kontinuität*

und Wandlung des Staatsbegriffs in der politischen Theorie Carl Schmitts (Frankfurt: Campus, 1980), esp. 100–137; Jürgen Fijalkowski, *Die Wendung zum Führerstaat. Ideologische Komponente in der Politische Philosophie Carl Schmitts* (Opladen, Ger.: Westdeutscher Verlag, 1958); Hasso Hofmann, *Legitimität gegen Legalität: Der Weg der politischen Philosophie Carl Schmitts* (Neuwied, Ger.: Luchterhand, 1964).

7. In developing his own more sociologically oriented critique of Weimar, Schmitt repeatedly cites Kirchheimer's writings from the late twenties. Schmitt's relationship to Kirchheimer was hardly one-way, and he seems to have learned a great deal from his pupil: see his "Wesen und Werden des Faschistischen Staates," 112; *Der Hüter der Verfassung,* 142. The essays collected in *Verfassungrechtliche Aufsätze aus den Jahren 1924–54* include numerous references to Kirchheimer and Neumann. The most interesting is a comment by Schmitt describing learning a great deal about left-wing legal theory (specifically, Karl Renner) from Kirchheimer and Neumann at a seminar they both attended in Berlin conducted by Schmitt in the summer of 1931 (pp. 167–68). What makes the story complicated is that Schmitt and Kirchheimer seem to have remained on friendly terms at least until 1932; they probably exchanged unpublished manuscripts (often directed at the views of the other) even then. Volker Neumann, "Verfassungstheorien politischer Antipoden," 238–39.

8. Schmitt, "Wesen und Werden des Faschistischen Staates," 112. If I seem to fuse my discussion of Schmitt's attack on the Weimar Republic with his more general critique of the liberal democratic welfare state, this is because Schmitt himself often seems to do so.

9. Schmitt, "Staatsethik und pluralistischer Staat," esp. 144–45. See also Schmitt's comments about English pluralism in the 1932 version of *The Concept of the Political,* 39–45.

10. Schmitt, *Der Hüter der Verfassung,* 71–91. Karl Korsch reviewed this study in the Institute for Social Research's *Zeitschrift für Sozialforschung,* vol. 1 (1932), 204–5; the review is interesting because Korsch's response to this moment in Schmitt's intellectual development is both more favorable and more traditionally Marxist than the young Kirchheimer's.

11. Rousseau, *The Social Contract,* ed. Roger Masters (New York: St. Martin's, 1978), 66.

12. Rousseau, "Political Economy," in *The Social Contract,* esp. 230–32. For a somewhat distinct exegesis of Rousseau's argument here, see Dennis Thompson, "Representation and the Welfare State," in *Democracy and the Welfare State,* ed. Amy Gutmann, (Princeton: Princeton University Press, 1988), 138–43.

13. Hegel grasps the centrality of the determinate character of law when contrasting nonformal Anglo-American common law (a "monstrous confusion") with the neatly codified and semantically coherent formal law then emerging on the continent: "making a law is not to be represented as merely the expression of a rule of behavior valid for everyone, though that is one moment in legislation; the more important moment, the inner essence of the matter, is knowledge of the content of the law in its determinate universality." Hegel understands that if law were to take the form of vague, undetermined resolutions, its seeming generality would be spurious: a legal standard based on a vague clause like "in the public interest" or "healthy popular sentiment" might appear to regulate a general category of objects, yet such legal norms are so imprecise that they not only are unlikely to provide any real direction to judges or administrators but probably will serve as a front for irregular, arbitrary individual state action. In such cases, the legal norm is no longer in fact general. For modern authors like Locke and Hegel, general law refers to an abstract

category of persons or objects—but it must do so in an adequately specific (or determinate) manner. In any event, for Hegel it is hardly the case that formal law and state regulation of social and economic affairs are inconsistent. G. F. Hegel, *The Philosophy of Right,* trans. T. M. Knox (New York: Oxford University Press, 1967), para. 211. On the complexities of this conception of the legal norm, see Franz Neumann, "The Change in the Function of Law in Modern Society," in *The Democratic and Authoritarian State,* 28–30.

14. Carl Schmitt, *Unabhängigkeit der Richter, Gleichheit vor dem Gesetz und Gewährleistung des Privateigentums nach der Weimarer Verfassung* (Berlin: Walter de Gruyter, 1926). Friedrich Hayek, *The Road to Serfdom,* esp. 54–65; Hayek, *Law, Legislation, and Liberty,* vols. 1–3 (London: Routledge and Kegan Paul, 1973). Hayek acknowledges his debt to Schmitt in an obscure yet revealing footnote on pp. 194–95 of vol. 3, where he notes that some facets of his analysis were anticipated by "the extraordinary German student of politics, Carl Schmitt." For an initial but inadequate comparison of Hayek and Schmitt, see F. R. Cristi, "Hayek and Schmitt on the Rule of Law," *Canadian Journal of Political Science,* vol. 17, no. 3 (September 1984).

15. Schmitt, *Legalität und Legitimität,* 87.

16. Schmitt, *Legalität und Legitimität,* 27.

17. For discussions of this theme in Weber's final writings and on his attempt to shape the Weimar Constitution, see Wolfgang Mommsen, *Max Weber und die deutsche Politik,* 1890–1920 (Tübingen, Ger.: J. C. B. Mohr, 1959), 324–413; Mommsen, *The Age of Bureaucracy: Perspectives on the Political Sociology of Max Weber* (Oxford: Basil Blackwell, 1974), 72–94. For a more general discussion, see David Beetham, *Max Weber and the Theory of Modern Politics* (Oxford: Polity, 1985), 215–49.

18. Mommsen, *Max Weber und die deutsche Politik,* esp. 379–86, 414–19.

19. Schmitt writes that the federal president should be allowed to rely on "measures" to "break through" *(durchbrechen)* constitutional norms, because not every facet of the Weimar Constitution is more important than "the protection of the constitution itself." Carl Schmitt, "Die staatsrechtliche Bedeutung der Notverordnung, insbesondere ihre Rechtsgültigkeit" (1931), in his *Verfassungsrechtliche Aufsätze,* 244–45. Of course, the question then is what makes up the constitution itself. On my reading, Schmitt's interpretation of this substance is overtly authoritarian. He explicitly dubs it a dictatorship in *Legalität und Legitimität.* He concludes by claiming that the basic decision to be made in Germany has to be for either the "substantial contents and forces of the German folk" or the "continuation" of "functionalistic value-neutrality." Schmitt associates the former with an unspecified "substantial kernel" of the Weimar Constitution's "Basic Rights and Basic Duties"; the latter refers in part to the formal procedures of parliamentary government. Schmitt, *Legitimität und Legalität,* 87, 96–98.

20. Schmitt, *Legalität und Legitimität,* 94.

21. The two most influential Schmitt scholars in the Anglo-American world, Joseph Bendersky and George Schwab, tend to trivialize much of Schmitt's argumentation from this period. Schmitt radicalizes some facets of the Weimar Constitution in a manner altogether alien to the constitution's underlying spirit in order to replace the genuinely democratic features of the republic with a form of mass-based dictatorship. "Saving" Weimar meant replacing a complex and contradictory, but nonetheless liberal-democratic, constitution with an executive-centered regime that would rely on easily manipulated forms of plebisci-

tary decision making. Schmitt ultimately endorses a revolutionary (sovereign) dictatorship and not a mere temporary (commissarial) one. True, Schmitt probably hoped that the reactionary and authoritarian General Schleicher would succeed in offering an alternative to the Nazis, and Schmitt certainly was not an active Nazi before 1933 (he joined the party on May 1, 1933). But Bendersky's attempt to transform Schleicher and the other authoritarian elites who eventually handed over power to Hitler into something close to principled antifascists badly obscures the role played by right-wing authoritarians (like Schmitt, who was an advisor to the semidictatorial presidential regimes during the early thirties) in preparing the way for the Nazi takeover. For a more accurate discussion of Schmitt's ally Schleicher, see Gotthard Jasper, *Die gescheiterte Zähmung*, esp. 88–126. Joseph Bendersky, *Carl Schmitt: Theorist for the Reich;* George Schwab, *The Challenge of the Exception.*

22. Morton J. Horwitz, "The Rule of Law: An Unqualified Good?" *Yale Law Journal*, vol. 86, no. 3 (January 1977).

23. Carl Schmitt, "Starker Staat und gesunde Wirtschaft," *Volk und Reich. Politische Monatshefte*, no. 2 (1933). For an overview of Schmitt's economic ideas, see Volker Neumann, *Der Staat im Bürgerkrieg*, 100–116. Herbert Marcuse perceptively recognized early on that Schmitt was a critic of political liberalism but by no means of capitalism in Marcuse's "Der Kampf gegen den Liberalismus in der totalitären Staatsauffassung," *Zeitschrift für Sozialforschung*, vol. 3, no. 2 (1934). Schmitt's anti-universalism undoubtedly has racist and fascist features; his apologists underplay all this. By the same token, it seems to me that his writings immediately before 1933 on pluralism develop the outlines for a reactionary authoritarian political program, but one that emphasizes social and economic features more than an explicitly racist one. If there is some kernel of truth to the claim that Schmitt was sympathetic to a somewhat less radical form of fascism than that represented by the Nazis, it has its basis here. In any case, Schmitt's activities and writings take on a far more viciously racist form as soon as the Nazis take power. Even if he might have preferred Mussolini over Hitler, Schmitt had few moral or political qualms about cultivating influence with the latter. On this, see Bernd Rüthers, *Carl Schmitt im Dritten Reich* (Munich: C. H. Beck, 1990), and my summary of it in "Carl Schmitt and the Nazis," *German Politics and Society*, no. 23 (summer 1991). See also my "The Fascism of Carl Schmitt: A Response to George Schwab," *German Politics and Society*, no. 29 (summer 1993). Schmitt's relationship to the Nazis was certainly a complicated one, and unfortunately I cannot discuss it in depth here. But it seems to me that a strong case (*contra* Schwab and Bendersky, and *pro* Rüthers and many others) can be made that demonstrates not only Schmitt's evident enthusiasm for the Nazis during the early years of the regime but also the apologetic structure of his writings after 1936.

24. Otto Kirchheimer, "Constitutional Reaction in 1932," in *PLSC*, 77–78, 80. See also "Die Verfassungslehre des Preussen-Konflikts" (1932), in Otto Kirchheimer, *Funktionen des Staats und der Verfassung. 10 Analysen* (henceforth *FSV*) (Frankfurt: Suhrkamp, 1972), where Kirchheimer attacks Schmitt's defense of the German federal government's blatantly unconstitutional removal of the Prussian state government in July 1932. Prussia was the largest (and, crucially, last SPD-governed) state in Germany, and the federal government's coup against it, enthusiastically defended by Schmitt in the courtroom (against the SPD's main lawyer, Hermann Heller) and in a number of publications, was an important step not only in cementing the authoritarian features of the then-existing presidential regime but in preparing the way for a more radical variety of authoritarianism. For the historical account, see Gotthard Jasper, *Die gescheiterte Zähmung*, 93–104. Schmitt's defense of the federal government's actions before the German constitutional court ("Schlussrede vor dem Staatsgerichtshof in Leipzig") can be found in his *Positionen und Begriffe im Kampf mit Weimar-Genf-Versailles.*

25. Otto Kirchheimer, "Legality and Legitimacy" (1932), in *Social Democracy and the Rule of Law,* 136.

26. Cited in Kirchheimer, "Constitutional Reaction in 1932," 78. Schmitt's views on direct democratic mechanisms are also sketched out in "Volksentscheid und Volksbegehren: Ein Beitrag zur Auslegung der Weimarer Verfassung und zur Lehre der unmittelbaren Demokratie," *Beiträge zum Äusländischen öffentlichen Recht und Völkerrecht* (1927).

27. Schmitt, "Staatsethik und pluralistischer Staat," 139–40.

28. Kirchheimer, "Constitutional Reaction in 1932," 78. Kirchheimer grasped what so many of Schmitt's contemporary apologists would like us to forget: Schmitt's is not the voice of a "traditional authoritarian conservative" or a Hobbesian, but a theorist who intimates many of the features of modern mass-based dictatorship. We should recall Hannah Arendt's painful realization that totalitarian regimes "are always preceded by mass movements and that they command and rest upon mass support up to the end," in her *Origins of Totalitarianism* (New York: Harcourt, Brace Jovanovich, 1951), 301.

29. Kirchheimer, "Constitutional Reaction in 1932," 80.

30. For Kirchheimer's answer to various attempts to alter Weimar's constitutional forms and corresponding institutional structures, see Otto Kirchheimer, "Die Verfassungslehre des Preussen-Konflikts," "Die staatsrechlichen Probleme der Reichtstagsauflösung" (1932), and "Verfassungsreform und Sozialdemokratie" (1933), all in *FSV;* "Die Verfassungsreform" (1932), in *WR.* Kirchheimer was concerned not simply with combating the authoritarian right's challenge to Weimar but also with developing arguments against proposals for constitutional reform that originated from the left. In a prominent debate with the social democrat Ernst Fraenkel, in *Die Gesellschaft,* he warned of the dangers of constitutional-reform proposals that might simply contribute to the further "devolution" of Weimar democracy. Because the Weimar Constitution represents, in Kirchheimer's view, a *normative* advance over a sad costellation of *de facto* power inequalities, careless changes in its structure might simply mean that the legal order would correspond more closely to those inequalities. The ambitious aspirations of the Weimar Constitution would then have been sacrificed in favor of an unfortunate political and social status quo; normativity would be surrendered to facticity.

31. Kirchheimer, "Remarks on Carl Schmitt's *Legalität und Legitimität,*" in *Social Democracy and the Rule of Law,* 149–57; "Constitutional Reaction in 1932," 86.

32. On Kirchheimer's reworking of Marx's theory of Bonapartism, see Wolfgang Luthardt, "Bemerkungen zu Otto Kirchheimers Arbeiten bis 1933," in *WR;* Otto Kirchheimer, "The Growth and Decay of the Weimar Constitution," *Contemporary Review,* vol. 144 (November 1933).

33. Kirchheimer, "Remarks on Carl Schmitt's *Legalität und Legitimität,*" 152.

34. Kirchheimer, "Constitutional Reaction 1932," 80. See also "Die Verfassungslehre des Preussen-Konflikts," 55–56, for a discussion of the advantages of heterogeneity, as well as Kirchheimer's review of a work by the Soviet legal scholar E. A. Korowine, "Review of Korowine," *Die Gesellschaft,* vol. 7 (1930), 575–78. When Kirchheimer later makes use of the term "social homogeneity," he means something distinct from Carl Schmitt's use of it. It refers to some relatively substantial degree of social and economic equality, but neither absolute value homogeneity nor social sameness. Though evocative of a social order far

more egalitarian than our own, it does not seem to have all the antipluralistic implications that Schmitt's use of it has. Homogeneity in this sense is closer to Hermann Heller's use of it in "Politische Demokratie und soziale Homogeneität," *Gesammelte Schriften,* vol. 2.

35. Kirchheimer, "Remarks on Carl Schmitt's *Legalität und Legitimität,*" 150.

36. Kirchheimer, "Remarks on Carl Schmitt's *Legalität und Legitimität,*" 150–52.

37. Kirchheimer, "Remarks on Carl Schmitt's *Legalität und Legitimität,*" 149–52. See also Kelsen, *Vom Wesen und Wert der Demokratie,* 3–13, 53–68.

38. The Weimar Constitution contained two main parts—the first describing decision-making procedures, the second containing nearly seventy (diverse) rights and "duties," which could not be altered by means of a simple parliamentary majority. Article 76 described the amendment procedures.

39. Schmitt, *Legalität und Legitimität,* 40–61.

40. Kirchheimer, "Remarks on Carl Schmitt's *Legalität und Legitimität,*" 161.

41. Kirchheimer, "Remarks on Carl Schmitt's *Legalität und Legitimität,*" 158.

42. Kirchheimer, "Remarks on Carl Schmitt's *Legalität und Legitimität,*" 159.

43. Kirchheimer, "Constitutional Reaction in 1932," 84.

44. The immediate issue at stake in these essays is the constitutional status of the Weimar Constitution's expropriation clause (article 153). Whereas conservative jurists interpreted it so as to make it a formidable check on state social and economic activity (and a de facto constitutional support for private capitalism), Kirchheimer sought to provide substantial possibilities for state economic intervention without requiring legislators to pay financial compensation. Otto Kirchheimer, "Reichsgericht und Enteignung: Reichsverfassungswirklichkeit des Preussischen Fluchtliniengesetzes" (1930), in *WR;* "Eigentumsgarantie in Reichsverfassung und Rechtsprechung" (1930), *Die Grenzen der Enteignung* (1930), both reprinted in Kirchheimer, *FSV.* The latter has also been translated under the title "The Limits of Expropriation," in *Social Democracy and the Rule of Law.*

45. See also Ernst Fraenkel, "Die Krise des Rechtsstaats und die Justiz," *Die Gesellschaft,* vol. 7 (1931).

46. Although echoes of Schmitt's thinking are still found here, Kirchheimer hinted at this answer to his former teacher as early as 1930, in "Eigentumsgarantie in Reichsverfassung und Rechtsprechung" (esp. p. 20) and in *The Limits of Expropriation,* 114–16. Kirchheimer does not mention the most obvious reason Schmitt underplays democratic law's general origins. Schmitt relies on a dramatic contrast between (universalistic) normativistic liberalism (where he locates the rule of law) and an explicitly anti-universalistic conception of democracy. For a similar criticism of Schmitt's emphasis on the generality of the legal norm, see Hermann Heller, "Der Begriff des Gesetzes in der Reichsverfassung" (1928), *Gesammelte Schriften,* vol. 2.

47. See Kirchheimer's earlier essay "Bedeutungswandel des Parlamentarismus" (1928), in *WR;* "Remarks on Carl Schmitt's *Legalität und Legitimität,*" 173.

48. Kirchheimer, "Remarks on Carl Schmitt's *Legalität und Legitimität*," 171–74.

49. Kirchheimer, "Remarks on Carl Schmitt's *Legalität und Legitimität*," 176.

50. Kirchheimer, "Remarks on Carl Schmitt's *Legalität und Legitimität*," 176–78. The conception of representation used here is very close to that described by Hannah Pitkin as "descriptive representation," in her *Concept of Representation* (Berkeley: University of California Press, 1977), 60–91.

51. Weber, *Economy and Society*, 217.

52. Weber, *Economy and Society*, 212–71, 952–54. David M. Trubek's "Max Weber on Law and the Rise of Capitalism," *Wisconsin Law Review*, no. 3 (1972), 720–53, is helpful.

53. As noted, Kelsen was one of Schmitt's central targets during the twenties and early thirties, chiefly because Kelsen's rather complicated quest to develop a pure theory of law, free from moral philosophy, demonstrated in Schmitt's mind how contemporary liberal democratic thinking and legal positivism was incapable of grounding itself morally. Yet as many of his eloquent essays from the period show, the "nihilist" Kelsen, unlike Schmitt, did his best to defend Weimar from its authoritarian critics. The finest example of this is Kelsen's brilliant response to Schmitt's *Der Hüter der Verfassung*. Hans Kelsen, *Wer soll der Hüter der Verfassung sein?* (Berlin: Rothschild, 1931).

54. Kirchheimer, "Legality and Legitimacy," 130. Kirchheimer suggests that democracy and formal equality are related on a number of occasions; see esp. p. 131, where the right's attack on rational legality is described as an attempt to "dispense with popular sovereignty." This essay was actually written before Schmitt's *Legality and Legitimacy*. Schmitt thus can refer to Kirchheimer's article (on p. 14) there. Kirchheimer's "Constitutional Reaction in 1932" and, of course, his "Remarks on Carl Schmitt's *Legalität und Legitimität*" constitute responses to Schmitt's book.

55. Kirchheimer, "Legality and Legitimacy," esp. 132–34.

56. Kirchheimer, "Legality and Legitimacy," 136, 147.

57. A number of recent historical accounts support this interpretation. See Ingo Müller, *Hitler's Justice: The Courts of the Third Reich* (Cambridge: Harvard University Press, 1991), 13–34. I summarize Müller's claims in my "Review of Ingo Müller," *German Politics and Society*, no. 29 (summer 1993). See also Martin Broszat, *Der Staat Hitlers* (Munich: DTV, 1989), 13–32. In an extremely interesting study, Ulrich Preuss shows the relevance of Kirchheimer's argument for German legal trends after 1945. Ulrich Preuss, *Legalität und Pluralismus. Beiträge zum Verfassungsrecht der Bundesrepublik Deutschland* (Frankfurt: Suhrkamp, 1973).

58. This seems to contradict other facets of Weber's massive oeuvre, in which he could be read as arguing that charismatic authority is not appropriate to modern political conditions. On this tension, see Wolfgang Mommsen, *Max Weber und die deutsche Politik*, 386–413.

59. Kirchheimer, "Legality and Legitimacy," 146–47.

60. Kirchheimer, "Constitutional Reaction in 1932," 78.

61. Kirchheimer, "Constitutional Reaction in 1932," 85–86.

62. Kirchheimer, "Constitutional Reaction in 1932," 80.

63. Kirchheimer, "Legality and Legitimacy," 142. Kirchheimer does suggest a qualification of his defense of a disenchanted mode of (democratic) parliamentary legality: one of the political consequences of disenchantment is the possibility of a radically instrumental view of politics that in some situations exacerbates political instability. As he thinks the example of the Weimar Republic demonstrates, there is a tendency among political and social interests to abandon democracy when they see another political instrument (like dictatorship) as better suited to their immediate social goals. The proliferation of "instrumental rationality" (Weber) poses a number of threats to democracy. Kirchheimer, "Remarks on Carl Schmitt's *Legalität und Legitimität*," 156–57.

64. Crucially, Kirchheimer now develops a fascinating critique of Leninism in "Marxism, Dictatorship, and the Organization of the Proletariat" (1933), in *PLSC*. Published just as the Nazis took power, the article is fascinating: despite his eloquent defense of formal democratic political mechanisms, Kirchheimer is not oblivious to the very real possibility of fascism's striking against democracy and that not only will (primarily working-class) democratic political groups be forced to "conquer executive political power by a civil war" (p. 27), but this struggle may require that they set up a transitional emergency dictatorship. Kirchheimer looks to the Soviet experience and deems it a disaster. After reminding the reader of Rosa Luxembourg's criticisms of Lenin, he insists that in figuring out what to do amidst such a crisis, the left should acknowledge Luxembourg's vision of a proletarian dictatorship as "defined by the way it applies democracy, not by the way it abolishes democracy; it consists of energetic, determined encroachments upon the duly vested rights and economic conditions of bourgeois society" (p. 31). Whatever its faults, the essay shows that some of those willing to defend allegedly formalistic parliamentary democracy were ready to take decisive action against its real foes.

65. Kirchheimer, "Legality and Legitimacy," 135.

66. Kirchheimer, "Legality and Legitimacy," 137.

67. Recall that classical authors always linked the demand for *generality* in law to the insistence on *clarity* in law. Does Kirchheimer's critique of general law here imply a dismissal of *both* features?

68. Roberto Unger, *Law In Modern Society* (New York: The Free Press, 1976), 193–94. Gianfranco Poggi similarly notes that "contemporary legislation has largely lost those features of generality and abstractness that made 'classical' legislation into the instrument par excellence of parliamentary legislation. Many laws are effectively ad hoc measures of an intrinsically administrative nature." Gianfranco Poggi, *The Development of the Modern State: A Sociological Introduction* (Stanford: Stanford University, 1978), 143.

69. Gunther Teubner, *Standards und Direktiven in Generalklauseln* (Frankfurt: Athenäum, 1971), 13–23. From what I have been able to decipher of Teubner's systems-theoretical jargon, he nonetheless thinks that blanket clauses of this type have a positive role to play in the legal order. See Gunther Teubner, "Generalklauseln als Sozionormative Modelle," in *Generalklauseln als Gegenstand der Sozialwissenschaften* (Baden-Baden: Nomos, 1973).

70. One of Hayek's early critics made this point long ago: see Harry M. Jones, "The Rule of Law and the Welfare State," *Columbia Law Review*, vol. 58, no. 2 (February 1958), 153. I think Judith Shklar was right to claim that the rule of law should not be reduced to a mere "football in a game between friends and enemies of free-market liberalism." See Judith

Shklar, "Political Theory and the Rule of Law," in *The Rule of Law: Ideal or Ideology,* ed. Allen Hutchinson and Patrick Monahan (Toronto: Carswell, 1987), 16. By the same token, it is in the sphere of social and economic life (where, despite neoconservative rhetoric, government even in the United States and Britain is extensively and often directly active) that citizens most commonly confront governmental action and agents. As Shklar was undoubtedly aware, to claim that the rule of law can have little to do with social and economic affairs in a world where the division between state and society has become increasingly unclear would amount to leaving a vast array of governmental institutions poorly regulated.

Chapter 4

1. Ernst Bloch, *Natural Law and Human Dignity* (Cambridge: MIT Press, 1986), 183. In 1935, Kirchheimer writes that fascist polemicists blame "alien" *(artfremdes)* Roman law for phenomena that, in fact, stem primarily from "unemployment, economic decline, and monopoly capital." Otto Kirchheimer, *Staatsgefüge und Recht des Dritten Reiches,* reprinted in *WR,* 154.

2. The Weberian structure of Neumann's project is most evident in *The Governance of the Rule of Law* (1936), reprinted under the title *Political Theory and the Legal System in Modern Society* (1936) (London: Berg, 1986), which served as Neumann's second doctoral dissertation (directed by Harold Laski and Karl Mannheim) at the London School of Economics. This work was the theoretical basis for "The Change in the Function of Law in Modern Society" (1937) and "Types of Natural Law" (1940), (both of which are reprinted in Franz Neumann, *The Democratic and Authoritarian State*), and *Behemoth: The Structure and Practice of National Socialism* (New York: Oxford University Press, 1942). Neumann's essay "A History of the Doctrine of Social Change" (coauthored with Herbert Marcuse) also includes helpful background information about the author's views of particular political theorists. (Available at the Herbert Marcuse Archives, Stadt- und Universitätsbibliothek, Frankfurt).

3. Franz Neumann, *Behemoth,* 49. See Matthias Ruete, "Post-Weimar Legal Theory in Exile," in Neumann, *The Governance of the Rule of Law,* xx.

4. Neumann, *The Governance of the Rule of Law,* 213.

5. The most relevant contrasting texts are Max Horkheimer, *The Eclipse of Reason* (New York: Continuum, 1974); Max Horkeimer and Theodor Adorno, *The Dialectic of Enlightenment* (New York: Continuum, 1972). But there are many parallels to the works from the Frankfurt school from the thirties. In "A Study on Authority" (1936), Marcuse tries to interpret the antinomies of the liberal concept of freedom as a consequence of bourgeois society's inability to live up to its universalistic aspirations, very much as Neumann links an analysis of the tension between law and sovereignty to capitalism. Marcuse's essay appears in his *From Luther to Popper* (London: Verso, 1973). In the 1936 "Entwurf zu einem Aufsatz über 'Das Rationale Recht in der Monopolwirtschaft,' " where Neumann offers a cogent summary of his argument, he remarks that the "starting point of the work is the comment by Horkheimer in the essay about philosophical anthropology . . . on the disappearance of the contract system and its replacement with commands in the monopoly economy" (p. 1). (Available at the Max Horkheimer Archives, Stadt- und Universitätsbibliothek, Frankfurt) Neumann is referring to "Bemerkungen zur philosophischen Anthropologie," *Zeitschrift für Sozialforschung,* vol. 4, no. 1 (1935), 14–15.

6. Weber, *Economy and Society,* 657. Recall Weber's definition of modern legal rational authority as a "system of abstract rules" capable of "generalized formulation" (p. 217).

7. On the "England problem" for Weber, see especially David Trubek, "Max Weber on Law and the Rise of Capitalism," and Sally Ewing, "Formal Justice and the Spirit of Capitalism: Max Weber's Sociology of Law," *Law and Society Review,* vol. 21, no. 3 (1987). Anthony Kronman's *Max Weber* (Stanford: Stanford University Press, 1983) is exclusively devoted to Weber's legal thought and offers a helpful summary, whereas Manfred Rehbinder, "Recht und Rechtswissenschaft im Werk von Max Weber," in *Max Weber Heute,* ed. Johannes Weiss (Frankfurt: Suhrkamp, 1989), nicely places Weber's contributions in the context of German legal debates during the period but is far too dismissive of Weber's anxieties about materialized law.

8. Weber, *Economy and Society,* 880–95. Weber's perceptive comment that "it is by no means certain that those classes which are negatively privileged today, especially the working classes, may expect safely from an informal administration of justice those results which are claimed for it" (p. 893) anticipates Neumann's critique of deformalized law.

9. See, for example, Philippe Nonet and Philip Selznick, *Law and Society in Transition: Toward Responsive Law* (New York: Harper and Row, 1978).

10. Neumann, *The Governance of the Rule of Law,* 58.

11. Karl Mannheim, *Ideology and Utopia* (New York: Harcourt and Brace, 1936). Like his colleagues at the Institute for Social Research, Neumann accepted a number of Marxist criticisms of Mannheim's sociology of knowledge. Yet he was clearly influenced by Mannheim's fascinating "Rational and Irrational Elements in Contemporary Society" (1934), where Mannheim relies on many Weberian views about rationalization, while insisting that the process remains incomplete until political democracy and radical social reform have been carried out. It has been reprinted in Mannheim's *Man and Society in an Age of Reconstruction* (New York: Harcourt, Brace and Jovanovich, 1950).

12. Neumann, *The Governance of the Rule of Law,* 58.

13. Neumann, *The Governance of the Rule of Law,* 25. Elsewhere he writes, "A more complete definition would . . . be the potentially highest power over a specific territory and a specific category of people." Neumann, *Behemoth,* 167.

14. Neumann, *The Governance of the Rule of Law,* 3.

15. In chapters 5 and 6, I analyze Neumann's conception of sovereignty in depth, but in order to avoid initial misunderstandings, let me distinguish, in a very preliminary manner, among its three central "moments": (1) on one level it simply means that law needs to be based on the possibility of state-based violence, so even the most cogent, predictable, normatively defensible system of law needs institutions (specifically, states) conceived of "as rationally operating machineries disposing of the monopoly of coercive power." (*Behemoth,* 467). In Neumann's view, such "machineries" have emerged in the West since the Renaissance. (2) For Neumann, this seems to imply a further and more problematic claim (as I will argue in chapter 6) that the political community's "highest power" is to be located in "the institution of the state: the legislative; executive (police, army, judiciary, bureaucracy)." This, indeed, is why Neumann generally talks about state sovereignty and not, for example, the normative principle of popular sovereignty, and why he agrees with Austin's claim that "the part truly independent . . . is not the society but the sovereign portion of the society. . . . The State is usually synonymous with the sovereign." *The Governance of the Rule of Law,* 23, 302. Law, in other words, presupposes "state sovereignty." (3) Finally, insofar as state power involves the idea of a highest power, it implies the possibility (and, too often in the history of the modern state, the reality) of normatively unregulated

power decisions in contradistinction to rational law. Sovereignty has always contained an irrational decisionist movement (which Schmitt's reconceptualization of sovereignty takes to its logical conclusion). In this chapter, I describe Neumann's aspiration to tame state power by means of law—or why he thinks we can tame or eliminate state sovereignty's third moment. In chapter 5, I recount Neumann's discussion of the "death of state sovereignty" in fascism—or why its first and second moments disappear but its third, decisionist, moment flourishes. In chapter 6, I criticize Neumann's own model of democratic state sovereignty—by focusing on the problematic structure of sovereignty's second moment.

16. For another view, see George Schwab, introduction to *Political Theology,* by Carl Schmitt, xviii. But Schwab trivializes Schmitt's views. The fact that Neumann acknowledges that (empirically) the "emergency" can provide important insights into a particular constellation of political power hardly makes him a Schmittian, any more than it does the *New York Times* reporter who focuses on the importance of a particular coup or putsch to understand the political dynamics of a specific setting. The fact that the thrust of the argument is directed against Schmitt comes out clearly at many junctures in Neumann's writings; see, for example, *The Governance of the Rule of Law,* 293–98.

17. This obsession with the problem of the individual command probably seems strange at first. Indeed, I will shortly suggest that it needs to be qualified. But before dismissing it, we would do well to appreciate its underlying intention. If the state is simply told "do what you please; deal with each specific case as you think fit," there is no longer even the most minimal check on the exercise of its power. That, as Neumann reminds us, was the view of Locke, Montesquieu, Rousseau, Kant, and Bentham. If the state can do whatever it wants with a particular individual, state authority is effectively unrestrained. For Neumann, "such a rule is not law but arbitrary decisionism." Neumann, *Behemoth,* 453. Vague legal standards are problematic for Neumann, because they are unlikely to provide sufficiently clear guidance to state agents; judges and administrators may then decide *similar* cases in *different* ways, which means that legal action would be potentially irregular and individual. We should recall Schmitt's definition of sovereignty in terms of power decisions undertaken during the (normless) exception. Neumann's attack on Schmitt culminates in the demand that the legal order *be rid of* arbitrary individual commands—in other words, forms of legal action like those associated by Schmitt with genuine acts of sovereignty.

18. The reader will discover some interesting parallels between Neumann's concerns here and those of Norberto Bobbio. Norberto Bobbio, *The Future of Democracy* (Minneapolis: Univ. of Minnesota, 1987), especially pp. 79–97. For Neumann, legal rationalization also involves the demise of ex post facto laws, which, as many liberal thinkers before him argued, provide excessive possibilities for arbitrary state action.

19. Karl Renner, *The Institutions of Private Law and Their Social Functions.* See also Neumann, *The Governance of the Rule of Law,* esp. 3–9.

20. Neumann, *The Governance of the Rule of Law,* 59. More generally on this part of the story, see 51–65, 72–76; "The Change in the Function of Law in Modern Society," 26–28; "Types of Natural Law," 81–83; "A History of the Doctrine of Social Change," (draft 1), 8–9.

21. Neumann, *The Governance of the Rule of Law,* 100–107; "Types of Natural Law," 86.

22. Neumann, *The Governance of the Rule of Law,* 45.

23. His reading of natural law is thus favorable: its legacy must be taken seriously by a disenchanted legal order. For similarly sympathetic views of natural law, see A. P. d'En-

trèves, *Natural Law* (London: Hutchinson, 1970); Ernst Bloch, *Natural Law and Human Dignity*.

24. Franz Neumann, "Review of Fuller, Radin, Llewellyn, Baumgarten and Bodenheimer," *Zeitschrift für Sozialforschung*, vol. 9, no. 1 (1941), 158. Neumann considers legal positivism's separation of legality and morality clearly superior to crude attempts (like those undertaken by the Nazis) to merge them, and he is ready to concede that positivism played a praiseworthy historical function in undermining traditionalistic natural law.

25. On the case of Britain, see Neumann, *The Governance of the Rule of Law*, 72–76, 117–25, 183–85, 219–22, 239–53, 263–65.

26. Neumann, "The Change in the Function of Law in Modern Society," 40. For example, a law setting the length of the working day at ten hours for some firms and eight hours for others contradicts "the principle of the equality of competitors."

27. Neumann, *The Governance of the Rule of Law*, 184. See also A. V. Dicey's original *Introduction to the Study of the Law of the Constitution* (New York: St. Martion's, 1961), as well as Jeffrey Jowell's excellent overview of the debates it spawned and their contemporary significance, "The Rule of Law Today," in *The Changing Constitution*, ed. Jeffrey Jowell and Dawn Oliver (Oxford: Clarendon Press, 1989).

28. Neumann, *The Governance of the Rule Of Law*, 125; "The Change in the Function of Law in Modern Society," 39. Howard Zinn repeated this facet of Neumann's argument in "The Conspiracy of Modern Law," in *The Rule of Law*, ed. Robert Paul Wolff, 18–19. Wolff's own essay in this volume ("Violence and the Law") provides an interesting contrast to Neumann's and Kirchheimer's studies during this period, because it so typically (for the radical tradition) refuses to take the problem of democratic legitimacy seriously: the idea of legitimate democratic authority is merely "the secular reincarnation of . . . religious superstition" (p. 71).

29. Neumann, *The Governance of the Rule of Law*, 239–53, 263–65; compare Weber, *Economy and Society*, esp. 814. On the relationship of capitalism and English common law, see Otto Kahn-Freund, introduction to *The Institutions of Private Law and Their Social Functions*, by Karl Renner.

30. Neumann, *The Governance of the Rule of Law*, 122, 124.

31. Neumann, *The Governance of the Rule of Law*, 124.

32. Neumann, *The Governance of the Rule of Law*, 257.

33. Neumann, *The Governance of the Rule of Law*, 150. On nineteenth-century Prussia, see also 138–50, 179–82, 199–205, 217–19, 257–66; "The Change in the Function of Law in Modern Society," 43–47; "A History of the Doctrine of Social Change" (draft 2), 25–27. For an excellent account of nineteenth-century German legal thought from a theoretical perspective sympathetic to Neumann, see Ingeborg Maus, *Rechtstheorie und politische Theorie im Industriekapitalismus* (Munich: Wilhelm Fink, 1986), 11–82. On the social context, see Hans-Ulrich Wehler, *The German Empire* (London: Berg, 1985).

34. Neumann, *The Governance of the Rule of Law*, 146.

35. Neumann, *The Governance of the Rule of Law*, 150. In "The Change in the Function of Law in Modern Society," Neumann qualifies his criticism, now writing that "if Kant's legal

theory is examined apart from his ethics" (p. 33) all the problems noted here follow. A helpful corrective to Neumann's view is provided by Leonard Krieger, who both acknowledges Kant's role as a theorist of the Prussian *Rechtsstaat* and demonstrates the centrality of Kant's moral philosophy to his political and legal thought. Leonard Krieger, *The German Idea of Freedom* (Chicago: University of Chicago Press, 1957), 86–125. The broader problem underlying Kant's formalism identified by Neumann here may plague contemporary neo-Kantians like Rawls and Habermas as well. As Seyla Benhabib notes, "the more minimal and general the conception of empirical and normative identity of persons from which the theory proceeds, the more unlikely that this will prove sufficient to yield normative principles of social and institutional arrangements." That is, the more minimal its substantive assumptions, the more trivial its conclusions. Unfortunately, Neumann's answer to this problem (as we will see) remains unsatisfying. Seyla Benhabib, "The Methodological Illusions of Modern Political Theory: The Case of Rawls and Habermas," *Neue Hefte für Philosophie,* vol. 21 (1982), esp. 51.

36. Neumann, *The Governance of the Rule of Law,* 136.

37. Neumann, "The Change in the Function of Law in Modern Society," 52.

38. Neumann, "The Change in the Function of Law in Modern Society," 50–52.

39. Neumann, "Types of Natural Law," 79; *The Governance of the Rule of Law,* 137. On this social democratic path, see *The Governance of the Rule of Law,* 126–37 (where, in contrast to the essays that appeared in the *Zeitschrift für Sozialforschung,* its utopian features clearly emerge); "Types of Natural Law," 78–80; "The Change in the Function of Law in Modern Society," 42–43. My exegesis should suggest why Habermas's charge that Schmitt's concept of the legal norm was introduced into left-wing legal discourse by Neumann is, at the very least, potentially misleading. First, the immediate inspiration for Neumann's valorization of the generality of the legal norm is Enlightenment political thought. Second, Habermas's comment ignores the fact that Schmitt *abandons* a defense of the classical liberal legal norm during the early thirties in favor of a system of profoundly deformalized, "flexible" law. Habermas's failure to mention this is rather convenient: Habermas belongs to a group of left-wing authors critical of "bourgeois" general law. Neumann's great contribution was to recognize that we should be suspicious of interpretations of the classical liberal legal norm that underplay its indispensable normative functions.

40. Neumann, *The Governance of the Rule of Law,* 234; more generally 224–39. Even in the contemporary legal order, "in the majority [of cases] the law is clear. . . . Every practical lawyer knows this" (p. 236). In a similar vein, Bentham once commented that legal experts tended to resist attempts at codifying and systematizing vague, amorphous legal standards "for the same reason that the Egyptian priest loved hieroglyphics" (cited in John Dinwiddy, *Bentham* [New York: Oxford University Press, 1989], 58).

41. Carl Schmitt, *Political Theology,* 28. For Schmitt, legal action necessarily includes an irrational, unpredictable, indeterminate "decision" that cannot be explained by reference to a legal norm; so-called normativistic modes of legal analysis allegedly ignore this. "A decision in the broadest sense belongs to every legal prescription. Every legal thought brings a legal idea, which in its purity can never become reality, into another aggregate condition and adds an element that cannot be derived either from the content of the legal idea or from the content of a general positive legal norm." *Political Theology,* p. 30. See also Schmitt, *Gesetz und Urteil. Eine Untersuchung zum Problem der Rechtspraxis.* Just as Schmitt relies on an idealized portrayal of classical liberal parliamentarism in order to claim that its mass democratic form represents a degradation, so, too, does he oftentimes

set up a sitting-duck version of liberal arguments about legal decision making, in order to criticize so-called normativistic legal thought.

42. Weber, *Economy and Society,* 979.

43. "We define administrative disputes as those disputes between individuals which are *exclusively or overwhelmingly decided on the basis of legal standards of conduct* [in other words: vague standards]; *that is to say, by free discretion.*" According to Neumann, such activity no longer deserves to be considered "judicial," in part because the judge is no longer meaningfully bound by law. For Neumann, this is an important distinction, because "administrative decisions are essentially more political than those of ordinary courts." Neumann, *The Governance of the Rule of Law,* 238–39.

44. Otto Kirchheimer, "The Legal Order of National Socialism," in *PLSC,* 98–99. Ingeborg Maus similarly notes that such a view "doesn't in any sense mean that the judge mediates as a subsumption-automaton between the law and concrete legal case—this was a caricatured invention. . . . Its method instead implies the priority of a grammatical and systematic interpretation during the concretization of a law. . . . The judicial decision thus doesn't legitimize itself by means of a logical deduction, but rather by reference to a law which has been produced by a set of legitimate procedures. According to this conception of the legal norm's capacity to constrain state actors *(Gesetzesbindung),* there are almost always several, but not as many as one might choose *(beliebig),* judicial decisions that are legitimate." Maus, " 'Gesetzesbindung' der Justiz und die Struktur der nationalsozialistischen Rechtsnormen," in *Recht und Justiz im Dritten Reich,* ed. Ralf Dreier and Wolfgang Sellert (Frankfurt: Suhrkamp, 1989), 85.

45. Even if such standards are then codified by administrators or judges, should not the profound fusion of legislative and bureaucratic authority that tends to result worry defenders of parliamentary democracy?

46. Neumann, *The Governance of the Rule of Law,* 226–28, and esp. 228, where he notes that the French revolutionaries' model of a *Referes legislatif* "really attempted to reduce the power of the judges as much as possible." See also: "Bemerkungen zu der Arbeit von Hans Mayer, 'Die nationalsozialistische Rechtsauffasung und ihre gesellschaftlichen Grundlagen' " (1937), 3–44 (available at the Max Horkheimer Archives, Stadt- und Universitätsbibliothek, Frankfurt). Still, Neumann never formulates an adequate theory of judicial decision making, and readers should be concerned about this gap. This is because he is chiefly concerned with the "politico-sociological problem of why in a certain historical period a certain theory [of legal decision making] became prevalent, and . . . what social functions it performed," and not with formulating a normative theory of legal decision making per se. Neumann, *The Governance of the Rule of Law,* 232). In his defense, Neumann seems to presuppose more than a "cookbook" view of law, according to which legal interpretation simply involves "reading off" a set of legal rules. He understands that legal action always implies a complicated interpretative process. His hope is that clear legal rules could help decision makers act in a relatively predictable manner and allow legal decision makers to decide as precisely as possible what a particular legislative body promulgated. Although a legislative norm is always an interpretative act, the legal norm has an important role to play in deciding how determinate such interpretations will be. Legal decision making may be more indeterminate than classical liberalism suggested, but—pace Schmitt—it need not be more or less arbitrary. The parliament-centered conception of the separation of powers (and, by implication, rule of law) like that Neumann suggests has been the object of vociferous criticism in recent years. Ronald Dworkin, *Taking Rights Seriously* (Cambridge: Harvard University Press, 1977); *A Matter of Principle* (Cambridge: Harvard

University Press, 1985). Like many on the German Left in their generation, Neumann and Kirchheimer were worried by the specter of activist judges and constitutional courts given the authority to test the constitutionality of legislative acts. The Weimar judiciary was a bastion of authoritarianism and the source of mean attacks on attempted parliamentary social reforms. Neumann would have been skeptical of views of the rule of law, like Dworkin's, that valorize the creative activity of judicial experts. As he might remind us, courts tend to be relatively elite and unrepresentative institutions and hardly a forum with a real generality of views or interests. Dworkin seems to dismiss this consideration by observing that contemporary legislatures tend to be dominated by privileged and well-organized social and economic groups anyhow (see *A Matter of Principle,* 27–28). Perhaps we need to ask whether his model of a Hercules-like judge risks reducing elected representative institutions to junior partners in a political system too often destined to be dominated by judicial experts.

47. Neumann, *The Governance of the Rule of Law,* 135, 138.

48. Neumann, *The Governance of the Rule of Law,* 130, 137.

49. Neumann, *The Governance of the Rule of Law,* 137.

50. Seyla Benhabib, "In the Shadow of Aristotle and Hegel: Communicative Ethics and Current Controversies in Practical Philosophy," *The Philosophical Forum,* vol. 21, nos. 1–2, (fall–winter 1989–90), 12. For a more general discussion, see Seyla Benhabib, *Critique, Norm and Utopia: A Study of the Foundations of Critical Theory* (New York: Columbia University Press, 1986), 309–16.

51. Neumann, *The Governance of the Rule of Law,* 7–8.

52. Neumann, "Types of Natural Law," 76.

53. Schmitt claims that only a pessimistic conception of human nature can ground a truly political theory that refuses to close its eyes to the mean and potentially violent character of the political sphere. Schmitt, *The Concept of the Political* (1932), 55–68. In "Types of Natural Law," Neumann implicitly challenges Schmitt by insisting that we need a view of human nature that insists on neither humanity's basic goodness nor its inevitable evilness.

54. Weber, *Economy and Society,* 868.

55. Benhabib, "In the Shadow of Aristotle and Hegel."

56. For a criticism of Weberian and neo-Weberian analyses of legal deformalization in a similar spirit, see Jürgen Habermas, "The Tanner Lectures." For Habermas (in contrast to Weber), legality does require normative legitimacy, but legitimacy needs to be conceptualized in terms of formal procedures supportive of the uncoerced exchange of opinions: law's reasonableness stems from the (universal) debate and exchange generative of it, and not law's (general) semantic form per se. Liberal political thought's emancipatory core lies in the social contract's implicit insight "that only those regulations can come about that have the uncoerced agreement of all" and in a concomitant "post-traditional" morality suggested by it. Habermas, "The Tanner Lectures," 594. Since the appearance of *The Theory of Communicative Action,* the basic contours of Habermas's legal theorizing otherwise parallel Neumann's during the late thirties and early forties in many ways. Very much in the shadow of his predecessor at the Institute for Social Research, Habermas has sought to develop a radically democratic and socially critical restatement of Weber's theory of

legal rationalization. Yet Habermas may be too unappreciative of legitimate anxieties about deformalized law. See my "Neumann v. Habermas: The Frankfurt School and the Case of the Rule of Law," *Praxis International*, vol. 13 (1993).

57. Neumann, *The Governance of the Rule of Law*, 275.

58. Neumann, *The Governance of the Rule of Law*, 256–57; "The Change in the Function of Law in Modern Society," 42–43.

59. Neumann, "Review of Fuller, Radin, Llewellyn, Baumgarten, and Bodenheimer," 159.

60. Rousseau, as cited in Neumann, "The Change in the Function of Law in Modern Society," 27–28.

Chapter 5

1. Barry M. Katz, *Foreign Intelligence: Research and Analysis in the Office of Strategic Services* (Cambridge: Harvard University Press, 1989); Alfons Söllner, ed. *Zur Archäologie der Demokratie in Deutschland*, vols. 1–2 (Frankfurt: Fischer, 1986).

2. On the dissolution of the early Frankfurt school, see especially Rolf Wiggershaus, *Die Frankfurter Schule* (Munich: DTV, 1988), 293–423. Horkheimer resisted Kirchheimer's plan to translate Neumann's study into German in the fifties. Back in Frankfurt, he seems to have been uninterested in getting an explicitly Marxist study of fascism in print in Adenauer's Germany.

3. Neumann, *Behemoth*, 261.

4. Neumann, *Behemoth*, 158–59.

5. In this vein, compare Karl Korsch's dismissal of *Behemoth*'s legalism (Korsch, "The Structure and Practice of Totalitarianism," *New Essays: A Quarterly Devoted to The Study of Modern Society*, vol. 6, no. 2 [fall 1942]) with the Texas rebel C. Wright Mills's positive assessment of *Behemoth* (Mills, "The Nazi Behemoth," in his *Power, Politics and People* [New York: Oxford University Press, 1972]). Even during this period, Neumann had a real appreciation of indigenous social thought in the United States, as demonstrated by many of his review articles in the pages of the Institute for Social Research's journal. In this way he was also distinct from his colleagues.

6. Neumann, *Behemoth*, 49.

7. Neumann, "Entwurf zu einem Aufsatz über das Recht in der Monopolwirtschaft," 3.

8. Increasingly, "the command" and "the administrative act" constitute an auxiliary guarantee for capitalist property. Neumann, *Behemoth*, 261, 446–47. See also Neumann, *The Governance of the Rule of Law*, 277–85; "The Change in the Function of Law in Modern Society," 58–59; "Die Ordnung der nationalen Arbeit," *Zeitschrift für Sozialismus*, vol. 1, no. 5 (February 1934); "The State and Labour in Germany," *The Contemporary Review*, vol. 146, (1934).

9. Competitive capitalism is based "on the assumption of a large number of entrepreneurs of about equal strength, freely competing with each other on the basis of freedom of

contract and freedom of trade, with the entrepreneur investing his [or her] capital and his [or her] labor for the purpose of his [or her] economic ends, and bearing the economic risks involved." Neumann, *Behemoth,* 258. One of the tasks of *Behemoth* is to show that this picture no longer fits the realities of contemporary capitalism and that legal institutions like the contract have, therefore, lost their original significance: "In the period of monopolization, the new auxiliary guarantee of property is no longer the contract but the administrative act," or individual measure (p. 260).

10. Fraenkel himself concedes in his study that there are signs of just such a radicalization of the destruction of classical law. Perhaps his sympathetic review of Neumann in a 1942 New York German exile newspaper was his roundabout way of conceding as much. Ernst Fraenkel, *The Dual State* (New York: Oxford, 1941). For Neumann's response, especially, see Neumann, *Behemoth,* 440. Much of the ongoing and very much unresolved debate in Germany on the nature of Nazi law continues to be defined by the Neumann-Fraenkel feud. The essays collected in *Justizalltag im Dritten Reich,* ed. Michael Stolleis and B. Diestelkamp (Frankfurt: Fischer, 1988) tend to side with Fraenkel; some of the authors in *Recht, Rechtsphilosophie und Nationalsozialismus,* ed. H. Rottleuthner (Wiesbaden: Franz Steiner, 1983) with Neumann. A helpful discussion of the Neumann-Fraenkel debate is found in Richard Saage, *Faschismustheorien* (Munich: C. H. Beck, 1976). Good empirical arguments can be made on both sides, but the real question is what institutions are essential to the rule of law. If cogent formal law is essential to legal certainty (as both authors seem to think), Neumann's view has much to be said in its favor: formal law undoubtedly did disintegrate in the sphere of civil law under the Nazis. If not, the story becomes more complex. For Fraenkel's review of Behemoth, see "Das Produkt des Grosskapitals," *New Yorker Neue Volkszeitung,* vol. 2, no. 16 (May 1942), 1.

11. Neumann, *Behemoth,* 24. See also *The Governance of the Rule of Law,* 269–73; Neumann, *European Trade Unionism and Politics* (New York: League for Industrial Democracy, 1936).

12. Neumann, *Behemoth,* 227. On Nazi Germany's economy, see Neumann, "Labor Mobilization in the National Socialist New Order," *Law and Contemporary Problems,* vol. 9, no. 3 (summer 1942); F. Neumann, O. Kirchheimer, and A. Gurland, *The Fate of Small Business in Nazi Germany* (Washington: U.S. Senate Special Commission on Small Business, 1943). See also (for the economic argumentation in *Behemoth*), A. Gurland, "Technological Trends Under National Socialism," *Zeitschrift für Sozialforschung,* vol. 9, no. 2 (1941).

13. Neumann, *Behemoth,* 444.

14. Neumann, *The Governance of the Rule of Law,* 286–98; "The Change in the Function of Law in Modern Society," 59–66. The references to Schmitt in *Behemoth* are too numerous to cite here. Neumann certainly recognized that there were important conflicts between Schmitt and the Nazis. Unlike many of Schmitt's contemporary defenders, however, he still thought there was a basic fit between key features of Schmitt's thinking and crucial Nazi legal practices.

15. On Nazi law, R. Dreier and W. Sellert, eds., *Recht und Justiz im Dritten Reich,* (Frankfurt: Suhrkamp, 1989); Kritische Justiz Redaktion, ed., *Der Unrechtsstaat: Recht und Justiz im Nationalsozialismus,* vols. 1–2 (Baden-Baden: Nomos, 1984). Bernd Rüthers does an especially good job of demonstrating the key role Schmitt plays in articulating some crucial aspects of Nazi law in *Die unbegrenzte Auslegung. Zum Wandel der Privatrechtsordnung im Nationalsozialismus* (Frankfurt: Athenäum, 1973); *Entartetes Recht. Rechtslehren und Kronjuristen im Dritten Reich* (Munich: C. H. Beck, 1988).

16. Neumann, *Behemoth,* xii. In 1938 Schmitt wrote *Der Leviathan in der Staatslehre Thomas Hobbes* (Cologne: Hohenheim, 1982). Neumann's *Behemoth* can be interpreted as an attempt to respond to Schmitt by showing that Nazism has nothing to do with the authoritarian (yet relatively calculable) "Leviathan." Instead, it possesses the terrifying features of Hobbes's "Behemoth."

17. Neumann, "The Change in the Function of Law in Modern Society," 57.

18. For Schmitt's revalorization of amorphous nonclassical legal standards *(Generalklauseln),* see Carl Schmitt, "Neue Leitsätze für die Rechtspraxis," *Juristische Wochenschrift,* vol. 62, no. 50 (December 16, 1933); Schmitt, *Staat, Bewegung, Volk,* 43–45; Schmitt, "Nationalsozialismus und Rechtsstaat," *Juristische Wochenschrift,* vol. 63, nos. 12–13 (March 24 and 31, 1934), esp. 717; Schmitt, *Über die drei Arten des rechtswissenschaftlichen Denkens,* 58–59. Schmitt's writings on this problem should be required reading for contemporary authors who, like Roberto Unger, see deformalized law as preparing the way for a new communitarian system of "customary law." Although the authors' political intentions obviously vary, the similarities in argumentation (Schmitt points to premodern Germanic *Gewohnheitsrecht* as an inspiration for what he calls a modern form of situation-specific law where *die Natur der Sache* determines decision making) are striking at times. Unger, *Law in Modern Society,* 238–42. Similarly, Schmitt's repeated emphasis on the profoundly indeterminate structure of the legal norm should remind us that there is nothing *necessarily* radical or left-wing about this idea.

19. For Schmitt's decisionist justification of Hitler's seizure of power, see his "Der Führer schützt das Recht" (1934), *Positionen und Begriffe im Kampf mit Weimar-Genf-Versailles;* "Ein Jahr Nationalsozialistischer Verfassungsstaat," *Deutsches Recht,* vol. 4, no. 2 (January 25, 1934).

20. Neumann, "The Change in the Function of Law in Modern Society," 29.

21. Schmitt, *Staat, Bewegung und Volk; Über die drei Arten des rechtswissenschaftlichen Denkens;* "Nationalsozialistisches Rechtsdenken"; "Nationalsozialismus und Rechtsstaat"; "Der Rechtsstaat," in *Nationalsozialistisches Handbuch für Recht und Gesetzgebung,* ed. H. Frank (Munich: NSDAP Zentralverlag, 1935); Schmitt's 1934 introduction to *Political Theology.*

22. Neumann, *Behemoth,* 150–71.

23. Neumann, "The Change in the Function of Law in Modern Society," 65. Much of the contemporary literature makes the same point.

24. Neumann, *Behemoth,* 468–69.

25. Neumann, *Behemoth,* 398.

26. Neumann, *Behemoth,* 166–69, 467–70. Much of the recent literature on Nazism supports this "polycratic" interpretation of its power structure. See Ian Kershaw, *The Nazi Dictatorship: Problems and Perspectives of Interpretation* (London: Edward Arnold, 1988); Martin Broszat, *Der Staat Hitlers;* Peter Hüttenberger, "Nationalsozialistische Polykratie," *Geschichte und Gesellschaft,* vol. 2, no. 4 (1976).

27. Neumann, *The Governance of the Rule of Law,* 4.

28. For some thoughtful reflections on this problem from a contemporary author, see Ulrich Preuss, "Zivilisation und das Gewaltmonopol—Über Linke wie Grüne Mißverständnisse," *Freibeuter*, no. 25 (1985).

29. Neumann, *Behemoth*, 397.

30. The idea of fascism as a mode of gangsterism appears in many of the early Frankfurt school's writings. Kirchheimer flirts with it in "In Quest of Sovereignty" (1944), in *PLSC*, 184, as do Horkheimer and Adorno in *The Dialectic of the Enlightenment*, 225–29.

31. Schmitt, *Political Theology*, 66.

32. Cited in Herbert Deane, *The Political Ideas of Harold J. Laski* (Hamden, Conn.: Archon, 1972), 14. For Laski's criticisms of the idea of state sovereignty, see his *Studies in the Problem of Sovereignty* (New Haven, Conn.: Yale University Press, 1917); *The Foundations of Sovereignty and Other Essays* (New York: Harcourt, Brace and Jovanovich, 1921). Neumann was on close intellectual and personal terms with Laski during the thirties. By then, Laski had abandoned his attack on the idea of state sovereignty and had embraced a rather statist variety of Marxism.

33. Although Neumann never embraced Laski's pluralism, this argument also has elements of a self-critique of his own endorsement of a relatively decentralized "economic democracy" during the twenties and early thirties. His postwar essay is much more explicit about this self-criticism. Franz Neumann, "Das Arbeitsrecht in der modernen Gesellschaft," *Das Recht der Arbeit*, vol. 4, no. 1 (January 1951).

34. Neumann, *Behemoth*, 10–11.

35. Neumann, *Behemoth*, 33–34;

36. Neumann, *Behemoth*, 522.

37. Neumann, *Behemoth*, 523.

38. See many of the early issues of the German journal *Kritische Justiz*.

39. Neumann, *The Governance of the Rule of Law*, 6.

40. On the discontents of Marxist legal theory, see Eugene Kamenka and Alice Erh-Soon Tay, "Marxism, Socialism, and the Theory of Law," *Columbia Journal of Transnational Law*, vol. 23 (1985).

41. For an excellent criticism of this thesis from a left-wing perspectice, see Tim Mason, "The Primacy of Politics—Politics and Economics in National Socialist Germany," in *Nazism and the Third Reich*, ed. Henry Turner (New York: Oxford University Press, 1972).

42. For a recent overview, see James Q. Wilson, ed., *The Politics of Regulation* (New York: Basic Books, 1980).

43. Wilson, *The Politics of Regulation*, 392.

44. Interestingly, Schmitt's view of democracy as a nonnormative category and his juxtaposition of it to the normativistic rule of law explains why he similarly emphasized the

centrality of liberal law's semantic generality while underplaying the generality of its democratic origins.

45. Jürgen Seifert, "Vom autoritären Verwaltungsstaat zurück zum demokratischen Verfassungsstaat," in *Die Zukunft der Aufklärung,* ed. P. Goltz and J. Rüssen (Frankfurt: Suhrkamp, 1988), 211.

46. John Rawls. *A Theory of Justice* (Cambridge: Harvard University Press, 1971), 238.

47. For some preliminary reflections on this difficult problem, see Jürgen Habermas, "The Tanner Lectures." Such a theory will have to acknowledge, as Habermas notes, that "the legitimating force of the rationality of legal procedures" is to be found "to a greater degree" in "the process of democratic legislation" than in the courtroom (p. 248). It seems to me that Neumann was correct to note that many early modern defenders of formal law implicitly grasped this point and that a defensible vision of judicial action—which Neumann never develops—will have to do credit to it.

48. Grant McConnell, *Private Power and American Democracy* (New York: Vintage, 1966), 297. We also need to take Kenneth Davis's observation seriously: "perhaps the most significant 20th century change in the fundamentals of the legal system has been the tremendous growth of discretionary power." Davis is correct to see that the contemporary legal order provides too many possibilities for poorly regulated forms of dicretionary decision making. Kenneth C. Davis, *Discretionary Justice: A Preliminary Inquiry* (Urbana: University of Illinois Press, 1979), 20

49. Theodore Lowi, *The End of Liberalism* (New York: Norton, 1979). According to Lowi, scholarship on the American welfare state "demonstrated that broad and vague delegations of power tend to put agencies too much under the influence of the most specialized and best organized interest groups." Lowi, "The Welfare State, The New Regulation, and The Rule of Law," in *The Rule of Law: Ideal or Ideology?,* ed. A. Hutchinson and P. Monahan, 19.

50. Ingeborg Maus, *Rechtstheorie und politische Theorie im Industriekapitalismus,* 280–91.

51. Although Marcus intends to make a point opposed to mine here, it seems to me that his empirical story could be interpreted as supporting my claim. Alfred Marcus, "Environmental Protection Agency," in Wilson, *The Politics of Regulation.*

52. Dworkin, *A Matter of Principle,* 9–32.

53. Neumann, "The Change in the Function of Law in Modern Society," 31. The right to free speech (for example) would be rendered meaningless if there were not auxiliary legal regulations guaranteeing citizens police protection for an unpopular demonstration, or protecting writers and publishers from being persecuted by public authorities. Every political right requires an array of complementary (and historically varying) legal rules, and the question then becomes what form such regulation can take. Modern defenders of formal law thought that they had part of the answer to this difficult question.

54. Martin Jay, *The Dialectical Imagination: A History of the Frankfurt School* (Boston: Little, Brown, 1973), 165–66. Leo Löwenthal accepts a similar interpretation. Leo Löwenthal, *An Unmastered Past* (Berkeley: University of California Press, 1987), 78. The institute's internal debate on the political economy of National Socialism has been extensively analyzed. David Held, *Introduction to Critical Theory: Horkheimer to Habermas* (London: Hutchinson,

1980), 40–76; Douglas Kellner, *Critical Theory, Marxism, and Modernity* (Oxford: Polity, 1989), 51–82; Rolf Wiggershaus, *Die Frankfurter Schule,* 314–26; Helmut Dubiel, *Theory and Politics: Studies in the Development of Critical Theory* (Cambridge: The MIT Press, 1985); *Kritische Theorie der Gesellschaft. Eine einführende Rekonstruktion von den Anfängen im Horkheimer-Kreis bis Habermas* (Weinheim, Ger.: Juventa, 1988).

55. See Franz Neumann, Letter to Horkheimer, July 23, 1941, reprinted in Rainer Erd, *Reform und Resignation. Gespräche über Franz Neumann,* 135–37.

56. Frederick Pollock, "Is National Socialism a New Order?" *Zeitschrift für Sozialforschung,* vol. 9, no. 3 (1941), 453.

57. Pollock, "Is National Socialism a New Order?" 445.

58. Frederick Pollock, "State Capitalism," *Zeitschrift für Sozialforschung,* vol. 9, no. 3 (1941), 207.

59. Pollock, "Is National Socialism a New Order?" 454.

60. Max Horkheimer, "The End of Reason," *Zeitschrift für Sozialforschung,* vol. 9, no. 3 (1941), 367. For a more general discussion, see Horkheimer, "Preface," *Zeitschrift für Sozialforschung,* vol. 9, no. 2 (1941); "Die Juden und Europa," *Zeitschrift für Sozialforschung,* vol. 8, nos. 1/2 (1940); "The Authoritarian State" (1942), in *The Essential Frankfurt School Reader,* ed. Andrew Arato and E. Gebhardt (New York: Continuum, 1982).

61. Horkheimer and Adorno, *The Dialectic of Enlightenment,* ix–x.

62. Neumann, *Behemoth,* 224. In an essay completed just before he committed suicide in a Nazi jail in Paris, Rudolf Hilferding made the same point against authors who were arguing that fascism and the Soviet Union represented state capitalist systems. Unlike Neumann, this did not lead him to insist on the monopoly capitalistic character of fascism. He opts for a picture of totalitarian economics strikingly like that provided by Pollock but insists that we should, therefore, simply dump the term "capitalism" altogether (to describe them) and refer instead to "totalitarian state economies." Hilferding's position may allow us better to recognize the particularities of Stalinist economies than either Neumann's or Pollock's, but it seems to me that in one respect he commits Pollock's error: he too indiscriminately groups together (profoundly distinct) fascist and Soviet-style economies. Rudolf Hilferding, "Staatskapitalismus oder totalitäre Wirtschaft" (1940), in *Zwischen den Stühlen. Schriften Rudolf Hilferdings 1904 bis 1940,* ed. Cora Stephan (Berlin: Dietz, 1982).

63. Axel Honneth, "Critical Theory," in *Social Theory Today,* ed. Anthony Giddens and Jonathan Turner (Oxford: Polity, 1987).

64. The case of Marcuse during the early forties is a somewhat more complicated one: he seems to have taken on the role of a mediator between Neumann and Kirchheimer on the one side and Horkheimer and Pollock on the other. See Marcuse, "Some Social Implications of Modern Technology," *Zeitschrift für Sozialforschung,* vol. 9, no. 3 (1941). In later years, clear echoes of Horkheimer's and Adorno's vision of a totally administered social order become evident in Marcuse's theory.

65. See Ian Kershaw, *Popular Opinion and Political Dissent in the Third Reich: Bavaria 1933–45* (Oxford: Oxford University Press, 1983); Detlev J. K. Peuckert, *Inside*

Nazi Germany: Conformity, Opposition and Racism in Everyday Life (London: Penguin, 1987).

66. Neumann, *Behemoth,* 225.

67. Neuamnn, "The Decay of German Democracy"; *Behemoth,* 3–34. Contrast Pollock's more functionalist argumentation in "Die gegenwärtige Lage des Kapitalismus und die Aussichten einer planwirtschaftlichen Neuordnung," *Zeitschrift für Sozialforschung,* vol. 1, no. 1 (1932); "Bemerkungen zur Wirtschaftskrise," *Zeitschrift für Sozialforschung,* vol. 2, no. 3 (1933).

68. Reprinted in Rainer Erd, *Reform und Resignation,* 145. In this context, the recently published transcript of a 1936 internal Institute for Social Research seminar on Marxist political economy is also quite interesting. There, Neumann criticizes his colleagues for suggesting that fascism might represent the "death" *(Untergang)* of capitalism: "Die Marxsche Methode und Ihre Anwenbarkeit," in Horkheimer, *Gesammelte Schriften,* vol. 12, 407.

69. Max Horkheimer, *Dawn & Decline: Notes 1926–31 and 1950–61* (New York: Continuum, 1978), 72.

70. Neumann, *The Governance of the Rule of Law,* 137.

Chapter 6

1. Otto Kirchheimer, "Changes in the Structure of Political Compromise" (1941), in *PLSC,* 140.

2. Kirchheimer himself uses the term at one juncture, referring to the "incipient state capitalism of our day," in "The Historical and Comparative Background of the Hatch Act," *Public Policy,* vol. 2 (1941), 346. More generally, he refers to monopoly capitalism.

3. Kirchheimer, "Changes in the Structure of Political Compromise," 140, 142–59. Neumann later sketched out similar ideas in the 1951 "Economics and Politics in the Twentieth Century," in *The Democratic and Authoritarian State* (henceforth *DAS*) (New York: The Free Press, 1957). See also Kirchheimer's comments in "Franz Neumann: An Appreciation," *Dissent,* vol. 4, no. 4 (1957), esp. 382–83. On the fusion of the "base/superstructure" in contemporary capitalism, see Jürgen Habermas, *Theory and Practice* (Boston: Beacon, 1973), 195.

4. This unpublished document was discovered in the Max Horkheimer Archives at the Stadt- und Universitätsbibliothek in Frankfurt. It is untitled but signed by Kirchheimer and dated May 1940. Henceforth I will refer to it as "Memo on State Capitalism".

5. Marcuse pursues a similar agrument in "Some Social Implications of Modern Technology," esp. 429–32.

6. Max Horkheimer, "The Authoritarian State" (1942), in *The Essential Frankfurt School Reader.*

7. Herbert Marcuse, *One-Dimensional Man* (Boston: Beacon, 1964). Of course, there are other important theoretical differences among Marcuse, Horkheimer, and Adorno.

8. Otto Kirchheimer, Letter to Marcuse, March 7, 1964, in the Kirchheimer File, German Emigré Collection, SUNY Albany Library, Albany, New York.

9. Robert Pippin and Andrew Feenberg, eds., *Marcuse: Critical Theory and the Promise of Utopia* (London: MacMillan, 1988); Jürgen Habermas, ed., *Antworten auf Marcuse,* (Frankfurt: Suhrkamp, 1968).

10. Walter Benjamin, "Theses on the Philosophy of History," *Illuminations* (New York: Schocken, 1969).

11. Kirchheimer, "Memo on State Capitalism," 1.

12. Kirchheimer, "Memo on State Capitalism," 2.

13. Kirchheimer, "Marxism, Dictatorship, and the Organization of the Proletariat," in *PLSC,* 31.

14. This is one of the essay's most curious claims. Presupposing a view that sees fascism as emerging when hegemonic bourgeois groups face radical challenges from below, Kirchheimer hopes that socialism could overcome the tendency of threatened economic interests to abandon democracy, by denying postcapitalist economic administrators (economic) incentives for acting in antidemocratic ways. Unfortunately, he has nothing to say about how an alternative economy could specifically institutionalize this advantage, and he probably presupposes an overly economistic Marxist view of power. Even more problematically, this line of argument helps explain why the essay's—admittedly, highly ambiguous and even murky—final paragraph may still be interpreted as implying the view that state socialism contains immanent features pointing toward a genuinely humane, democratic socialism. Kirchheimer may accept this problematic view—*despite* his prescient critique of Leninism and the essay's suggestion that integral statism is dominated by a new ruling class (p. 4).

15. Kirchheimer's related writings on criminal law include "Remarques sur la statistique criminelle de la France d'apres-guerre," *Revue de Science criminelle et la Droit penal compare,"* vol. 1 (1936); "Recent Trends in German Treatment of Juvenile Delinquency," *Journal of Criminal Law and Criminology,* vol. 29 (1938); "Criminal Law in National Socialist Germany" (1940), in *PLSC;* "Criminal Omissions," *Harvard Law Review,* vol. 54 (1942). The history of *Punishment and Social Structure* (New York: Columbia University Press, 1939) is itself intriguing, chiefly because Rusche lost touch with the Institute for Social Research, and Kirchheimer was then given the task of revising Rusche's original text for publication. Dario Melossi, "George Rusche and Otto Kirchheimer: *Punishment and Social Structure,"* *Crime and Social Justice: Issues in Criminology,* no. 9 (spring-summer 1978). The work's central theses were earlier developed by Rusche in "Arbeitsmarkt und Strafvollzug," *Zeitschrift für Sozialforschung,* vol. 2, no. 1 (1933). The German writer Karl F. Schumann rightly criticizes many of the work's overly economistic features, in "Produktionsverhältnisse und staatliches Strafen. Zur aktuellen Diskussion über Rusche und Kirchheimer," *Kritische Justiz,* vol. 14 (1981).

16. Kirchheimer and Rusche, *Punishment and Social Structure,* 193–205.

17. Kirchheimer and Rusche, *Punishment and Social Structure,* 6.

18. Kirchheimer and Rusche, *Punishment and Social Structure,* 78, 83. This is one of the more obvious differences between Kirchheimer's study and Foucault's *Discipline and Pun-*

ishment: The Birth of the Prison (New York: Pantheon, 1977). While acknowledging the importance of *Punishment and Social Structure* for his own work, Foucault disregards Kirchheimer and Rusche's appreciation for the achievements and aspirations of the modern rule of law and rather crudely sees it as little more than another repressive "disciplinary" mode of power. I wonder if those who do not enjoy the benefits of due process would see it that way.

19. Kirchheimer and Rusche, *Punishment and Social Structure,* 79.

20. Benjamin, "Theses on the Philosophy of History," 257.

21. Kirchheimer and Rusche, *Punishment and Social Structure,* 207.

22. Kirchheimer and Rusche, *Punishment and Social Structure,* 179.

23. Kirchheimer and Rusche, *Punishment and Social Structure,* 207.

24. Kirchheimer, "Decree Powers and Constitutional Law in France under the Third Republic" (1940), in *PLSC,* 110. Background information on legal trends in the French Third Republic is also to be found in Kirchheimer's unpublished "Die wirtschaftliche Betätigung der französischen Gemeinden und die Rechtsprechung des Conseil Détat" (1937?). Otto Kirchheimer File, German Emigré Collection, SUNY Albany Library, Albany, New York.

25. Kirchheimer, "Decree Powers and Constitutional Law in France under the Third Republic," 118.

26. Kirchheimer, "Decree Powers and Constitutional Law in France under the Third Republic," 122–25.

27. Kirchheimer, "Decree Powers and Constitutional Law in France under the Third Republic," 126–30.

28. Kirchheimer, "Decree Powers and Constitutional Law in France under the Third Republic," 130.

29. Kirchheimer, "The Growth and Decay of the Weimar Constitution," 566.

30. Kirchheimer, "The Growth and Decay of the Weimar Constitution," 566; on Schmitt and Nazi law, see "Staatsgefüge und Recht im Dritten Reich" (1935), in *WR;* "Criminal Law in National Socialist Germany," in *PLSC.* "Staatsgefüge und Recht im Dritten Reich" has a particularly curious history. Smuggled into German under the pseudonym Hermann Seitz, so as to look like part of a series of Nazi pamphlets (on "Der Deutsche Staat der Gegenwart") edited by Schmitt, and given a title similar to one of Schmitt's own recent Nazi pamphlets (the 1934 *Staatsgefüge und Zusammenbruch des zweiten Reiches*), it was quickly denounced in the Nazi legal press by, it seems, none other than Carl Schmitt himself. For details, see Wolfgang Luthardt, "Einleitung zu Kirchheimer, Staatsgefüge und Recht des Dritten Reiches," *Kritische Justiz,* vol. 9, no. 1 (1976). True, Kirchheimer's subsequent writings on fascist law seem to place somewhat less emphasis on Schmitt's role in it; this *might* suggest that he believed that Schmitt's influence declined after his feud with the SS in 1936.

31. Kirchheimer and Rusche, *Punishment and Social Structure,* 179. Kirchheimer sides with

Neumann against Ernst Fraenkel, arguing as well that fascism had shed the dual norm/prerogative structure characteristic in Neumann's and Kirchheimer's view of every bourgeois legal order in favor of a system in which arbitrary prerogatives become dominant. Kirchheimer writes that Fraenkel overestimates "the importance of some isolated judicial decisions of the earlier epoch" of fascist law. Kirchheimer, "The Legal Order of National Socialism," 99; "Review of Ernst Fraenkel, *The Dual State," Political Science Quarterly,* vol. 56, no. 3 (1941), 434–36.

32. Kirchheimer, "The Legal Order of National Socialism," 103.

33. Whereas liberal law "confined" itself to an "ethical minimum," Nazi law propagates a (crude) "identity between law and morality," realized in part by troublesome moralistic legal standards like "in good faith" *(Treu und Glaube).* In turn, such standards facilitate the disintegration of traditional forms of legal decision making and the emergence of a judiciary malleable to the needs of dominant political and economic interests. Otto Kirchheimer, *Staatsgefüge und Recht des Dritten Reiches,* in *WR,* 154–55.

34. Kirchheimer, "The Legal Order of National Socialism," 99.

35. Kirchheimer, "The Legal Order of National Socialism,," 88.

36. Kirchheimer, "The Legal Order of National Socialism," 88. Fascism thus radicalizes the "absorption of individual rights by monopolistic groups," which Kirchheimer thinks is foreshadowed in the increasingly corporatist decision making structure of contemporary representative government. Kirchheimer, "Changes in the Structure of Political Compromise," 141.

37. Kirchheimer, "Changes in the Structure of Political Compromise," 151.

38. Neumann, *Behemoth,* 447. Kirchheimer's argument here complements much of Neumann's in *Behemoth.*

39. Another unpublished essay from the early forties by Kirchheimer is particularly interesting in this respect. In "Schutzhaft, Internment, Confinio, Arrestations Administrative," he describes the liberal legal order's sad reliance on instruments of "preventive arrest" as a way of thwarting incipient challenges to the law. In Kirchheimer's view, such trends constitute a prehistory of sorts for fascist law. Although an otherwise familiar argument from his repertoire, the example he uses here (female prostitution) is one that might have suggested to him the inadequacies of his Marxist conception of power. Rather traditionally, Neumann and Kirchheimer neither acknowledge the limitations of a Marxist view of social conflict nor grasp the autonomy of gender inequalities. For an excellent critique of Marxism's blindness to this problem, see Linda Nicholson, "Feminism and Marx: Integrating Kinship with the Economic," in *Feminism as Critique,* Seyla Benhabib and Drucilla Cornell (Minneapolis: University of Minnesota Press, 1987). The (undated) manuscript is on hand at the Max Horkheimer Archives, Stadt- und Universitätsbibliothek, Frankfurt.

40. Kirchheimer, "Remarques sur la théorie de la souveraineté nationale en Allemagne et en France," *Archives de Philosophie du Droit et de la Sociologie juridique,* vol. 4 (1934), 252–54.

41. For a more recent discussion in a similar vein, see Ingeborg Maus, *Rechtstheorie und politische Theorie im Industriekapitalismus,* 280–90.

42. Kirchheimer, "In Quest of Sovereignty," in *PLSC,* 184, 185–86.

43. Kirchheimer, "In Quest of Sovereignty," 180.

44. Jacques Maritain, "The Concept of Sovereignty," *American Political Science Review*, vol. 44, no. 2 (1950), 357.

45. On the evolution of the idea of sovereignty, see Otto von Gierke, *The Development of Political Theory* (New York: Norton, 1939); F. H. Hinsley, *Sovereignty* (New York: Cambridge University Press, 1986).

46. Hannah Arendt, *The Human Condition* (Chicago: University of Chicago Press, 1958), 234.

47. Neumann probably reproduces one of Laski's most serious failings. For Laski, sovereignty refers primarily to the sovereignty of state organs, and he is strikingly insensitive to the fact that many Enlightenment-era versions of the concept were more complex than his simple attack on "grim Hegelian" state sovereignty suggests. Even for Rousseau, the idea of the sovereignty of the general will referred not simply to the supremacy of a particular institutional complex but to a normative conception of the rules and procedures according to which legitimate authority could emerge. Terrified by the implications of the fascist behemoth, Neumann criticizes Laski but may implicitly accept much of Laski's reading of sovereignty in terms of the state as a unified "highest power."

48. Neumann, *The Governance of the Rule of Law*, 302.

49. Neumann, *The Governance of the Rule of Law*, 27.

50. Hans Kelsen, *Reine Rechtslehre* (1934) (Darmstadt, Ger.: Scientia Verlag, 1985), 64.

51. Hans Kelsen, *Allgemeine Staatslehre* (Berlin: Springer, 1925), esp. 102–3; Kelsen *Das Problem der Souveranität und die Theorie des Völkerrechts* (Tübingen, Ger.: J. C. B. Mohr, 1928).

52. Neumann, "Review of Fuller, Radin, Llewellyn, Baumgarten, Bodenheimer." The emphasis on the "ethical" structure of the general legal norm in Neumann's analysis is one result of this view.

53. Neumann, *The Governance of the Rule of Law*, 11.

54. Neumann, *Behemoth*, 47. See also *The Governance of the Rule of Law*, 13, 23–24.

55. Cited in Carl Friedrich, *The Philosophy of Law in Historical Perspective* (Chicago: University of Chicago Press, 1963), 176, where Friedrich offers a number of similar criticisms of Kelsen. See also Wolfgang Schluchter, *Entscheidung für den sozialen Rechtsstaat*, 25–52, which does an excellent job of tracing the consequences of the problems identified by Hermann Heller (and Franz Neumann) in Kelsen's theory.

56. Neumann, *The Governance of the Rule of Law*, 16. For a discussion in a similar vein, see Kirchheimer, "Remarques sur la théorie de la souveraineté nationale en Allemagne et en France," 25–51.

57. Neumann, *The Governance of the Rule of Law*, 17.

58. Neumann, *The Governance of the Rule of Law*, 23.

59. Neumann's views about political decentralization undergo a clear evolution. As noted in chapter 2, during the twenties and early thirties he is sympathetic toward programs for decentralizing political authority. After witnessing the collapse of the Weimar Republic and coming to believe that its demise stemmed in part from its institutionalization of some ideas like those found in pluralist political theory, he clearly becomes much more skeptical of plans for extensive legislative decentralization. Neumann, "The Concept of Political Freedom," in *DAS*, 192.

60. Hermann Heller, *Die Souveranität* (Berlin: Walter de Gruyter, 1927), 75.

61. Rousseau, *The Social Contract*, 100.

62. See, for example, Dicey's classic discussion of the English idea of the "Sovereign in Parliament," in A. V. Dicey, *Introduction to the Study of the Law of the Constitution*, esp. 39–85.

63. Claude Lefort, *Democracy and Political Theory* (Minneapolis: University of Minnesota Press, 1988), esp. 17–19.

64. Cited in Edmund Morgan, *Inventing the People: The Rise of Popular Sovereignty in England and America* (New York: Norton, 1988), 61.

65. For a recent restatement of the principle of democratic legitimacy with a similar intent, see Bernard Manin, "On Legitimacy and Political Deliberation," *Political Theory*, vol. 15 (1987).

66. Kirchheimer, "In Quest of Sovereignty," 181. My analysis here has to focus on the problem of sovereignty as an internal or domestic issue, but it certainly has implications for the international setting as well. Is it too naive to aspire today to an international federation of (desubstantialized) modern democratic "sovereigns"?

67. Kirchheimer, "Changes in the Structure of Political Compromise," 140. The Frankfurt authors were hardly mere observers of the New Deal. Neumann gave lectures (in 1938 and 1939) at the U.S. Senate for Thurman Arnold and the Antitrust Division of the Justice Department on the Weimar cartel system and its lessons for the United States, and both he and Kirchheimer seemed to have maintained some ties to Felix Frankfurter. Kirchheimer's "Die wirtschaftliche Betätigung der französischen Gemeinden" was intended for Frankfurter. Theirs was a critique of the New Deal from a sympathetic left viewpoint.

68. Kirchheimer, "In Quest of Sovereignty," 182.

69. Kirchheimer, "In Quest of Sovereignty," 183.

70. Kirchheimer, "In Quest of Sovereignty," 187–88.

71. Kirchheimer, "In Quest of Sovereignty," 188–92; "Remarques sur la théorie de la souveraineté nationale en Allemagne et en France," 251–52.

72. Kirchheimer, "In Quest of Sovereignty," 187–88.

73. Kirchheimer, "In Quest of Sovereignty," 189.

74. After describing parliament's decline, he notes that "new devices and institutions must

take the place of parliament." But he never describes what those devices should be. Kirchheimer, "In Quest of Sovereignty," 182.

75. J. A. Schumpeter, *Capitalism, Socialism and Democracy* (New York: Harper and Row, 1942). For a critique, see Carole Pateman, *Participation and Democratic Theory* (Cambridge: Cambridge University Press, 1970).

76. Kirchheimer, "In Quest of Sovereignty," 182, 187.

77. Kirchheimer, "The Historical and Comparative Background of the Hatch Law," 359.

78. Kirchheimer, "In Quest of Sovereignty," 182.

Chapter 7

1. In fact, he may see it as a direct counterpode to Schmitt's *Die Diktatur;* see Franz Neumann, "Notes on The Theory of Dictatorship," in *DAS,* 254, no. 1. Two related unpublished manuscripts support this interpretation: "Zur Theorie der Diktatur" (1953) (Otto Kirchheimer File, German Emigre Collection, SUNY Albany Library, Albany, New York); "Die Diktatur: Frankfurter Vortrag vom 7. Juli 1954" (Max Horkheimer Archives, Stadt- und Universitätsbibliothek, Frankfurt). A central thesis of these pieces is that a plebiscitary dictatorship like that advocated by Schmitt in the twenties and early thirties necessarily tends to become ruthlessly totalitarian under modern conditions. Schmitt's idea of a democratic dictatorship is an irresponsible myth.

2. Neumann, "Notes on the Theory of Dictatorship," 253. Neumann seems to think that any distinctions between "fear" *(Angst)* and "anxiety" or "discontent" *(Unbehagen)* is unimportant to his analysis; the German original of "Anxiety and Politics" carried the title "Angst und Politik"; it was reprinted in *DAS.*

3. As Alfons Söllner has pointed out to me, an interesting contrast from the same period is Marcuse's more utopian *Eros and Civilization: A Philosophical Inquiry into Freud* (New York: Vintage, 1955). Was Marcuse trying to provide some type of response to his friend Neumann?

4. Neumann, "Anxiety and Politics" (1954), in *DAS,* esp. 273–76; "Notes on the Theory of Dictatorship," 252–53.

5. Neumann, "Anxiety and Politics," 279.

6. Neumann, "Anxiety and Politics," 279.

7. Neumann, "Anxiety and Politics," 287.

8. Neumann, "Anxiety and Politics," 299, n. 84.

9. Neumann, "Anxiety and Politics," 294.

10. Neumann, "Anxiety and Politics," 270.

11. Neumann, "The Concept of Political Freedom," in *DAS,* 194.

12. Neumann, "The Concept of Political Freedom," 193. The title, as we see, is no accident. The fit also works in the original German: Neumann refers to his "Begriff der Politischen Freiheit" (versus Schmitt's "Begriff des Politischen"). Despite the centrality of this essay, its main argument is worked out or at least suggested in others as well. "Die Wissenschaft der Politik in der Demokratie" (1950), in Neumann, *Wirtschaft, Staat, und Demokratie, Aufsätze 1930–54,* ed. A. Söllner (Frankfurt: Suhrkamp, 1978); the radio address "Die Wissenschaft von der Politik in der Demokratie" (1952) (which, importantly, is distinct from the 1950 essay with a similar title), in *Internationale wissenschaftliche Korrespondenz zur Geschichte der deutschen Arbeiterbewegung,* vol. 25 (1989), 512–20; "Approaches to the Study of Political Power" (1950), "Economics and Politics in the Twentieth Century" (1951), and "Intellectual and Political Freedom" (1954), all in *DAS;* somewhat more distantly, "The Social Sciences," in *The Cultural Migration: The European Scholar in America,* ed. William Rex Crawford (Philadelphia: University of Pennsylvania Press, 1953). As we will also see, it provides the backdrop to all of Neumann's more ambitious writings during this period. My view that Neumann himself saw the "concept of political freedom" as the centerpiece of his postwar program is buttressed by Martin Fleischer's perceptive comments in Rainer Erd, ed., *Reform und Resignation,* 206–7.

13. Neumann, "The Concept of Political Freedom," 193.

14. Neumann, "Anxiety and Politics," 270.

15. Neumann, "The Concept of Political Freedom," 190. See also "Approaches to the Study of Political Power," 5–7. Neumann goes so far as to write that "the concept of the 'community,' even if it sounds beautiful . . . should be driven out of Germany. A community can only exist where there is an identity of interests: in the family, perhaps in the labor union, when and insofar as solidarity is genuinely and deeply experienced there. When there is no identity of interests, the concept of the community can very easily become an ideological instrument of authoritarian domination." Neumann, "Arbeitsrecht in der modernen Gesellschaft," 2. Contemporary communitarian theorists, by the way, would do well to heed Neumann's warnings about the perils of an inflationary use of the term "community."

16. Neumann, "Montesquieu," in *DAS,* 116–17. The key passage here has been reprinted in virtually every one of Neumann's postwar theoretical essays.

17. Neumann, "On the Limits of Justifiable Disobedience," 156.

18. In other words, what I described as the first moment in Neumann's concept of sovereignty (see chapter 4, n. 15) does not require its further moments, nor does his argument here necessarily presuppose much more than the first moment—the idea that "by its coercive character law can be distinguished from custom and morality"—and that a particular institutional configuration is responsible for assuring law's coercive character. Neumann, *The Governance of the Rule of Law,* 11. Why that first moment should lead us to embrace the further idea of the state as an all-powerful, undivided "highest power," as Neumann thinks, remains unconvincing to me for reasons sketched out in chapter 6.

19. Neumann, "Intellectual and Political Freedom," 202.

20. Neumann, "Economics and Politics in the Twentieth Century," esp. 264–65.

21. Neumann, "On the Limits of Justifiable Disobedience," 156.

22. Neumann, "Economics and Politics in the Twentieth Century," 264.

23. Neumann, "The Concept of Political Freedom," 172.

24. Neumann, "Intellectual and Political Freedom," 202.

25. Neumann, "The Concept of Political Freedom," 200, n. 87.

26. Neumann, "Intellectual and Political Freedom," 202–6.

27. In particular, Neumann, "Intellectual and Political Freedom."

28. Neumann, "Die Wissenschaft von der Politik in der Demokratie," 517.

29. Neumann, "Die Wissenschaft von der Politik in der Demokratie," 514–15, 517–20.

30. Neumann, "The Concept of Political Freedom," 162.

31. Neumann, "Die Wissenschaft von der Politik in der Demokratie," 519; "The Concept of Political Freedom," 190.

32. Neumann, "The Concept of Political Freedom," 190–92; many other junctures as well. For a more recently discussion of the limits of Marxist analyses of bureaucracy, see Wolfgang Schluchter, *Aspekte bürokratischer Herrschaft* (Frankfurt: Suhrkamp, 1985), 34–64.

33. Neumann, "Approaches to the Study of Political Power," 3. For Arendt's argument, see especially *On Violence*.

34. Neumann, "Approaches to the Study of Political Power," 4; "The Concept of Political Freedom," 161.

35. Neumann, "Approaches to the Study of Political Power," 18.

36. Neumann, "Die Wissenschaft der Politik in der Demokratie," 391.

37. Neumann, "Approaches to the Study of Political Power," 13.

38. Neumann, "Approaches to the Study of Political Power," 13; 21, n. 21.

39. Neumann, "Die Wissenschaft der Politik in der Demokratie," 392.

40. Neumann, "The Concept of Political Freedom," 184.

41. Neumann, "The Concept of Political Freedom," 186.

42. Neumann, "The Concept of Political Freedom," 184–85.

43. Neumann, "The Concept of Political Freedom," 162.

44. Neumann, "Economics and Politics in the Twentieth Century," 264.

45. Schmitt, *Political Theology*, 66.

46. Neumann, "Die Wissenschaft von der Politik in der Demokratie," 517.

47. Seyla Benhabib has shown how the early Frankfurt school remained trapped in what she describes as "the philosophy of the subject," and she argues that critical theory needs to break with this tradition in favor of an intersubjective or "communicative" theoretical paradigm. It seems to me that especially at this juncture, her analysis takes on a direct significance for us here. The "concept of political freedom" shows more clearly than any other aspect of Neumann's thinking how he struggled to break with a (subject-centered) Marxist philosophy of history in favor of an (intersubjective) theory of democracy, how he strained to appreciate the importance of (communicative) political deliberation while failing to work out its implications—in short, how he managed to break, if only implicitly, with the "philosophy of the subject" far more extensively than his Frankfurt colleagues did. The same, I believe, can be said for Otto Kirchheimer. Seyla Benhabib, *Critique, Norm, and Utopia.*

48. Neumann, "The Concept of Political Freedom," 185.

49. Neumann, "The Concept of Political Freedom," 185–86.

50. Neumann, "On the Theory of the Federal State," in *DAS,* 224.

51. Neumann, "Economics and Politics in the Twentieth Century," 268–69.

52. Martin Jay, "Franz Neumann and the Frankfurt School," in Neumann, *The Governance of the Rule of Law;* H. Stuart Hughes, "Franz Neumann: Between Marxism and Liberal Democracy," in *The Intellectual Migration: Europe and America, 1930–60,* ed. Donald Fleming and Bernard Bailyn (Cambridge: Harvard University Press, 1969). See also Alfons Söllner, "Politische Dialektik der Aufklärung: Zum Spätwerk von Franz Neumann und Otto Kirchheimer," in *Sozialforschung als Kritik,* ed. Wolfgang Bonß and Axel Honneth (Frankfurt: Suhrkamp, 1982).

53. Neumann, "Review of A. Vyshinsky, *The Law of the Soviet State,* " *Political Science Quarterly,* vol. 64 (1949), 128; "Approaches to the Study of Political Power," 11. For a more general discussion, see "Economics and Politics in the Twentieth Century." Both "Wandlungen des Marxismus" and "Marxismus und Intelligenz" (both radio addresses reprinted in *Internationale wissenschaftliche Korrespondenz zur Geschichte der deutschen Arbeiterbewegung,* vol. 25 [1989], 501–11) reveal the complexities of Neumann's postwar relationship to Marxism: while rightly critical of much of classical Marxism there, Neumann thinks critical theory can still learn a great deal from some facets of Marxism.

54. Rainer Erd, ed. *Reform und Resignation.*

55. He does so at many junctures, but especially in "Montesquieu," 116–17, 138–43.

56. Neumann, "The Concept of Political Freedom," 165.

57. Neumann, "Das Arbeitsrecht in der modernen Gesellschaft," 1. This is one reason why Kirchheimer's description, in the fifties, of his friend as a "critical" or "libertarian socialist" seems accurate to me. Kirchheimer, "Franz Neumann: An Appreciation."

58. Neumann, "The Concept of Political Freedom," 170–71.

59. Neumann, "The Concept of Political Freedom," 172.

60. Neumann, "Intellectual and Political Freedom," 202.

61. Neumann, "The Concept of Political Freedom," 170.

62. Neumann, "The Concept of Political Freedom," 192.

63. Weber, *Economy and Society,* 1402.

64. Neumann, "The Concept of Political Freedom," 189.

65. Few today deny that, for example, "positive" governmental regulations undermining private monopolies or rules guaranteeing the representation of an adequate diversity of political views on television are necessary for preserving freedom of the press.

66. Ulrich Preuss, in *Die Verfassungsdiskussion im Jahre der deutschen Einheit, ed.* Bernd Guggenberger and Tine Stein (Munich: Carl Hanser, 1991), 363.

67. The idea of social rights in postwar political discourse can be traced to T. H. Marshall, *Citizenship and Social Class* (Cambridge: Cambridge University Press, 1950).

68. See Cass R. Sunstein, "Constitutionalism after the New Deal," *Harvard Law Review,* vol. 101 (1987–88); Sunstein, *After the Rights Revolution: Reconceiving the Regulatory State* (Cambridge: Harvard University Press, 1990).

69. Wilson, *The Politics of Regulation,* 392.

70. Lowi, *The End of Liberalism,* esp. chap. 5. See also Theodore Lowi, "The Welfare State, the New Republic, and the Rule of Law," in *Rule of Law: Ideal or Ideology?*

71. Robert Lieberman, "Race and the Administration of Old-Age Insurance and Aid to Dependent Children, 1930s–1960s," unpublished paper presented at the Workshop on American Political Development, Harvard University, April 7, 1993, 26–27.

72. Most recently in *Critique of Economic Reason* (New York: Verso, 1989), 191–215.

73. Thomas Schmid, ed., *Befreiung von falscher Arbeit. Thesen zum garantierten Mindesteinkommen* (Berlin: Wagenbach, 1986).

74. Lowi, *The End of Liberalism,* 275. As those familiar with contemporary law know, countless similar examples could be named. Lowi mentions many of them.

75. Neumann, *The Governance of the Rule of Law,* 275–86; Maus, *Rechtstheorie und politische Theorie im Industriekapitalismus,* 280–91.

76. Ingeborg Maus, "Sinn und Bedeutung der Volkssouveranität in der modernen Gesellschaft," *Kritische Justiz,* vol. 24, no. 2 (1991), 148–49.

77. Maus, "Sinn und Bedeutung," 146.

Chapter 8

1. Herbert Marcuse, "Repressive Tolerance," in *Critical Sociology,* ed. Paul Connerton (New York: Penguin, 1976), 320.

2. Marcuse, "Repressive Tolerance," 320.

3. Benjamin, "Theses on the Philosophy of History," 257.

4. Kirchheimer, "The Rechtsstaat as Magic Wall," in *PLSC,* 452.

5. Otto Kirchheimer, *Political Justice: The Use of Legal Procedure for Political Ends* (henceforth *PJ*) (Princeton: Princeton University Press, 1961), 322. A somewhat expanded German version also appeared: *Politische Justiz. Verwendung juristischer Verfahrensmöglichkeiten zu juristischen Zwecken* (Neuwied, Ger.: Luchterhand, 1965).

6. But this should not imply that Kirchheimer was not as outraged as Marcuse at the course of American politics in the sixties. A few months before Kirchheimer's sudden death in 1965, he jotted down a nasty letter to the editor for the *New York Times* critical of American foreign policy in Southeast Asia and Latin America: "US behavior takes so much more the appearance of an asserted right of permanent intervention into the internal affairs of third countries in order to prevent the rise of groups or governments not in accordance with official ideologies or policies of the US . . . . In a democracy there should be some, however vague correspondence between major campaign themes and subsequent political action by the winner. How many of those who voted for the incumbent President have been given to understand that they were endorsing a candidate who was to sponsor a super-Goldwater foreign policy? In point of fact, millions voted for the Democratic candidate as an insurance against the very policies of which, along with the rest of the world—they are now becoming helpless spectators." (Letter to the *New York Times,* May 27, 1965, Otto Kirchheimer File, German Emigré Collection, SUNY Albany Library, Albany, New York.)

7. Let me explain more precisely what I mean by the term "between the norm and the exception." On one level, when I refer to "norms" in law, I simply mean *cogent, formal rules.* But as we saw in chapter 4, the normative core of contemporary law must be conceptualized more broadly so as to refer to the potential *universal* or *general* participatory *origins* of law. Thus, my defense of Kirchheimer's claim that contemporary law finds itself "between the norm and the exception" means both (1) that state action is decreasingly guided by cogent rules and (2) that its participatory roots tend to be inadequately democratic. One consequence is that law increasingly seems highly discretionary—that is, cases seem to be decided as though they were individual or exceptional. Jon Elster has a similar concern in mind when he notes that from the perspective of welfare state clients, "vague and complex criteria lead to what appears at best to be a meddlesome paternalism and at worst a Kafkaesque nightmare." Jon Elster, "Is There (or Should There Be) a Right to Work?" in *Democracy and the Welfare State,* ed. Amy Gutmann (Princeton: Princeton University Press, 1988), 62.

8. Kirchheimer, "The Rechtsstaat as Magic Wall," 429. It first appeared in *The Critical Spirit: Essays in Honor of Herbert Marcuse,* ed. Barrington Moore. (Boston: Beacon, 1967).

9. See, for example, his reflections on legal decision making in *PJ,* 178–88.

10. Kirchheimer, "The Rechtsstaat as Magic Wall," 435.

11. For the critique of the right-wing argument, see Kirchheimer "The Rechtsstaat as Magic Wall," 432–37.

12. Kirchheimer, "The Rechtsstaat as Magic Wall," 434.

13. Kirchheimer, "The Rechtsstaat as Magic Wall," 435.

14. Otto Kirchheimer, "Notes on the Political Scene in West Germany" (1954), in *PLSC,* 201–2. See also "The Political Scene in West Germany," *World Politics,* vol. 9 (1957), 444; "German Democracy in the 1950s," *World Politics,* vol. 13, no. 2 (1961), 255–57, 261–62. He also seems to endorse the French Fourth Republic's attempt to constitutionalize basic social rights, in *A Constitution for the Fourth Republic* (Washington: Foundation For Foreign Affairs, 1947).

15. Kirchheimer, "German Democracy in the 1950s," 262.

16. Kirchheimer, "Notes on the Political Scene in West Germany," 203.

17. Kirchheimer, "Notes on the Political Scene in West Germany," 209. But subsequent essays can be interpreted as sharing the widespread faith in the possibility of an unlimited capitalist economic boom.

18. Kirchheimer, "Germany: The Vanishing Opposition," 331.

19. Kirchheimer, "German Democracy in the 1950s," 262.

20. Otto Kirchheimer, "European Parliaments," paper delivered at the Ninth National Conference of the United States National Commission for UNESCO (Chicago: October 23–26, 1963), 7. Otto Kirchheimer File, German Emigré Collection, SUNY Albany Library, Albany, New York.

21. Kirchheimer, "German Democracy in the 1950s," 261.

22. This is a basic problem with Joachim Hirsch's *Der Sicherheitsstaat* (Frankfurt: EVA, 1980).

23. Kirchheimer, "Rechtsstaat as Magic Wall," 438–44. Neumann discussed the issue of German war criminals, in "The War Crime Trials," *World Politics,* vol. 2 (1949). For the historical background, see the still quite helpful: John Herz, "The Fiasco of Denazification in Germany," *Political Science Quarterly,* vol. 63 (1948).

24. Kirchheimer, "The Rechtsstaat as Magic Wall," 438, 451.

25. Kirchheimer, "The Rechtsstaat as Magic Wall," 441.

26. Kirchheimer, "The Rechtsstaat as Magic Wall," 441; Kirchheimer, "Majorities and Minorities in Western European Governments" (1959), in *PLSC,* 291.

27. Kirchheimer does raise one criticism of this minimalistic reading: "to ride together in a bus while wanting to go to different places may be all right, provided that the

destinations are not too different from each other." Kirchheimer, "Private Man and Society," in *PLSC,* 454.

28. Kirchheimer, "Private Man and Society," 456.

29. Kirchheimer, "Private Man and Society," 462.

30. Kirchheimer, "German Democracy in the 1950s," 265.

31. Kirchheimer, "German Democracy in the 1950s," 265.

32. Lefort, *Democracy and Political Theory,* 29.

33. Otto Kirchheimer, "The Waning of Opposition" 294.

34. Kirchheimer, "The Waning of Opposition," esp. 295; *PJ,* esp. 14–18, 30–36.

35. Kirchheimer, *PJ,* esp. 30–36.

36. For the most complete analysis of this theme, see Kirchheimer "European Parliaments," 2–4.

37. Kirchheimer, *PJ,* 16–19; on the role of the press, see Kirchheimer "The Waning of Opposition," 312–13. This thesis anticipates some important features of the basic argument of Habermas's subsequent (1962) *Structural Transformation of the Public Sphere* (Cambridge: MIT Press, 1989.)

38. The remainder of the passage is worth citing. In describing Schmitt's theory, Kirchheimr refers to its "lack of any clear-cut criteria for differentiating between *nomos* and violence, the discrepancy between the traditional liberal concepts of classical international law and the decisive rejection of *artfremd* and disintegrating liberalism as part of the domestic constitutional order, the broody omnipresence of the people's constituent power and its incapacity to act as a constituted organ, the indeterminate character of the values underlying concrete decisions, and the conjunction of a relativistic openness to a variety of historical interpretations with an ever-present negation of the rule of law." Kirchheimer, "The Political Scene in West Germany," 438–39. In an interesting letter to the editor of the *American Political Science Review,* Kirchheimer restates some of his criticisms of Schmitt. Letter to Harvey Mansfield, June 4, 1964, Otto Kirchheimer File, German Emigré Collection, SUNY Albany Library, Albany, New York.

39. This is one of the basic ambiguities of *Political Justice.* It seems at times that Kirchheimer only wants to contrast the aspirations of the liberal rule of law in its most radical forms with contemporary legal practices, whereas at other times he really does suggest that eighteenth- and nineteenth-century constitutionalist reality was superior to our own. The former view is probably the more defensible one.

40. This expression appears in "Confining Conditions and Revolutionary Breakthroughs" (1965), in *PLSC,* 405.

41. Kirchheimer, "Review of Kaiser," 257.

42. See, most importantly, Schmitt, *The Concept of the Political.*

43. See, in particular, *PJ,* 16, 25. It is difficult for me to assume that Kirchheimer's Schmittian language here is accidental, even if the work is not explicitly intended as an "anti-Schmitt."

44. Otto Kirchheimer, "Politics and Justice" (1955), first published in *Sociologica. Aufsätze, Max Horkheimer zum 60. Geburtstag gewidmet* (Frankfurt: 1955), but reprinted in *PLSC,* 408. Kirchheimer does think that justice can be seen as political from a somewhat broader perspective, and this is why he wants to differentiate between them but not see them as perfectly separate. What worries him about attempts to blur this distinction is that they risk abandoning the minimum of autonomy that an independent judiciary can help provide (in particular, see *PJ,* 47–53). See also Judith Shklar, *Legalism: Law, Morals, and Political Trials* (Cambridge: Harvard University Press, 1986), 111–221; Shklar argues that we should see legalism as a matter of degree and a continuum (p. 156) and probably wants to go further than Kirchheimer in overcoming any clear-cut break between law and politics. The question for Shklar, from Kirchheimer's perspective, would be whether or not she can fuse law and politics so extensively without, if only inadvertently, undermining some of the achievements of liberal legalism that both authors appreciate. For a more recent discussion, see Ulrich Preuss, "Politische Justiz im demokratischen Verfassungsstaat," in *Verfassung, Souveranität, Pluralismus,* ed. Wolfgang Luthardt and Alfons Söllner (Opladen, Ger.: Westdeutscher Verlag, 1986).

45. Kirchheimer, *PJ,* 3.

46. Kirchheimer, *PJ,* 323–47, esp. 341. For a discussion in a similar vein but in greater depth, see Judith Shklar, *Legalism,* esp. 143–200.

47. Kirchheimer, *PJ,* 119–20, 167–72.

48. Kirchheimer discusses in depth the shocking example of how a vague and repressive concept of treason that reemerged in postwar Germany was used by the governing Christian Democrats to close down the newsweekly *Der Spiegel,* because it published articles critical of Defense Minister Franz Josef Strauß. Otto Kirchheimer (with Constantine Menges), "A Free Press in a Democratic Society? The *Spiegel* Case," in *Politics in Europe,* ed. A. F. Westin and G. M. Carter (New York: Harcourt, Brace & World 1965). See also his contribution to *Ich lebe nicht in der Bundesrepublik,* ed. Hermann Kesten (Munich: List, 1964), 85–90.

49. It would be a mistake to chalk the ugliest forms of political justice up to the Cold War. For some of its more recent manifestations, a bare but more or less accurate summary is offered by John Finn (who uncritically accepts much of Carl Schmitt's self-interpretation of his views and actions during Weimar's final days) in *Constitutions in Crisis: Political Violence and the Rule of Law* (New York: Oxford University Press, 1991). More reliable as far as the continuing legacy in Germany goes is the special issue dedicated to "Unser Rechtsstaat" of the journal *Kursbuch,* no. 56 (June 1979).

50. John Herz and Erich Hula, "Otto Kirchheimer: An Introduction to His Life and Work," in *PLSC,* xxxvii.

51. Kirchheimer, *PJ,* 431, 169.

52. Kirchheimer, *PJ,* 170.

53. Kirchheimer, *PJ,* 169. For an interesting gloss on Tocqueville's analysis of this

theme emphasizing his (aristocratic) hostility to bourgeois society, see Roger Boesche, *The Strange Liberalism of Alexis de Tocqueville* (Ithaca, N.Y.: Cornell University Press, 1986), 229–59.

54. For Kirchheimer, one of the most worrisome forms of this spillover is the modern-day secret police, "a cancer plaguing almost all governments . . . enveloping, since its unhappy beginning in Russia, all social systems and largely contributing to their conformist zeal." Kirchheimer, "Expertise and Politics in The Administration" (1961), in *PLSC,* 375.

55. Kirchheimer, *PJ,* 37.

56. Kirchheimer, *PJ,* 430. For the broader argument, see 16–18, 36–45.

57. Kirchheimer, "The Realities of Political Responsibility: Parliament and Party in Western Europe (Outline for a Research Project)," esp. 2, undated but probably from the early sixties, Otto Kirchheimer File, German Emigré Collection, SUNY Albany Library, Albany, New York.

58. Kirchheimer, "German Democracy in the 1950s," 255. See also "Expertise and Politics in the Administration," 372.

59. Kirchheimer, "European Parliaments," 6.

60. Faced with nasty attacks on the contemporary welfare state from the right, Kirchheimer's thinking about parliamentarism does sometimes take a rather conciliatory tone. See, for example, "The Rechtsstaat as Magic Wall," 435–36.

61. Otto Kirchheimer, "Diskussionsbeitrag," *Verhandlungen des deutschen Juristentages* (1964), ed. Ständige Deputation des Deutschen Juristentages (Munich: C. H. Beck, 1965), E96–E105.

62. Otto Kirchheimer, "Party Structure and Mass Democracy in Europe," in *PLSC,* 253–54, 257.

63. Kirchheimer, "European Parliaments," 7.

64. Kirchheimer, "European Parliaments," 8.

65. On these trends in the United States, see Arthur Schlesinger, *The Imperial Presidency* (Boston: Houghton Mifflin, 1973).

66. Otto Kirchheimer, "France from the Fourth to Fifth Republic" (1958), in *PLSC,* 243.

67. Kirchheimer, "In Quest of Sovereignty," 182.

68. Kirchheimer, "German Democracy in the 1950s," 265. Does not this demand for referenda contradict Kirchheimer's hostility of the early thirties toward plebiscitary forms of decision making? Perhaps he understands that we need to distinguish personal plebiscites, in which the public is asked to do little more than say "yes" or "no" to a political leader representing a medley of oftentimes disconnected political positions, from issue referenda, in which voters are asked to say "yes" or "no" to a particular question; the former are probably more problematic than the latter. Ingeborg Maus, "Die Kontrolle von unten nach oben in Gang halten. Zum Verhältnis von institutionalisierter und nichtinstitutionalisierter Volkssouveranität," *Links,* vol. 24, no. 262 (March 1992).

69. If we are to believe much of the more recent empirical literature, Kirchheimer's worries here remain legitimate. In 1979 Suzanne Berger reported that "the decline of parliament as the locus of policy-making in contemporary European states has continued over the past fifteen years." "Politics and Antipolitics in the Seventies," *Daedelus*, vol. 108, no. 1 (winter 1979), 46.

70. Kirchheimer, "Germany: The Vanishing Opposition," 331.

71. Otto Kirchheimer, "The Transformation of the Western European Party System" (1966), in *PLSC*, esp. 362–65.

72. Kirchheimer, "The Transformation of the Western European Party System," 370–71; "Party Structure and Mass Democracy," esp. 265–66.

73. Kirchheimer, "Majorities and Minorities in Western European Governments" (1959), 271; "The Waning of Opposition," 313; "The Transformation of the Party System in Western Europe," 370–71.

74. Kirchheimer, "The Waning of Opposition," 313; "Private Man and Society," esp. 476–77. For an opposing interpretation, see Alfons Söllner, "Politische Dialektik der Aufklärung: Zum Spätwerk von Franz Neumann und Otto Kirchheimer"; on the Frankfurt school's critique of the "culture industry," see Douglas Kellner, "Kulturindustrie und Massenkommunikation. Die Kritische Theorie und ihre Folgen," both in *Sozialforschung als Kritik*, ed. W. Bonß and A. Honneth.

75. Kirchheimer, "Germany: The Vanishing Opposition," 332.

76. Some countries—most notably, the German Federal Republic—did constitutionalize a commitment to the welfare state; I am referring to the *Sozialstaatsgebot* of article 20 of the Basic Law. Certainly, this development has had many meaningful consequences for legal experience in Germany. At the same time, it is noteworthy that recent attempts to *supplement* the Basic Law's rather general commitment to the welfare state with a set of *specific* constitutional social rights (to social security, a job, or an apartment) have been roundly defeated. Even if the welfare state has gained constitutional status, that commitment remains vague and tentative in many ways. For the recent German debate on social rights, see the essays collected in Bernd Guggenberger and Tine Stein, eds., *Die Verfassungsdiskussion im Jahr der deutschen Einheit.*

77. Kirchheimer, "Rechtsstaat as Magic Wall," 435.

78. Kirchheimer, "Private Man and Society," 463. Perhaps this comment suggests that Kirchheimer came to be as worried about the "private woman" as about her male counterpart.

79. For helpful criticisms of idealized accounts of nineteenth-century parliamentarism, see Ernst Fraenkel, *Deutschland und die westlichen Demokratien*, esp. 35–37, 79–80; Wolfgang Jäger, *Öffentlichkeit und Parlamentarismus. Eine Kritik an Jürgen Habermas* (Stuttgart: Kohlhammer, 1973).

80. For another recent criticism of social rights from the political Left, see Jon Elster, "Is There (or Should There Be) a Right to Work?"

81. In the recent German debate, reform-minded jurists argued that the best way of realizing the idea of social rights would be by means of constitutional "goals of state activity"

(Staatsziele). An unemployed worker would not be able to appear before a court and demand, for example, a government job. But just as the Basic Law's more general commitment to the welfare state *(Sozialstaatsgebot)* has long played a significant role in judicial decision making, it was hoped that a set of more specific, constitutionally endorsed social policy goals (stating, for example, that government should try to attain full employment) would have to be taken into consideration by judges forced to weigh different legal principles when resolving conflicts. Such proposals led some authors to argue that the addition of vague constitutional standards, allegedly implied by the idea of constitutional "governmental goals," might simply increase the already excessive influence of the German judiciary. The judiciary, of course, would possess the power to interpret the meaning of such clauses. Despite the noble goals of the constitutional reformers, might not their proposals simply increase the significance of potentially irregular forms of judicial decision making? Ingeborg Maus, "Kontrolle von unten nach oben in Gang halten."

82. Cited in Boesche, *The Strange Liberalism of Alexis de Tocqueville*, 251.

Conclusion

1. Mark Kelman, *A Guide to Critical Legal Studies* (Cambridge: Harvard University Press, 1987), 59–61, 258.

2. Duncan Kennedy, "Form and Substance in Private Law Adjudication," in *Essays on Critical Legal Studies* (Cambridge: Harvard Law Review, 1986). See also Duncan Kennedy, "Legal Formality," *The Journal of Legal Studies*, vol. 2 (June 1973).

3. Roberto Unger, *Law in Modern Society*, 221–22, 238–42.

4. For a thoughtful recent attempt at such analysis, see Andrew Altman, *Critical Legal Studies: A Liberal Critique* (Princeton: Princeton University Press, 1990).

5. Otto Kirchheimer, "Vorbemerkung," in Kirchheimer, *Politik und Verfassung* (Frankfurt: Suhrkamp, 1964), 7.

Bibliography

Selected Primary Texts

Publications are ordered chronologically. For full bibliographies, see Franz Neumann, *Wirtschaft, Staat, und Demokratie;* and Otto Kirchheimer, *Von der Weimarer Republik zum Faschismus. Die Auflösung der demokratischen Rechtsordnung.*

Otto Kirchheimer

"Review of E. A. Korowine, *Das Völkerrecht der übergangszeit.*" *Die Gesellschaft,* vol. 7 (1930).

"Nazi, Auslandsdeutsche, und Proleten." *Das Freie Wort,* vol. 4, no. 21 (1932).

"Review of Curzio Malaparte, *Der Staatsreich.*" *Die Gesellschaft,* vol. 9 (1932).

"The Growth and Decay of the Weimar Constitution." *The Contemporary Review,* vol. 144 (November 1933).

"Remarques sur la théorie de la souveraineté nationale en Allemagne et en France." *Archives de Philosophie du Droit et de la Sociologie juridigue,* vol. 4 (1934).

"Zur Geschichte des Obersten Gerichtshofes der Vereinigten Staaten." *Zeitschrift für öffentliches Recht,* vol. 14 (1934).

"Remarques sur la statistique criminelle de la France d'après-guerre." *Revue de Science criminelle et la Droit pénal comparé,* vol. 1 (1936).

"Die wirtschaftliche Betätigung der französischen Gemeinden und die Rechtsprechung des Conseil d'État" (1936/37). Otto Kirchheimer File, German Emigré Collection, SUNY Albany Library, Albany, New York.

"Recent Trends in German Treatment of Juvenile Delinquency." *Journal of Criminal Law and Criminology,* vol. 29 (1938).

Punishment and Social Structure. New York: Columbia University Press, 1939.

"Memo on State Capitalism." New York: Institute for Social Research, 1940. Available at the Max Horkheimer Archives, Stadt- und Universitätsbibliothek, Frankfurt, Germany.

"Schutzhaft, Internment, Confinio, Arrestations Administrive." (1940?). Available at the Max Horkheimer Archives, Stadt- und Universitätsbibliothek, Frankfurt, Germany.

"The Historical and Comparative Background of the Hatch Act." *Public Policy,* vol. 2 (1941).

"Review of Ernst Fraenkel, *The Dual State.*" *Political Science Quarterly,* vol. 56 (1941).

"Criminal Omissions." *Harvard Law Review,* vol. 54 (1942).

The Fate of Small Business in Nazi Germany. (Written with F. Neumann, A. Gurland). Washington: U.S. Senate Special Commission on Small Business, 1943.

A Constitution for the Fourth Republic. Washington: Foundation for Foreign Affairs, 1947.

"The Act, The Offense and Double Jeopardy." *Harvard Law Review,* vol. 58 (1949).

"The Decline of Intra-State Federalism in Western Europe." *World Politics,* vol. 3 (1951).

"Franz Neumann: An Appreciation." *Dissent,* vol. 4, no. 4 (1957).

"The Political Scene in West Germany." *World Politics,* vol. 9 (1957).

"Ein kritischer Sozialist." *Die neue Gesellschaft,* vol. 5, no. 4 (1958).

"The Party in Mass Society," *World Politics,* vol. 10 (1958).

"Asylum." *American Political Science Review,* vol. 53 (1959).

"German Democracy in the 1950s." *World Politics,* vol. 13, (1961).

Political Justice: The Use of Legal Procedure for Political Ends. Princeton: Princeton University Press, 1961.

"Prinzipien der Verfassungsinterpretation in den Vereinigten Staaten." *Jahrbuch des öffentlichen Rechts,* vol. 11 (1962).

"European Parliaments." Address at the Ninth National Conference, United States National Commission for UNESCO, Chicago, Illinois, October 23–36, 1963. Otto Kirchheimer File, German Emigré Collection, SUNY Albany Library, Albany, New York.

"Brief an Hermann Kesten." *Warum ich nicht in der Bundesrepublik lebe.* Edited by H. Kesten. Munich: List, 1964.

Politik und Verfassung. Frankfurt: Suhrkamp, 1964.

"Diskussionsbeitrag." *Verhandlungen des 45. Deutschen Juristentages Karlsruhe 1964.* Edited by Ständige Deputation des Deutschen Juristentags. Munich: C. H. Beck, 1965.

"A Free Press in a Democratic Society? The *Spiegel* Case." In *Politics in Europe.* Edited by A. F. Westin and G. M. Carter. New York, 1965.

Politische Herrschaft. Fünf Beiträge zur Lehre vom Staat. Frankfurt: Suhrkamp, 1967.

"Einleitung." In *Die Justiz in der Weimarer Republik. Eine Chronik.* Edited by E. Fraenkel and Hugo Sinzheimer. Neuwied, Ger.: Luchterhand, 1968.

"Political Justice." In *Encyclopedia of the Social Sciences,* vol. 12 (1968).

Politics, Law and Social Change: Selected Essays of Otto Kirchheimer. Edited by F. Burin and Kurt Schell. New York: Columbia University Press, 1969.

Funktionen des Staats und der Verfassung. 10 Analysen. Frankfurt: Suhrkamp, 1972.

Von der Weimarer Republik zum Faschismus: Die Auflösung der demokratischen Rechtsordnung. Edited by Wolfgang Luthardt. Frankfurt: Suhrkamp, 1976.

Social Democracy and the Rule of Law. Written with Franz Neumann. Edited by Keith Tribe. Translated by Keith Tribe and Leena Tanner. London: Allen and Unwin, 1987.

Franz L. Neumann

Rechtsphilosophische Einleitung zu einer Abhandlung über das Verhältnis vom Staat und Strafe. Unpublished doctoral thesis, Faculty of Law, University of Frankfurt, 1923. Available at the Stadt- und Universitätsbibliothek, Frankfurt, Germany.

"Der Kampf um den Zwangstariff." *Die Arbeit,* vol. 2, no. 11 (November 1925).

"Zur öffentlichen-rechtlichen Natur des Tarifvertrags." *Arbeitsrecht,* vol. 13, no. 1 (January 1926).

"Gesellschaftliche und staatliche Verwaltung der monopolistischen Unternehmungen." *Die Arbeit,* vol. 5, no. 7 (July 1928).

"Betriebsrisiko." *Arbeitsrecht-Praxis,* vol. 1, no. 10 (October 1928).

"Der Salzburger Juristentag." *Die Arbeit,* vol. 5, no. 10 (October 1928).

"Lohnzahlungen bei Betriebsstockungen." *Juristische Wochenschrift,* vol. 57, no. 46 (November, 1928).

"Recht und Eisenkampf." *Die Justiz,* vol. 4, no. 2 (December 1928).

Die politische und soziale Bedeutung der arbeitsgerichtlichen Rechtsprechung. Berlin: E. Laubsche, 1929.

"Gegen ein Gesetz zur Nachprüfung der Verfassungsmässigkeit von Reichsgesetzen." *Die Gesellschaft,* vol. 6 (June 1929).

"Richterliches Ermessen und Methodenstreit im Arbeitsrecht." *Arbeitsrecht,* vol. 16 no. 6 (June 1929).

"Der Entwurf eines Monopol- und Kartellgesetzes." *Die Arbeit,* vol. 7, no. 12 (December 1930).

Tarifrecht auf der Grundlage der Rechtsprechung des Reichsarbeitsgerichts. Berlin: Deutscher Baugewerkschaft, 1931.

"Kartell- und Monopolkontrolle." *Gewerkschafts-Zeitung,* vol. 41, no. 6 (February 1931).

"Bankenkontrolle." *Gewerkschafts-Zeitung,* vol. 41, no. 32 (August 1931).

"Gewerkschaften und Wirtschaftsverfassung." *Marxistische Tribüne,* vol. 1, no. 2 (November 1931).

"Der Lübecker Juristentag." *Die Arbeit,* vol. 8, no. 11 (November 1931).

Koalitionsrecht und Reichsverfassung. Die Stellung der Gewerkschaften im Verfassungssystem. Berlin: Carl Heymanns Verlag, 1932.

"Betriebsgeheimnisschutz." *Arbeitsrecht-Praxis,* vol. 5, no. 5 (May 1932)

"Fünf Jahre Arbeitsgerichtbarkeit." *Soziale Praxis,* vol. 41, no. 35 (September 1932).

"Recht ohne Grundlage." *Vorwärts* (morning edition), September 7, 1932.

"Reichsverfassung und Wohlfahrtsstaat." *Das Freie Wort,* vol. 4, no. 26 (1932).

"Rechtswirksamkeit der Notverordnungen, Kampffreiheit oder Friedenspflicht." *Arbeitsrecht-Praxis,* vol. 5, no. 10 (October 1932).

"Das geschichtliche Verhältnis von Staat und Koalitionen." *Gewerkschafts-Archiv,* vol. 9, no. 17 (December 1932).

Das gesamte Pressenotrecht vom 4. Februar 1933. Berlin: Dietz, 1933.

Preface to *Das Strafrecht als politische Waffe,* by Philipp Loewenfeld. Berlin: Vereinigung sozialdemokratischer Juristen, 1933.

"The Decay of German Democracy," *The Political Quarterly,* vol. 4, no. 1 (1933).

"Die Gewerkschaften im faschistischen Deutschland." *Zeitschrift für Sozialismus,* vol. 1, no. 4 (January 1934).

"Die Ordnung der nationalen Arbeit." *Zeitschrift für Sozialismus,* vol. 1, no. 5 (February 1934).

"Faschismus in Großbritannien." *Deutsche Freiheit,* vol. 2, nos. 57–59 (March 1934).

"The State and Labour in Germany." *The Contemporary Review,* vol. 146 (1934).

"Entwurf zu einem Aufsatz über 'Das Rationale Recht in der Monopolwirtschaft.' " New York: Institute for Social Research, 1936. Available at the Max Horkheimer Archives, Stadt- und Universitätsbibliothek, Frankfurt, Germany.

European Trade Unionism and Politics. New York: League for Industrial Democracy, 1936.

"Bemerkungen zu der Arbeit von Hans Mayer." New York: Institute for Social Research, 1937. Available at the Max Horkheimer Archives, Stadt- und Universitätsbibliothek, Frankfurt, Germany.

"A History of the Doctrine of Social Change." Written with Herbert Marcuse. New York: Institute for Social Research, 1941. Available at the Max Horkheimer Archives, Stadt- und Universitätsbibliothek, Frankfurt, Germany.

"Labor Mobilization in the National Socialist New Order." *Law and Contemporary Problems,* vol. 9, no. 3 (summer 1942).

Behemoth: The Structure and Practice of National Socialism. New York: Oxford University Press, 1944.

"Review of A. Vyshinsky, *The Law of the Soviet State.*" *Political Science Quarterly,* vol. 64 (1949).

"The War Crimes Trials." *World Politics,* vol. 2 (1949).

"Das Arbeitsrecht in der modernen Gesellschaft." *Das Recht der Arbeit,* vol. 4, no. 1 (January 1951).

"Review of Joseph Buttinger, *Am Beispiel Österreichs.*" *Political Science Quarterly,* vol. 67 (1952).

"The Social Sciences." In *The Cultural Migration: The European Scholar in America.* Edited by William Rex Crawford. Philadelphia: University of Pennsylvania Press, 1953.

"Zur Theorie der Diktatur." Unpublished manuscript, 1953. Otto Kirchheimer File, German Emigre Collection, SUNY Albany Library, Albany, New York.

The Democratic and Authoritarian State. Edited by Herbert Marcuse. New York: The Free Press, 1957.

Wirtschaft, Staat, und Demokratie. Aufsätze 1930–54. Edited by A. Söllner. Frankfurt: Suhrkamp, 1978.

The Rule of Law: Political Theory and the Legal System in Modern Society. Leamington Spa, Eng.: Berg, 1986.

"Wandlungen des Marxismus"; "Marxismus und Intelligenz"; "Die Wissenschaft von der Politik in der Demokratie." In *Internationale wissenschaftliche Korrespondez zur Geschichte der deutschen Arbeiterbewegung,* vol. 25 (1989).

Secondary Texts

Altman, Andrew. *Critical Legal Studies: A Liberal Critique.* Princeton: Princeton University Press, 1990.

———. "Legal Realism, Critical Legal Studies and Dworkin." *Philosophy and Public Affairs,* vol. 15, no. 3 (summer 1986).

Adler, Max. *Politische oder soziale Demokratie.* Berlin: Laubsche, 1926.

———. *Die Staatsauffassung des Marxismus.* Darmstadt, Ger.: Wissenschaftliche Buchgesellschaft, 1964.

Adler, Michael, and Stewart Asquith. *Discretion and Welfare.* London: Heinemann, 1981.

Adorno, Theodor. *Soziologische Schriften.* Frankfurt: Suhrkamp, 1979.

Agnoli, Johannes, and Peter Brückner. *Die Transformation der Demokratie.* Frankfurt: EVA, 1968.

Anderson, Benedict. *Imagined Communities: Reflections on the Origins and Spread of Nationalism.* New York: Verso, 1983.

Anderson, Perry. "Roberto Unger and the Politics of Empowerment." *New Left Review,* no. 173 (January–February 1989).

Apel, Karl-Otto, "Ist die Ethik der idealen Kommunikationsgemeinschaft eine Utopie: zum Verhältnis von Ethik, Utopie und Utopiekritik." In *Utopieforschung.* Edited by Wilhelm Vosskamp. Frankfurt: Suhrkamp, 1985.

Arato, Andrew, and E. Gebhardt, eds. *The Essential Frankfurt School Reader.* New York: Continuum, 1982.

Arendt, Hannah. *The Human Condition.* Chicago: University of Chicago Press, 1958.

———. *On Revolution.* London: Penguin, 1973.

———. *On Violence.* New York: Harcourt, Brace and Jovanovich, 1970.

———. *The Origins of Totalitarianism.* New York: Harcourt, Brace and Jovanovich, 1951.

Avineri, Shlomo. "Toward a Socialist Theory of Nationalism." *Dissent,* vol. 37, no. 4 (fall 1990).

Bauer, Otto. "Das Gleichgewicht der Klassenkräfte." In *Austromarxismus.* Edited by H. J. Sandkühler and Rafael de la Vega. Frankfurt: EVA, 1970.

Beetham, David. *Max Weber and the Theory of Modern Politics.* Oxford: Polity, 1985.

Bendersky, Joseph. *Carl Schmitt: Theorist for the Reich.* Princeton: Princeton University Press, 1983.

Benhabib, Seyla. *Critique, Norm and Utopia: A Study of the Foundations of Critical Theory.* New York: Columbia University Press, 1986.

———. "In the Shadow of Aristotle and Hegel: Communicative Ethics and Current Controversies in Practical Philosophy." *The Philosophical Forum,* vol. 21, nos. 1–2 (fall–winter 1989–90).

———. "The Methodological Illusions of Modern Political Theory: The Case of Rawls and Habermas." *Neue Hefte für Philosophie,* vol. 21 (1982).

———. "Modernity and the Aprioris of Critical Theory." *Telos,* no. 49 (fall 1981).

Benhabib, Seyla and Drucilla Cornell, eds., *Feminism as Critique*. Minneapolis: University of Minnesota Press, 1987.

Benjamin, Walter. *Illuminations*. New York: Schocken, 1969.

———. *Reflections*. New York: Harcourt Brace Jovanovich, 1978.

Berger, Suzanne. "Politics and Antipolitics in the Seventies." *Daedulus*, vol. 108, no. 1 (Winter 1979).

Berghahn, V. R. *Modern Germany*. Cambridge: Cambridge University Press, 1982.

Blanke, Thomas, ed. *Streitbare Juristen: Eine andere Tradition*. Baden-Baden: Nomos, 1989.

Blau, Joachim. *Sozialdemokratische Staatslehre in der Weimarer Republik*. Marburg, Ger.: Verlag der Arbeiterbewegung, 1980.

Bloch, Ernst. *Natural Law and Human Dignity*. Cambridge: MIT Press, 1986; German edition, 1961.

Bobbio, Norberto. *Democracy and Dictatorship: The Nature and Limits of State Power*. Oxford: Polity, 1989.

———. *The Future of Democracy*. Minneapolis: University of Minnesota, 1987.

Böckenförde, E. W. *Recht, Staat und Freiheit: Studien zur Rechtsphilosophie, Staatstheorie und Verfassungsgeschichte*. Frankfurt: Suhrkamp, 1991.

Boesche, Roger. *The Strange Liberalism of Alexis de Tocqueville*. Ithaca: Cornell University Press, 1986.

Boldt, Hans. "Article 48 of the Weimar Constitution: Its Historical and Political Implications." In *German Democracy and the Triumph of Hitler*. Edited by A. Nichols and E. Matthias. London: Allen and Unwin, 1971.

Bonß, Wolfgang, and Axel Honneth, eds. *Sozialforschung als Kritik*. Frankfurt: Suhrkamp, 1982.

Borkenau, Franz. *Der Übergang vom feudalen zum bürgerlichen Weltbild*. Paris: Libraire Felix Alcan, 1934.

Brand, Donald R. *Corporatism and the Rule of Law: A Study of the National Recovery Administration*. Ithaca, N.Y.: Cornell University Press, 1988.

Breuer, Stefan. "Nationalstaat und pouvoir constituant bei Sieyes und Carl Schmitt." *Archiv für Rechts- und Sozialphilosophie*, vol. 70 (1984).

Broszat, Martin. *Der Staat Hitlers*. Munich: DTV, 1989.

Brunkhorst, Hauke. "Demokratische Frage und volonte generale." *Links*, vol. 23, no. 252 (May 1991).

Burnheim, John. *Is Democracy Possible?* Cambridge: Polity, 1985.

Cairns, Huntington. *Legal Philosophy from Plato to Hegel.* Baltimore: John Hopkins Press, 1967.

Carnoy, Martin. *The State and Political Theory.* Princeton: Princeton University Press, 1984.

Chayes, Abraham. "The Role of the Judge in Public Law Litigation." *Harvard Law Review,* vol. 89, no. 7 (May 1976).

Cohen, Ira. "The Underemphasis on Democracy in Marx and Weber." In *A Marx-Weber Dialogue.* Edited by Roberto J. Antonio and Ronald M. Glossman. Lawrence: University of Kansas Press, 1985.

Cohen, Jean. "Discourse Ethics and Civil Society." *Philosophy and Social Criticism,* vol. 14, nos. 3–4 (1988).

———. "Why More Political Theory?" *Telos,* no. 40 (summer 1979).

Coker, Francis. "The Technique of the Pluralistic State." *American Political Science Review,* vol. 15, no. 2 (1921).

Connerton, Paul, ed. *Critical Sociology.* New York: Penguin, 1976.

Cristi, F. R. "Hayek and Schmitt on the Rule of Law." *Canadian Journal of Political Science,* vol. 17, no. 3 (September 1984).

Davis, Kenneth C. *Discretionary Justice: A Preliminary Approach.* Urbana: University of Illinois Press, 1979.

Deane, Herbert A. *The Political Ideas of Harold J. Laski.* Hamden, Conn.: Archon, 1972.

d'Entrèves, Alexander Passerin. *Natural Law.* London: Hutchinson, 1970.

———. *The Notion of the State.* Oxford: Oxford University Press, 1967.

Dewey, John. *The Public and Its Problems.* Chicago: Swallow Press, 1954.

Dicey, A. V. *Introduction to the Study of the Law of the Constitution.* New York: St. Martin's, 1961.

Dreier, Ralf, and Wolfgang Sellert. *Recht und Justiz im Dritten Reich.* Frankfurt: Suhrkamp, 1989.

Dubiel, Helmut. *Kritische Theorie der Gesellschaft: Eine einführunde Rekonstruktion von den Anfängen im Horkheimer-Kreis bis Habermas.* Weinheim, Ger.: Juventa, 1988.

———. *Theory and Politics: Studies in the Development of Critical Theory.* Cambridge: MIT Press, 1985.

Dubiel, Helmut, and Alfons Söllner, eds. *Wirtschaft, Recht und Staat im Nationalsozialismus: Analysen des Instituts für Sozialforschung, 1939–42.* Frankfurt: EVA, 1981.

Dworkin, Ronald. *Law's Empire.* Cambridge: Harvard University Press, 1986.

———. *A Matter of Principle.* Cambridge: Harvard University Press, 1985.

———. *Taking Rights Seriously.* Cambridge: Harvard University Press, 1977.

Eder, Klaus. "Zur Rationalisierungsproblematik des modernen Rechts." *Soziale Welt,* vol. 29, no. 2 (1979).

Eley, Geoff. "What Produces Fascism: Preindustrial Traditions or a Crisis of the Capitalist State?" *Politics and Society,* vol. 12, no. 1 (1983).

Elliot, W. Y. "The Pragmatic Politics of Mr. Harold J. Laski." *American Political Science Review,* vol. 18, no. 2 (1924).

Elster, John, and Rune Slagstad. *Constitutionalism and Democracy.* New York: Cambridge University Press, 1988.

Ely, John Hart. *Democracy and Distrust: A Theory of Judicial Review.* Cambridge: Harvard University Press, 1980.

Erd, Rainer, ed. *Reform und Resignation. Gespräche über Franz L. Neumann.* Frankfurt: Suhrkamp, 1985.

Esping-Andersen, Gosta. *Politics against Markets: The Social Democratic Road to Power.* Princeton: Princeton University Press, 1985.

Ewing, Sally. "Formal Justice and the Spirit of Capitalism: Max Weber's Sociology of Law." *Law and Society Review,* vol. 21, no. 3 (1987).

Fetscher, Iring. *Rousseaus Politische Philosophie.* Frankfurt: Suhrkamp, 1975.

Fijalkowski, Jürgen. *Die Wendung zum Führerstaat. Ideologische Komponente in der Politische Philosophie Carl Schmitts.* Opladen, Ger.: Westdeutscher Verlag, 1958.

Finn, John E. *Constitutions in Crisis: Political Violence and the Rule of Law.* New York: Oxford University Press, 1991.

Forester, John, ed. *Critical Theory and Public Life.* Cambridge: MIT Press, 1985.

Foucault, Michel. *Discipline and Punishment: The Birth of the Prison.* New York: Pantheon, 1977.

———. *Power/Knowledge: Selected Interviews and Other Writings, 1972–77.* New York: Pantheon, 1980.

Fraenkel, Ernst. *Deutschland und die westlichen Demokratien.* Frankfurt: Suhrkamp, 1991.

———. *The Dual State.* New York: Oxford, 1941.

———. "Die Krise des Rechtsstaats und die Justiz." *Die Gesellschaft,* vol. 7 (1931).

———. "Das Produkt des Grosskapitals." *New Yorker Neue Volkszeitung,* vol. 2, no. 16 (May 1942).

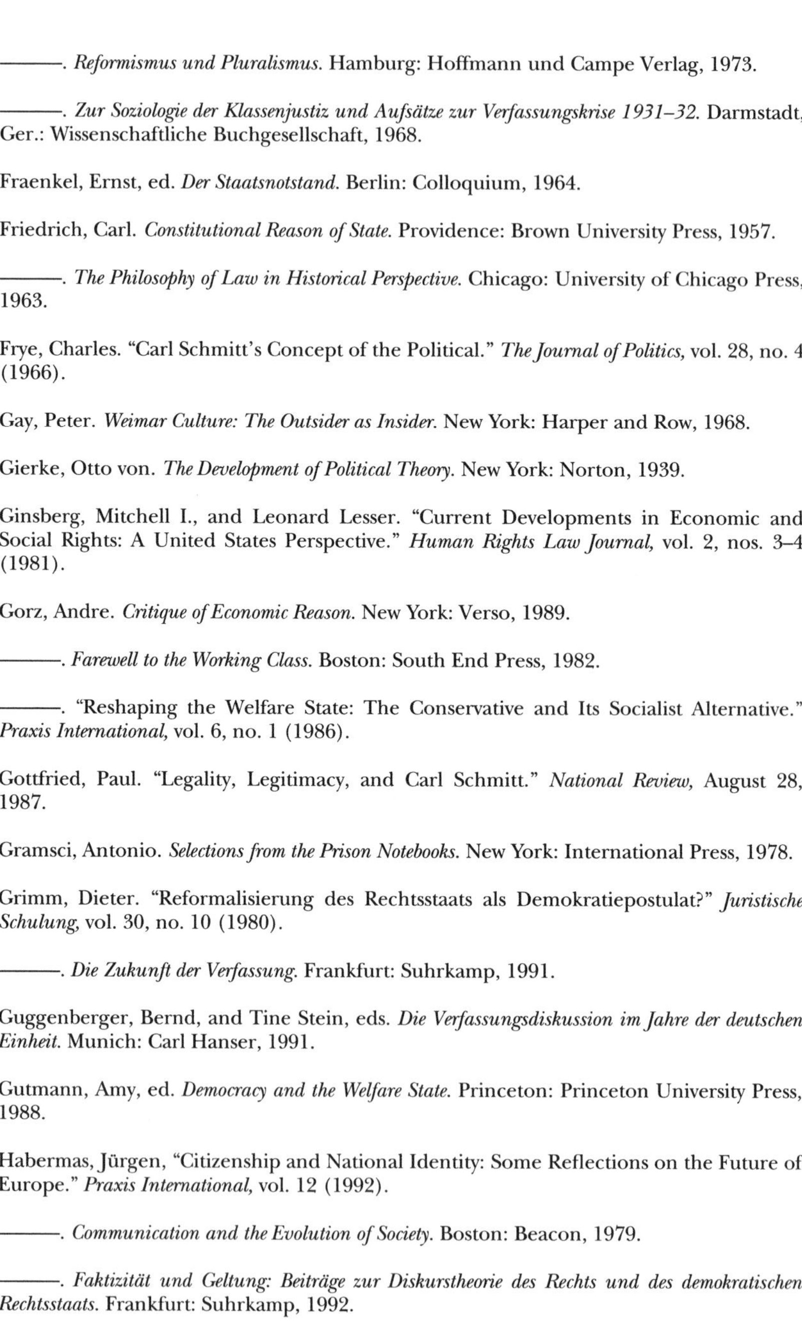

———. *Reformismus und Pluralismus.* Hamburg: Hoffmann und Campe Verlag, 1973.

———. *Zur Soziologie der Klassenjustiz und Aufsätze zur Verfassungskrise 1931–32.* Darmstadt, Ger.: Wissenschaftliche Buchgesellschaft, 1968.

Fraenkel, Ernst, ed. *Der Staatsnotstand.* Berlin: Colloquium, 1964.

Friedrich, Carl. *Constitutional Reason of State.* Providence: Brown University Press, 1957.

———. *The Philosophy of Law in Historical Perspective.* Chicago: University of Chicago Press, 1963.

Frye, Charles. "Carl Schmitt's Concept of the Political." *The Journal of Politics,* vol. 28, no. 4 (1966).

Gay, Peter. *Weimar Culture: The Outsider as Insider.* New York: Harper and Row, 1968.

Gierke, Otto von. *The Development of Political Theory.* New York: Norton, 1939.

Ginsberg, Mitchell I., and Leonard Lesser. "Current Developments in Economic and Social Rights: A United States Perspective." *Human Rights Law Journal,* vol. 2, nos. 3–4 (1981).

Gorz, Andre. *Critique of Economic Reason.* New York: Verso, 1989.

———. *Farewell to the Working Class.* Boston: South End Press, 1982.

———. "Reshaping the Welfare State: The Conservative and Its Socialist Alternative." *Praxis International,* vol. 6, no. 1 (1986).

Gottfried, Paul. "Legality, Legitimacy, and Carl Schmitt." *National Review,* August 28, 1987.

Gramsci, Antonio. *Selections from the Prison Notebooks.* New York: International Press, 1978.

Grimm, Dieter. "Reformalisierung des Rechtsstaats als Demokratiepostulat?" *Juristische Schulung,* vol. 30, no. 10 (1980).

———. *Die Zukunft der Verfassung.* Frankfurt: Suhrkamp, 1991.

Guggenberger, Bernd, and Tine Stein, eds. *Die Verfassungsdiskussion im Jahre der deutschen Einheit.* Munich: Carl Hanser, 1991.

Gutmann, Amy, ed. *Democracy and the Welfare State.* Princeton: Princeton University Press, 1988.

Habermas, Jürgen, "Citizenship and National Identity: Some Reflections on the Future of Europe." *Praxis International,* vol. 12 (1992).

———. *Communication and the Evolution of Society.* Boston: Beacon, 1979.

———. *Faktizität und Geltung: Beiträge zur Diskurstheorie des Rechts und des demokratischen Rechtsstaats.* Frankfurt: Suhrkamp, 1992.

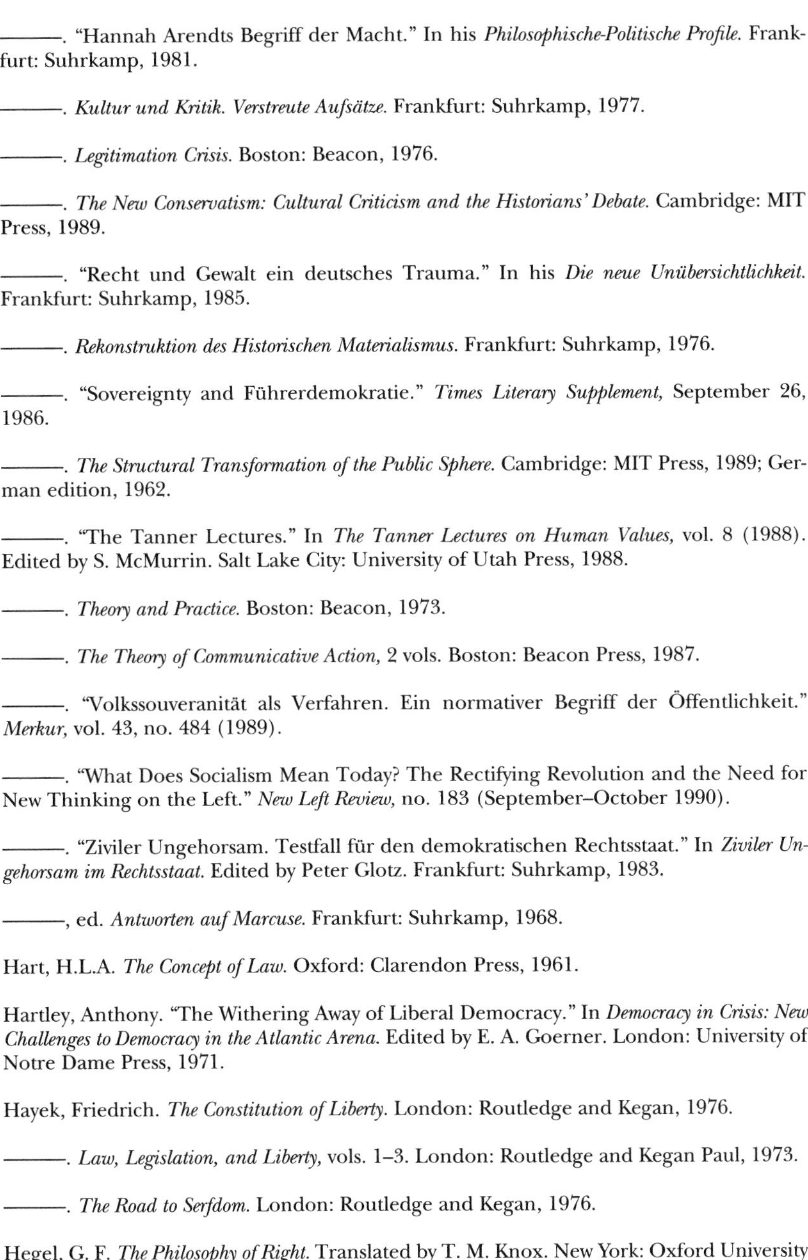

———. "Hannah Arendts Begriff der Macht." In his *Philosophische-Politische Profile.* Frankfurt: Suhrkamp, 1981.

———. *Kultur und Kritik. Verstreute Aufsätze.* Frankfurt: Suhrkamp, 1977.

———. *Legitimation Crisis.* Boston: Beacon, 1976.

———. *The New Conservatism: Cultural Criticism and the Historians' Debate.* Cambridge: MIT Press, 1989.

———. "Recht und Gewalt ein deutsches Trauma." In his *Die neue Unübersichtlichkeit.* Frankfurt: Suhrkamp, 1985.

———. *Rekonstruktion des Historischen Materialismus.* Frankfurt: Suhrkamp, 1976.

———. "Sovereignty and Führerdemokratie." *Times Literary Supplement,* September 26, 1986.

———. *The Structural Transformation of the Public Sphere.* Cambridge: MIT Press, 1989; German edition, 1962.

———. "The Tanner Lectures." In *The Tanner Lectures on Human Values,* vol. 8 (1988). Edited by S. McMurrin. Salt Lake City: University of Utah Press, 1988.

———. *Theory and Practice.* Boston: Beacon, 1973.

———. *The Theory of Communicative Action,* 2 vols. Boston: Beacon Press, 1987.

———. "Volkssouveranität als Verfahren. Ein normativer Begriff der Öffentlichkeit." *Merkur,* vol. 43, no. 484 (1989).

———. "What Does Socialism Mean Today? The Rectifying Revolution and the Need for New Thinking on the Left." *New Left Review,* no. 183 (September–October 1990).

———. "Ziviler Ungehorsam. Testfall für den demokratischen Rechtsstaat." In *Ziviler Ungehorsam im Rechtsstaat.* Edited by Peter Glotz. Frankfurt: Suhrkamp, 1983.

———, ed. *Antworten auf Marcuse.* Frankfurt: Suhrkamp, 1968.

Hart, H.L.A. *The Concept of Law.* Oxford: Clarendon Press, 1961.

Hartley, Anthony. "The Withering Away of Liberal Democracy." In *Democracy in Crisis: New Challenges to Democracy in the Atlantic Arena.* Edited by E. A. Goerner. London: University of Notre Dame Press, 1971.

Hayek, Friedrich. *The Constitution of Liberty.* London: Routledge and Kegan, 1976.

———. *Law, Legislation, and Liberty,* vols. 1–3. London: Routledge and Kegan Paul, 1973.

———. *The Road to Serfdom.* London: Routledge and Kegan, 1976.

Hegel, G. F. *The Philosophy of Right.* Translated by T. M. Knox. New York: Oxford University Press, 1967.

Held, David. *Introduction to Critical Theory: Horkheimer to Habermas.* London: Hutchinson, 1980.

———. *Models of Democracy.* Cambridge: Polity Press, 1987.

Held, David, and Christopher Pollitt. *New Forms of Democracy.* London: Sage, 1986.

Heller, Agnes. "Past, Present, and Future of Democracy." *Social Research,* vol. 45, no. 4 (winter 1978).

Heller, Hermann. *Europa und der Fascismus.* Berlin: Walter de Gruyter, 1929.

———. *Gesammelte Schriften.* Leiden: A. W. Sijthoff, 1971.

———. *Die Souveranität.* Berlin: Walter de Gruyter, 1927.

———. "Staat." In *Handwörterbuch der Soziologie.* Stuttgart: Ferdinand Enke Verlag, 1955.

Henkin, Louis, and Albert J. Rosenthal, eds. *Constitutionalism and Rights: The Influence of the United States Constitution.* New York: Columbia University Press, 1990.

Herf, Jeffrey. *Reactionary Modernism: Technology, Culture and Politics in Weimar and the Third Reich.* New York: Cambridge University Press, 1984.

Herz, John. "The Fiasco of Denazification in Germany." *Political Science Quarterly,* vol. 63 (1948).

———. "Looking at Carl Schmitt from the Vantage Point of the 1990s." *Interpretation,* vol. 19, no. 3 (spring 1992).

Hilferding, Rudolf. "Staatskapitalismus oder totalitäre Wirtschaft." In *Zwischen den Stühlen. Schriften Rudolf Hilferdings 1904 bis 1940.* Edited by Cora Stephan. Berlin: Dietz, 1982.

Hinsley, F. H. *Sovereignty.* Cambridge: Cambridge University Press, 1986.

Hirsch, Joachim. "The New Leviathan and the Struggle for Democratic Rights." *Telos,* no. 48 (summer 1981).

———. *Der Sicherheitsstaat.* Frankfurt: EVA, 1980.

Hoffmann, Stanley. "Some Notes on Democratic Theory and Practice." *The Tocqueville Review,* vol. 2, no. 1 (winter 1980).

Hofmann, Hasso. *Legitimität gegen Legalität: Der Weg der politischen Philosophie Carl Schmitts.* Neuwied, Ger.: Luchterhand, 1964.

Holmes, Stephen. "The Scourge of Liberalism." *The New Republic,* August 22, 1988.

Honneth, Axel. "Critical Theory." In *Social Theory Today.* Edited by Anthony Giddens and Jonathan Turner. Oxford: Polity, 1987.

———. *Critique of Power: Reflective Stages in Critical Social Theory.* Cambridge: MIT Press, 1991.

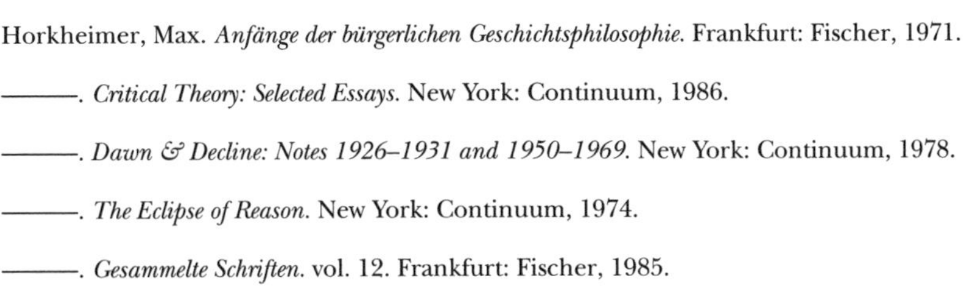

Horkheimer, Max. *Anfänge der bürgerlichen Geschichtsphilosophie.* Frankfurt: Fischer, 1971.

———. *Critical Theory: Selected Essays.* New York: Continuum, 1986.

———. *Dawn & Decline: Notes 1926–1931 and 1950–1969.* New York: Continuum, 1978.

———. *The Eclipse of Reason.* New York: Continuum, 1974.

———. *Gesammelte Schriften.* vol. 12. Frankfurt: Fischer, 1985.

Horkheimer, Max, and Theodor Adorno. *The Dialectic of Enlightenment.* New York: Continuum, 1972.

Horwitz, Morton J. "The Rule of Law: An Unqualified Good?" *Yale Law Journal,* vol. 86, no. 3 (January 1977).

Hughes, H. Stuart. "Franz Neumann between Marxism and Liberal Democracy." In *The Intellectual Migration: Europe and America, 1930–60.* Edited by Donald Fleming and Bernard Bailyn. Cambridge: Harvard University Press, 1969.

Hutchinson, Allen, and Patrick Monahan, eds. *The Rule of Law: Ideal or Ideology.* Toronto: Carswell, 1987.

Hüttenberger, Peter. "Nationalsozialistische Polykratie." *Geschichte und Gesellschaft,* vol. 2, no. 4 (1976).

Institute for Social Research. *Zeitschrift für Sozialforschung.* Edited by Alfred Schmidt. Munich: DTV reprint, 1980.

Intelmann, Peter. "Zur Biographie von Franz L. Neumann." *1999: Zeitschrift für Sozialgeschichte des 20. Jahrhunderts und 21. Jahrhunderts,* vol. 5, no. 1 (January 1990).

Jäger, Wolfgang. *Öffentlichkeit und Parlamentarismus. Eine Kritik an Jürgen Habermas.* Stuttgart: Kohlhammer, 1973.

Jasper, Gotthard. *Die gescheiterte Zähmung. Wege zur Machtergreifung Hitlers 1930–34.* Frankfurt: Suhrkamp, 1986.

Jay, Martin. *Adorno.* Cambridge: Harvard University Press, 1984.

———. *The Dialectical Imagination: A History of the Frankfurt School.* Boston: Little, Brown, 1973.

———. "Reconciling the Irreconcilable? A Rejoinder to Kennedy." *Telos,* no. 71 (spring 1987).

Jellinek, Georg. *Allgemeine Staatslehre.* Bad Homburg, Ger.: Gertner Verlog 1960.

Jones, Harry M. "The Rule of Law and the Welfare State." *Columbia Law Review,* vol. 58, no. 2 (February 1958).

Jowell, Jeffrey and Oliver, Dawn, eds. *The Changing Constitution.* Oxford: Clarendon Press, 1989.

Kairys, David, ed. *The Politics of Law: A Progressive Critique.* New York: Pantheon, 1982.

Kamenka, Eugene, and Alice Erh-Soon Tay. "Marxism, Socialism and the Theory of Law." *Columbia Journal of Transnational Law,* vol. 23 (1985).

Kant, Immanuel. *Metaphysik der Sitten.* Leipzig: Felix Meiner, 1945.

———. *Political Writings.* Edited by Hans Reiss. Cambridge: Cambridge University Press, 1983.

Katz, Barry M. *Foreign Intelligence: Research and Analysis in the Office of Strategic Services.* Cambridge: Harvard University Press, 1989.

Kelman, Mark. *A Guide to Critical Legal Studies.* Cambridge: Harvard University Press, 1987.

Kellner, Douglas. *Critical Theory, Marxism, and Modernity.* Oxford: Polity, 1989.

Kelly, Michael, ed. *Hermeneutics and Critical Theory in Ethics and Social Theory.* Cambridge: MIT Press, 1990.

Kelsen, Hans. *Allgemeine Staatslehre.* Berlin: Springer, 1925.

———. *Demokratie und Sozialismus.* Darmstadt, Ger.: Wissenschaftliche Buchgesellschaft, 1967.

———. *General Theory of Law and Society.* Cambridge: Harvard University Press, 1946.

———. *Das Problem der Souveranität und die Theorie des Völkerrechts.* (Tubingen, Ger.: J.C.B. Mohr, 1928).

———. *Reine Rechtslehre.* Darmstadt, Ger.: Scientia Verlag, 1985.

———. *Sozialismus und Staat.* Leipzig: C. L. Hirschfeld, 1923.

———. *Vom Wesen und Wert der Demokratie.* Tübingen, Ger.: J. B. Mohr, 1929.

———. *Wer soll der Hüter der Verfassung sein?* Berlin: Rotschild, 1931.

Kennedy, Duncan. "Form and Substance in Private Law Adjudication." In *Essays on Critical Legal Studies.* Cambridge: Harvard Law Review, 1986.

———. "Legal Formality." *The Journal of Legal Studies,* vol. 2 (June 1973).

Kennedy, Ellen. "Carl Schmitt and the Frankfurt School." *Telos,* no. 71 (spring 1987).

———. "Carl Schmitt and the Frankfurt School: A Rejoinder." *Telos,* no. 73 (fall 1987).

———. "The Politics of Toleration in Late Weimar: Hermann Heller's Analysis of Fascism and Political Culture." *History of Political Thought,* vol. 5 (1984).

Kern, Fritz. *Kingship and Law in the Middle Ages.* Oxford: Basil Blackwell, 1948.

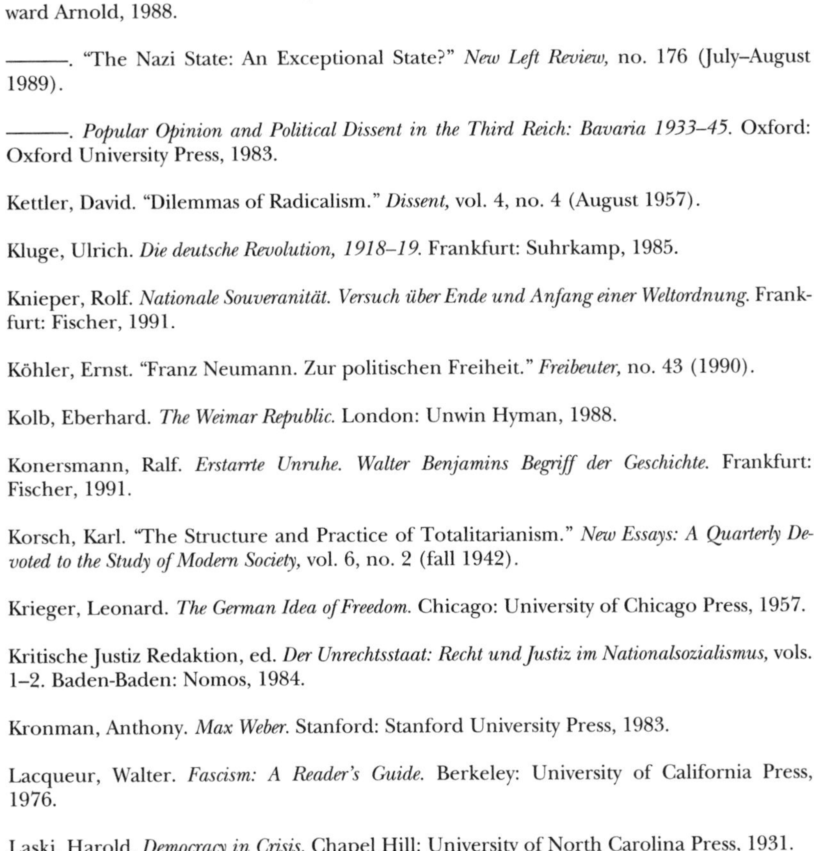

Kershaw, Ian. *The Nazi Dictatorship: Problems and Perspectives of Interpretation*. London: Edward Arnold, 1988.

———. "The Nazi State: An Exceptional State?" *New Left Review*, no. 176 (July–August 1989).

———. *Popular Opinion and Political Dissent in the Third Reich: Bavaria 1933–45*. Oxford: Oxford University Press, 1983.

Kettler, David. "Dilemmas of Radicalism." *Dissent*, vol. 4, no. 4 (August 1957).

Kluge, Ulrich. *Die deutsche Revolution, 1918–19*. Frankfurt: Suhrkamp, 1985.

Knieper, Rolf. *Nationale Souveranität. Versuch über Ende und Anfang einer Weltordnung*. Frankfurt: Fischer, 1991.

Köhler, Ernst. "Franz Neumann. Zur politischen Freiheit." *Freibeuter*, no. 43 (1990).

Kolb, Eberhard. *The Weimar Republic*. London: Unwin Hyman, 1988.

Konersmann, Ralf. *Erstarrte Unruhe. Walter Benjamins Begriff der Geschichte*. Frankfurt: Fischer, 1991.

Korsch, Karl. "The Structure and Practice of Totalitarianism." *New Essays: A Quarterly Devoted to the Study of Modern Society*, vol. 6, no. 2 (fall 1942).

Krieger, Leonard. *The German Idea of Freedom*. Chicago: University of Chicago Press, 1957.

Kritische Justiz Redaktion, ed. *Der Unrechtsstaat: Recht und Justiz im Nationalsozialismus*, vols. 1–2. Baden-Baden: Nomos, 1984.

Kronman, Anthony. *Max Weber*. Stanford: Stanford University Press, 1983.

Lacqueur, Walter. *Fascism: A Reader's Guide*. Berkeley: University of California Press, 1976.

Laski, Harold. *Democracy in Crisis*. Chapel Hill: University of North Carolina Press, 1931.

———. *The Foundations of Sovereignty and Other Essays*. New York: Harcourt, Brace and Jovanovich, 1921.

———. *Studies in Law and Politics*. New York: Greenwood Press, 1968.

———. *Studies in the Problem of Sovereignty*. New Haven, Conn.: Yale University Press, 1917.

Lefort, Claude. *Democracy and Political Theory*. Minneapolis: University of Minnesota Press, 1988.

———. *The Political Forms of Modern Society*. Cambridge: MIT Press, 1986.

Levinson, Sanford. "Escaping Liberalism: Easier Said Than Done." In *Essays on Critical Legal Studies*. Cambridge: Harvard Law Review, 1986.

Lieberman, Robert. "Race and the Administration of Old-Age Insurance and Aid to Dependent Children, 1930s–1960s." Unpublished paper presented at the Workshop on American Political Development, Harvard University, April 7, 1993.

Locke, John. *Two Treatises on Government.* Edited by Peter Laslett. Cambridge: Cambridge University Press, 1967.

Loewenstein, Karl. *Max Weber's Political Ideas in the Perspective of Our Time.* Amherst: University of Massachusetts Press, 1966.

Löwenthal, Leo. *An Unmastered Past.* Berkeley: University of California Press, 1987.

Lowi, Theodore. *The End of Liberalism.* New York: Norton, 1979.

Löwith, Karl (alias Hugo Fiala). "Politischer Dezionismus." *Revue Internationale de la Theorie du Droit,* vol. 9 (1935).

Lukács, Georg. *History and Class Consciousness.* Cambridge: MIT Press, 1971.

Luthardt, Wolfgang. "Einleitung zu Kirchheimer, *Staatsgefüge und Recht des Dritten Reiches.*" *Kritische Justiz,* vol. 9, no. 1 (1976).

———. "Kontinuität und Wandel in der Theorie Franz L. Neumanns." *Internationale Wissenschaftliche Korrespondenz zur Geschichte der deutschen Arbeiterbewegung.* vol. 19. (1983).

———. *Sozialdemokratische Verfassungstheorie in der Weimarer Republik.* Opladen, Ger.: Westdeutscher, 1986.

Luthardt, Wolfgang, and Alfons Söllner, eds. *Verfassung, Souveranität, Pluralismus.* Opladen, Ger.: Westdeutscher Verlag, 1986.

Maier, Charles. *The Unmasterable Past: History, Holocaust, and German National Identity.* Cambridge: Harvard University Press, 1988.

Manin, Bernhard. "On Legitimacy and Political Deliberation." *Political Theory,* vol. 15 (1987).

Mann, F. A. "Outlines of a History of Expropriation." *Law Quarterly Review,* vol. 75 (1959).

Mannheim, Karl. *Ideology and Utopia.* New York: Harcourt and Brace, 1936.

———. *Man and Society in an Age of Reconstruction.* New York: Harcourt, Brace and Jovanovich, 1950.

Marcuse, Herbert. *Eros and Civilization: A Philosophical Inquiry into Freud.* New York: Vintage, 1955.

———. *One Dimensional Man.* Boston: Beacon, 1964.

Maritain, Jacques. "The Concept of Sovereignty." *American Political Science Review,* vol. 44, no. 2 (1950).

Marshall, T. H. *Citizenship and Social Class*. Cambridge: Cambridge University Press, 1950.

Maus, Ingeborg. *Bürgerliche Rechtstheorie und Faschismus: Zur sozialen Funktion und aktuellen Wirkung der Theorie Carl Schmitts*. Munich: Wilhelm Fink, 1976.

———. "Die Kontrolle von unten nach oben in Gang halten. Zum Verhältnis von institutionalisierter und nichtinstitutionalisierter Volkssouveranität." *Links,* vol. 24, no. 262 (March 1992).

———. *Rechtstheorie und politische Theorie im Industriekapitalismus*. Munich: Wilhelm Fink, 1986.

———. "Sinn und Bedeutung von Volkssouveranität in der modernen Gesellschaft." *Kritische Justiz,* vol. 24, no. 2 (1991).

———. *Zur Aufklärung der Demokratietheorie. Rechts- und demokatietheoretische Studien im Anschluss an Kant*. Frankfurt: Suhrkamp, 1992.

McCarthy, Thomas. "Complexity and Democracy: The Seducements of Systems Theory." In *Ideals and Illusions: On Reconstruction and Deconstruction in Contemporary Critical Theory*. Edited by Thomas McCarthy. Cambridge: MIT Press, 1991.

McConnell, Grant. *Private Power and American Democracy*. New York: Vintage, 1966.

McIlwain, Charles H. *Constitutionalism: Ancient and Modern*. Ithaca: Cornell University Press, 1947.

Mehring, Reinhard. *Carl Schmitt*. Hamburg: Junius, 1992.

———. "Vom Umgang mit Carl Schmitt." *Geschichte und Gesellschaft,* vol. 19 (1993).

Melossi, Dario. "George Rusche and Otto Kirchheimer: *Punishment and Social Structure*." *Crime and Social Justice: Issues in Criminology,* no. 9 (spring–summer 1978).

Michelman, Frank. "Political Truth and the Rule of Law." *Tel Aviv University Studies in Law,* vol. 8 (1988).

Mills, C. Wright. "The Nazi Behemoth." In *Power, Politics and People*. New York: Oxford University Press, 1972.

Mommsen, Hans. "Die Sozialdemokratie in der Defensive. Der Immobilismus der SPD und der Aufstieg des Nationalsozialismus." In *Sozialdemokratie zwischen Klassenbewegung und Volkspartei*. Edited by Hans Mommsen. Frankfurt: Athenäum, 1974.

Mommsen, Wolfgang. *The Age of Bureaucracy: Perspectives on the Political Sociology of Max Weber*. Oxford: Basil Blackwell, 1974.

———. *Max Weber und die deutsche Politik, 1890–1920*. Tübingen, Ger.: J. C. B. Mohr, 1959.

Montesquieu, Baron de. *The Spirit of the Laws*. New York: Hafner, 1949.

Moore, Barrington. *The Social Origins of Democracy and Dictatorship*. Boston: Beacon, 1966.

Morgan, Edmund. *Inventing the People: The Rise of Popular Sovereignty in England and America.* New York: Norton, 1988.

Mouffe, Chantal. "Radical Democracy or Liberal Democracy?" *Socialist Review,* vol. 90, no. 2 (April–June 1990).

Müller, Christoph, and Ilse Staff. *Staatslehre in der Weimarer Republik. Hermann Heller zu Ehren.* Frankfurt: Suhrkamp, 1985.

Müller, Ingo. *Hitler's Justice: The Courts of the Third Reich.* Cambridge: Harvard University Press, 1991.

Münkler, Herfried. "Carl Schmitt in der Diskussion." *Neue politische Literatur,* vol. 35 (1990).

———. *Im Namen des Staats. Die Begründung der Staatsräson in der frühen Neuziet.* Frankfurt: Fischer, 1987.

———. "Die politischen Ideen der Weimarer Republik." In *Pipers Handbuch der politischen Ideen,* vol. 5. Edited by H. Münkler and Iring Fetscher. Munich: Piper, 1987.

Neumann, Volker. *Der Staat im Bürgerkrieg. Kontinuität und Wandel des Staatsbegriffs in der politischen Theorie Carl Schmitts.* Frankfurt: Campus, 1980.

———. "Verfassungstheorien politischer Antipoden: Otto Kirchheimer und Carl Schmitt." *Kritische Justiz,* vol. 14 (1981).

Nonet, Philippe, and Philip Selznick. *Law and Society in Transition: Toward Responsive Law.* New York: Harper and Row, 1978.

Offe, Claus. *Contradictions of the Welfare State.* Cambridge: MIT Press, 1984.

———. "Democracy against the Welfare State." *Political Theory,* vol. 15 (1987).

———. *Disorganized Capitalism.* Cambridge: MIT Press, 1985.

———. "Die Staatstheorie auf der Suche nach ihrem Gegenstand. Beobachtungen zu aktuellen Diskussion." In *Jahrbuch zur Staats- und Verwaltungswissenschaft.* Baden-Baden: Nomos, 1987.

Pateman, Carole. *Participation and Democratic Theory.* Cambridge: Cambridge University Press, 1970.

Payne, Stanley. *Fascism.* Madison: University of Wisconsin Press, 1980.

Perels, Joachim, ed. *Recht, Demokratie und Kapitalismus: Aktualität und Probleme der Theorie Franz L. Neumanns.* Baden-Baden: Nomos, 1984.

Peuckert, Detlev J. K. *Inside Nazi Germany: Conformity, Opposition and Racism in Everyday Life.* London: Penguin, 1987.

———. *Die Weimarer Republik.* Frankfurt: Suhrkamp, 1987.

Piccone, Paul, and G. L. Ulmen. "Introduction to Carl Schmitt." *Telos,* no. 72 (summer 1987).

Pippin, Robert, and Andrew Feenberg. *Marcuse: Critical Theory and the Promise of Utopia.* London: MacMillan, 1988.

Pitkin, Hannah. *The Concept of Representation.* Berkeley: University of California Press, 1977.

Poggi, Gianfranco. *The Development of the Modern State: A Sociological Introduction.* Stanford: Stanford University Press, 1978.

———. *The State: Its Nature, Development, and Prospects.* Stanford: Stanford University Press, 1990.

Polan, A. J. *Lenin & the End of Politics.* Berkeley: University of California Press, 1984.

Potthof, Heinrich. "Das Weimarer Verfassungswerk und die deutsche Linke." *Archiv für Sozialgeschichte,* vol. 12 (1972).

Preuss, Hugo. *Staat, Recht, und Freiheit.* (Tübingen, Ger.: J. B. Mohr, 1926.

Preuss, Ulrich. "Aktuelle Probleme einer linken Verfassungstheorie." *Prokla,* vol. 15, no. 4 (1985).

———. "The Critique of German Liberalism: A Reply to Kennedy." *Telos,* no. 71 (spring 1987).

———. *Legalität und Pluralismus. Beiträge zum Verfassungsrecht der Bundesrepublik Deutschland.* Frankfurt: Suhrkamp, 1973.

———. "Politischer Ethos und Verfassung." In *Über den Mangel an politische Kultur in Deutschland.* Edited by H. Brüggemann and H. Gerstenberger. Berlin: Wagenbach, 1978.

———. "Rechtsstaat und Demokratie." *Kritische Justiz,* vol. 22 (1989).

———. *Revolution, Fortschritt und Verfassung. Zu einem neuen Verfassungsverständnis.* Berlin: Wagenbach, 1990.

———. "Was heisst radikale Demokratie heute?" In *Die Ideen von 1789.* Edited by Forum für Philosophie. Frankfurt: Suhrkamp, 1989.

———. "Zivilisation und das Gewaltmonopol—über linke wie grüne Mißverständnisse." *Freibeuter,* no. 25 (1985).

———. "Zum Begriff des Politischen bei Carl Schmitt." In *Politische Verantwortung und Bürgerloyalität. Von den Grenzen der Verfassung und des Gehorsams in der Demokratie.* Edited by U. Preuss. Frankfurt: Fischer, 1984.

Pross, Helge. "Einleitung." In *Demokratischer und autoritärer Staat.* Edited by Franz Neumann. Frankfurt EVA, 1967.

Rawls, John. *A Theory of Justice.* Cambridge: Harvard University Press, 1971.

Rehbinder, Manfred. "Recht und Rechtswissenschft im Werk von Max Weber." In *Max Weber Heute.* Edited by Johannes Weiss. Frankfurt: Suhrkamp, 1989.

Reich, Charles. "The Law of the Planned Society." *Yale Law Review,* vol. 75, no. 8 (July 1966).

———. "The New Property." *Yale Law Journal,* vol. 73, no. 5 (April 1964).

Renner, Karl. *The Institutions of Private Law and Their Social Functions.* London: Routledge and Kegan Paul, 1949.

Rittstieg, Helmut. *Eigentum als Verfassungsproblem.* Darmstadt, Ger.: Wissenschaftliche Buchgesellschaft, 1975).

Rödel, Ulrich, ed. *Autonome Gesellschaft und libertäre Demokratie.* Frankfurt: Suhrkamp, 1990.

Rödel, Ulrich, Günther Frankenberg, and Helmut Dubiel. *Die demokratische Frage.* Frankfurt: Suhrkamp, 1989.

Rosenberg, Arthur. *Geschichte der Weimarer Republik.* Frankfurt: EVA, 1961.

Rosenberg, Hans. *Bureaucracy, Aristocracy and Autocracy: The Prussian Experience.* Boston: Beacon, 1958.

Rottleuther, H., ed. *Recht, Rechtsphilosophie und Nationalsozialismus.* Wiesbaden: Franz Steiner, 1983.

Rousseau, Jean Jacques. *The Social Contract,* Edited by Roger Masters. New York: St. Martin's, 1978.

Rüthers, Bernd. *Carl Schmitt im Dritten Reich.* Munich: C. H. Beck, 1990.

———. *Entartetes Recht. Rechtslehren und Kronjuristen im Dritten Reich.* Munich: C. H. Beck, 1988.

———. *Die unbegrenzte Auslegung. Zum Wandel der Privatrechtsordnung im Nationalsozialismus.* Frankfurt: Athenäum, 1973.

Saage, Richard. *Faschismustheorien.* Munich: C. H. Beck, 1976.

Saage, Richard, ed. *Solidargemeinschaft und Klassenkampf.* Frankfurt: Suhrkamp, 1986.

Sartori, Giovanni. "The Essence of the Political in Carl Schmitt." *Journal of Theoretical Politics,* vol. 1, no. 1 (1989).

Schäfer, Gert. Introduction to *Behemoth: Struktur und Praxis des Nationalsozialismus 1933–44,* by Franz Neumann. Frankfurt: Fischer, 1984.

Scheuerman, William E. "Carl Schmitt and the Nazis." *German Politics and Society,* no. 23 (summer 1991).

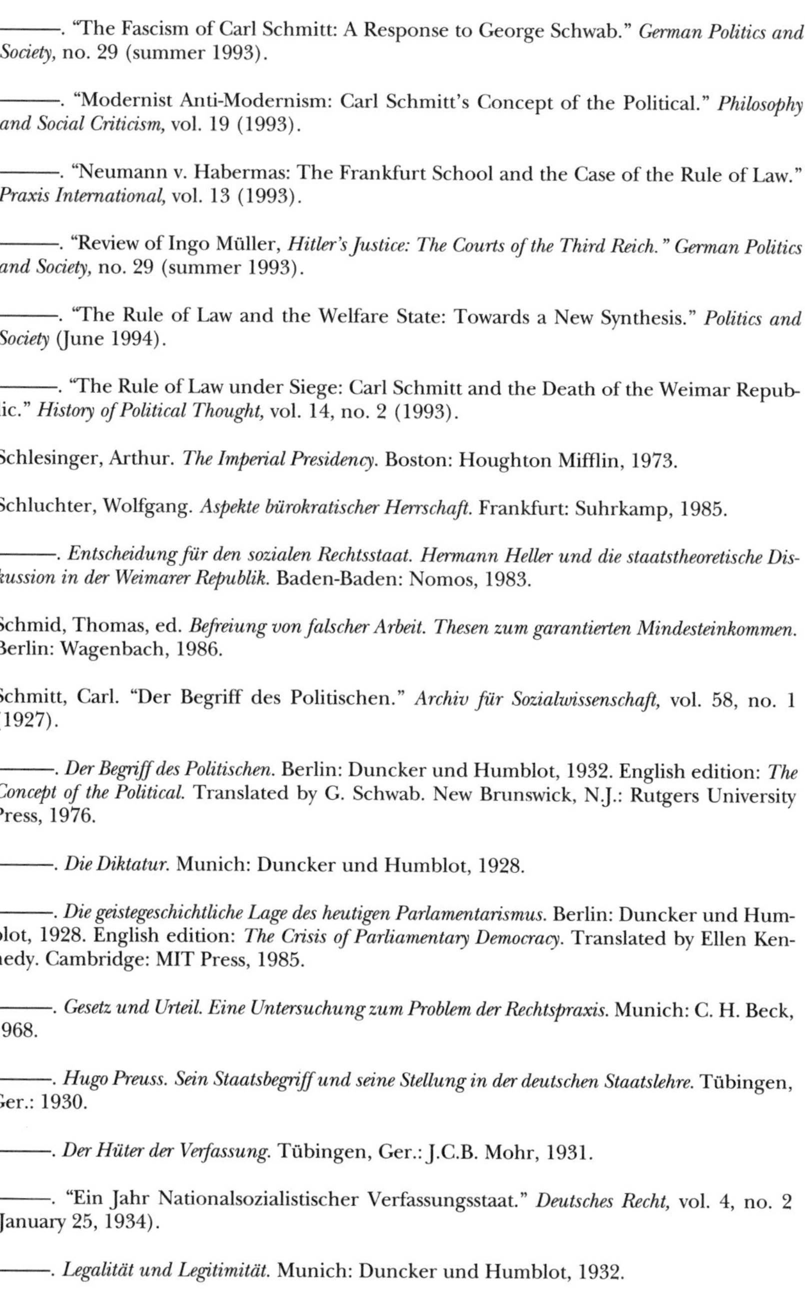

———. "The Fascism of Carl Schmitt: A Response to George Schwab." *German Politics and Society,* no. 29 (summer 1993).

———. "Modernist Anti-Modernism: Carl Schmitt's Concept of the Political." *Philosophy and Social Criticism,* vol. 19 (1993).

———. "Neumann v. Habermas: The Frankfurt School and the Case of the Rule of Law." *Praxis International,* vol. 13 (1993).

———. "Review of Ingo Müller, *Hitler's Justice: The Courts of the Third Reich.*" *German Politics and Society,* no. 29 (summer 1993).

———. "The Rule of Law and the Welfare State: Towards a New Synthesis." *Politics and Society* (June 1994).

———. "The Rule of Law under Siege: Carl Schmitt and the Death of the Weimar Republic." *History of Political Thought,* vol. 14, no. 2 (1993).

Schlesinger, Arthur. *The Imperial Presidency.* Boston: Houghton Mifflin, 1973.

Schluchter, Wolfgang. *Aspekte bürokratischer Herrschaft.* Frankfurt: Suhrkamp, 1985.

———. *Entscheidung für den sozialen Rechtsstaat. Hermann Heller und die staatstheoretische Diskussion in der Weimarer Republik.* Baden-Baden: Nomos, 1983.

Schmid, Thomas, ed. *Befreiung von falscher Arbeit. Thesen zum garantierten Mindesteinkommen.* Berlin: Wagenbach, 1986.

Schmitt, Carl. "Der Begriff des Politischen." *Archiv für Sozialwissenschaft,* vol. 58, no. 1 (1927).

———. *Der Begriff des Politischen.* Berlin: Duncker und Humblot, 1932. English edition: *The Concept of the Political.* Translated by G. Schwab. New Brunswick, N.J.: Rutgers University Press, 1976.

———. *Die Diktatur.* Munich: Duncker und Humblot, 1928.

———. *Die geistegeschichtliche Lage des heutigen Parlamentarismus.* Berlin: Duncker und Humblot, 1928. English edition: *The Crisis of Parliamentary Democracy.* Translated by Ellen Kennedy. Cambridge: MIT Press, 1985.

———. *Gesetz und Urteil. Eine Untersuchung zum Problem der Rechtspraxis.* Munich: C. H. Beck, 1968.

———. *Hugo Preuss. Sein Staatsbegriff und seine Stellung in der deutschen Staatslehre.* Tübingen, Ger.: 1930.

———. *Der Hüter der Verfassung.* Tübingen, Ger.: J.C.B. Mohr, 1931.

———. "Ein Jahr Nationalsozialistischer Verfassungsstaat." *Deutsches Recht,* vol. 4, no. 2 (January 25, 1934).

———. *Legalität und Legitimität.* Munich: Duncker und Humblot, 1932.

———. *Der Leviathan in der Staatslehre Thomas Hobbes.* Cologne: Hohenheim, 1982.

———. "Nationalsozialismus und Rechtsstaat." *Juristische Wochenschrift,* vol. 63, nos. 12–13 (March 24/31, 1934).

———. "Nationalsozialistisches Rechtsdenken." *Deutsches Recht,* vol. 4, no. 10 (May 25, 1934).

———. "Neue Leitsätze für die Rechtspraxis." *Juristische Wochenschrift,* vol. 62, no. 50 (December 16, 1933).

———. *Political Romanticism.* Translated by Guy Oakes. Cambridge: MIT Press, 1986.

———. *Political Theology.* Translated by George Schwab. Cambridge: MIT Press, 1988.

———. *Positionen und Begriffe im Kampf mit Weimar-Genf-Versailles.* Hamburg: Hanseatische Verlagsanstalt, 1940.

———. "Der Rechtsstaat." In *Nationalsozialistisches Handbuch für Recht und Gesetzgebung.* Edited by H. Frank. Munich: NSDAP Zentralverlag, 1935.

———. *Staat, Bewegung, und Volk: Die Dreigliederung der politischen Einheit.* Hamburg: Hanseatische Verlagsanstalt, 1933.

———. *Staatsgefüge und Zusammenbruch des zweiten Reiches Der Sieg des Bürgers über den Soldaten.* Hamburg: Hanseatische Verlagstanstalt, 1934.

———. "Starker Staat und gesunde Wirtschaft." *Volk und Reich, Politische Monatshefte,* no. 2 (1933).

———. *Über die drei Arten des rechtswissenschaftlichen Denkens.* Hamburg: Hanseatische Verlagsanstalt, 1934.

———. *Ünabhängigkeit der Richter, Gleichheit vor dem Gesetz und Gewährleistung des Privateigentums nach der Weimarer Verfassung.* Berlin: Walter de Gruyter, 1926.

———. *Die Verfassungslehre.* Munich: Duncker und Humblot, 1928.

———. *Verfassungsrechtiche Aufsätze* aus den Jahren 1924–54. Berlin: Duncker und Humblot, 1973.

———. "Volksentscheid und Volksbegehren. Ein Beitrag zur Auslegung der Weimarer Verfassung und zur Lehre der unmittelbaren Demokratie." *Beiträge zum ausländischen öffentlichen Recht und Völkerrecht* (1927).

Schmitz, Matthias. *Die Freund-Feind Theorie Carl Schmitts.* Cologne: Westdeutscher, 1965.

Schumann, Karl F. "Produktionsverhältnisse und staatliches Strafen. Zur aktuellen Diskussion über Rusche und Kirchheimer." *Kritische Justiz,* vol. 14 (1981).

Schumpeter, Joseph. *Capitalism, Socialism and Democracy.* New York: Harper and Row, 1942.

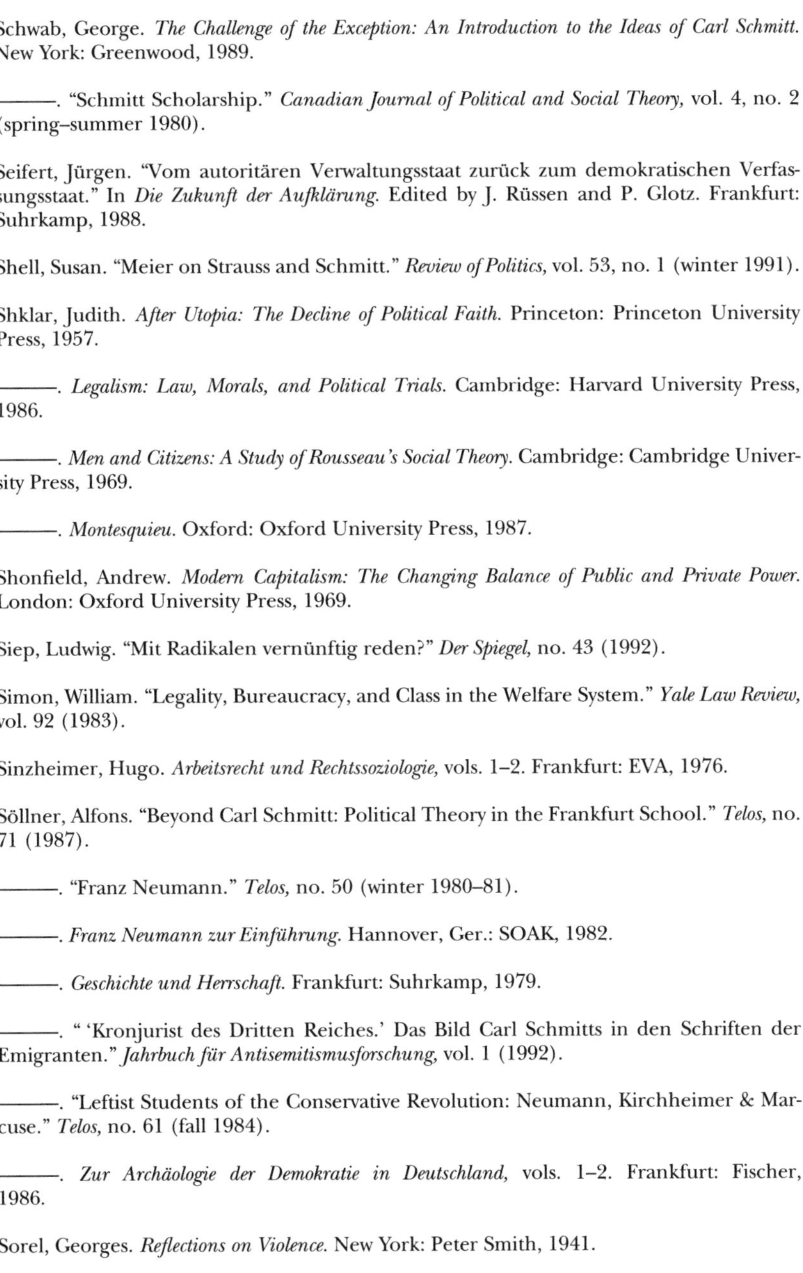

Schwab, George. *The Challenge of the Exception: An Introduction to the Ideas of Carl Schmitt.* New York: Greenwood, 1989.

———. "Schmitt Scholarship." *Canadian Journal of Political and Social Theory,* vol. 4, no. 2 (spring–summer 1980).

Seifert, Jürgen. "Vom autoritären Verwaltungsstaat zurück zum demokratischen Verfassungsstaat." In *Die Zukunft der Aufklärung.* Edited by J. Rüssen and P. Glotz. Frankfurt: Suhrkamp, 1988.

Shell, Susan. "Meier on Strauss and Schmitt." *Review of Politics,* vol. 53, no. 1 (winter 1991).

Shklar, Judith. *After Utopia: The Decline of Political Faith.* Princeton: Princeton University Press, 1957.

———. *Legalism: Law, Morals, and Political Trials.* Cambridge: Harvard University Press, 1986.

———. *Men and Citizens: A Study of Rousseau's Social Theory.* Cambridge: Cambridge University Press, 1969.

———. *Montesquieu.* Oxford: Oxford University Press, 1987.

Shonfield, Andrew. *Modern Capitalism: The Changing Balance of Public and Private Power.* London: Oxford University Press, 1969.

Siep, Ludwig. "Mit Radikalen vernünftig reden?" *Der Spiegel,* no. 43 (1992).

Simon, William. "Legality, Bureaucracy, and Class in the Welfare System." *Yale Law Review,* vol. 92 (1983).

Sinzheimer, Hugo. *Arbeitsrecht und Rechtssoziologie,* vols. 1–2. Frankfurt: EVA, 1976.

Söllner, Alfons. "Beyond Carl Schmitt: Political Theory in the Frankfurt School." *Telos,* no. 71 (1987).

———. "Franz Neumann." *Telos,* no. 50 (winter 1980–81).

———. *Franz Neumann zur Einführung.* Hannover, Ger.: SOAK, 1982.

———. *Geschichte und Herrschaft.* Frankfurt: Suhrkamp, 1979.

———. " 'Kronjurist des Dritten Reiches.' Das Bild Carl Schmitts in den Schriften der Emigranten." *Jahrbuch für Antisemitismusforschung,* vol. 1 (1992).

———. "Leftist Students of the Conservative Revolution: Neumann, Kirchheimer & Marcuse." *Telos,* no. 61 (fall 1984).

———. *Zur Archäologie der Demokratie in Deutschland,* vols. 1–2. Frankfurt: Fischer, 1986.

Sorel, Georges. *Reflections on Violence.* New York: Peter Smith, 1941.

Staff, Ilse, "Zum Begriff der Politischen Theologie bei Carl Schmitt." In *Christentum und modernes Recht.* Edited by Gerhard Dilcher and Ilse Staff. Frankfurt: Suhrkamp, 1984.

———. "Zur Rezeption der Ideen der Französischen Revolution von 1789 in der deutschen Staatslehre des 20. Jahrhunderts." In *Die Ideen von 1789.* Edited by Forum für Philosophie. Frankfurt: Suhrkamp, 1989.

Stolleis, Michael, and B. Diestelkamp, eds. *Justizalltag im Dritten Reich.* Frankfurt: Fischer, 1988.

Strauss, Leo. "Anmerkungen zu Carl Schmitt, *Der Begriff des Politischen.*" In *Carl Schmitt, Leo Strauss und der Begriff des Politischen.* Edited by H. Meier. Stuttgart: J. B. Metzler, 1988.

Sunstein, Cass. *After the Rights Revolution: Reconceiving the Regulatory State.* Cambridge: Harvard University Press, 1990.

———. "Constitutionalism after the New Deal." *Harvard Law Review.* vol. 101 (1987–88).

Sypnowich, Christine. *The Concept of Socialist Law.* Oxford: Clarendon, 1990.

Telos, Special Issue on Carl Schmitt, no. 72 (summer 1987).

Teubner, Gunther. "Juridification: Concepts, Aspects, Limits, Solutions." In *The Juridification of Social Spheres.* Edited by G. Teubner. New York: Walter de Gruyter, 1987.

———. *Standards und Dirketiven in Generalklauseln.* Frankfurt: Athenäum, 1971.

———. "Substantive and Reflexive Elements in Modern Law." *Law and Society Review,* vol. 17, no. 2 (1983).

Thompson, E. P. *Whigs and Hunters.* London: Penguin, 1977.

Tigar, Michael, and Madeleine Levy. *Law and the Rise of Modern Capitalism.* New York: Monthly Review, 1972.

Tohidipur, Mehdi. *Der bürgerliche Rechtsstaat,* vols. 1–2. Frankfurt: Suhrkamp, 1978.

Tommissen, Piet. *Schmittiana II.* Weinheim, Ger.: VCH, 1990.

Tribe, Keith. "Franz Neumann in der Emigration: 1933–42." In *Die Frankfurter Schule und die Folgen.* Edited by Axel Honneth and Albrecht Wellmer. Berlin: de Gruyter, 1986.

———. "Symposium on the Work of Otto Kirchheimer." *History of Political Thought,* vol. 3, no. 1 (spring 1987).

Trubek, David M. "Max Weber on Law and the Rise of Capitalism." *Wisconsin Law Review,* no. 3 (1972).

Turner, Henry, ed. *Nazism and the Third Reich.* New York: Oxford University Press, 1972.

Ulmen, G. L. "Return of the Foe." *Telos,* no. 72 (summer 1987).

———. "Review of Bendersky." *Telos,* no. 59 (spring 1984).

———. "The Sociology of the State: Carl Schmitt and Max Weber." *State, Culture, and Society,* vol. 1, no. 2 (1985).

Ulmen, G. L., and Paul Piccone. "Schmitt's 'Testament' and the Future of Europe." *Telos,* no. 83 (spring 1990).

Unger, Roberto. *The Critical Legal Studies Movement.* Cambridge: Harvard University Press, 1975.

———. *Knowledge and Politics.* New York: The Free Press, 1975.

———. *Law in Modern Society.* New York: The Free Press, 1976.

———. *Social Theory: Its Situation and Its Task.* Cambridge: Cambridge University Press, 1987.

Vile, M. J. C. *Constitutionalism and the Separation of Powers.* Oxford: Clarendon Press, 1967.

Voigt, Rüdiger. *Abschied vom Recht?* Frankfurt: Suhrkamp, 1983.

von Krockow, Christian Graf. *Die Entscheidung. Eine Untersuchung über Ernst Jünger, Carl Schmitt, Martin Heidegger* Stuttgart: Ferdinand Enke, 1965.

Weber, Max. *Economy and Society.* Berkeley: University of California Press, 1978.

———. *From Max Weber: Essays in Sociology.* New York: Oxford University Press, 1946.

Wehler, Hans-Ulrich. *The German Empire.* London: Berg, 1985.

Wiggershaus, Rolf. *Die Frankfurter Schule.* Munich: DTV, 1988. English edition: *The Frankfurt School.* Cambridge: MIT Press, and Oxford: Polity Press, 1994.

Willms, Bernard. "Politics as Politics. Carl Schmitt's 'Concept of the Political' and the Tradition of European Political Thought." *History of European Ideas,* vol. 13, no. 4 (1991).

Wilson, James Q., ed. *The Politics of Regulation.* New York: Basic Books, 1980.

Wippermann, Wolfgang. *Europäischer Faschismus im Vergleich 1922–1982.* Frankfurt: Suhrkamp, 1983.

Wolf, Robert Paul, ed. *The Rule of Law.* New York: Random House, 1971.

Wolfe, Alan. *The Limits of Legitimacy: Political Contradictions of Contemporary Capitalism.* New York: Free Press, 1977.

Wolin, Richard. "Carl Schmitt—The Conservative Revolutionary: Habitus and the Aesthetics of Horror." *Political Theory,* vol. 20, no. 3 (1992).

———. "Carl Schmitt, Political Existentialism, and the Total State." *Theory and Society*, vol. 19, no. 4 (1990).

Wolin, Sheldon. "Democracy and the Welfare State." *Political Theory*, vol. 15 (1987).

———. *Politics and Vision: Continuity and Innovation in Western Political Thought*. Boston: Little, Brown, 1960.

———. "Violence and the Western Political Tradition." *American Journal of Orthopsychiatry*, vol. 33, no. 1 (January 1963).

Zeitschrift für Sozialforschung. See Institute for Social Research.

Index

Studies in Contemporary German Social Thought
Thomas McCarthy, General Editor

Theodor W. Adorno, *Against Epistemology: A Metacritique*
Theodor W. Adorno, *Hegel: Three Studies*
Theodor W. Adorno, *Prisms*
Karl-Otto Apel, *Understanding and Explanation: A Transcendental-Pragmatic Perspective*
Seyla Benhabib, Wolfgang Bonß, and John McCole, editors, *On Max Horkheimer: New Perspectives*
Seyla Benhabib and Fred Dallmayr, editors, *The Communicative Ethics Controversy*
Richard J. Bernstein, editor, *Habermas and Modernity*
Ernst Bloch, *Natural Law and Human Dignity*
Ernst Bloch, *The Principle of Hope*
Ernst Bloch, *The Utopian Function of Art and Literature: Selected Essays*
Hans Blumenberg, *The Genesis of the Copernican World*
Hans Blumenberg, *The Legitimacy of the Modern Age*
Hans Blumenberg, *Work on Myth*
Susan Buck-Morss, *The Dialectics of Seeing: Walter Benjamin and the* Arcades Project
Craig Calhoun, editor, *Habermas and the Public Sphere*
Jean Cohen and Andrew Arato, *Civil Society and Political Theory*
Maeve Cooke, *Language and Reason: A Study of Habermas's Pragmatics*
Helmut Dubiel, *Theory and Politics: Studies in the Development of Critical Theory*
John Forester, editor, *Critical Theory and Public Life*
David Frisby, *Fragments of Modernity: Theories of Modernity in the Work of Simmel, Kracauer and Benjamin*
Hans-Georg Gadamer, *Philosophical Apprenticeships*
Hans-Georg Gadamer, *Reason in the Age of Science*
Jürgen Habermas, *Justification and Application: Remarks on Discourse Ethics*
Jürgen Habermas, *Moral Consciousness and Communicative Action*
Jürgen Habermas, *The New Conservatism: Cultural Criticism and the Historians' Debate*
Jürgen Habermas, *On the Logic of the Social Sciences*
Jürgen Habermas, *The Philosophical Discourse of Modernity: Twelve Lectures*
Jürgen Habermas, *Philosophical-Political Profiles*
Jürgen Habermas, *Postmetaphysical Thinking: Philosophical Essays*
Jürgen Habermas, *The Structural Transformation of the Public Sphere: An Inquiry into a Category of Bourgeois Society*
Jürgen Habermas, editor, *Observations on "The Spiritual Situation of the Age"*
Axel Honneth, *The Critique of Power: Reflective Stages in a Critical Social Theory*
Axel Honneth and Hans Joas, editors, *Communicative Action: Essays on Jürgen Habermas's* The Theory of Communicative Action
Axel Honneth, Thomas McCarthy, Claus Offe, and Albrecht Wellmer, editors, *Cultural-Political Interventions in the Unfinished Project of Enlightenment*
Axel Honneth, Thomas McCarthy, Claus Offe, and Albrecht Wellmer, editors, *Philosophical Interventions in the Unfinished Project of Enlightenment*
Max Horkheimer, *Between Philosophy and Social Science: Selected Early Writings*
Hans Joas, *G. H. Mead: A Contemporary Re-examination of His Thought*
Michael Kelly, editor, *Critique and Power: Recasting the Foucault/Habermas Debate*
Reinhart Koselleck, *Critique and Crisis: Enlightenment and the Pathogenesis of Modern Society*
Reinhart, Koselleck, *Futures Past: On the Semantics of Historical Time*
Harry Liebersohn, *Fate and Utopia in German Sociology, 1887–1923*
Herbert Marcuse, *Hegel's Ontology and the Theory of Historicity*

Gil G. Noam and Thomas E. Wren, editors, *The Moral Self*
Guy Oakes, *Weber and Rickert: Concept Formation in the Cultural Sciences*
Claus Offe, *Contradictions of the Welfare State*
Claus Offe, *Disorganized Capitalism: Contemporary Transformations of Work and Politics*
Helmut Peukert, *Science, Action, and Fundamental Theology: Toward a Theology of Communicative Action*
Joachim Ritter, *Hegel and the French Revolution: Essays on the* Philosophy of Right
William E. Scheuerman, *Between the Norm and the Exception: The Frankfurt School and the Rule of Law*
Alfred Schmidt, *History and Structure: An Essay on Hegelian-Marxist and Structuralist Theories of History*
Dennis Schmidt, *The Ubiquity of the Finite: Hegel, Heidegger, and the Entitlements of Philosophy*
Carl Schmitt, *The Crisis of Parliamentary Democracy*
Carl Schmitt, *Political Romanticism*
Carl Schmitt, *Political Theology: Four Chapters on the Concept of Sovereignty*
Gary Smith, editor, *On Walter Benjamin: Critical Essays and Recollections*
Michael Theunissen, *The Other: Studies in the Social Ontology of Husserl, Heidegger, Sartre, and Buber*
Ernst Tugendhat, *Self-Consciousness and Self-Determination*
Georgia Warnke, *Justice and Interpretation*
Mark Warren, *Nietzsche and Political Thought*
Albrecht Wellmer, *The Persistence of Modernity: Essays on Aesthetics, Ethics and Postmodernism*
Rolf Wiggershaus, *The Frankfurt School: Its History, Theories, and Political Significance*
Thomas E. Wren, editor, *The Moral Domain: Essays in the Ongoing Discussion between Philosophy and the Social Sciences*
Lambert Zuidervaart, *Adorno's Aesthetic Theory: The Redemption of Illusion*